JAMES K. LYON
BERTOLT
BRECHT
IN AMERICA

PRINCETON UNIVERSITY PRESS   PRINCETON, N.J.

ADDENDUM

Citations from Brecht's published and unpublished works used by permission of the
Bertolt Brecht heirs and Suhrkamp Verlag, Frankfurt/Main, Germany. All unpublished
material by Brecht cited in this volume copyright 1980 by Stefan S. Brecht.

FOR DOROTHY ANN

CONTENTS

LIST OF ILLUSTRATIONS

PREFACE

Bertolt Brecht took part in that spectacular migration of art, culture, and intellect from Germany to America during the Hitler era which included names like Thomas Mann and Albert Einstein. Not since the influx of scholars into Western Europe after the fall of Constantinople in 1453 had the world seen such an enormous and sudden enrichment of one culture at the expense of another. In some ways Brecht's experiences were perhaps not typical of Mann's, Einstein's, and those of a few other luminaries who enjoyed special recognition. To a considerable extent, however, his experiences reflected what happened to a large number of gifted and brilliant émigrés in America. And, while Brecht did not remain in America, his delayed-action impact on Western drama and film today is as profound as any made by the great émigrés of the 1930's and 1940's in their time.

In the words of Peter Brook in *The Empty Space*, Brecht now ranks as the "strongest, most influential, and most radical theater man of our time," one whose ideas have decisively influenced American theater and film-making. Throughout his life the theater man Brecht understood how to "produce" himself. While living in American exile, however, between 1941-1947, this "production" failed, and his influence passed almost unnoticed. Yet exile in America for him was perhaps one of the most significant periods in one of the fascinating lives of our age.

Brecht has interested me since I became acquainted with him in 1960. I admired his works, but I was also perplexed by the lore surrounding his person. Much of this had begun to spring up before he died in 1956. Anecdotes fascinate me, but so does historical fact, and I became interested in learning more. In April 1969 I met Ernst Halberstadt of Onset, Massachusetts, who showed me a number of letters Brecht had written to Halberstadt's cousin, Ferdinand Reyher, while the dramatist was living in America. When I learned that Brecht scholarship knew nothing of who or what Reyher was, I realized how little was known about the years Brecht spent in America. After living here for nearly six and one-half years, I inferred, Brecht must have left behind other traces. My curiosity, and the hope of finding more documents, launched a project that was to last nearly ten years. It grew beyond what I had originally planned. A race against the clock also enlivened a piece of detective work that carried me through America and Europe. Many of Brecht's contemporaries were still alive when I began, but most were over seventy, and I was eager to reach them as soon as possible for information and documents. My haste proved justified, for many who contributed generously to this work are no longer here to read it.

Two main considerations shaped this treatment of Brecht as a human being. To a considerable degree his thought and writings dictated the approach I took. In his private life, as in his works, he attempted to escape from emotion. For the tough-minded Brecht, excessive concern with one's own psyche was self-indulgent sentimentality that stupified rational thought. Subscribing to this view, I have attempted to characterize him in non-psychological descriptive terms which correspond roughly to his own view that visible social experiences, seen in previously unknown combinations, reveal the essence of what is real about a person or a society. My own appreciation of Brecht also shaped this study. In my opinion, he is not only the most gifted and important German writer in the twentieth century; the quality of his writings, not to mention his world-wide impact, convince me that he is one of the great writers of our century in any language.

Having stated these biases in favor of Brecht, I also admit an aversion to an international Brecht "cult" which has grown up recently. For me, admiration stops short of adulation, and I consider attempts to canonize him and his pronouncements repugnant. If my treatment at times seems critical of him, it represents an attempt to counterbalance this excessive glorification and remind the reader that he was, after all, human. I trust that, while attempting to rescue Brecht from this bear-hug of fanatical devotees as well as from his critics, my basic sympathy toward him will still be evident. Lest these statements leave any question as to where I stand, it is strongly on the side of critical sympathy. I feel that, in spite of obvious human error and frailty, Brecht was essentially right in what he did and the way he did it.

Jerry Tallmer has called Brecht "one of the most complicated human beings of the past fifty years," a characterization with which I agree. Dealing with such complexity of character has affected my method of description. In addition to Brecht's literary works, I draw on conventional biographical sources such as journals and letters. Further, in order to understand some of the complexities of the man, I interviewed numerous friends and acquaintances, ranging from his widow and children to political enemies (see appendix for a complete list of names and dates of interviews). This type of oral history, while highly useful at times, has well-known pitfalls. To avoid them, I did not accord the same status to information and anecdotes from living informants as I did to documentary material unless at least two persons who had no contact with each other provided the same information, or unless documents corroborated it. Occasionally I relate anecdotes obtained from these interviews and allow the reader to decide on their veracity by labelling them as anecdotes. But the reader should remember that informants were recalling events which happened nearly three decades earlier, with all the problems inherent in such recall. For ease of reading, and to reduce the number of footnotes, statements ascribed to someone who is not further identified in a footnote derive from these interviews.

Translations from the German (unless otherwise noted) are mine. In the case of Brecht's lyrics, I have attempted to render them close to the original rather than to produce the "imitations" which are the essence of great translations.

Many more details could be added to a book already too long. Because of space limitations, much material (from Brecht's FBI files, for example, and from his work on "Hangmen also Die") could not be reported. Some readers may miss a fuller account of what Brecht learned from America and what impact he had on the USA in the years immediately following his departure. Considerations of length demanded that these and other topics be limited or deleted. Out of deference to the wishes of Brecht's living heirs, almost nothing is said about the lives of his two children, who lived with him in America, unless it is important for his own activities.

Exceptional kindness by an unusually large number of people and organizations helped me to carry out this work. My thanks to all who allowed me to interview them about their association with Brecht; their names appear at the beginning of the footnote section. The American Council of Learned Societies; the University of Florida; and the University of California, San Diego, each gave me generous financial support for travel in the United States, Canada, and Europe necessary to interview people, obtain documents, and work in archives. A grant from the John Simon Guggenheim Memorial Foundation enabled me to write most of the manuscript. The following persons and institutions helped in locating or copying documents, photos, and information: Eric Bentley, Ruth Berlau, Arthur Braunmuller, Egon Breiner, Joseph Breitenbach, Bruce Cook, Brainerd Duffield, Leo Fiedler, Wolfgang Gersch, Mordecai Gorelik, Lotte Goslar, H. R. Hays, Vincent Homolka, Faith Reyher Jackson, Clarence Kelley, James Laughlin, Elsa Lanchester, Kate Drain Lawson, Dorothy Norman, Walter Nubel, Naomi Replansky, Joseph Starobin, Helene Weigel, Douglas Youngkin, and the staff of the Bertolt Brecht Archives, East Berlin; the Beinecke Library, Yale University; the Dramatist's Guild of America; the Wisconsin State Historical Society; and the University of Illinois, Carbondale Library.

Donald and Barbara Barber, Barbara Frank, Lane and Margaret Jennings, and Jonathan and Clare Johnson provided physical assist-

ance during the research, while Richard Astle, Sara Cooper, Christa
Eichhorn, Kathryn Hafner, Greg Hidley, Monika Ihlenfeld, Frank
Langer, Virginia Magnus, Brigitte Schmidt, and Irmela Spelsberg all
helped at some stage in the preparation of the manuscript. Barbara
Schall-Brecht, Stefan Brecht, and Suhrkamp publishers in Frankfurt/
Main, Germany generously allowed me to see and to quote from un-
published documents by Brecht. Special encouragement and sugges-
tions came from Eric Bentley, R. G. Davis, Victor Lange, Roy Harvey
Pearce, and John Viertel, all of whom read the manuscript at some
stage in its development. To all of them, and to John Spalek and John
Willett for useful information, I express my gratitude for unusual
generosity and support.

Finally, my special thanks go to Bernhard Blume, a friend, scholar,
and inspiring teacher, who first introduced me to the works of Brecht,
and whose interest in this work sustained and stimulated me; and to
my wife Dorothy Ann for helpful insights, gentle criticism, and un-
complaining involvement. I have dedicated this work to her as an expression of the gratitude that "thank you" fails to convey.

JAMES K. LYON
La Jolla, California
September 1979

I. PROLOGUE TO AMERICAN EXILE

1 BRECHT AND AMERICA — THE NEW ATLANTIS

Bertolt Brecht surely knew better.

In his mind he had been to America many times as a young man. To live there was quite another matter. When Hitler's advancing troops forced him to flee Europe in 1941, he was a mature man with few illusions about the fabled "New Atlantis" of his youth. But necessity and lack of options compelled him to come and stay from 1941 to 1947. Out of that exile experience arose some of his most significant works. It also brought out the worst in him as he fought to maintain himself in an alien culture. He spoke of this period as his "exile in paradise" and wondered how long it would last.[1] In American exile Bertolt Brecht, whose dramas are said to have done more to shape the modern theater than any playwright since Ibsen,[2] suffered more financial deprivation, greater intellectual and emotional isolation, and more resounding failure and indifference toward his genius than he had known for years, or would know again in his lifetime.

After Hitler came to power, Brecht initially chose exile in Europe. But it was probably inevitable that one day he would come to the land of his youthful fantasies. He had grown up in a generation of Germans born around the turn of the century that was fascinated by and eager to imitate anything American. No sociologist can accurately measure what the idea called "America" did to the consciousness of a certain youth counter-culture in Germany. For many this exotic word carried a thousand overtones: gangsters and flappers; boxing and the latest dance steps; Prohibition and Charlie Chaplin films; auto racing and labor violence; jazz and Wild West films; an inventive language full of slogans that entered the vocabulary of many German youth; runaway technology that transformed radios, airplanes, gramophones, and automobiles from minor miracles into accustomed conveniences. All of these and anything practical, useful, experimental, or new were considered "American." "America" was in the air. In Germany, books about its life and culture proliferated. Publishers rushed to translate any title that sounded as though it came from the mythical continent.

"America," at least the exotic land conceived by the German imagination and transmitted by its popular media of the twenties, presented to Brecht and many of his generation an exciting alternative to a Europe which they thought to be depleted of its imaginative resources. Speaking for that generation in 1920, he wrote a poem about "blonde, pale Germany." He labelled it the "carrion pit" of Europe and announced that its young people had directed their creative powers elsewhere:

In the young men you
have not corrupted
America awakens.[3]

The same year his diary notes: "How this Germany bores me." Bewailing his lot of living in a mediocre land with its obese middle class and languid intelligentsia, he asks: "What's left? America!" (*GW* xx, 10)

This young man considered many of the traits he associated with America to be compatible with his own personality, or with the way he wanted to mold it. In America's sober pragmatism and toughness, combined with its imagination and vitality, he found a reflection of his own desire for toughly realistic behavior designed to challenge the existing world. The fascination boxing held to this young scarecrow, who had been hospitalized for malnutrition in 1922, bespoke the "hard bravado of soft youth" so characteristic of his early years. Boxing, to Brecht's thinking the quintessential American sport, symbolized life in the modern age. His play *In the Jungle of the Cities*, a portrayal of the "struggle of everyone against everyone" in a mythical Chicago, emphasized his obsession with contemporary life as a struggle between combatants. Beneath Brecht's interest in the cold-bloodedness of American gangsters, robber barons, and similar "tough guys" lay a clear desire to identify. In all probability this facade concealed a sensitive makeup. Just as his well-known theory of epic theater attempts to reduce emotion on the stage in favor of reasoned analysis, in his personal life Brecht generally tried to eliminate or escape from feeling in favor of what he called a "rational" mode of thought or behavior.[4] Everything from his leather jacket, short cropped hair, and ubiquitous cigar, to his Anglicized name (he changed the German "Berthold" to "Bertolt" and went by "Bert") cultivated this image that he worked so hard to maintain.

For Brecht and his contemporaries, America of this period stood for a mode of modern experience rather than for a geographical location. He intentionally stylized or exaggerated America as the locale in his plays *In the Jungle of the Cities, Mahagonny, Happy End, St. Joan of the Stockyards, The Flight of the Lindberghs, The Bread Shop*, and in the unpublished dramatic fragments *The Man from Manhattan, Dan Drew, The Fall of the Paradise City Miami*, and *Joe Fleischhacker*, as well as in the fragmentary libretto *Prairie* and many poems and short stories set in America. Most critics agree that many of these settings are little more than Americanized portrayals of life in Berlin. Just as gross exaggeration to make a point was an important facet of his personality, so the inclination to mythologize or remove the familiar to exotic places became essential to his art. This, too, was part of his theory of "estrangement." Elizabethan dramatists before Brecht often set their tragedies of revenge in Spain or Italy (which were practically indistinguishable in the popular mind) because of preconceived English attitudes toward these exotic lands. For Brecht, America fulfilled a similar function—it evoked preconceptions as well as a fascination in his audience based on an America that Germany of the day had invented for itself. To critics who faulted him for a fixation based on second-hand experience, he declared self-assuredly in a poem from his "Reader for Big-City Dwellers" written around 1926:

> I hear you say:
> He talks about America
> He doesn't understand anything about it
> He was never there.
> But believe me
> You understand me very well when I talk about America
> And the best thing about America is:
> That we understand it.
> (*GW* viii, 286)

But there was much that Brecht did not understand. As he came to understand America better, its glamour began to fade. After reading Frank Norris's *The Pit*, he tried unsuccessfully in 1926 to write a play about the Chicago Wheat Exchange. Not understanding its workings, he immersed himself in Marx's economic theory. This reading triggered his interest in that ideology. As his Marxist convictions solidified after 1926, his enthusiasm for America waned. Convinced that the Marxism of Soviet Russia represented the system of the future, he turned to that country as the utopia America once symbolized.[5] Yet the myth of America never let go of his imagination, and he continued to locate plays there. But by 1930 America had come to embody capitalism in its most highly developed, sinister form. Now "America" stood for a doomed country and system. A poem written that year under the impact of the Great Depression, "Forgotten Fame of the Metropolis New York" (*GW* ix, 475), refers to it mordantly as "God's own country." The poem goes on to describe the collapse of American culture from the perspective of a future observer reflecting on the now-forgotten center of capitalism. Little wonder that Brecht waited so long to come to America, or that he came so reluctantly.

On February 28, 1933, the day after the Reichstag fire, Brecht joined hundreds of artists and intellectuals who fled Germany for fear of their lives. Later he insisted that he had been number five on a Nazi death list.[1] That story probably had its origin in his imagination, but clearly he was in jeopardy. After a flight that took him through Prague and Vienna, he stopped briefly in Switzerland and in Paris before beginning nearly six years of exile in Denmark on the island of Fyn near the town of Svendborg. With him were his wife and his two children, eight-year-old Stefan and three-year-old Barbara. Soon two women collaborators joined the family on a more or less permanent basis— Margarete Steffin and Ruth Berlau.

On April 13th, six weeks after he fled Germany, an English-language version of his *Threepenny Opera* opened at New York's Empire Theatre in a weak production that closed after twelve performances. This was not his first work to reach America. That occurred on April 4, 1931, when Leopold Stokowski and the Philadelphia Symphony Orchestra performed *The Flight of the Lindberghs* with Kurt Weill's music.[2] In Salem, Massachusetts, an unidentified school also produced Brecht's and Weill's *He Who Says Yes*[3] in 1933, while in New York City that year the Music School of the Henry Street Settlement House performed the same opera. Yet Brecht remained essentially unknown in America. The failure of his *Threepenny Opera* in New York galled him, for he recognized that theatrical success in America meant New York City. To an exile without his own stage, Broadway, in spite of its reputation for commercialism, stood for real audiences and live performances. And Brecht preferred living theatergoers to the audience of posterity for which many exiles were writing. For the next fourteen years, the notion of conquering Broadway became an obsession.

The first opportunity for a New York performance came when the composer Hanns Eisler, who had collaborated with Brecht on several plays in the thirties, made a tour of the United States early in 1935. Highly regarded in leftist circles, Eisler had urged the Executive Board of the New York Theatre Union, the most famous "workers' theater" of the day, to perform Brecht's dramatic adaptation of Gorki's novel *Mother*. The Theatre Union, whose advisory and executive boards consisted of a cross-section of Stalinists, Trotskyists, socialists, and liberals, was known as a leftist theater that followed no party line. Its aim was to present plays with a progressive, socially conscious message at drastically reduced ticket prices to as wide an audience as possible, which ranged from labor unions to upper-middle-class New

York theater patrons. *Mother* had that kind of message, and the Theatre Union quickly decided to produce it.

Set in Russia at the turn of the century, *Mother* portrays the radicalization of Peleagea Vlassova, mother of a metal-worker named Pavel. Initially hostile to her son's involvement in the revolutionary movement, she is gradually drawn in when she distributes leaflets to help him to avoid arrest. After taking part in a peaceful demonstration where Pavel is arrested and sent to Siberia, she learns to read, helps striking peasants, and runs an illegal press in her apartment. Her son escapes from Siberia and is shot, and she carries on alone. When the World War breaks out, she is beaten up for protesting it, but continues to resist. At one point she is seen arguing against the war with women waiting in line to surrender their copper kettles for the war effort. The play ends as she carries a red flag during an anti-war demonstration in the winter of 1916.

In mid-1935 the Theatre Union, which was enthusiastic about using the play, wrote Brecht in Denmark. After some delay he finally agreed to a production, whereupon Paul Peters of the Theatre Union translated and adapted *Mother* for American audiences. Production was started and a copy of the translation was mailed to Brecht. When he saw it, he exploded. In his view, Peters had transformed his play into the kind of hypnotic theater he abhorred. The result appeared to be something resembling a well-made "naturalistic" play, instead of what he had written as a loosely structured "epic" piece.

By the time Brecht received the controversial translation, the Theatre Union could not turn back from its production. An exchange of letters explaining each side's viewpoint got nowhere,[4] and the Theatre Union finally dispatched Manuel Gomez to Denmark, where he negotiated a verbal agreement with Brecht which he thought gave the Theatre Union production rights. After initially refusing for financial reasons, the Theatre Union reluctantly agreed to pay Brecht's passage to America. As eager for a New York performance as the Theatre Union was to do it, Brecht apparently construed assurances that the play could be modified during rehearsal to mean he would get his own way once he was there. Not knowing the playwright, Theatre Union members miscalculated by thinking that on their own ground they could control him. But they had as little concept of Brecht's epic theater style as they had of his personality.

To Theatre Union officials, Brecht's primary qualifications appear to have been his achievements as a Marxist dramatist and the popular success of his *Threepenny Opera* in Europe. But they were ignorant of his reputation for controversial behavior as a director who insisted on the last word wherever he was involved in a production of his own plays. This reputation for troublemaking sprang in large part from his perception of himself as a pioneer in a new type of theater. Some years earlier he had begun to promote a new kind of "epic" theater, as he called it, which he opposed to conventional or "Aristotelian" theater. With enormous conviction of his own ideas, he began a frontal assault on the entire western mode of thinking about and viewing theater as it existed in the early twentieth century. Though he continued to refine and restate his theories, he remained to the end a maverick and innovator in the theater. Of course Brecht had his forerunners, and often he was quite willing to acknowledge his debt to them. But just as frequently he conveyed the impression that the theories he propounded were totally original. With characteristic self-certitude he called himself the "Einstein of the new stage form."[5] If he was contentious, it was principled contentiousness, with one end in mind—to inaugurate precisely and perfectly his own style of theater in an alien world. Today we know he was right, but in 1935 the Theatre Union was unprepared for his dramatic ideas or his means of implementing them.

In coming to New York, Brecht clearly hoped to introduce his name and theories to the theater world. On board the *S.S. Acquitania* he wrote an autobiographical poem entitled "When the Classic Departed on Monday, October 7, 1935, Denmark Wept" (*GW* IX, 559). With characteristic brashness he compared himself to Columbus about to embark for the New World. Noting that America represented the most advanced country in everything, he wondered if it was prepared for his new kind of "learning play." The answer was not long in coming.

From the moment he and the young director, Victor Wolfson, met at the pier on October 15th, they struck up a strong mutual dislike.[6] Rehearsals had already begun, but Brecht found nothing to his liking. He proceeded to demand changes in everything from the script and the sets to the actress portraying Peleagea Vlassova. The Theatre Union acceded to some of his demands, including the one for a new lead, but in the process Brecht antagonized nearly everyone associated with the production. Writing to Helene Weigel in Denmark early in November he admitted that by exercising a "nice little dictatorship" he had managed to restore the script to its original version. But he failed to realize how badly the situation had deteriorated, and how far he was from resolving differences.

Albert Maltz, a member of the executive board, remembers how Brecht constantly badgered Wolfson. He thundered out "in a voice that would have humiliated the fight announcer at Madison Square Garden" that " 'this is shit.' . . . We had in our midst a screaming banshee. . . . I can still hear . . . his Prussian drill master's call, *Sitzung*, i.e., meeting. We often had several a day."[7] Brecht's pet phrases for the actors and their acting (*Das ist Scheisse! Das ist Dreck!* i.e., "That's shit!" "That's crap!") required no translation after the first time, and his tantrums triggered several fights a day, each of which demanded a council of peace. Erroneously assuming that the Communist Party controlled the Theatre Union, he at one point appealed in vain to V. J. Jerome, the party's chief cultural officer, for binding arbitration. In little more than two weeks from the time he signed a contract with the Theatre Union, his behavior was considered so abusive that on November 8th he and Eisler were finally thrown out of the theater after the most recent victim of his insults, a pianist, threatened to "break every bone in his body."[8]

From an apartment he shared with Elisabeth Hauptmann at 225 West 69th Street, Brecht continued to bombard the Theatre Union with letters and phone calls threatening court action and withdrawal of his script if it ignored his wishes. In a letter of November 9th he reserved for himself "the right to take whatever steps are necessary . . . because of the threat of physical violence by a pianist whom I justifiably criticized." He went on to assert that his contract secured him the rights to "give instructions to the director." Perhaps he had in mind the oral agreement made with Gomez in Denmark, but his written contract with the Theatre Union said nothing about this.[9] On the other hand, the Theatre Union did not construe any agreement made by Gomez to mean interference with their adaptation, regardless of how they altered it. And there was the rub, for in his eyes they had butchered it.

After Brecht was excluded from the theater, Wolfson reverted to a modified version of the script that Paul Peters had prepared. It was closer to Gorki's original novel, since it eliminated scenes Brecht had added to Gorki's plot, including one showing the mother persuading women not to surrender copper kettles for the war effort, and one in which she defiantly tears a page from the Bible. But some of Brecht's theater ideas and parts of his text were retained. The result was a hybrid production which satisfied no one. Brecht and Eisler continued to protest that their text and music were being altered or handled so ineptly that they did not want the play to open, though they realized they could not prohibit it. They declined an invitation to attend further rehearsals, and the compromise stage version opened on November 19, 1935, with predictable results.

While recognizing it as "experimental" or a "new kind of theater," most critics demolished *Mother*: "an animated lecture on the theme of revolution, which may have an educational value, but which is desultory theater" (Brooks Atkinson, *New York Times*); "a Marxian primer, slightly illustrated" (Richard Lockridge); "an unhappy marriage of revolutionary exhortation and stage experimentation" (Howard Barnes); "a series of animated pictures of pre-Soviet Russia" (Burns Mantle); and "poor stuff, amateurishly presented" (*Daily Mirror*). Brecht himself, who was angry that the Theatre Union had not presented his play on his terms, later intimated that it was produced primarily for commercial gain: "The Theatre Union behaved like any other Broadway theater that treats a play like goods or the raw material for easily marketable goods."[10] *The Daily Worker* devoted two-thirds of a page to a perceptive, balanced review that noted a "struggle of two styles, two tendencies in the production." M. J. Olgin, the reviewer, obviously had been privy to the pre-production battles, and he carefully pointed out the separate qualities of the play and the production. But nothing could alter the fact that Brecht's first try at an American stage production had failed. In the process, it dealt a financial blow to the Theatre Union from which it never recovered.[11] The executive secretary wrote him (December 9, 1935) that increasing losses would force the Theatre Union to close *Mother* on the 15th. Advance ticket sales to workers' organizations had brought in sizable audiences, but ultimately the theater's survival depended on box-office sales to the general public, and poor reviews in the press effectively stopped those. It stands as a harsh irony in theater history that one of the strongest (and certainly the best) spokesmen for proletarian theater in this century contributed so decisively to the demise of one of America's most progressive workers' theaters.

Did Brecht learn anything from the experience? One interpreter believes that after returning to Europe, and as a result of these events, he wrote several scenes in *Private Life of the Master Race*, the American title of his *Fear and Misery of the Third Reich* (1935-1938), and the entire play *Señora Carrar's Rifles* (1937) with a middle-class audience in mind.[12] The more conventional "Aristotelian" dramatic structuring of these two works suggests that he may have begun to tailor his plays to available audiences and theaters. Constitutionally, Brecht was poorly equipped to do this, especially for a middle-class American audience, but he later admitted to an American friend that he had precisely that in mind.[13] To say that his American experience helped him to break out of the rigid Marxist schematic of his learning plays goes too far. But he was realistic, and while he proposed to change the dramatic realities he saw, he was not blind to them.

In the New York production, Brecht had recognized certain elements of his own "epic" acting style in Helen Henry,[14] the lead in *Mother*, whom he liked very much. Perhaps her background in vaudeville made her his kind of actress, for he saw in vaudeville affinities with his own epic theater.[15] Most American actors nauseated Brecht with their playing. The exceptions were those who shared with vaudeville players the traits which made them "performers" rather than "actors." He had genuine affection for this kind of "performing," probably because it communicated and entertained simultaneously, without swindling the audience into a state of belief.

An inveterate theater man, Brecht attended several Broadway plays during his New York stay. Writing in his journal years later, he described a political mass meeting in Madison Square Garden in December 1935 where he saw several scenes of Clifford Odets's *Waiting for Lefty* performed. The play appealed to him as much as Madison Square Garden, that "thin, elegant, intimate structure that is so splendidly appropriate for mass theater," as he later wrote.[16] Soon afterward, he also saw a performance of Odets's *Paradise Lost*. By this time he probably had met Odets personally, for, to vent his dissatisfaction with *Paradise Lost*, he wrote an occasional poem entitled "Letter to the Playwright Odets" (*GW* x, 846) that sounded as if he knew him personally. It addressed him as "comrade," a honorific Brecht would not have used with Odets during the forties (Odets left the American Communist Party in 1936). The poem scolded Odets for his excessive sympathy with the rich who were suffering from the Depression: "Perhaps the families of the exploiters/fall to ruin. What if they did not?/Would exploitation be easier for us if they/Did not?" he asked. Because Brecht's sympathies lay completely with the exploited classes, he not only found Odets's sympathy misplaced; he considered the step from *Waiting for Lefty* to *Paradise Lost* tantamount to ideological treason: "From compassion for the taxi driver to compassion for those who soon will not be able to afford a cab—for which damnable capitalism is responsible. The invisible enemy of the small capitalist is the big capitalist,"[17] he told V. J. Jerome in a letter. Though social protest probably shaped the attitudes of American theater history more strongly in the thirties than at any other time, as a socially conscious play *Paradise Lost* was found wanting when weighed in the balance by this Marxist playwright.

Theatre Union people recall what they perceived to be a superiority complex in matters of Marxist ideology as one personal trait that did not endear Brecht to them.[18] Manuel Gomez remembers him to have been "enormously vain . . . enormously energetic, enormously stubborn, enormously sarcastic, enormously difficult."[19] Albert Maltz, who took umbrage at his "contentious arrogance," openly admits that he came to loathe him as a person, in part because the stench of his unwashed body (Brecht disliked bathing) made it an ordeal to sit next to him.[20] George Sklar compared Brecht to Hitler and perceived in him at the time "the same apoplectic indulgence, the same ranting and shrieking associated with the German dictator."[21] This would not be the first or last time someone would make this unflattering comparison.

Virtually no one was able to see that they were dealing with something more than a disgusting, disruptive lout. Only one person seems to have recognized that Brecht's theatrical ideas had merit, and that his behavior was dictated by a stubborn self-certainty about these views—Mordecai (Max) Gorelik, the set designer for *Mother*.

When Brecht first saw Gorelik's sets for the production, he objected that they were too "picturesque."[22] Gorelik tolerated such remarks and grew to be the only member of the Theatre Union who was friendly to Brecht and his ideas. Such sympathy in hostile surroundings appealed to Brecht, and he won a disciple in this eager student of theater. For hours they talked of their craft, and, though Gorelik did not always agree with him, he recognized in him a master craftsman of the theater. Later in 1936 Gorelik, who then had a Guggenheim fellowship, went to Denmark, where he observed Brecht in Copenhagen assisting in a production of his *Round Heads and Peak Heads*. He then spent two weeks talking theater with him at his converted farmhouse on the isle of Fyn. From these conversations sprang the idea for an "International Diderot Society," an organization Brecht hoped to establish in 1937 devoted to the theater of the scientific age, or what he termed "inductive theater." In the encyclopedist, revolutionary, and playwright Diderot, Brecht recognized a kindred spirit whose views on non-emotional, didactic theater coincided with many of his own.[23]

Plans for this society arose in part from Brecht's frustrating failure with the Theatre Union and his determination to find others, especially in English-speaking countries, who shared or would be willing to try his ideas on theater. Without production pressure, he also wanted to hear more from Gorelik about the conventions he had flouted during the *Mother* production. In response to Brecht's request for more information on theater life in America, Gorelik sent, among other things, two issues of *Theatre Workshop*. They ignited a response that illustrated how alien everything happening on the American stage was to Brecht.

From this theatrical magazine, Brecht realized how strongly American theater was becoming committed to "method-acting," with its basis in the concepts and models of Stanislavsky. Most of the Theatre Union people had been with the Group Theatre, the company that first propagated Stanislavski's system in America. In a letter thanking Gorelik for the reading matter, Brecht called the Group Theatre "progressive" only because it offered *some* method.[24] Otherwise, he mocked the actor "serving" his art in a "creative" setting (wasn't God the creator?) and "transforming" himself much like the manner in which the eucharist became the body of Christ. Action in these "well-made plays" must be "justified," according to Brecht, just like earthly behavior at the Last Judgment. He continued that the actor's "concentration" or "immersion" in his role became similar to the introspection of the mystic, and he served "truth," which came through proper "feeling," just as Truth might be gained through the Jesuits' spiritual exercises.[25] The public in turn must be "hypnotized by this type of actor." But he found not a word about classes, society, or economics, he said, and the revolution had not taken place. He praised the efforts of *Theatre Workshop* as a magazine and encouraged Gorelik to continue on its editorial board, but for him the theorists in its pages were nothing but "incorrigible intellectuals, jaded bourgeois."

This was more than a clash of two national cultures. Brecht drew the battle lines between what he saw as disparate theater traditions—his, with its roots in classical Greek, Elizabethan, and Counter-Reformation Jesuit drama,[26] generously seasoned with modern socio-economic philosophical theories; and, on the other hand, a distinctly bourgeois-style drama and playing that arose in the eighteenth and nineteenth centuries and perpetuated a mode of social consciousness and behavior which he considered incompatible with the modern scientific age. Because he habitually overstated his theories, he appeared at this time to be an implacable foe of feeling in the theater. In his view it destroyed the rational thought that he insisted must prevail in our age. Later Brecht modified this position, but from 1936 until the end of his American exile he appeared to be uncompromising in his views. More than anything else, it was this single-mindedness which barred him from the American stage. The information Gorelik furnished on Broadway did little to make him eager to compromise with the norms of American theater. Until he achieved success with his ideas after the war, his efforts to change prevailing theater practice struck those who knew him as total opposition rather than the shift in emphasis he really intended.

Gorelik himself subscribed to many main-line ideas of American theater, a position which later led to disagreements with Brecht. At this time, however, his genuine interest in understanding the playwright's theories made him an open-minded listener, which Brecht desperately needed during his exile. In the April/June, 1937 issue of *Theatre Workshop* he published his own translation of some early theoretical formulations. Entitled "Epic Realism: Brecht's Notes on the Threepenny Opera," it was accompanied by Gorelik's explication of these theories.

Gorelik's advocacy of Brecht invited two quick attacks. In the following issue of *Theatre Workshop* John Howard Lawson wrote a letter to the editor dismissing Brecht's views as "nonsense" and "theoretical material . . . of an extremely meretricious character," while Edmund Fuller assailed them later that year in *One Act Play Magazine*.[27] Three years later Gorelik published his book *New Theatres for Old*, which represented the first major scholarly work on drama in the Anglo-Saxon world to give a well-rounded survey of Brecht's poetics. Read today, his six-page exposition of Brecht's theories seems obvious, since Brecht's ideas are known; at the time, Gorelik's presentation must have struck the reader as revolutionary, if in fact it was intelligible. In January of 1940, this was the most advanced exposition of Brechtian theater available in any language, and a reasonably accurate one at that. Gorelik had gleaned most of the material from conversations and correspondence with the exiled playwright, who would not publish many of these ideas until years later. Any shortcomings must be attributed to Brecht himself. His dramatic theories were still evolving, and later he contradicted or superseded much that he said or wrote at this time. Nevertheless Gorelik's discipleship stands as one of the few positive results of the New York Theatre Union experience. In contrast to his relationship with V. J. Jerome, the ranking cultural officer in the American Communist Party, it held up well for many years.

Privately, Brecht and Jerome appear to have been cordial. Jerome considered the German to be the great hope of proletarian drama. When asked to referee the playwright's dispute with the Theatre Union, he made the cause his own, and Brecht appreciated it. Jerome also saw a good deal of Brecht socially, taking him to parties where he introduced the visitor to cultural figures of the American left, such as Marc Blitzstein and Eva Goldbeck. Further, he helped to promote Brecht's writings. During a visit to Brecht's apartment, the playwright showed him a copy of his poem "How the Carpet Weavers of Kujan-Bulak Honored Lenin." Jerome, who read German, arranged immediately to have Eva Goldbeck translate the poem in time for the anniversary issue of *The Daily Worker* commemorating Lenin's death, which was to appear two days later.[28] Goldbeck made the deadline, and the translation appeared on January 21, 1936. Eight days after Brecht departed, Goldbeck sent Jerome a letter with the statement that "Bert Brecht told me that you have taken charge of certain of his works and translations," which sounds as though Brecht empowered him to act in some way as his literary agent.[29] A letter from Jerome to Goldbeck two days later confirms that Brecht asked him to arrange for translations and productions of his works in America.[30] What Brecht had in mind is unclear, but it is evident that he trusted Jerome and appreciated his assistance. Shortly before Brecht left, Jerome gave him a briefcase. A warm letter from the exile's "Danish Siberia" (as he called it), in February 1936, thanked Jerome and regretted that they had missed, among other things, having "a talk about American literature, at least drama.[31] They corresponded over the next years, and in 1939 Brecht thoughtfully sent a poem he had adapted from the Chinese poet Tung-Po congratulating the Jeromes on their son's birth.[32] But Brecht's journal from the years 1941 to 1947 fails to mention Jerome, and there is no record of correspondence or contact between them after 1939.

One suspects that politics, not friendship, moved Brecht to address "comrade" Jerome with the intimate *Du* form used only with close friends or party members. In spite of an uncanny ability to attract certain people to aid him and his projects, Brecht never had many close "friends" during his life time. For him friendship was defined in terms not only of political compatibility, but of usefulness in making a name or getting a production, availability to collaborate, and willingness to be a disciple. When Jerome no longer functioned in those roles, their association lapsed.

In November 1935 Jerome conducted a formal interview with Brecht and Eisler in German that Elisabeth Hauptmann recorded and transcribed into English.[33] Jerome struggled to comprehend as Brecht explained dramatic theories so alien to him that repeatedly he missed Brecht's point. Announcing that he wished to write an article on dramaturgical methods he found common to Archibald MacLeish and Brecht, Jerome listed points of contact, such as the use of chorus, verse, symbolism, and metaphysics. Brecht sharply denied any similarities and ignored the comparison to MacLeish as he argued his own theories. He elaborated on the parable as a theatrical teaching form (making comparisons with Jesus, Buddha, and Lenin), expressed his aversion to Ibsenesque theater, and discussed his ideas of using dialect in the theater.

Jerome asked how he would treat the language in a play about a slave insurrection in nineteenth-century America led by an educated slave (later correspondence confirms that it was Nat Turner). The German dramatist's inquiry at this point about the language used in *Porgy and Bess* and *Green Pastures*, plays with all-black casts which Brecht saw while in New York, foreshadows another idea he tried to realize later in American exile—to have all-black productions of his plays. His solutions here constituted a striking example of his now famous "estrangement" or "distanciation" effect, where the familiar is cast in a new light. Brecht would have had the slaves, who normally spoke dialect, employ standard English. "This is revolutionary," he claimed. Verisimilitude mattered little to him, but the mode of speech used to delineate social classes in a striking manner did. Jerome objected and, though willing to learn, he seemed unable to accept what Brecht was proposing.

The playwright did not return to Denmark immediately after *Mother* closed, but stayed until early February 1936, reconnoitering the cultural landscape and cultivating people in America who might help him. A letter from the Theatre Union (December 6, 1935) had invited him to a symposium it was sponsoring on "Poetry and Music in the Labor Theatre." Scheduled for December 11th, it was to help stimulate lagging ticket sales for the *Mother* production. There is no record that he knew the participants (Archibald MacLeish, Aaron Copeland, John Gassner, and Fannia M. Cohn) before this time, but later correspondence confirms that sometime in the winter of 1935-1936, and probably there, he met Gassner and MacLeish.[34] Neither helped him especially in his later American exile, but MacLeish wrote in 1938 that Brecht's play *Mother* "failed with more distinction in its Theatre Union production in New York than most successes gain in years of glory,"[35] and Gassner became a Brecht admirer at this time, in spite of an unfavorable review he wrote of *Mother*.[36]

At least one young American whom Brecht met in New York succumbed to the immense intellectual pull the dramatist exerted on many of those he did not antagonize—the composer Marc Blitzstein. Brecht's direct influence helped give birth to his opera *The Cradle Will Rock*.

When Hanns Eisler completed his tour of the United States in the spring of 1935, he took a teaching position at the New School for Social Research. Almost from the moment that he met Blitzstein and his wife Eva Goldbeck, Eisler promoted Brecht's cause. In December 1935 the Blitzsteins invited friends in to meet Brecht. Minna Lederman recounts how she came hoping to arrange an article on Brecht's and Eisler's songs to be published in *Modern Music*.[37] After drinks, they listened to Blitzstein play "The Nickel Under Your Foot," a song about prostitution. Brecht commented, "Very good so far, but why not a whole play about all forms of prostitution—the press, the clergy, and so on," an idea Brecht himself developed later in a novel and play about prostituted intellectuals.[38] A week later Blitzstein called Lederman and reported, "I've taken up his idea and am making an opera of it." Lederman further insists it was "Brecht's influence on Marc's youthful *Weltanschauung* that effected the synthesis of his disparate resources—his awareness of the American scene, his feeling for popular speech and music idioms, his militant social consciousness, and his skill as a serious composer." In a word, Brecht was "the solvent of his career."[39] The two men had only occasional contact after 1936, but Blitzstein memorialized his gratitude to Brecht in several forms: he dedicated *The Cradle Will Rock* to him; he later translated *The Threepenny Opera* version that opened in New York's Theatre De Lys in 1954 and ran until 1961; and he translated *Mother Courage, Mahagonny*, and a number of Brecht poems set to Eisler's music.

At the Blitzsteins Brecht became acquainted with another young man who would figure prominently in the history of American film and theater—John Houseman. Houseman recalls discussing Brecht's play *Round Heads and Peak Heads* with the dramatist and hearing how he wanted it performed in America.[40] Brecht had derived the original idea from Shakespeare's *Measure for Measure*, and, though his own play had become something quite different in its final form, Shakespeare's comedy also came up for discussion. According to Houseman, Brecht proposed having it done in America with an all-black cast. Neither idea materialized, but it was the beginning of a productive association between them that lasted for years and would assist Brecht materially during his American exile.

Houseman had been introduced to Brecht by Joseph Losey, a young American director whom Brecht had met in Moscow the previous year, where both were visiting out of political conviction coupled with artistic interest. As one of the directors of the Federal Theater Project's "Living Newspaper" productions in 1936, Losey had staged its first play, *Triple-A Plowed Under*, and its third, *Injunction Granted*. Losey reports that Brecht attended one of these "Living Newspaper" productions and "loved it,"[41] perhaps because in them Losey had unwittingly created a style that came as close as anything in America to Brechtian theater. Immediately the two sensed an affinity in theatrical views and style which later critics were quick to note.[42] Losey recalls listening to Brecht in their apartment "expounding his enthusiasms, articulating his 'eye,' which was our eye, too. But none of us was conscious then of the parallels."[43] Soon after this visit, he tried to bring Brecht's works to the United States, but without success.

Eva Goldbeck, Blitzstein's wife, also deserves credit as an important translator and early proponent of Brecht's works. Except for her death in 1936, America might have known more of them earlier, and in better translations. She had done several Brecht poems before he arrived in New York, and he asked her to render others after he met her. In collaboration with him, she re-translated some of the songs from

Mother, which the *Daily Worker* published. Under Brecht's supervision she wrote a two-page essay on his ideas that appeared in *New Masses* (December 31, 1935) with the title "Principles of 'Educational' Theater." This lucid exposition of Brechtian dramaturgy still ranks as one of the most intelligible summaries of his principles. Several items among Goldbeck's posthumous papers mirror the degree of her involvement in Brecht's literary activities—a translation she prepared (probably with Brecht's assistance) of a speech he delivered in 1935 before the International Congress of Writers in Paris entitled "A Needed Inquiry Regarding the Struggle Against Barbarism," and several letters stating that Brecht had authorized her to translate his anti-war poem "The Three Soldiers" and the choruses for his play *The Measures Taken*, which was being considered for production in New York.[44] Brecht seems to have had high regard for her translations. Before leaving, he followed what was to become a familiar pattern by giving authority simultaneously to her and to V. J. Jerome to translate and arrange for publication of his poems and stories (in a document he executed for Goldbeck, he did exclude the plays from this arrangement).[45]

Mild irony surrounds another encounter where Brecht met and failed to recognize a potential adversary. Among his contacts with left-wing and avant-garde theater circles, he managed to meet Harold Clurman and his wife Stella Adler, two leading figures in the Group Theatre. Clurman maintains that he knew little and saw less of him, but Adler, always curious about new modes of theater, asked Brecht to expound his acting theories to her.[46] Brecht did so by rehearsing her in a scene from his *Saint Joan of the Stockyards*. The playwright was unaware that she had met Konstantin Stanislavski the previous year and had received lengthy instruction from him on his method of acting. At this point, too, he was probably not aware that the Group Theatre was using and promoting the principles of Stanislavski acting, which, as he interpreted them, were anathema to him. Adler listened to Brecht and learned, but she seems to have made no more impact on her than he had on American theater generally.

In America in 1935-1936 Brecht's name reached only a limited number of artists and readers of the American left and failed generally to justify his international reputation. The summer 1935 issue of *Music Vanguard* carried a translation of his "Notes on Translating Songs of Protest" (pp. 67-68), and the *Daily Worker* printed an interview on October 31, 1935, which he gave Martha Dreiblatt of the Theatre Union upon arriving in the States.[47] In *New Masses* Stanley Burnshaw had published a favorable article (December 3, 1935) entitled "The Theatre Union Produces 'Mother,'" which was more about

Brechtian theater than about that specific production. Translations of Brecht's poems as texts to Hanns Eisler's songs began to turn up in leftist publications and song books.[48] Except for a limited circle, however, he was probably best known as the author of the texts to protest songs from the international Communist movement of the thirties.

Only once did Brecht find a platform to reach a wider New York audience. In its theater section, the Sunday edition of the *New York Times* of November 24, 1935, carried an article by "Bert Brecht" entitled "The German Drama: Pre-Hitler." Presumably someone at the Theatre Union arranged it. The English suggests that Eva Goldbeck or another native speaker familiar with his theories translated it, but under Brecht's supervision. One reads, for example, the German title of his works (*Versuche*) followed by the English translation "experiments," or an explanation that the nearest English equivalent for his *Lehrstücke* is "learning plays," a term no translator would have hit upon without the author's assistance.

After a brief summary of the technological and dramaturgical innovations of German theater in the Weimar Republic, Brecht in this article contrasts his own type of "non-Aristotelian" or epic playing with conventional "Aristotelian" drama and insists that the latter is essentially static, i.e., its task is to depict the world as it is. His theater, he claims, is essentially dynamic, i.e., it shows the world as it is changing (and how it can be changed). Audiences must remain thinking individuals and not dissolve into a "mob" that can be reached only through emotions. Theater should be "fun," the fun being a by-product of learning. Brecht urges those who had seen *Mother* to revisit it and give him their opinions, because both he and they would learn from it. But he would have had as much effect if he had talked to the wind. By the time he left, the middle-class New York theater world neither knew nor cared about the "Einstein of the New Theater" or his theories.

Initially, New York, or at least his troubles with the Theatre Union, depressed Brecht. Hanns Eisler recalls that his ascetic friend, who seldom drank more than a glass of beer a day, carried a small whiskey flask with him in New York: "I can't stand it here without whiskey," he complained.[49] Instead of sulking, Brecht set out to experience New York and America. An undated note sent to the theater columnist Wilella Waldorf by Martha Dreiblatt of the Theatre Union states that he was "going about town seeing all the detective plays and movies he can in spare time between rehearsals. Says he prefers them to almost anything else here, as they give the most realistic picture of the American, particularly New York scene . . . and are also technically and artistically the best done of our theater entertainments."[50] Others confirm that he saw nearly every gangster movie in town.[51] His view that

they were the most accurate documentary representations of social reality in America explains why Brecht returned to Denmark with a suitcase full of clippings from New York papers reporting on the murder
of the famous gangster Dutch Schultz and two of his bodyguards,
which happened while he was there, and articles on gangland wars
and slayings, loan-sharking, robberies, corrupt public officials, murders of respected citizens, and other ills of life in the capitalistic metropolis.[52]

In addition to attending parties with non-Theatre Union leftists,
Brecht frequented Broadway and saw a number of plays, including the
two by Odets mentioned earlier, *Porgy and Bess*, and *Green Pastures*.
In her note to Wilella Waldorf, Martha Dreiblatt records his reaction
to one evening in the theater with the statement that Brecht "admires
extremely the direction of [Rouben] Mamoulien in *Porgy and Bess*."
Finally, on February 1, 1936, he and Eisler heard their songs from
Mother performed by the New Singers in a farewell concert for Eisler
at Steinway Hall.

But much of Brecht's stay is not documented. His paternal aunt
and her husband, Mr. and Mrs. William Zaiss, lived at 12-S Bay 17th
Street, in Brooklyn. On his immigration records he listed a cousin,
DeWitt Bronard, at 1198 Ocean Avenue in Brooklyn.[53] Did he visit
this favorite aunt? And did he produce any poems, stories, or plays
during the days and weeks in his apartment? Immigration and Naturalization Service records show that he renewed his German passport
in New York early in 1936.[54] Apparently he found an unsuspecting
consular official, since on June 8, 1935 the Nazi regime had stripped
him of German citizenship "for behavior in violation of the obligation
of loyalty toward Reich and people."[55]

A letter to Erwin Piscator written five months after Brecht's return
to Europe intimates that he met at least some theater people receptive
to his ideas. "You cannot imagine," he says, "how greedily many
people in New York seized on our new methods after realizing that
traditional theater and ideology cannot solve the new problems."[56]
Clearly he was not speaking of Theatre Union people, but of Blitzstein,
Goldbeck, Losey, Houseman, and Gorelik. Yet even these associations
with sympathetic theater people did little to relieve his disappointment. *Mother* had flopped, and the "Einstein of the new stage form"
had failed to capture the capital of American theater.

3 "CHANGING COUNTRIES MORE OFTEN THAN SHOES"

Except for the multitude of enemies and handful of friends he left behind, the only mark Brecht made on America at this time was on *Pins and Needles*, the musical review presented by the Labor Stage and the International Ladies' Garment Workers' Union in 1936. Emanuel Eisenberg, a well-known figure in the New York leftist theater, wrote a satire entitled "The Little Red School House" based on what had happened in rehearsals and production of Brecht's *Mother*. Like many leftists, he had had no sympathy for Brecht as a person or for his type of theater. Presented as one of the skits that comprised *Pins and Needles*, this satire suggests that had he not been so disliked, Brecht might have been forgotten entirely.

Europe, especially Germany, was still the center of Brecht's universe, and he wanted to be near his German-language stage and the struggle against the Nazis. During eight years of exile in Denmark, Sweden, and Finland, he devoted himself to anti-fascist activities that included writing radio broadcasts, giving lectures, staging his anti-fascist plays, and turning out pamphlets to be smuggled into Germany. In this period he also wrote some of his most brilliant poetry and many plays, among them several of the dramas that later would bring him international recognition—*Galileo; Mother Courage and Her Children; The Good Woman of Setzuan; Round Heads and Peak Heads; Private Life of the Master Race; The Resistible Rise of Arturo Ui*; and *Puntila and His Servant Matti*.

During his Scandinavian exile, Brecht traveled to Russia, France, and England. He had not forgotten America, but he had no desire to settle there. In mid-1936, a few months after returning from New York, he wrote Erwin Piscator, the German stage director living in Russian exile, and suggested that they travel to America and try to sell a film story. But not until Hitler marched into Czechoslovakia in October 1938, and free Europe began to shrink, did he seriously entertain the idea of America as a refuge.

After the Stalin purges began, Brecht never considered the Soviet Union a haven. Two trips there in 1932 and 1935 convinced him that by now he would be associated too closely with the "Formalist" heretics Meyerhold, Eisenstein, and his Soviet friend, Sergei Tretyakov. By 1937, when Tretyakov was arrested and tried on a trumped-up charge (he was executed in 1939), Brecht's survival instinct told him to look elsewhere. One by one his acquaintances in Moscow, both German exiles and Soviets, disappeared.[1] In July 1938 he replied to an inquiry about his friends in the Soviet Union: "I really don't have any friends there. Nor do the Muscovites—like the dead."[2]

Late in 1938 the Hollywood screen writer Ferdinand Reyher visited Brecht in Copenhagen. Before he went to Hollywood in 1931, Reyher, a brilliant raconteur, not only enjoyed a reputation as a gifted writer himself; he maintained close ties to Sinclair Lewis, Wallace Stevens, Ford Maddox Ford, John Rodker, and a large number of important literary figures on each side of the Atlantic. When he and Brecht first met in Berlin in 1927, they discovered a kinship which grew into one of the closest friendships Brecht experienced in his lifetime.[3] With America very much on his mind during Reyher's visit between October 28 and November 4, 1938, Brecht now recounted to him his plans for a drama on the life of Galileo. Ruminating on it with Reyher, he cocked an eye toward Hollywood's hills of gold and agreed first to write a film story, which Reyher would try to sell, and then to do a drama. From Reyher or others, he learned that to have a film or play of his produced in America would simplify immigration matters greatly. On December 2, 1938 he wrote Reyher saying that within a period of three weeks he had written a play about Galileo instead of the film story they agreed upon. Could Reyher arrange an American production of it? "It has a monumental role," he went on, "and if one could get an important, influential actor for it, it might help get a production. But perhaps productions in America aren't dependent on actors as they are in Europe." His obsession with succeeding on Broadway, coupled with fear for his own safety, now spelled one word—America.

As Nazi agents moved freely throughout Denmark and as the Danish government's ability to resist Nazi demands for deportation of German exiles weakened, Brecht decided to apply for an American quota immigration visa for his family and himself, which he did in Copenhagen sometime before March 1939.[4] Like many who wanted to come, Brecht had been stripped of his German citizenship by Hitler and no longer qualified as a "German national." Not only were he and others like him refused special consideration; they were penalized by being placed on a much longer waiting list for those without nationality. Further, American xenophobic and isolationist popular opinion supported pointlessly harsh immigration policies which allowed many State Department foreign service officers to obstruct the entry of German refugees. For many like Brecht, consular whim became a matter of life and death.[5]

From information he received in 1939, Brecht informed friends in America that he would have to wait two years for a normal quota visa.[6] In the meantime, as Reyher wrote a friend, "Bert Brecht's little green isle of Denmark is getting hot, and I believe will soon be untenable for him. He is trying everything to get out and wants to come to America."[7] With his little Danish isle becoming, in his own words, "increasingly like a mousetrap,"[8] he moved to Sweden in April 1939, where he spent another year before continuing his exile in Finland after April 1940. Like thousands of other refugees from Nazi Germany, Brecht found America's golden door opened to him through the exertions and largesse of kind friends and generous strangers, not to mention a substantial portion of good luck.

In mid-1939, the exiled German film director Fritz Lang began soliciting funds from Hollywood personalities expressly to support the Brecht family for a six-month period.[9] In the next two years, Fritz Kortner, Dorothy Thompson, Kurt Weill, Oskar Homolka, Bruno Frank, and Lion Feuchtwanger all helped financially at one point or another.[10]

In June 1939 Erwin Piscator, the German stage director known as the founder of "political theater," wrote from New York and asked if Brecht remembered encouraging him to go to New York "because of the enormous opportunities there." He urged him to heed his own counsel and asked if Brecht would help with Piscator's fledgling Theatre Workshop at the New School for Social Research.[11] Later this became a solid invitation that resulted in a quota immigration visa. And in Mexico in the summer of 1939, Hanns Eisler told a young American writer named H. R. Hays, who had seen and admired *Mother* in 1935, about Brecht's genius and plight. Hays offered to help, sight unseen, and Brecht now had someone who later provided an affidavit of support for his party.[12]

On April 17, 1940, shortly after Nazi troops occupied Denmark and Norway, Brecht sailed for Finland and again "took up the exile's trade: hoping" (*GW* IX, 822). On the same day he left Sweden, Dr. Alvin S. Johnson, president of the New School for Social Research and father of the "University in Exile" at that school, cabled him in Stockholm with an invitation to "join our faculty . . . as Lecturer in Literature, with a salary of $1500, the appointment to run from May 1940 (or the earliest date on which you can arrive) to January 1941."[13] Many Europeans owed their lives to Dr. Johnson and his idea for a "University in Exile," born out of dismay at what he saw in Germany in 1932. Normally he invited distinguished refugee scholars and teachers for one to two years at stipends of $3,000 to $4,000 annually, solely to help them get into the United States.[14] Piscator, one of the few refugees to secure a permanent position at the New School, persuaded Dr. Johnson to invite the distinctly non-academic Brecht on the basis of his poetic and dramatic reputation. While this invitation was not enough to bring Brecht to America immediately, it probably saved his life, for it prompted him to go to the American embassy in Helsinki

(May 17, 1940) and re-enter the names of his family and a collaborator, Margarete Steffin, on the consul's waiting list.

Brecht wrote Piscator the same day, thanked him and his friends for
intervening in his behalf with Dr. Johnson, and stated his plans to
come soon on a visitor's visa. Could the New School do anything to
speed up approval of that visa? His name, he said, had been on a list
for a quota visa since March 1939, but now the situation had become
urgent—his wife's and children's Danish refugee papers would expire
in August 1940.

Why did Brecht hesitate this long before pressing for quota visas?
The most apparent answer lies in the desperate hope that the fight
against Hitler would not be a losing battle. Few optimists have had
fewer illusions than Brecht and remained optimists. He refused to quit
Europe until the situation was hopeless. Only after the Nazi invasion
of Holland that same month and the fall of France the next month did
he decide to leave for good.

A letter to Piscator of May 27, 1940 reveals a more compelling reason for hesitation—his collaborator Margarete Steffin. Remarking
that "I believe the United States is one of the few countries where one
still has the freedom to do literary work and show plays like my Master Race," he asks if the New School could not request a visa for Steffin from the American consul in Helsingfors, Finland. "She, in fact, is
the only one who has an overview of my thousands of manuscript
pages. Without her, preparing lectures would mean an enormous loss
of time. . . . I cannot simply leave her here. For ten years she has been
my closest collaborator and is personally much too close."

Margarete (Grete) Steffin, the intellectually gifted daughter of a Berlin worker, began collaborating with Brecht in Berlin in the early thirties and followed him into Danish, Swedish, and Finnish exile. In
many ways she resembled the scores of women who became entranced
by this man whose generally unsavory appearance belied a legendary
reputation for being sexually attractive. Like many of his women, she
played several roles for him—editor, secretary, collaborator, teacher,
librarian, and sexual partner. Nor did Brecht maintain a conventional
ménage à trois. Often he had more than one female collaborator. At
this time at least one other woman belonged to his entourage—Ruth
Berlau, an actress trained in the Royal Danish Theater who had left
her husband, a professor of medicine in Copenhagen, in the mid-
thirties and followed him. She, too, played the same roles Steffin and
Brecht's other women did. It was unthinkable to leave without them.

At this time, Steffin was by all odds the favorite. In contrast to his
feelings for the women involuntarily drawn into his orbit without special effort on his part, Brecht appears to have felt a profound depend-

ence on and tenderness toward her. Her frail health (she had only one lung) caused him a dilemma, for it eliminated her from consideration for an immigration visa. He, however, was unwilling to leave without her. According to his own account, in December 1940 he, his wife, and his children received immigration visas for Mexico, where a number of his German friends had settled.[15] Steffin's visa was denied on grounds of poor health. Against the urging of friends in America to leave immediately for Mexico, he risked everything on obtaining an American visa for her, even if it was a visitor's visa. Throughout his exile years, this unexpected tenderness would intrude into Brecht's coolly rational behavior often enough to amend his "tough-guy" image. In his relationship to Steffin one sees his ability to care deeply for something beyond his own work. To her and to a few close friends he committed himself with the same irrational devotion which, in promoting his ideas in the theater, brought him the reputation of refractoriness and intractability.

In June 1940 Piscator wrote him that the New School could do nothing to accelerate the visa process. If and when one were issued depended entirely on the American consul in Helsingfors. Mentioning his great difficulty in securing an appointment for Brecht, Piscator urged him to thank Dr. Johnson. Brecht did so later that month: "You can imagine," he wrote Johnson, "what it means here in war-ravaged Europe to be given such a prospect of continuing cultural activities."[16]

In late November 1940 Brecht announced to Piscator that the American consul now had promised the visas, but his appointment at the New School was about to expire. Could it be extended? Dr. Johnson quickly sent a letter to "Dr. Brecht," tendering him an appointment from February through September 1941.[17]

Brecht's journal says almost nothing about the struggle to secure visas for himself, his wife, his children, Steffin, and Berlau. But his penchant for writing occasional poetry preserved some details. A poem entitled "Ode to a Lofty Dignitary" catches the frustration of one moment while sitting across from Lawrence von Hellens, vice-consul in charge of immigration matters. He, no doubt, is one of the few U.S. Foreign Service officers to be memorialized in a poem in any language. Brecht begins his unflattering portrait with a caustic greeting:

> Exalted vice-consul, deign
> To accord this trembling louse
> The blessed stamp.

Four times, he continues in a mock dignified tone, I have managed to come into your exalted presence; twice I cut my hair for you. I hid my shabby cap, and I wore a hat. I hope some of my words have reached your ears. Then changing the tone abruptly, he demands:

> Don't be afraid, little man behind the desk.
> Your superiors
> Won't mind your stamp.
> ....
> Slap it on, your superiors
> Won't devour you.
> (*GW* IX, 811-12)

Brecht's indignation at this degrading treatment while trying to obtain visas also comes out in one of his *Refugee Dialogues*, semi-autobiographical conversations between an exiled German physicist, Ziffel, and an exiled metal worker, Kalle, which he wrote in Finland in 1941. Speaking of attempts to get an American immigration visa, Kalle describes being sent from one office to another until a consul finally demands that he crawl around the block on hands and knees four times and then get medical certification that he has no callouses. Then he has to take an oath that he "never had any opinions," but when asked to prove it, he falters, and the visa is not issued.[18] However exaggerated, this account represents Brecht's reactions to the many questions asked to determine that he was never in prison or an almshouse; that neither he nor his parents had been in a mental institution; that he was not an idiot, imbecile, epileptic, chronic alcoholic, polygamist, procurer, vagrant, criminal, or any one of twenty other categories not allowed to enter the United States; and, above all, that he was not excluded by a 1918 law forbidding "anarchists and similar classes" from entering and conducting political activity against the established order.

Affidavits of support for his family, Berlau, and Steffin also complicated matters at a time when his family noticed growing numbers of German "tourists" appearing in Finland. In March 1941, Brecht wrote H. R. Hays asking for an affidavit to support Berlau's immigration.[19] The previous month Hays had sent him his own English renderings of Brecht's poems, one of which had appeared in *New Masses*, and his translation of the *Lucullus* radio play. In the kind of charming letter he was capable of writing, Brecht replied quickly about the affidavit. He explained that Berlau, a Danish citizen, could secure a visa more easily than he and his family. Would Hays forward it to the American consul in Mexico City, their intermediate destination on the way to America? The next day he wrote and changed instructions: Would Hays please send the affidavit to the American consul in Finland? Hays responded quickly, and on March 29, 1941, Berlau received a quota immigration visa.

Brecht in the meantime had been soliciting help from others in America for affidavits and ship passage. Perhaps never before has there been so much humanitarian misrepresentation to U.S. immigration and consular officials as there was in bringing exiles from Nazi Germany to the United States at this time. Many Hollywood personalities inflated their financial statements in order to provide dozens of affidavits of support for exiles stranded in Europe.[20] William Dieterle, a successful director at Warner Brothers who had come from Germany in 1930, and his wife Charlotte, probably assisted over one hundred Europeans personally this way,[21] and friends testify that they contributed up to a half million dollars of their own funds to this cause.[22] Dieterle gained a reputation for the mass scenes in his films designed specifically to employ non-English speaking German exiles in them.[23] Sometime in April 1941 the exile obtained an affidavit of support signed by Dieterle.

With German motorized divisions visible everywhere in Finland and the invasion of Russia somewhat over two months away, Brecht still lacked a sure escape route. In a poem he describes his plight:

Curiously, I examine the map of the continent.
High up in Lapland,
Toward the Arctic Ocean
I still see a small door.
(GW ix, 819)

On his visa application he wrote that he would depart from Bassia, Persia. But, in fact, nearly every exit seemed blocked. He notified Hays that he heard Japan would not let him through via Russia, and that Turkey was also closed off because of the war.

On May 3, 1941 the "lofty consul" finally stamped and issued immigrant quota visa number 1936 to Eugen Berthold Friedrich Brecht, who was listed as having "no nationality."[24] He now possessed what Kalle in the *Refugee Dialogues* had called the noblest part of a human-being—a passport (GW xiv, 1383). Two days later, word came that Steffin, who could not pass the physical for a quota visa, would receive a visitor's visa as Helene Weigel's "secretary." Though time as well as his "means of production" (as he called cigars and English murder mysteries)[25] were running low, Brecht delayed another week, waiting for Steffin's visa. He packed, stored the books and manuscripts he could not transport, and purchased railroad tickets to Moscow for the six persons in his party.

Shortly before leaving, Brecht wrote Gorelik saying: "Where Columbus succeeded, I'll be successful too, though I won't have it as easy as he did."[26] He also mentions the new play he is bringing (*Arturo Ui*), "which really ought to stand a chance over there."

On May 13, 1941, one day after Steffin's visa finally came, Brecht, his wife, his son, his daughter, Berlau, and Steffin boarded a train for Moscow. They had scarcely arrived when Steffin collapsed with tuberculosis and had to be hospitalized.

After great difficulties, Brecht managed to secure tickets for a Swedish ship that sailed for America from Vladivostok on June 14th. Not knowing this would be the last ship he could take, he noted in his journal that he had tried to exchange his tickets for a later ship in order to wait for Steffin.[27] But he was unable to do so, or his concern for her and assurances of friends that the Stalin-Hitler pact of the previous year guaranteed peace in Russia for a considerable time might have lulled him into a fatal postponement. Leaving many of his manuscripts with her, and with arrangements made for her to come as soon as she could travel, he, his family, and Berlau departed Moscow on May 30, 1941, for the ten-day trip across Russia on the trans-Siberian railroad. Daily telegrams reported Steffin's decline, and on June 5th news reached him that she had died the previous day. Her death cast him into a depression that lasted well into American exile. One of several poems on the topic reads:

> Since you died, my little teacher,
> I wander aimlessly, restlessly
> Benumbed in a gray world,
> Without work, like one discharged.
> (*GW* x, 827-8)

In what became a leitmotif in many of his exile poems, he speaks further of his guilt at having survived her.

After Nazi U-boats made the North Atlantic unsafe for ship passage, the Swedish Johnson line had dispatched its small freighter, the *S.S. Annie Johnson*, to the Pacific. Flying a neutral flag which the Japanese respected, it was allowed to shuttle between Russia and America, carrying fifty-one refugees to freedom on each trip. When it sailed, its manifest listed Brecht, his family, and Ruth Berlau among its passengers. Though the voyage was interrupted by a five-day stop in Manila to load copra, the ship spent more than a month on the high seas before arriving in San Pedro, California, on July 21, 1941.

In his poem "The Landscape of Exile" (*GW* x, 830) Brecht claims he took the last ship to cross the Pacific before the bombing of Pearl Harbor on December 7, 1941.[28] Perhaps this was poetic license, though he repeated the claim to friends after his arrival. But another set of circumstances was very real. In June 1941, while his ship was somewhere in the Pacific and while Germany prepared to launch its invasion of Russia later that month, the U.S. Government declared that no one with close relatives in Germany could henceforth enter the United States.[29] Having a father and brother in Germany certainly would have made this the last ship for Brecht. His narrow escape might have been reason enough to rejoice, but by instinct and inclination he seldom permitted himself any feelings that dulled his critical habit of mind, and his approach to America was no exception. Calling himself in the same poem the "messenger of misfortune," he describes his joy at various sights on their trip—the rolling dolphins, the horse-drawn carts of "doomed Manila," the pink armbands of the matrons there. But of the oil rigs, gardens, and ravines in his new southern California home, he could bring himself to say only that they "didn't leave him cold."[30] Soon, however, they would. His exile in paradise, and one of the most difficult periods of his life, had begun.

4   CULTURE SHOCK

Shortly after Marta Feuchtwanger, wife of the émigré novelist Lion Feuchtwanger, and the refugee actor Alexander Granach picked up his party at the San Pedro harbor and drove them to the small apartment the Dieterles had arranged for them at 1954 Argyle Avenue in Hollywood,[1] Brecht began to suffer from symptoms of the culture shock experienced by most people transplanted into an alien environment. A year passed before he overcame the initial trauma, and there is some question if he ever felt completely at ease. Comparing Los Angeles to Europe, he inevitably found it wanting. He suffered from the summer heat and longed for the more temperate European climate; he discovered it was impossible to buy decent bread in America; he hated the short-order food which he occasionally bought in drugstores; he railed against the artificiality of life in a verdant region that would revert to desert if sprinkling and irrigation ceased ("scratch a bit, and the desert comes through").[2] He abhorred the "cheap prettiness" of a consumer-oriented capitalism which depraved everything about it; he resented its superficiality and the underlying commercial ethos. Even the architecture of an automobile-oriented society where the "houses are additions built onto the garages"[3] mirrored a society out of joint.

Arriving at a time of great physical mobility in the population touched off by the expanding war industry, he observed that Americans are nomads who build homes with no intention of living out their years there, and who change jobs like boots.[4] He saw no evidence of a cultural past, and this rootlessness produced a life-style completely lacking in style. But perhaps his greatest shock was his collision with the English language.

Though he read English fairly fluently (primarily murder mysteries) and now began to speak it as required, Brecht failed to master spoken English or to talk in it extensively until after 1944, when he and Charles Laughton became friends. He considered himself constitutionally incapable of ever using English as he did German. He subscribed to the views of his fellow-exile, the philosopher Ernst Bloch, that "as a general rule, the more intimate a person is with his native language, the more he has learned in and from it, the harder he finds it to change over to another language." Few writers of this century have been more intimate with German than the poet and dramatist Brecht. Demonstrating how the experience of exile disrupts the language of German writers in America, Bloch points to changes that occur when a writer tries to substitute his own language for one evolved by another culture and related to another world of perception. It is only in the words and word-relationships of his own language, Bloch says, that he has experienced and known something. He recalls that few writers have moved about in a foreign language with the same sureness and productivity they had in their own.[5]

Brecht echoed some of these ideas himself in an interview he gave to the *New Yorker Staats-Zeitung und Herold*, a German-language newspaper in New York City, on March 7, 1943. After spending nearly two years in America, he said that he doubted he would ever write in English. Of all German émigrés, he thought this was possible for perhaps two groups—journalists and scholars.

Behind this reluctance to speak lay more than lack of confidence. For a man whose life was the word, groping for the right one in another language or mangling it while trying to pronounce it seemed like playing a fine instrument that was slightly out of tune. Friends concede that Brecht's spoken English lacked the subtle humor and the clarity of his brilliant German, and no one knew it better than he himself.

The psychology of American English also went against his grain. The last thing this writer committed to changing the world wanted to be was a "nice guy." Yet that, he claimed, is precisely what English demanded of him. An essay written five years after he settled in America called "Letter to an Adult American" devotes one section to American popular speech.[6] In it he acknowledged that he had been studying English, but he expressed his frustration at being able to say only what he had learned, rather than what he wanted to say. He despaired of ever learning it to his satisfaction. With effort, he could express superficial thoughts in correct English sentences. But, he continued, he simply lacked the manner necessary to make his behavior conform to what he saw as the implicit demands of proper spoken English. For him, that meant being a "nice fellow," "easy to get along with."

While this suggests something about the German language ("In German, one lies if one's polite," Goethe had said in *Faust*), it also raises a question about Brecht's personality. Who and what kind of man was the forty-three-year old exile when he arrived in the United States?

This is a difficult question to answer, since Brecht guarded his private person in a way to confuse the most skilled analyst. Martin Esslin's influential interpretation of him as a man torn between reason and instinct, a "person basically tender, driven to suppress his emotion, to appear hard and rational" by submitting to Marxism and political engagement,[7] captures only two facets of his enormously complex personality. There were others, among them a fundamental oppositional stance which was one of the dominant features of his makeup. Earlier it had motivated him to accept Marxist thought, since Marxism's attitude of opposition to the world as it exists coincided in many ways with his own. It was also at the root of his approach to theater. Had Hitler not driven him from Germany, Brecht might have translated this attitude into a productive revolution in the European theater. But eight years in exile had prevented that. A trip across the Atlantic did nothing to change an attitude which persisted throughout his life; even within a Marxist framework in his last years, Brecht remained at bottom essentially a dissident, though a cunning one. Elsa Lanchester, Charles Laughton's widow, who disliked Brecht, formulated it negatively but with considerable accuracy: "If Brecht had belonged to the Communist Party, he would be anti-Communist. He was anti-everything, so that the moment he became part of a country he was anti- that country. . . . I think he was a professional 'anti.' "[8]

In his dialogues on the theater entitled *Buying Brass*,[9] Brecht allows the philosopher, a spokesman for himself, to admit autobiographically: "I have another passion besides curiosity. It's contentiousness. I like to examine carefully everything I see and then 'speak my mind' as they say" (*GW* xvi, 510). Because of this spirit of contradiction, which in his writings produces the abrupt reversals of thought and zig-zag logic that he called "dialectics," Brecht's attitude toward America was destined from the outset to be critical. But it was never dreary criticism, for he had at his disposal a keen sense of humor, which in turn was tempered by abiding skepticism and distrust of himself.

From Europe Brecht had brought a Chinese wall hanging portraying a Confucian-like sage he called "the skeptic." This glowering visage constantly reminded him to be critical.[10] A complementary character trait became the subject of a poem written at this time describing another Oriental wall-hanging—a Japanese mask. In Japan the mask is worn by a dramatic character who, in English translation, would be called "The Angry One." In German, Brecht uses the ambiguous word *böse*, which means "evil," but in certain contexts can also mean "ill-tempered" or "angry":

THE MASK OF EVIL
On my walls hangs a Japanese wood carving
Mask of an evil demon, lacquered in gold.
With empathy I see
The swollen veins on the forehead, suggesting
How strenuous it is to be evil.
(*GW* x, 850)

This mask reminded him of a basic principle. Brecht believed that goodness or friendliness, not evil or anger, was man's normal state,

and that indignation over injustice tended to wear off in time. Therefore he resolved to remain critical by exerting himself to keep his anger
alive, i.e., to be the "evil" one by playing the role of the adversary.
This, combined with intense interest in everything about him, made
him a born critic. Life in the most advanced capitalist country of the
world contained enough new experiences to transform culture shock
into mordant social criticism.

In European exile, Brecht seldom criticized his host societies. Instead he turned to an imaginative world and historicized his experience of exile. A number of his poems proudly identify him with great
literary exiles of the past: Homer, Dante, Li-Po, Tu-Fu, Lucretius, and
Heine.[11] In America, this changed. In contrast to Joyce, Hemingway,
Pound, or other well-known literary expatriates of this century, this
inveterate European had been involuntarily banished, and he was
determined not to make the best of it. Repeatedly he attributed his
present unhappy state to the host culture.

Nine days after arriving, Brecht wrote in his journal about the
American life style: "In almost no other place was my life more difficult than here in this mortuary of easy going. I especially miss Grete
here. It's as though they'd taken away my guide just as I entered the
desert."[12] One week later he notes: "I get the impression of having
been removed from my age. This is Tahiti in metropolitan form."[13] A
letter to H. R. Hays echoes the same motif: "I'm here [in Hollywood]
as if in Tahiti, among palm trees and artists. It makes me nervous."[14]
Eight months later he is still not at home: "I have the feeling of being
like Francis of Assisi in an aquarium, Lenin at the Prater (or the Ok-
toberfest), or a chrysanthemum in a coal mine."[15]

Another journal entry written nine months after his arrival mentions his ongoing difficulties in adjusting: "Since June, 1941, there's
much I haven't gotten over: the loss of Grete, the new environment,
not even the mild climate here . . . and being penniless. For the first
time in ten years, I'm not working well, both as a consequence of these
things, and with the expected results."

Other journal entries and letters in the first year complain of depression and non-productivity. He cannot breathe in this climate, Brecht
claims, and he has abandoned his life-long habit of going to the window after arising and breathing the air—in California there is nothing
to smell.[16] To read, as he had done in Denmark and Finland, Caesar's
Bellum Gallicum in a setting where "cheap prettiness depraves everything," would be the worst sort of snobbery;[17] to write poetry, even
on topical themes, would be withdrawal into an ivory tower. He dis-
likes American food. The sickness of his eleven-year-old daughter
Barbara, who spent the winter in bed with tuberculosis, also affects

him. Most of all, the progress of the war in Europe depresses him. In his mind the world's destiny is being decided on distant European battlegrounds.

For Brecht, "not working well" meant he was engaged in only six or eight writing projects instead of his customary two dozen. By most standards he was highly productive, in spite of his seeming emotional disequilibrium. Few Calvinists have subscribed to a sterner work ethic than this atheist. He once boasted that "even when fleeing the Gestapo, I never missed a day's work."[18] "Work is good medicine," he advised Hans Tombrock, a refugee friend in 1940;[19] "work is the best drug," he reiterated later;[20] and "to be wise is to be productive," he told Tombrock again that year.[21] In his autobiographical *Me-ti/Book of Changes* he has Me-ti state his distaste for phrases that began with "Thou shalt." The sole exception he allows is the dictum: "Thou shalt be productive."[22] "Productivity," by this time the cardinal commandment in Brecht's life, meant purposeful work. Through it, he says, people become wiser and gain confidence.[23] But, for the first time in years, his productivity lacked purpose. With no German language audience to address, and no stage on which to try out his plays, he spent the first year writing essentially for the desk drawer. The reason for his productivity had shifted. With little prospect of reaching an audience, he needed to combat the boredom of exile, for, as Hanns Eisler noted, boredom made him physically ill.[24] Yet it also became a prime production force during his years in America, and Eisler's claim that both he and Brecht produced more in exile than at any other time in their lives is probably valid.[25]

Brecht's life, especially now, was his writing, or his rewriting, which for him was the same thing—he considered everything he wrote to be unfinished and subject to revision, even after it was printed. There is no way to measure everything he wrote or rewrote during the first year in America, but what can be measured is impressive. In addition to his work on more than a dozen film stories and extensive revision of the play *The Resistible Rise of Arturo Ui*,[26] he wrote additional sections of his *Refugee Dialogues*; he added to his theatrical dialogues called *Buying Brass*; he worked on his *Tui* novel; he revised parts of his novel *The Business Affairs of Mr. Julius Caesar*; he composed a number of epigrams for his *Primer of War*; and journal entries confirm that by December 20, 1941, he had finished the initial outline for a play *Jeanne d'Arc 1940* (completed in 1943 as the full-length play *The Visions of Simone Machard*).[27]

Letters, too, were a significant part of his first year's productivity. The need to see friends in New York and Boston, his desire to gain a foothold on Broadway, and financial circumstances that limited travel forced him to correspond. During the first year he wrote a relatively large number for a non-letter writer. Thus, necessity and boredom combined to make his American years among the best documented of his life.

By far the largest number of his letters in the American years, or any time in his life, went to Ruth Berlau, who gradually began to fill the void left by Grete Steffin's death. Early in May 1942 she left Santa Monica for Washington, D.C., where she was to address an anti-fascist group of Danish refugees. Unexpectedly, she settled in New York City and took a job making Danish language broadcasts for the Office of War Information. Though Brecht was accustomed to her erratic behavior, her failure to return surprised and disturbed him. For the first time since November, 1924 he was without at least one close female collaborator. No one sensed more strongly than he how important they were to his writing—he considered them, along with cigars and murder mysteries, an indispensable "means of production" for his works.

Brecht took pains to cast himself in the role of an involuntary exile, not an immigrant who came to stay. In 1937 his poem "On the Designation 'Emigrants' " (GW ix, 718) objected to the term "emigrant." He did not emigrate voluntarily, he insisted, but was driven out, an exile, banished, forced to flee. In 1943 that poem would appear at least twice in FBI files as grounds for suspicion. The files stated "It is believed that the substitution of the word 'exile' for 'emigration' is an indication that persons connected with Brecht do not consider themselves immigrants here, but look upon themselves rather as exiles who wait to return to Europe." This is one of many times the FBI appeared to have understood Brecht's writings exactly as he intended them.

A number of factors compounded the normal effects of culture shock. In early August 1941 his family moved to a house at 817-25th Street in Santa Monica. Because of inadequate room for large tables, Brecht disliked these new quarters. But the flow of workers into Southern California's booming aircraft and ship-building industries had made housing scarce. This, and their limited finances, forced them to stay there a year.

Neighbors must have puzzled over this odd foreigner. Five feet eight inches tall and one hundred thirty pounds; a gaunt face with a scar on his left cheek; short-cropped brown hair cut straight across the forehead; penetrating deep-set brown eyes behind steel-rimmed glasses; a fine, aquiline nose over thin, tight lips; decayed teeth; always a day or two's growth of beard; mufti or a gray flannel shirt and baggy trousers; and the omnipresent five-cent cigar—at first sight he resembled a runaway monk. On October 15, 1941 he submitted a statement of facts to be used in becoming an American citizen.[28] He signed a formal declaration of intent, his so-called "first papers," on December 8, 1941. Three days later the United States declared war on Germany, an act that automatically made him an "enemy alien." Like thousands of other German refugees in the United States, Brecht and his family did not escape the suspicion of patriotic American neighbors.

A family that lived in Santa Monica a few houses away from the Brechts during these years became convinced they were enemy agents engaged in espionage. They had seen a steady stream of German-speaking visitors at the house, and they felt certain they heard "Heil Hitler" uttered. They also recall maps of Europe on the walls of Brecht's study, plotting the progress of the war. Brecht's daughter Barbara, they said, sometimes ate at a lunch stand frequented by workers from Douglas Aircraft, and they saw her returning books to the Santa Monica public library with messages on slips inserted in them. Later FBI inquiries about the Brechts, whom other neighbors initially described as decent, hard-working people, convinced them that they were agents working for the Russians.[29] The idea that the Brechts were probably not simultaneously Nazis and Communist spies eluded them.

Brecht either ignored or was ignorant of these xenophobic fantasies about him. His journal and letters say almost nothing about them, and he accepted his status as an "enemy alien" with surprising stoicism. Dutifully he registered as enemy alien no. 7624464[30] and accepted the restrictions on him with uncharacteristic equanimity. Like thousands of other German refugees, he was not allowed to travel more than five miles from home except to a job. A curfew imposed in March 1942 that required him to be off the streets between 8 p.m. and 6 a.m. resulted in many overnight stays with friends. During the first few months both requirements were strictly observed, but compliance grew lax in later months, and they were lifted within a year. His journal note about a visit by the FBI on May 29, 1942 reveals how little all this troubled him: "Evening . . . two FBI people come and look at my registration booklet, apparently a curfew check." Even FBI inquiries about him with friends and neighbors failed to excite any protest when he heard of them.

The death of Steffin still depressed him. In a letter dated "end of January, 1942" Brecht wrote to Hays excusing his long silence: "The move, together with the loss of my closest collaborator, the unusual calm and isolation from all world affairs in which I've been placed, have paralyzed me to such a degree that in six months I've written only a few letters. . . . I couldn't even bring myself to thank the people who helped me come over, which still weighs heavily on me." Though far more productive than his claim of "paralysis" allowed, he was still not himself. On March 16, 1942 his journal notes: "Often I see Grete with her things that she packed over and over in her suitcase." On June 4, 1942 his only entry reads: "Anniversary of Grete's death," while another on June 30, 1942 states: "I have not done and will not do anything to 'get over' Grete's death." An undated notation admits the conflict his depression over her death was causing him. He tries to avoid thinking of her death, he writes, not so much because he fears the pain, but because he is ashamed of feeling it.[31] Of the six poems he wrote about her shortly after arriving, one uses simple metaphors to describe their complex relationship:

My general has fallen
My soldier has fallen
My pupil has gone
My teacher has gone. . . .
(*GW* x, 826)

In August 1941 news of another friend's death added to his "personal casualty list." In desperation Walter Benjamin, philosopher, critic, scholar, and man of letters, had taken his own life on the Spanish border while fleeing the Nazis. Two poems Brecht wrote about Benjamin at this time, especially a four-line commemorative, give the appearance of an objective statement. By refusing to express grief, these poems, like scenes in some of his plays, become that much more powerful through their control of undeniable emotion.

The death and suffering of German refugees preoccupied Brecht from 1933 on. In late April or early May 1942 his own guilt at surviving while other innocent but unlucky persons died prompted him to write one of the most moving poems he ever composed:

I, THE SURVIVOR
Of course I know: only through luck
Have I survived so many friends. But last night in a dream
I heard these friends saying of me: "Those who are stronger
    survive"
And I hated myself.
(*GW* x, 882)

Like almost every poem Brecht wrote in America, this one was triggered by a concrete event. Salka Viertel remembers the horror they shared as she, Brecht, and Berlau discussed a report by Soviet Commissar for Foreign Affairs Molotov which had appeared in American newspapers during the spring of 1942. Learning of the murder of over 7,000 Russian civilians by German occupation troops in the city of

Kerch, she expressed her guilt at having been spared when so many died. The next morning, she reports, Brecht had written this poem and slipped it under her door.[32] The same concern for those who were weaker translated itself into Brecht's belief in the survival of the unfittest in the social sphere, which found its most satisfying support in the teachings of Marxism.

Because of its geographic location, America inflicted on Brecht a sense of helplessness and isolation. In Scandinavia he lived close to Germany and was intensely involved in the fight against Fascism. In America, thousands of miles from the battlefields, and where Europe's destiny caused only "a faint echo in the hurly-burly of the art market,"[33] he had the impression of being on another planet.

In September 1941 Brecht wrote the philosopher Karl Korsch in Boston that in the remotest part of Finland he was not so removed from the world. And in October he wrote again complaining: "the intellectual isolation here is enormous. In comparison to Hollywood, Svendborg [the location of his Danish exile] was a world center."[34] He felt isolated in a double sense—he had little contact with Americans, and few of the German exiles with whom he associated shared his artistic or political views, not to mention his consuming hatred of Fascism.

Equally frivolous in his view were the distinguished members of the Marxist-oriented Frankfurt Institute for Social Research whom he had known and despised personally or by reputation from Europe, and who were now in America. An undated journal entry from his first month in the States mentions a garden party where he met Max Horkheimer and Friedrich Pollock, two of its luminaries. Acidly he describes their wealth and cites their claim that "their major revolutionary duty through all the years was to preserve the Institute's money."[35] Social intercourse with these financially independent academic Marxists later provided ammunition for Brecht's bitter parodies of "prostituted intellectuals."

But he reserved his greatest scorn for émigrés who tried to turn him into an American. From the day he arrived, Brecht resisted becoming "Americanized." True, he did not violate legal requirements that might have jeopardized his stay, such as the restrictions placed on enemy aliens. At age forty-four he conscientiously registered with the Local Draft Board in Santa Monica, where age and nationality resulted in a 4-A classification.[36] And his wife dutifully sewed blackout curtains for the occasional air-raid scares and alerts Los Angeles experienced. In matters of the law, he conformed to prevailing norms.

But in most other things Brecht kept his fingers crossed. In August 1941 he mentioned to Hays his biggest complaint about other refugees: "Here everyone tries to turn themselves and everyone else into thoroughbred Americans in record time. It makes me seasick."[37] And in February 1942, after an evening of argument and conversation about America with Ferdinand Reyher, he complained in his journal of two views which irritated him: "Everywhere one meets apostles of the Great Melting Pot, advertisers of the Paradise City New York . . . and German émigrés, in wild indignation at the demands to be assimilated, let fly with Biblical invectives."[38] In effect, Brecht cursed both houses. In his typically tough-minded view, he believed that chest-beating and self-righteous resistance to assimilation into the host culture were as inappropriate for refugees as eagerness was to become an American. Only one principle mattered—survival.

II. BRECHT AND HOLLYWOOD

5 "SPELL YOUR NAME"

In his "Sonnet in Emigration" (*GW* x, 831) written during his first year in America, Brecht described how he was forced to go out and "sell what I think." Though uncertain where to go, he perceived himself to be treading "the old ways worn smooth by the steps of those without hope." Wherever he went he always encountered the same response: "Spell your name." Sardonically he added: "This name once belonged to the great ones."

Though he exaggerated his fame, Brecht did enjoy a considerable European reputation before arriving in America. In the thirties he had found doors open wherever he went. Workers' theaters and leftist theater people in Moscow, London, Paris, Copenhagen, and Stockholm recognized his talent, received him warmly, and welcomed discussions of his ideas and works. His New York Theatre Union experience had been the only occasion when his charisma failed to win over those he met. Like many creative geniuses, Brecht possessed an unmistakable personal magnetism that captivated most of those who knew him. Even while isolated on a tiny Danish island in the Baltic, he managed to draw a steady stream of collaborators and important visitors there for discussions and working sessions.

All this changed in America. Except in the German refugee community where he enjoyed a reputation as a gifted playwright, Brecht at age forty-three was obliged to begin again and "sell himself" and his works to American film and theater people who had never heard of him. In spite of a talent for self-publicity, he experienced far greater difficulty organizing his fame than he ever had in Europe.

Within days after taking up the study of American colloquial speech, Brecht grasped the importance of the word "to sell." He noted that just as a girl at the lunch counter in a drugstore "sells" you a sandwich (where they also "sell" vitamins to supplement the inadequate nutrition in the sandwich), virtually everything else must be "sold."[1] Someone "sells" someone else his ideas on surrealism; the President must "sell" the people on the war; in New York, dramatists "sell" their plays to potential producers; in Hollywood writers "sell" stories to the studios. Few roles were more poorly suited to Brecht than that of the persuasive salesman.

A journal note confesses that it is unlike him to be so dissatisfied with his surroundings: "But perhaps it's the working conditions that make me impatient. Here it's customary to 'sell' everything, from a shrug to an idea, i.e., always to be concerned about a buyer; thus you are constantly a buyer or a seller."[2]

In selling himself, Brecht faced a country which, at least since World

War I, was not given to excessive Germanophilia. Relative to French literature, works by German authors, especially dramas, had fared poorly. With the exception of Thomas Mann's writings, they were a book of seven seals to most educated Americans in the early forties. Though Broadway had performed a considerable number of German plays during the twenties and thirties,[3] almost none was canonized in the standard theatrical repertory as were the works of Molière, Ibsen, Chekhov, or Strindberg. To most American theater and film people in 1941, Brecht's reputation as a leading German dramatist was non-existent.

There were a few exceptions. Following his 1935-1936 visit, one performance and isolated publication of his work occurred in disparate locations.[4] And the enthusiasm with which a few cognoscenti, among them Gorelik, Reyher, and H. R. Hays, began to promote his name, reflects the strong spell his writings or his personality cast over many who knew them. In the case of Hays, who had translated and published *Mother Courage* in the 1941 edition of *New Directions in Prose and Poetry*, it was the works that captivated him, since he had not met Brecht. In a letter to James Laughlin, publisher of New Directions, written shortly before Brecht came to America, Hays shows prophetic insight into the dramatist's stature: "He is, I think, the only poet to really absorb Marxism and use it creatively in the theatre . . . he . . . believes in getting away from the worn out symbolist-naturalist theatre of illusion and getting back to the formal, heroic, and didactic . . . his characters are philosophical yet not allegorical, they are real people acting in social situations which are inherently ironic. And his poetry is really functional . . . of course he has no use for artifical suspense and well-made play structure, hence the Broadway managers throw up their hands in horror. I know, for I've tried to get Mother Courage produced."[5]

But Hays was an exception. Awareness of Brecht's works was too diffuse to establish a reputation. Hollywood personalities listened incredulously to refugee friends who singled him out as a brilliant poet and playwright. Don Ogden Stewart, a past president of the League of American Writers and later a film director, insists that he, like others in Hollywood, had no inkling when he met Brecht in 1942 that he was so famous, or that his wife was a noted actress. This reaction was typical. Most had never heard Brecht's name. If they had, it was as the librettist for Kurt Weill's *The Threepenny Opera*, since Weill's Broadway musical successes with *Johnny Johnson, Knickerbocker Holiday* and *Lost in the Stars* had already made him a celebrity.

Another phenomenon significantly affected Brecht's American exile—financial deprivation. Though raised in comfortable middle-class circumstances in Augsburg, he had in fact known malnutrition and near-poverty while trying to establish himself in Berlin in the early twenties. But after the success of his *Threepenny Opera* in 1928, he was able to maintain a living standard which, for the time, bordered on the affluent. Among other things he owned a car and bought a home. Throughout his Scandinavian exile he continued to be able to afford modest comforts and to travel beyond the means of most Europeans.

This, too, changed in America. Supported totally from money given by the "European Film Fund," which Charlotte Dieterle, wife of the Hollywood director, and Liesl Frank, wife of the Novelist Bruno Frank, collected in the film capital to aid refugees, Brecht and his family subsisted on $120 a month for somewhat over the first year in America. This amount equalled what the average unskilled industrial worker in California earned at the time, and about half of what a carpenter made.[6] Of that $120, $48.50 a month went for rent. In a metropolitan area where, as one émigré put it, "people are born as drivers," and "the breed called pedestrians has either died out or been killed off,"[7] the Brechts had no car and depended for a time on limited public transportation or on friends to take them everywhere. Weigel completely furnished her house and clothed her children from Salvation Army and Good Will stores in Los Angeles. Free medical treatment from another German refugee, Dr. Schiff, helped them that first year when their daughter Barbara was in bed recovering from tuberculosis.

Though by nature frugal, Brecht did not accept such deprivation stoically. At a time when he needed to "sell himself" most vigorously, economic problems restricted him. This, combined with his relegation to the status of an unknown writer, intensified his oppositional attitude to a degree that probably made his behavior in relation to his environment, in this case Hollywood, more extreme and more uncompromising than at any time in his life.

Financial considerations had weighed heavily in Brecht's original decision to settle in Los Angeles rather than to go to New York for the lectureship at the New School. The day after disembarking, he recorded in his journal Lion Feuchtwanger's advice to stay near Hollywood, "where it's cheaper than New York, and there are more prospects to earn money."[8] A letter to Karl Korsch written at the end of September 1941 announced that Brecht planned to remain and build himself a small financial base. The same month he wrote to Piscator in New York inquiring about the minimum subsistence level if he were to come—"we live simply and could live outside the city."[9] Soon he discovered that remaining near Hollywood provided him the best possible access to Broadway outside of New York City. There were those who viewed Broadway as an adjunct to Hollywood, and, while Brecht did not share that attitude, it is true that most of the important figures of the American theater whom he met during his American exile spent at least as much time in the film capital as they did working in New York.

To Brecht, New York City offered fewer opportunities for a writer like him than did the film world. Hollywood was full of successful émigré German writers, among them Erich Remarque, Vicki Baum, Franz Werfel, George Froeschel, Salka Viertel, Kurt Siodmak, Robert Thoeren, and dozens of others. By one count in 1944 there were fifty-nine refugee German screen writers in Hollywood, thirty-three directors, twenty-three producers, ten actors, and nineteen composers working for the film industry.[10] According to George Froeschel, an émigré writer who won an Academy Award for his work on the screenplay of "Mrs. Miniver" (1942), Hollywood studios considered German language writers to have a special gift for storytelling. "We were gods in those days," recalls Froeschel of successful writers in this golden era of the American screen.[11] Brecht knew this, and he thought that, with his talent, it would be easy to break in. But as a relative latecomer, he found the Olympus of American popular entertainment occupied, and its affluent inhabitants second-rate European writers. When he was confronted with this situation, the two major irritants of his American exile—non-recognition and lack of money—became a near-obsession. Convinced that he was better than they, he bitterly asserted: "If Arthur Koestler can make money writing pornography, I can do it writing films."[12]

Brecht's letters and journal of this period abound in references to money and prominent people. Whether he was speaking of actors, producers, directors, Broadway plays, Jewish emigrants, Hollywood films, intellectuals of the Frankfurt Institute for Social Research, or prominent acquaintances, financial details of their lives intrude themselves almost involuntarily into Brecht's accounts. Never one to rejoice in the success of others, he did not normally allow their success to bother him unduly if he, too, succeeded. But in a society that equated failure with lack of talent, their success galled him deeply. Thus his entry into "the marketplace where lies are bought," as he called the film world,[13] to perform what he repeatedly called *Brotarbeit*—the bread-and-butter work of writing for Hollywood—in many ways brought out the worst in him. In a reflexive oppositional response heightened by envy, frustration, and lack of recognition, he seemed determined to write for Hollywood on his own terms or not at all. For someone who wanted to change the structure of society by world revolution and the landscape of modern theater by his own revolutionary dramatic writings, it was logical that he should also want to revolutionize a major art form that had fascinated him since youth. From his impact on numerous film makers of the sixties and seventies, it is clear that Brecht achieved delayed-action success. At the time, however, Hollywood was unreceptive to the ideas of this obscure émigré.

The tradition that writing for Hollywood is fatal for literary talent never affected Brecht. Absolutely sure of his own genius, he tenaciously wrote the only kind of film stories he could. Inevitably, they were not what Hollywood wanted. Though he learned the norms of Hollywood writing quickly, he was constitutionally unable to adjust to them.

Within weeks of disembarking from the "Annie Johnson," Brecht undertook several story projects that he hoped to sell to studios. Hollywood called this "writing on spec," i.e., without a contract or firm offer. To do this required the optimism of a gambler, and Brecht seized on the analogy. Several times his journal compares the movie industry to a huge gambling casino and his own writing and selling of film stories to a game of roulette. In his first two attempts, it seems he failed to understand the rules of that game as played in Hollywood. "Misfortunes are due mainly to miscalculations," Galileo had stated in his play of that name.[1] In these cases, Brecht's ignorance of the rules contributed to those miscalculations.

While he was looking at a copy of *Life*, which he read regularly and drew on for film stories, poems, and journal entries, an article entitled "A Model Family in a Model Home" struck him.[2] It reported that after competition throughout rural Ohio, Frank Engels, his wife, and their three children had emerged as Ohio's "most typical farm family." Consequently they were "put on display" for one week at the Ohio State Fair, where they lived in a model home, tried to follow their normal daily routine, and allowed thousands of visitors to march through their parlor and peer into their lives. Brecht's wry wit seized on this display of all-American domestic bliss and conceived a film story based on the idea of a huge quarrel taking place the night before the fair opened. Visitors the next day would see rooms that had been destroyed when the couple had run amuck and a letter on the table from an attorney announcing divorce proceedings.[3]

Brecht's failure to develop the story beyond the outline stage is not the only reason it would not have sold. Attacking the American family then was attacking Mom and Apple Pie, and no Hollywood studio would have looked at it. If he did not realize it then, a journal entry less than three months later suggested he had grasped a fundamental truth about writing for the movie industry: "The directors and actors here want stories with a 'message,' i.e., a moral, a Metro-Goldwyn-Mayer Gospel for the Little Man."[4]

Another journal entry shortly after reaching the States describes how a conversation about the lack of good bread in America generated a second film story, one which he completed: "Looking for film materials, I tell Reyher the plan for Joe Fleischhacker in Chicago, and in a few hours we develop a film story, 'The Bread King Learns to Bake.' There's no real bread in the States, and I like to eat bread. . . ."[5] "Joe (or Jae) Fleischhacker" was the unfinished drama about the Chicago wheat exchange based on Frank Norris's *The Pit*, which he put aside in 1926 to study Marxist economics. Modelling his protagonist "Jae" after the rich wheat dealer Curtis Jadwin, whom friends called "J," Brecht recast him now as the "bread king" of Chicago and, with Reyher's help, proceeded to write a new story line.

Though he read and understood English without excessive difficulty, Brecht at this point needed a native speaker to help him to write. Instinctively he turned to Reyher, whom he saw frequently that first year. This established screen writer knew his way around Hollywood and understood what the movie industry wanted. More important, Brecht felt a spiritual intimacy with him that was almost unique in his life and especially welcome at this time. Together they wrote a story that no Hollywood studio would have touched. The plot of this unpublished typescript illustrates why. Drawing on the earlier play where a destitute farmer, his wife, a 21-year-old daughter, and 11-year-old son are stranded in Chicago, Brecht introduces a new element by having the wife bake a loaf of bread for Fleischhacker in the naive hope of persuading the baking magnate, who controls production in the city, to finance her in her own bakery. The next scene inverts the Joan of Arc episode Brecht enjoyed using. When minor executives in the organization try to pass off someone else as the bread king and keep the real Fleischhacker from her, the woman abandons her loaf of bread and flees. Fleischhacker, who has witnessed the farce, makes the mistake of tasting her seductively good bread and realizes he must have more. He gets in touch with her, sets her up in business, and comes regularly to buy it for his wealthy friends. While visiting her anonymously, he often sits in her back room, eating her bread and berating the ruthless Fleischhacker, whom she still does not know.

Her bakery prospers until Fleischhacker goes on vacation and forgets her. The daughter's fiancé introduces a plan to increase production, but it also adulterates the quality of the bread. The bakery thrives, but an outraged Fleischhacker returns and discovers a new business rival in the place of his home-baked bread. Ruthlessly smashing his new competitor, he demands that his chemists re-create the woman's recipe from an old crust. When they fail, he desperately waves a checkbook and demands her recipe, only to hear that making good bread takes more than good flour; it involves "one day of good work; one world of good neighbors; a heart of good will; and a good appetite." Again he sets up her bakery, hires her ambitious son-in-law in his own organization, and joins with her in the back room, where they eat bread and berate the Fleischhacker dynasty.

Though Reyher wrote the English, Brecht's ideas shaped this story. The clash between a big capitalist and a proletarian family comes straight from his *St. Joan of the Stockyards*. Fleischhacker, the capitalist with a soft spot in his stomach and heart, reminds the reader of J. Pierpont Mauler in the same play, while the unnamed mother resembles mother figures in several other plays. In writing this story, however, Brecht had overlooked a major element—the mandatory Hollywood love story. In addition, he had violated a major taboo by portraying antagonistic class differences in the clash between the ugly capitalist and a noble proletarian mother.

After finishing the story on Saturday night, October 4, 1941, Brecht personally visited the MGM studios the following Tuesday and tried to "sell" the story to Gottfried Reinhardt, son of the famous exiled European stage director Max Reinhardt. The young Reinhardt, who had come to the USA in 1934, was on his way to becoming a producer at MGM; at this time he was working as an assistant to MGM producer Bernard Heyman. Reinhardt claims he did his best to help Brecht, as he had done with dozens of émigrés whose material he sold to MGM or whom he put on the payroll. But privately he knew this story, as he put it, "had as much chance of being sold to MGM as 'Gone With the Wind' had of being played at the Berliner Ensemble" (Brecht's brilliant postwar theater in East Berlin): "For an hour and a half, Brecht fascinated me in his unalloyed Augsburg dialect with a film story about the production, distribution, and enjoyment of bread. . . . He had the right man, but the wrong place, and he had no illusions when I said as he left that I would try my best to sell the story."[6] A stamp of the Screen Writers Guild shows that Brecht registered the story idea to protect it, and Reinhardt did attempt to interest MGM officials. Their reaction, according to his account, left him feeling like a Don Quixote jousting with windmills.

Why did Reyher, whom Brecht called a "good Cicerone for the States," and who had worked as a film doctor at every major Hollywood studio, collaborate without protest on a story so alien to Hollywood norms? The answer illuminates something of Brecht's personality and his relationship to his collaborators. Virtually all who worked with him recognized his genius, and it often mesmerized them. Though Reyher was not easily awe-struck (all his life he had worked closely with great writers), he, too, experienced that, by sheer force of personality, Brecht assumed the dominant role in a creative relationship. Nor did Brecht have a reputation for doing things on anyone's terms but his own. If he had asked Reyher about the conventions of Hollywood film writing, chances are he would have ignored them anyway. Convinced of his own superiority as a writer, he wanted to change public taste, not pander to it. This attitude handicapped him as much in Hollywood as it had two decades earlier when he wrote silent film scripts in Germany. His work for film then was also out of step with prevailing film-making formulas, and the results were identical—an almost total lack of success. His tirades against German film companies in the twenties had employed the same arguments he later aimed at Hollywood, e.g., that they made film writing a closed shop for second-rate writers, and that they catered to the public's taste for *kitsch* instead of producing something "effective," i.e., instructive. He had roundly cursed them all by comparing the competition among their films, the most advanced in Europe, to a race among draft horses (*GW* XVIII, 137).

For the next two years, Brecht worked mainly with German-speaking refugee actors and writers on film projects. After the fiasco with "The King's Bread," he apparently tried to penetrate the secret of successful Hollywood writing. Sometime late in 1941 he borrowed from Dieterle a film "treatment," i.e., a 50-75-page prose narrative, on the life of Samuel Gompers that Dieterle hoped to turn into a full-length screen play.[7] Soon after his journal announced four different film stories in progress besides "The King's Bread": an unidentified work called "Days of Fire," and a paraphrase of Schnitzler's *Reigen*, both of which he and Fritz Kortner were writing for Charles Boyer; "The Snowman," which he was doing with Ruth Berlau; and "Bermuda Troubles," a film story on which Robert Thoeren, a refugee writer at MGM, assisted him.[8] Except for fragmentary sketches, nothing remains of these stories, and probably they were not finished.

From this point on, more and more journal entries reproduce bits of film-writing lore and Brecht's own perceptions of Hollywood. Many conversations with friends also focused on film writing. Anyone remotely connected with Hollywood served as an informant, and he weighed everything he read as potential film material. Dozens of notes and ideas (seldom exceeding a title and a few lines) from the period reveal how active he was. A few such titles (all written in English) read: "Refugees Both," "Boy Meets Girl, So What," "The Senator's Conscience," "Love Story," and "The Traitor."[9]

The more Brecht learned, the more steadfastly he resolved to write film stories for Hollywood on his own terms or not at all. He reports with approval the assertion of Fritz Kortner, an unsuccessful German exile actor whose abrasive personality estranged everyone in Hollywood and endeared him to Brecht, that Southern California's "eternal sunshine" shriveled up the brains of gifted writers, leaving them incapable of anything but film writing.[10] And he scoffs at the movie moguls who, in claiming to speak for the wishes of the popcorn-eating public, use and re-use stories based on formulas that had previously worked and bring in teams of writers to enliven them. After working with Robert Thoeren at the MGM studios, he wrote in his journal of Thoeren's villa, his chicken ranch, his pretty wife, his endless chatter "which painstakingly avoids any reflection," and of what he must have learned from him about "the biggest film company in the world": " 'right' is anything which was filmed once and got through; 'good' is anything that increased receipts; these riddles and guessing games, this mindless chatter, the ongoing incest of what has been liked and bought with something else that has been liked and bought (simply rear-ranged) have flourished to the point where the simplest comedy (such as the new Garbo film) consumes $250,000 for the script alone be-cause it requires an army of writers and producers to put together a mediocre plot."[11] Then this impoverished refugee remarked on the immense waste produced by the most expensive art form in human history. Reflecting on the innumerable films that were made and never released, he noted wistfully that "in the process, MGM earns $17 mil-lion a year."

In these lines, Brecht summarized the attitudes that insured his fail-ure as a film writer—his disdain of the formula stories required by most Hollywood films, and his scorn for a world that was hypersensi-tive to criticism. John Houseman remembers that he "was absolutely open in his contempt for the movies as a medium for *him* to work in, and this was kind of a racket, and he hoped he could collect some dol-lars to keep him alive because he had a very hard time in those days."[12] Had he concealed his contempt better, Hollywood per-sonalities might have helped him more willingly. But if Brecht's jour-nal is accurate, he expressed openly what he wrote privately in the poem "Deliver the Goods." Several lines in the poem allegedly quote some of Hollywood's ruling figures:

> Show yourself as one of us, we
> Will call you The Best.
> We can pay, we have the means
> No one besides us can
> Deliver the goods
>
> ....
> Know this: our big shows
> Show what we want to have shown.
> Play our game, we divide the loot.
> Deliver the goods, be honest with us.
>
> ....

When I see their rotting faces
My hunger goes away.
(GW x, 851)

Dieterle, the German director who came to Hollywood in 1930 and built a solid reputation with films such as *The Story of Louis Pasteur* (1935), *The Hunchback of Notre Dame* (1938), and *Dr. Ehrlich's Magic Bullet* (1940), and who had his finger on Hollywood's pulse as well as anyone Brecht knew, fired his discontent over the film industry. Because theirs was more a personal than a professional relationship (the Dieterles sent a Christmas goose to the Brechts each year and regularly had them to dinner at their ranch in the San Fernando Valley), Dieterle spoke with surprising candor. Early in 1942 he showed the dramatist an uncut version of his independently produced film on the history of jazz, *Syncopation*. In early March 1942 Brecht compiled a list of suggestions for sharpening the story line and making the history of jazz the history of the Negro. Dieterle claims he followed some of Brecht's recommendations, but he states that the banks financing the film demanded he reduce the number of scenes showing Blacks and strengthen the obligatory love story. This, and objections by the so-called Hays office, Hollywood's self-appointed censor, which had to approve the release of all films, mutilated it and neutralized Brecht's suggestions. As a consequence, Brecht showed uncharacteristic sympathy with Dieterle when he noted in his journal that "the banks . . . are forcing him to cut as many Negroes as possible and to insert as much 'boy-meets-girl' as he can."[13]

Repeatedly Dieterle had asked Brecht for potential film stories. One day Brecht showed him a treatment he had written called "Caesar's Last Days." Drawn from his fragmentary novel written during his Danish exile, *The Business Affairs of Mr. Julius Caesar*, it depicted events in the last three days of Julius Caesar's life from two perspectives—that of the dictator, and that of a retired army veteran named Terentius Scaper, who wanted to enlist in Caesar's latest campaign. Now Brecht returned to his pet notion that great men's fame was built by the nameless common man of history. Scaper came to Rome to plead for Caesar's help, but ended up trying in vain to save the dictator from his assassins. In an apparent concession to Hollywood, Brecht contrived a rather lame love story between one of Caesar's minor secretaries, Rarus, and Scaper's daughter. In his journal he noted that because of the war, which had awakened the public's sense of history and grand politics, his film story should find a ready-made audience.[14] Dieterle soon disabused him of that notion. Because of a recent quarrel he had had with Louis B. Mayer, head of MGM studios at the time, he informed Brecht that "the industry isn't making any costume-films," meaning historical films.

From Dieterle, Brecht probably also heard the anecdote about Louis B. Mayer that turns up unexpectedly in his unfinished *Tui* novel. There he relates how the "executioner" or head of the largest studio in the "holly" wood called together his 700 assistants and asked them to name the greatest topic of all time—a topic that interested everyone in every situation. After a public opinion survey of thousands— housewives, arctic explorers, beer brewers, Catholics, service station attendants, and astrologers—he had determined that the answer was "love." That, he announced, was to be the dominant topic in this, the biggest studio.[15] From his slightly embittered friend Dieterle, who in later years insisted that success in Hollywood would have harmed Brecht immeasurably, he also heard a Hollywood maxim for survival: "You can lose everything, but don't lose the connection."[16]

A poem Brecht wrote in the thirties begins: "The thief screams: I've been robbed."[17] This poem was to become prophetic. In 1942 Brecht, who all his life admitted to the same "laxity in matters of intellectual property" characteristic of many of the world's greatest writers, uttered a similar cry when someone pilfered one of his ideas for a film story and earned $35,000 with it. Early in 1942 his journal reports on one of several evenings he spent with the noted German actress Elisabeth Bergner and her husband, the producer Paul Czinner.[18] He indicates that Bergner suggested a film story about the strange actions of a hypnotized girl. According to Bergner, the proposed story, set in San Francisco, was to deal with a girl who, after pretending to be hypnotized at a party, committed certain radical political acts that she would not have done otherwise. Reminding himself that Hollywood directors and actors wanted stories with a "message," i.e., a moral, Brecht remarked how difficult it would be to accept Czinner's challenge to finish this plot. But he undertook it anyway.

For several weeks in February and March Brecht met daily with Czinner and Bergner and worked on the plot. In the meantime Bergner tested the response of Hollywood friends to their story. Their critique discouraged her, and she gave up. Her husband, however, told the story to the director Billy Wilder (a "German film writer in Hollywood," as Brecht caustically noted), and one of Wilder's friends "bought" the story idea for $35,000. Bergner claims that the new story had only remote similarities to Brecht's plot, and that it had discarded the hypnosis idea. Brecht's journal agrees that the hypnosis introduction was gone, but claims that otherwise the new story corresponds in every detail to his plot. He fails to name the culprit or the film that came from it, but, judging by internal evidence, this or a similar incident inspired the acerbic poem "Shame" written that same year:

> When I was robbed in Los Angeles, the city
> Of merchandisable dreams, I noticed
> How I kept the theft, performed
> By a refugee like me, a reader
> Of all my poems,
> Secret, as though I feared
> My shame might become known,
> Let's say, in the animal world.
> (GW x, 858)

During the first half of 1942, Brecht probably also wrote the film story "Rich Man's Friend," a stylized account of how his friend Peter Lorre convinced a Hollywood producer in London to hire him in 1934.[19] Probably Brecht heard it from Lorre personally, whom he saw frequently. Another successful refugee actor, Oskar Homolka, who had played in some of Brecht's European productions and who admired him tremendously, invited him frequently to his Bel Air home, where they played chess and discussed theater and films. From a conversation with the well-read Homolka, Brecht gleaned the idea for a film story on the life of Henri Dunant, founder of the International Red Cross.[20] As background, it is possible that Brecht read a biography of Dunant by the émigré Martin Gumpert, a German doctor living in New York. Not long after his conversation with Homolka he wrote a story outline based on this, a favorite theme of his—the fatality of doing and being good in a hostile world. In his completed film outline with the English title "The Malady of Monsieur Dunant," this querulous idealist ultimately becomes a tragic victim of his own obsession with relieving suffering.[21]

Early that summer, Eisler brought the dramatist and screen writer Clifford Odets to Brecht's house. When Odets spoke of the decline of the American theater and of Hollywood film writing, Brecht concurred, though he privately noted that Odets, too, was sinking to the level of other Hollywood writers. His plays, Brecht's journal observes, follow the naturalistic model of Chekhov which dominated the American stage in the early forties.[22] He abhorred it, but Odets meant an important connection to the film industry. A few days later he again met Odets for lunch with Eisler and the German film director Fritz Lang, at which time they discussed a film version of *Private Life of the Master Race*.[23] Eisler recalls that Odets contributed an excellent concept for the film,[24] but Brecht's deep-grained aversion to the psychological probing in Odets's dramas made the American playwright's suggestions unacceptable. His journal entry that "Odets is looking for something uplifting"[25] damned any hope of collaboration. Again Brecht had failed to convince an important Hollywood connection that his ideas were worth being filmed.

This was by no means the sum of Brecht's film writing during the first year. Two brief but complete plot summaries, and a lengthy story outline for a film on Walter Reed's struggle against malaria entitled "The Fly," probably date from that period, as well as notes for film stories to be called "Horoscope," "The Traitor," and "The Mexican."[26] A journal notation of June 1, 1942, also intimates that he had spoken with someone at the MGM studios about filming his *The Threepenny Opera*, though nothing came of it beyond an entry which reads: "Chances: (1) MGM is seriously considering filming *The Threepenny Opera*. (2) Jean Renoir would like to write a film with me." Renoir, already a famous film director, had known Brecht since the late twenties in Berlin. Arriving in Hollywood in 1940, Renoir had found work with Twentieth Century Fox, but at this time he still lacked the influence with studios to help Brecht sell his stories.

An inveterate movie-goer since his youth, Brecht held firm opinions about Hollywood films long before 1941. In 1936 he knew its films well enough to classify them as part of "the world narcotics trade."[27] He considered most Hollywood films to be an opiate of the masses. To him, meaningless diversions anesthetized the mind through their attempt to entertain or to "grip" viewers with stories unrelated to their own lives. Consonant with his revolutionary theatrical theories, he demanded that films as well as dramas not hypnotize audiences (*GW* XVI, 563). Hence he rejected empathy, identification, and other sentimental devices which he classified as "laxatives of the soul." Instead he insisted on non-escapist films (and dramas) that were entertaining and instructive, i.e., that provoked thinking. The double features he saw two or three times a week at local movie house matinees before the prices changed convinced him that Hollywood was consciously narcotizing a country at war. He accurately sensed what later statistics partially bear out: 20 percent of films in production by Hollywood studios at the beginning of 1942 were musical comedies; by the end of the year it was 40 percent.[28] For Brecht, 99 percent of Hollywood films had the same stupefying effect on the audience. Appropriately, his journal laments being "here in the world center of the narcotic trade."[29]

"World center of the narcotic trade," "marketplace of lies," "gambling casino"—Brecht's epithets for Hollywood did not end there. A letter to Berlau the following year speaks of fleeing Hitler and having to hide "in this sewer."[30]

A critic who speaks of Brecht's "unhappy love-hate relationship" to the film world describes his attitude in categories alien to his make-up.[31] One might speak instead of contempt mitigated by ambition to control the object of that contempt. While despising Hollywood, Brecht also recognized its enormous influence, some of which he hoped to capture for himself and for his own artistic and political views. "Change the world, it needs it" demands a song in his play *The Measures Taken*,[32] and Brecht was burning to do that with film. His chance came near the end of his first year in America when he suddenly won big at Hollywood roulette.

7 A QUALIFIED WINNER—
THE FILM *HANGMEN ALSO DIE*

On one spin of the wheel that looked no more promising than a dozen others that year, Brecht in mid-1942 hit the right number with a story that became one of the best anti-fascist films produced in Hollywood during World War II—*Hangmen Also Die*. Contrary to claims that he disavowed the final film version after seeing his efforts mutilated, Brecht in fact tried to gain more credit for it than he received. And more of his presence remains in the film than many Brecht purists care to admit.

Following the pattern of a common Hollywood mistake, his work on it began when two important names teamed up as a writer and director in the expectation of great results. On May 27, 1942, the Nazi "Reichsprotector of Bohemia/Moravia," the notorious "hangman" Reinhard Heydrich, died from the bullets of unidentified Czech resistance fighters. The following day, Brecht's journal remarks: "With Lang on the beach thinking about a hostage film (on the occasion of Heydrich's execution in Prague)."

Fritz Lang, a noted film director in the Weimar Republic (*Dr. Mabuse, Metropolis, M*), left Germany in 1933 after Goebbels asked him to head the production of films there. He came to Hollywood (via Paris) in 1934, where he soon re-established himself with films which added to his international reputation. He called his second Hollywood film, *You and Me* (1938), "a fairy tale inspired by Brecht" and attributed its concept to the style of that writer's learning plays.[1] He had known Brecht before 1933 and had great respect for his work. Brecht also knew Lang and his European films, for his wife, Helene Weigel, had appeared as an extra in some of them and had played a small role in *Metropolis*, while his actor-friend Peter Lorre had taken the lead in *M*.

Many European theater people, including Brecht, viewed film as a legitimate art form. Actors from the theater often took movie roles, especially in silent films, without regard for the distinction made in America at the time between Hollywood and Broadway actors. In his own theoretical writings Brecht, too, sometimes blurred the line between theater and film. He claims, for example, that Charlie Chaplin's acting coincided almost exactly with his demands for epic theater (*GW* XVII, 987). In other writings on his non-Aristotelian dramaturgy, Brecht repeatedly refers to film to corroborate his theories, at one point even speaking of "the new dramaturgy (for film or theater)" (*GW* XV, 274) as if they were synonymous. Film for him constituted an art form separate from but equal to much that he did in the theater.

Not so, however, with American film, which is probably why Brecht chose to work with Fritz Lang, a European whose outlook he felt might have been similar to his.

In twenty-two journal entries between the end of May and December 1942 Brecht preserved more of his reactions to the development of this film than to any single work he wrote. Initially it was another try at roulette. But a journal notation in late June sounds optimistic: "It appears the story I'm writing with Lang has some prospects. Lang told it to a producer, who was impressed."[2] Arnold Pressburger, a refugee Lang knew from Europe, had been urging him for months to make a film (Lang was free-lancing at the time), and here Lang discovered an appealing topic. Engaging Brecht because of what he called his "political knowledge" of the underground situation in Europe, Lang met with him, and together they wrote a story outline in German based on the pursuit of Heydrich's assassin by the Nazis and the execution of Czech hostages as they imagined that these events happened.[3] Drawing on Lang's film *M*, where both the police and the criminals of a city pursue a murderer, they finished what Lang calls an "exact outline," which probably meant a ten- to fifteen-page version of the story.[4]

Hans Viertel, the German-born son of Brecht's friends Berthold and Salka Viertel, insists that Brecht and Lang completed a full-length treatment of roughly one-hundred pages in German and had him translate it into English with the help of three secretaries provided by Lang. This is what they sold to Pressburger, and this, according to Viertel, was the basis for the screenplay. Lang denies this, but acknowledges that a manuscript existed when John Wexley, who began work with Brecht in early August, arrived. Wexley, on the other hand, maintains that Brecht and Lang had written no more than a page of rough notes.[5]

Soon after they began their story, Brecht's journal notes: "Normally Lang and I work from nine in the morning until seven in the evening on the hostage story."[6] Given his speed in writing and a journal note of July 20th which speaks of spending full time on the story ("The entire time bread-and-butter work on the hostage story with Lang"), they must have written a good deal before Wexley came. One entry contains story details that scarcely could have existed in the single-page outline. Writing to Berlau in late June, Brecht complains how exhausting it is writing with Lang. Again in July he grumbles about the hectic pace of writing this story, which, he states, is "manual labor." He also reports to her that he has received $250 for preliminary work on it.[7]

Brecht's collaboration during June and July 1942 severely damaged his opinion of Lang. He felt that this European artist had succumbed to Hollywood values, and he illustrates it in his journal on June 29th by quoting a remark Lang made repeatedly while working on the story: "the public will accept this." For Brecht, what the public would accept had nothing to do with how they should write their story. His bitter complaint to Berlau in a letter of July 1942 about the "thousand taboos" of film-making is a reaction against daily warnings he heard from Lang to avoid what producers and directors felt the public would not accept. This extreme caution, he felt, proved that Lang had capitulated to prevailing movie industry norms.

Brecht's assessment, while perhaps objectively unfair, was at least subjectively accurate. Throughout their collaboration, Lang apparently failed to grasp the playwright's profound contempt for anything that smacked of conventional film, an attitude that came to include the director himself. Lang did not share this contempt for Hollywood pictures, since he not only felt himself capable of making good ones that went against the grain of conventional films; he also considered film to be (in his own words) "*the* art of our century. A theater play reaches only a very limited audience; a book, if it is a bestseller, a much wider one; but neither comes close to the audiences to which a film appeals."[8] Brecht would have agreed only if this were one of *his* films, done totally on *his* terms. Once before he had accomplished this in his film *Kuhle Wampe* (Engl. *Whither Germany*, 1931). In it, he not only incorporated many of his "epic" theories of drama, but his close supervision over production kept his own vision intact from his screenplay to the screen. Critics today recognize it as one of the innovative films of the thirties. But neither Hollywood nor Lang was in a position at the time to accommodate his unconventional vision.

A journal note on August 5th first mentions John Wexley, a prominent screen writer and dramatist whom Lang brought in from the East to help Brecht do an English screenplay. Wexley claims Lang promised him sole credit for the screenplay.[9] He did not consider it a collaboration of peers, since Brecht knew little English and less about Hollywood film writing. Wexley's background suited Brecht well—his screenplay for the anti-fascist film *Confessions of a Nazi Spy* (1939) represented a daring step for Hollywood at the time; he had a good command of German; he had travelled extensively in Europe and knew Prague; and, politically, he was a known leftist, which presumably would have made him a compatible colleague. But Brecht knew nothing of the alleged agreement Wexley had with Lang and rightly thought he was working as an equal partner, with a voice in all decisions.

According to Wexley, when he arrived early in August 1942 Brecht and Lang gave him a few written notes on a single sheet of paper, but there was no film story, no plot, no scenes, etc. Brecht's journal entries, and independent statements by Lang and Viertel, contradict him. At least one finished version of a story existed in some form. At first, Wexley's attempts to make it his own screenplay irritated Brecht, who in his journal on August 5th mentions the new arrival's reputation as "very leftist and decent" and then mitigated his observation by noting two incidents. First, he had told one sequence in the film story to Wexley, who dictated it in English to a secretary and then hesitated to give Brecht a copy because the name "John Wexley" appeared on the top of each page as sole author. And when Brecht took away a page with notations to translate it (at Wexley's request) into German, Wexley phoned and said he needed it back immediately, since he could not work without it. Brecht may not have realized that Wexley was accumulating every piece of paper they wrote to protect himself in any future dispute over credits, but he did sense that Wexley was taking advantage of him. "These tricks," his journal notes, "appear to be well paid."

Throughout August, Lang often sat with the two writers in their working sessions. By now, according to Brecht's journal, he travelled the twelve miles from Santa Monica to begin work at nine a.m. each day in the old Chaplin studios that Pressburger had rented for the film. They also met some evenings at Brecht's home, where the curfew confined him after 8 p.m. Wexley states that often he had to mediate between Brecht and Lang, since the director resisted anything that violated Hollywood norms and might jeopardize releasing the picture. For example, in keeping with a Hollywood dictum to avoid appearing philo-Semitic (studios were sensitive because of the number of Jewish executives and artists on their payrolls), Lang objected to scenes showing Czech Jews wearing the star of David or to Nazis maltreating Jewish resistance fighters. In a journal note written shortly after they had completed the screenplay, Brecht confesses that much of the work nearly made him ill. He quotes one dispute with Lang, from which he recalls the director's indignant rejoinder concerning two characters in the story: "Why should I give that line to a worker, whom I'm paying $150, when the professor, whom I'm paying $5000, is standing next to him?"[10]

Brecht and Wexley had another kind of difference. Speaking of Wexley, Joseph Losey, who later knew and understood Brecht well, writes that "one cannot imagine anyone farther removed from Brecht's world, from what he wanted, and from the values he stood for."[11] Wexley, who says that he knew and admired Brecht from the 1935 performance of *Mother* in New York, usually failed to understand Brecht's theories during their collaboration and rejected them when he did. "He (Brecht) couldn't get used to American methods or the ideological approach demanded by this special time in history," Wexley remembers. Brecht wanted to teach by appealing to his viewers' reason and common sense. Wexley did also, but in a different manner: "I maintain (and still do) that the audience must be moved, emotionally held in the Greek sense, must experience catharsis." In another difference of opinion, he faulted Brecht for trying to introduce alien dramatic devices from his epic theater into the screenplay, e.g., film clips, posters, songs, even a chorus.

Because of these differences, Wexley believed at the outset that the refugee writer knew "little or nothing about the technical aspects of film." Certainly Brecht was ignorant, for example, of English technical terms used to give camera instructions in a Hollywood screenplay. But much of his "ignorance" arose from his disgust with the kind of screenplay Wexley wanted to write. In a journal entry, he admits that he often finds it an effort "not to participate in solving these dirty little problems, to find these smooth, smart lines, these transitions from nothing to nothing, and not to write 'outpourings.' I left that to others. That kind of work can really impair one's handwriting."[12]

In spite of differing outlooks and temperaments, the two men apparently got along in the ten weeks they worked on the screenplay. In what must have pained Brecht slightly, Wexley invoked the Hollywood privilege of instant intimacy by calling him "Bert" (all his European friends, including his wife, called him "Brecht"). He visited Brecht's home frequently, and they wrote, discussed, ate, and played chess together.

On September 14th, Brecht's journal mentions that work is progressing better since Lang has left him alone with Wexley. They had completed an outline (Wexley maintains they wrote two) and were now transferring the contents into a screenplay. Wexley wrote it down in English and then, according to Brecht, "I correct his work." He adds that he has persuaded Wexley to meet him in the evening at his home and write a "completely new ideal script" which he proposes to show Lang. By Wexley's account they had already finished 120 pages of the screenplay when they began this project.

This lost "ideal script" still exercises those who are convinced that, in contrast to the film, it contained unadulterated Brecht. According to a journal notation it was to feature "scenes of people."[13] Wexley recalls that Lang feared this deliberate propagandistic tendency, for he knew how sensitive Hollywood was to such matters. Their dissatisfaction with Lang's timidity prompted them to fantasize on scenes they would like to include and to write out some of them. Later they showed a few to Lang. As an artist he liked them, but his instinct for prevailing film industry norms sounded an alarm against injecting too many into a film that had to pass Joe Breen of the Hays office.

Lang himself recalls nothing about the existence of a separate "ideal script," though he remembers Brecht's plans for something which sounded like that. By now the dramatist knew that, in producing a motion picture, directors often shoot twenty to forty times as much footage as appears in the released version. Brecht suggested to Lang that they expand the hostage scenes they would be filming anyway so he might show them separately in Germany after Hitler's defeat. Apparently he hoped to use these as quasi-documentary films to re-educate his countrymen after the war.

Brecht's journal mentions one scene in which hostages taken from different social classes after Heydrich's assassination fail to set aside class or racial differences and make a common front against the enemy. Five minutes before their execution, anti-Semitic incidents still break out among them.[14] Since this scene does not exist in any extant version of the screenplay, it must have belonged to the "ideal script." That script probably included other sequences which expanded on scenes already in the film, some of which were totally unrelated to the released film. In all likelihood, these apparently unrelated scenes lacked any plot line, much like the series of vignettes from life in Nazi Germany in his play *The Private Life of the Master Race*. On October 10th Brecht's journal records that they have completed seventy pages of this "ideal script," but that Wexley refuses to write any more. Wexley agrees with that number of pages, but he thinks scholars have exaggerated their importance, for in reality they never really were a coherent script.

The loss of this allegedly pure Brechtian opus, however, cannot alter another fact—at least one version of the completed screenplay contained enough unalloyed Brecht that he was willing to acknowledge it unequivocally as his own work. Probably this was the first mimeographed version dated October 16, 1942, for in a journal notation two days later he writes: "If I could continue publishing the *Versuche* [the collective title for his works published in Germany before 1933], I would print a few scenes from *Trust the People* [his working title for the film]. . . ." He then mentions the scene in which Heydrich confronts Czech industrialists. Had Brecht disapproved of the screenplay at this date, or had the work not been his own, it seems curious that he hoped to canonize in future editions of his work this scene, which appeared unchanged in the released film, as well as others of the hostage camp.

Far from being dissatisfied, Brecht seems to have sensed at least qualified pride in what he thought was the finished product. Writing to the émigré political philosopher Karl Korsch after he had seen one version of the screenplay, he is delighted over the money earned on it and says he does not know how it will look on the screen, "but at least the script is no run-of-the-mill thing."[15] A journal entry of October 18th applies the highest compliment in his vocabulary to the screenplay—"epic": "the film is constructed on epic lines, employing three stories that alternate: the story of an assassin; the story of a girl whose father is taken hostage; and the story of a quisling who is hunted down by an entire city. That, for example, is not bad. Not bad, either, that the underground makes mistakes, which the people at large correct, etc."

The collaboration had been punctuated with periodic disputes over money. Initially, according to Lang, Brecht asked if $3000 would be too much to request for work on the screenplay. Lang promised to get him $5000, whereupon he says he requested $7500 for Brecht. Pressburger, who considered it too much for a writer who had never written an American screenplay and who would need help, succumbed only after strenuous objection.

Brecht's journal reflects his obsession with the potential money to be made on the film, though the amounts he listed conflict with Lang's recollections. He records in July that he is to receive $5000 initially and $3000 for "additional work."[16] But a notation the following month that Wexley is earning $1500 a week for his work on the screenplay is not one of gracious acceptance, as another entry some weeks later confirms.[17] Having heard, he says, that Wexley had demanded a bonus for working evenings and Sundays, he told Lang that unless he, too, received the same bonus from Pressburger, he would quit. Wexley recalls that he helped Brecht to obtain the additional bonus, though Brecht's journal mentions that the idea came from Lang. Lang denies that he initiated the request and recalls his dismay at Brecht's crude attempt to blackmail Pressburger, who finally approved the bonus but never forgave the playwright. Whether Brecht received a $2500 (Lang) or a $2000 (Wexley) bonus is immaterial. The total sum he earned on the film (between $8000 and $10,000) helped him to achieve what he insisted was his only purpose in writing for film. A journal entry of June 24, 1943, reads: "The Lang film . . . gave me breathing space for [writing] three plays: *Simone, Duchess, Schweyk*."

Sometime early in October 1942 Pressburger informed Lang that pressure from the banks required them to begin shooting three weeks earlier than planned. The script, not quite complete, already had a girth of 280 pages at a time when screenplays averaged around 150 pages. Originally Lang wanted to have Brecht and Wexley abridge the screenplay after they had completed a first draft. While they rushed to

finish, Lang covertly hired an unknown writer, Henry Guinsberg, to
help him trim it down. Wexley exploded when he discovered what he
claims was an outlawed practice, and he insists that Brecht shared his
anger. Lang hastily terminated Guinsberg, who had done little on the
script, and Brecht and Wexley concluded it. Brecht's participation in
the writing ended at this point (around the middle of October) while
Wexley, without consulting him, spent the next two weeks alone reducing the screenplay to shooting length. Brecht saw him at a dinner
once during this two-week period, and he notes in a later journal entry
that Wexley was a "living bad conscience."[18] From it he inferred that
something was amiss. But he did not know what it was until he received a call from Lang's secretary on November 1st announcing that
shooting was to begin, and "you're invited, more than invited."

Several journal entries between November 2nd, when Brecht began
to watch Lang shooting, and December 17th, his last entry dealing
with a film which was shot in 52 days, express his rage at what he
observed.[19] The first scene he saw filmed, which portrayed the heroine
arguing with her aunt about how low her wedding dress should be cut,
was one he and Wexley had deleted. After two more days of observation he concluded that while collaborating with Wexley, "I was able to
remove the main stupidities from the story. Now they're all back in."
For two weekly paychecks totalling $3000, he observed, Wexley, with
Lang's assistance, had restored all the weak scenes they had eliminated
in ten weeks of work.[20]

The filming of one scene drew unexpected kudos from Brecht—a
brutal fight between Gestapo inspector Gruber and Jan Horek: "something almost resembling art comes out of it, and the work has dignity,
respectability of the craft. Artistically it's not uninteresting how precisely and elegantly a prostrate man is kicked in the chest and then the
ribs."[21] But generally he damned without the faintest praise. In a song
written for the hostages to sing while awaiting execution, he had used
the image of passing an invisible flag in the fight against fascist rule.
For $500 Lang had hired the songwriter Sam Coslow, known for the
hits "Cocktails for Two" and "My Old Flame," to render it in English.
To quote Brecht's words, he produced "incredible filth." In reality he
changed only two images with Communist implications: "comrade"
became "brother," and "invisible flag" became "invisible torch."
Brecht opposed "invisible torch," claiming that invisible light bulbs
(he knew a "torch" in British-English was a flashlight) could not be
visualized too well. He further objected to Lang's casting of the Czech
poet according to bourgeois stereotypes—vain, pale, kindly. Brecht
wanted him to be drunken and obese.

In essence, Brecht's dissatisfaction arose from a simple fact of film producing—it was collective work, but not Brecht's kind. For nearly two decades he had surrounded himself with a collective of writers who fed him ideas or wrote for and with him. There he was clearly *primus inter pares*. But as his work on *Hangmen* passed through the hands of second, third, and fourth parties, he lost control over it. To lose the chance of realizing his unique vision, which he believed was superior to that of anyone working on the film, embittered him toward Lang and Wexley, not to mention toward the film industry. His unswerving conviction of his own genius made him construe the results as a criminal act against his person and work. Nor would it be the last time he would refer to those who subverted his creative efforts as "criminals" (*Verbrecher*).

Before shooting, Wexley and Lang had introduced changes in at least 70 of the 192 pages of what Brecht thought was the final version. This, of course, was standard practice. Various extant versions show newly inserted pages dated October 28th, 30th, 31st, and November 2nd, 16th, and 27th. In some cases they were trivial changes, involving a line or two, or at most a shot. In other cases they were major, such as one revision which deleted shots 130-150. Brecht himself always changed and rewrote the script of his own plays when they were in rehearsal, but here he had no control over emendations. When shooting began, he felt the final revised script had subverted much of what he originally intended.

To make matters worse in his eyes, Lang, like most good directors, followed the screenplay as a guide rather than as sacred writ. While shooting, he made changes that inevitably arose as he saw visual possibilities the screenplay did not offer. Lang liked to involve his writers in shooting, but now he consulted only Wexley, who stayed throughout. When Lang edited the film, more of Brecht's scenes ended up on the cutting-room floor. What Brecht saw in the final edited film version struck him as containing more than "minor changes." Justifiably or not, he felt Lang had mutilated a work with which he was once satisfied, and he was technically correct in telling an interviewer in 1943 that he had not written the screenplay for the final film version.[22]

Even the title *Never Surrender* had to be dropped when a book by that name appeared. The final title also failed to capture the idea of resistance implicit in others Brecht had considered: *Silent City, The Hostages of Prague, Unconquered*, and *Trust the People*. In response to competition which Lang and Pressburger announced among their staff, a nameless secretary won $100 for suggesting *Hangmen Also Die* as a title that had box-office appeal, though little relationship to the film's central action.

In spite of these frustrations, Brecht, who still viewed the film as at least partially his own, had no intention of disclaiming it. When he learned shortly before release that Lang and Pressburger had given him no credit for the screenplay because Wexley opposed it,[23] he telephoned the Screen Writers Guild and demanded an arbitration hearing. Wexley later came to feel that Hollywood had corrupted the refugee—knowing what other writers earned, Brecht had become jealous. Wexley also thinks that Lang and Brecht's Hollywood agent, Paul Kohner, encouraged him to seek credit in order to get more film writing jobs. If one believes Brecht, his demands were dictated by his survival instinct. In his journal he admits that "credit for the film would possibly put me in a position to get a film job if the water gets up to my neck."[24]

The Screen Writers Guild at this time arbitrated picture credit disputes (which sometimes reached 100 a year) by assigning three experienced writers to review the material each collaborator had written. To be entitled to credit, a writer had to establish that he had contributed 25 percent of the screen story. Wexley showed them manuscript pages with his name on them; Brecht submitted only a written report of discussions and working sessions along with a few pages. Lang and Eisler, who wrote the music for the film and who spent many hours with the two writers, testified to Brecht's substantial contribution, with Lang citing examples of things "only Brecht could have written." He later stated in print that he believed Brecht wrote a significant portion of the screenplay.[25] But Pressburger declined Lang's invitation to defend the refugee writer—he had not forgotten what he saw as a blackmail attempt. At the hearing, Brecht's journal reports, Wexley "sat in front of half a hundredweight of manuscripts and claimed he had hardly spoken with me."[26] The decision went against Brecht.

The paradox of Brecht's dissatisfaction with something for which he demanded more credit raises a basic question—how much of his effort remained in the final film version? Among those who minimize his contribution are the editors of his film writings, who refused to admit it to the canon of his works.[27] But based on examination of the released film version, with which he was not pleased but which he did not disown, it is clear that many ideas must have originated with Brecht.

First, he wrote dozens of German lines spoken throughout, not to mention the entire first scene, or "shot," in the film. Here, where Heydrich berates Czech industrialists in German and announces he is putting the Skoda works under Gestapo control, is the scene Brecht referred to as the "intelligent portrayal of a modern tyrant."[28] Further, he wrote the original version of the "Song of Freedom" sung by the hostages waiting to be shot. He concealed from Lang that he and

Eisler had set part of it to Eisler's "Comintern" song. Unwittingly, millions of American movie-goers who saw this resistance film heard Czech hostages in a Nazi prison singing a few bars from a political song well known in the Communist movement throughout the world. Brecht must have smiled.

A number of scenes or speeches also carried Brecht's distinctive trademark, or derived directly from his own writings. Lang points to lines in shot number 65, where Professor Novotny addresses his daughter about the need for silence on political matters: "Example: you tell it to A—A entrusts it to B—B confides in C—C reposes the secret in D. It's not very far from E to F—so F breathes it to G . . . and *G stands for Gestapo.*" This, Lang insists, is something only Brecht could have written.[29] The text continues as the professor defines "no one" for his daughter: "not any—not one—no single one—none!" This probably originated with Brecht. His Herr Keuner, a philosophical alter ego in his anecdotes and aphorisms written in the thirties, had a name that in the Swabian dialect meant "no one." The "no one" concept also played an important role in his early play *A Man's a Man.* Here Brecht apparently was borrowing from himself.

Lang also insists that Brecht wrote or decisively formed all the scenes in the hostage prison camp. At least one shot confirms this. Shortly before Professor Novotny is to be executed, he dictates to his daughter Mascha a letter for his son, which serves as a last testament and a charge to resist the Nazis. In the scene "Plebiscite" from Brecht's play *The Private Life of the Master Race,* written several years earlier, a letter is read which a father, about to be executed by the Nazis, has smuggled out of prison urging his son to fight on. In tone and content it corresponds in many details to the one in the film. Firsthand accounts of the terror of Gestapo prisons, of occupation troops, underground operations, and executions had made Brecht something of an expert on such matters. This, and the manner in which shot 260 elevates an anonymous worker to the poet of the Czech rebellion (a worker shows his poem to the country's leading poet, who lets his verses stand in spite of their roughness), all argue that Brecht contributed significantly to the prison camp scene in the film.

Even names show Brecht's hand. Heydrich's assassin, Dr. Franz Svoboda, assumes a false name when he goes into hiding—Karel Vaněk. Brecht encountered the name "Karel Vaněk" when he read Jaroslav Hašek's novel *The Good Soldier Schweik,* which he helped to dramatize in 1927-1928. The name Karel Vaněk had appeared on the title page of that work, for it was he who completed Hašek's fragmentary novel. It did not appear in the English translation of *Schweik.* Instead of inventing a name, Brecht appropriated this familiar one for the film. The name of the Gestapo inspector, Alois Gruber, also sounds like Brechtian punning with its proximity to "Schickelgruber," the derisive term sometimes applied to Hitler after his father's original name.

One could mine the script for more subterranean evidence besides that already recovered.[29a] It may not have been Brecht at his best, but it was unquestionably Brecht within the limitation of a genre which, at least in Hollywood, was fundamentally alien to him. Dieterle conjectures that Wexley prevailed in the *Hangmen* arbitration because he was known and liked in Hollywood.[30] The justification for the decision against Brecht did nothing to dilute that suspicion, for the Screen Writers Guild awarded the decision to Wexley on the grounds that Brecht planned to return to Germany, whereas for an American writer like Wexley (who already owned a number of film credits), recognition was essential to his existence.

In spite of Wexley's and Lang's statements that they admired Brecht's talent, they never asked him to work with them again on a film. Nor did Brecht forgive or forget, at least not Lang. In later years, friends heard him name the director as the villain who had mutilated a screenplay he and his wife considered to be very good,[31] and Brecht broke off contact with him in a rift which was known to the entire émigré community.[32] Others heard him identify Wexley as a "nice guy, but a hack,"[33] though this judgment, too, was dictated in part by the frustrations of exile. In 1948 Wexley visited him in Switzerland, where, according to Wexley, Brecht offered an apology for the "unfortunate credit stupidity." While it was probably not a formal apology (Brecht seldom apologized), it was probably an expression of the natural generosity he often displayed when not suffering from the nonrecognition and financial stress that plagued him in America. Wexley would not be the last to find a different Brecht in Europe from the one he had known in America.

If the tone of Brecht's journal entries dealing with this experience reflects what he said in the presence of Hollywood figures, one understands why many in the film world who knew him came to consider him a difficult person to work with. A few days after he completed the *Hangmen* screenplay, he wrote: "Even the most experienced Hollywood writers, who turn out one script after another, sense at a certain point in every script the hope that, by one trick or another, or thanks to this or that stroke of luck, they can produce something better, something not quite so cheap. This hope is always disappointed, but without it they couldn't do their work—and there would be no cheap, vulgar films."[34] And after his hearing before the Screen Writers Guild, he wrote of those present that "the sight of intellectual deformity makes me physically ill. I can scarcely stand to be in the same room with these intellectual cripples and moral casualties."[35]

In spite of these reflections, work on the film was far from a total loss. In addition to securing him financially for a time, it supplied him with many proper and place names, with insights into conditions in Nazi-occupied Prague, and with much local color, some of which he transplanted into the *Schweik* comedy he wrote the following summer. As background for the film, he and Wexley had requested information from the Czech exile government in London. Among the materials they received were crudely printed leaflets distributed by the Czech underground among workers in munitions factories. Beneath the drawing of a turtle was a message calling for a slowdown of production. Brecht transformed this symbol into a resistance poem, "In the Sign of the Turtle" (1943), in which this small and seemingly harmless member of the animal kingdom devoured the eggs of the imperial German eagle. Indirectly, his work on a Hollywood film was the catalyst for this poem, just as nearly every poem he wrote in America originated from a particular experience.

Before the credit dispute, Wexley had tried to convince Brecht that in the final film version Lang had preserved 90 percent of the original ideas and had not mutilated it as badly as Brecht had imagined. From one vantage point, Wexley was right. A large number of American movie-goers liked *Hangmen* well enough to make it a box-office success during a time when war movies were competing with comedies and escape-to-nostalgia musicals for the attention of audiences. Brecht's and Lang's influence not only gave the film an authentically European look; German-speaking refugee actors playing Nazi roles (Reinhold Schunzel, Hans von Twardowski, Tonio Selwart, and Brecht's friend Alexander Granach, who was inspector Gruber) lent credibility by playing their parts with sadism and thick accents. It stands as one of the amusing ironies of history that the American popular image of ugly Germans and malevolent Nazis was fixed for decades to come by World War II films like this in which German Jews like Granach played the parts of their Nazi tormentors with a passion fired by hatred and desire for revenge. But the questionable morality of capitalizing on these Nazi film roles caused the opposite reaction in another of Brecht's acquaintances, the Jewish actor Oskar Homolka, who declined the role of inspector Gruber that Brecht originally offered him because he would have to portray a Nazi.[36]

Confirmation that Lang had not watered down Brecht's message excessively comes from another quarter—the FBI. After the USA entered the war against Germany, the FBI routinely monitored the activities of Brecht and thousands of other German aliens in the USA.

Sometime in 1943 they transferred his dossier from the category "enemy alien control" to the more ominous "internal security." At a time when most American readers had never heard Brecht's name, the FBI compiled considerable information about his works that included perceptive bits of literary analysis. One of these in 1943 illustrates that at least one FBI informant, as well as the agents assessing Brecht's potential danger, understood his intentions in *Hangmen*. Quoting source T-23, the file states: "The effect of the picture was that it emphasized the importance of underground work, the sacrifice necessary thereto, and the methods used by the underground. When viewed in the light of previous writings of Bert Brecht, 'Hangmen Also Die' takes on something of the complexion of Brecht's education plays in that it emphasizes the conduct required of persons working in an underground movement. In general, the individuals in the story are made to see that their position and even their safety and the safety of their families is completely subordinate to the work of the underground movement. This principle is that which Brecht in his play 'The Disciplinary Measure' [*The Measures Taken*] mentioned previously, emphasized."

Fritz Lang reports that scenes portraying this attitude caused a quarrel with Joe Breen of the Hays office. Breen did not want to allow the film to be released. In the film, a series of pre-arranged lies by members of the underground "betray" the Czech quisling Czaka to the Nazis and cause his death. Initially Breen refused to approve a picture that "glorified a lie." Only after a day-long argument with Lang did he relent.[37]

According to Wexley, critics have since praised *Hangmen* as one of the best anti-fascist films made during World War II. Lang recalls it as the best anti-fascist film he ever made. Compared with cliché-ridden anti-Nazi films of the period, it does hold up today, even in the abbreviated version often shown on television.

Brecht's work on this film had far-reaching effects on the remainder of his exile. In addition to securing him financially for the next two years, it intensified his contempt for Hollywood and closed a few more doors in the film world. And, while he received no credit as the screen writer, his name did appear (with Lang) as the co-author of the original story. This would be enough in 1947 to bring him to the attention of the House Committee on Un-American Activities. A statement he made before that committee summarized not so much his view of himself as a writer, but the realities of his life in the film world: "I am not a film writer, and I am not aware of any influence I have had on the film industry, either politically or artistically."[38]

Until the end of his exile, Brecht looked on film-writing as many people do gambling. He knew the odds against him, but, knowing that he stood to win big money for a small expenditure of time and effort, he went right on playing. Interspersed with playwriting, his major activity in 1943-1945, were interludes devoted to writing notes, sketches, and outlines for film stories. Some never progressed beyond the talking stage, such as an idea Brecht discussed with Hans Viertel for a film showing Shakespeare's struggle to keep his theater afloat financially. Reading Ward's *History of English Dramatic Literature* against the backdrop of Hollywood may have sparked this idea. Earlier his journal had called Elizabethan theater "the cradle of capitalistic dramatic art" and Hollywood its "grave."[1] Now in mid-1943 he adduced their common features: "collective writing, fast writing-on-order, the same motifs used over again, the lack of influence writers have over their products, fame only among the writers themselves, then the violent action, the plots, the new milieus, the political interests, etc., etc. . . . Even Shakespeare's curious flight at the end into tavern-keeping corresponds to the flight to a ranch which everyone here is planning."[2]

Brecht sketched out other ideas for film stories in more detail, among them a three-page German text with the English title "Uncle Sam's Property," which treats the wanderings of a bayonet from the hands of a soldier through the ranks and social classes of American society until it finds its way back to its owner.[3] But by this time film-writing without a specific contact in mind was an exception. After Brecht's work on *Hangmen*, solid connections to someone who could help "sell" his stories triggered most of his "spec" writing.

In May 1943, while discussing his recently completed play *Schweyk in the Second World War* with Peter Lorre, whom he wanted to recruit for the title role, Brecht learned that the actor was a close friend of Ernest Pascal, past president of the Screen Writers Guild. Pascal had built a reputation on a number of successful screenplays, including *Lloyds of London, Kidnapped*, and *The Hound of the Baskervilles*. With Pascal in mind, Brecht conceived the idea for a film story that he mentions in a letter to Berlau early in June 1943. In it he states he hopes to sell it through Lorre "because we could really use the money."[4] Later that month he notifies her that he and Lorre are discussing a second story "which I would work on in July and August so there would be some money in our purse again. Something permanent *could* develop out of it, one or two films each year with United Artists. If that happened, I'd bring you here."[5]

Lorre, who was interested in Brecht's ideas, invited him to his Lake Arrowhead resort home to work on them and "sell" them to Pascal. After securing travel permission from the Assistant United States Attorney in Los Angeles (he was still an alien), Brecht went to Lake Arrowhead from July 3rd to 6th. The four days he spent with two figures who had succeeded in the world's most expensive art form generated some caustic observations.

Describing the forested private recreation area on the shores of Lake Arrowhead where Lorre and other Hollywood figures owned homes, Brecht notes: "it's as quiet here as in a forest next to two steam-driven sawmills—speedboats keep thundering across the lake.... A little girl asks me if I'm a chauffeur, then if I'm an actor, then if I'm a writer. Her instinct is infallible—I must belong to the servant class. They discuss the story in the morning as a concession to me, because it's not customary to do any work when you go off somewhere to work."[6]

Though he left Lake Arrowhead with no firm promise, Brecht had enough hope for a story idea he called "The Crouching Venus" to work it out later that month with Hans Viertel. Modeling his main character on a magazine photo of Toulouse-Lautrec in a top hat and cut-away, Brecht treats the individual resistance of Mr. Totin, an art museum curator in Marseilles in 1940. The plot, as recounted by Viertel, illustrates the kind of story Brecht hoped to sell at a time when anti-Nazi resistance films were flourishing in Hollywood.

The day after the Vichy government takes over, the apolitical Totin, in order to protect his museum, pledges his loyalty to the new regime. Soon afterward a Nazi art commission, headed by a German art historian who happens to be an old friend, appears at his museum. They select his favorite work, a seventeenth-century wooden statue called "The Crouching Venus," for export to Germany. Totin sets about to save the statue, and his former friend becomes a mortal enemy. He contacts the Marseilles underworld, and, with their help, and the aid of the proprietress of a bistro, they steal the statue and arrange for it to be shipped away in a coffin. At a critical juncture the German art commissioner discovers the ruse, and Totin is forced to kill him with a sword cane. The statue is saved, but Totin disappears into the underworld. Following the war he is seen in a cafe having an aperitif with the proprietress. As a criminal, he had lost his identity and become an adjunct to the bourgeois society to which he once belonged.[7]

In a letter to Berlau written after his return from Lake Arrowhead, Brecht indicates that he and Viertel are still working on what must have been a "treatment," i.e., a 50-75 page narrative version of the film's action. They placed it with the Paul Kohner agency in Hollywood, which handled many émigré writers. Brecht, who was consid-

ered a "small fry" relative to other successful émigrés, was turned over
to Ilse Lahn, who remembers trying to sell this and several other of his
film stories.[8] But Hollywood was not interested. The title itself, as
Berthold Viertel told his son in an argument over a story he considered
too "brechtian" for the film world, disqualified it (they later changed it
to "The Fugitive Venus"). Compared to most Hollywood formula
stories of the period, the protagonist's unhappy fate—i.e., his loss of
middle-class identity—reflected too daring a departure from box-
office certainties for potential buyers to gamble on it. Today it counts
among several lost film stories Brecht wrote for Hollywood.

Conversations with Lorre and Pascal also gave Brecht reason to go
ahead with the second story he mentioned to Berlau, which has been
found only recently. Among some of Lorre's posthumous papers
owned by Ernest Pascal's widow is a nine-page outline in German
sketching out a film version of his balladesque anti-war poem "Children's Crusade 1939."[9]

Originally in 1941 Brecht had planned it as a film story, but had
written the poem instead.[10] Now he returned to his original concept.
Set in a rural New England school, Brecht's outline begins with a
frame story describing how new snow threatens to interrupt a "war
stamp campaign" the school children are conducting. After deciding
to go sleigh-riding, they invite along a five-year-old immigrant boy
who has joined them recently. Their teacher, however, uses the occasion to explain that, to some children, snow can mean something besides fun. He narrates a tale of children displaced by the war in Poland
in 1939 who set out on a crusade in the middle of winter to find a land
where there is peace. In the end, as the story goes, they all perish.

From the film outline it is evident that Brecht understood considerably more about the technical details of film-writing than Wexley
believed while they were collaborating on *Hangmen*. In addition to
dividing the action into thirty-three separate scenes or shots, he also
prescribed visual effects, music, and even certain camera angles he
wanted. His outline ends with the immigrant boy falling asleep on the
teacher's lap during a description of the "visions" which precede the
death of the children who have never found their destination. Following the final vision, blow-ups of twelve individual children's heads are
to appear on the screen.

Several aspects reflect Brecht's attempts to make his story reach
American audiences. The setting in New England, the cradle of American democracy, and the children's "war stamp campaign" are obvious
appeals to patriotism, while the small immigrant child adopted by the
other children is intended to arouse America's traditional sympathy
for the underdog. Likewise, the suffering of the children in war-torn

Poland is intended to generate compassion for them and, by extension, revulsion against the war that caused it. This may be one reason Brecht never found a buyer, for at a time when Hollywood was distributing many successful war films and most Americans believed they were fighting a just war against fascism, Brecht was sending a thinly veiled pacifistic message. Whether by miscalculation or because of his oppositional nature, the film stories he wrote failed to meet the "taste" of American audiences as defined by the film industry.

An undated letter to Berlau written while Brecht was at Lake Arrowhead reports on a meeting with a producer from Universal Studios shortly before he came there. Brecht had attempted to sell him a story that he had helped Berlau to write a few years earlier. He fails to mention the producer's name, but he identifies the story as one from the "suffragette movement" about a female teacher who was fired for being secretly married, and whose dismissal results in a "marriage strike in the town." The producer, according to his letter, is "very interested," and he added: "perhaps you'll earn something from it."

Two weeks later Brecht wrote to Berlau that he had spent the evening with a producer named Goldsmith and the actor Fritz Kortner.[11] Isidor Goldschmidt, who headed Gloria Film studios in Germany before 1933 and who spelled his name Goldsmith after he became a producer at Columbia Studios, was now free-lancing in Hollywood. His widow recalls that he and Brecht had worked together around this time on a modern version of *Lysistrata* that they hoped to sell to a studio.[12] The theme of a marriage strike common to their unfinished story and the one Brecht told the unidentified producer from Universal Studios a few weeks earlier suggests that it was that same material, and that Goldsmith was the producer with whom he discussed it. But their story was never sold, and it, too, has disappeared.

Most of Brecht's flesh-and-blood contacts with Hollywood at this time took place in a home on Mabery Road in Santa Monica. Here Salka Viertel, who had written a number of screenplays for Greta Garbo, presided with wit and charm over an old-world literary salon unique in America at the time.[13] Her guest lists resembled a pantheon of European and American writers, intellectuals, artists, and musicians, as well as the rulers, the gods, and the goddesses of Hollywood and Broadway. Through contact with Aldous Huxley, W. H. Auden, Christopher Isherwood, John Houseman, Charlie Chaplin, Otto Klemperer, Igor Stravinsky, Dimitri Tomkin, and many more, Brecht after 1942 began to associate with people he otherwise might not have met. Here, for example, he first met Charles Laughton, who from 1944 till 1947 was to become the most powerful promoter of his dramatic works in America. This contact with prominent Hollywood personalities, coupled with Brecht's habit of regularly seeing the latest releases, kept him reasonably well informed about the tastes and mores of the film community.

In October 1944 he collaborated with Salka Viertel and the screen writer Vladimir Pozner on a film story entitled "Silent Witness." In the matter-of-fact way he often used to conceal his generosity, Brecht told Viertel, whose temporary financial distress had prompted him to offer his collaboration, that he wanted to do it to make some money himself. This was not altogether true, for recently he had received a large sum. But clearly he wanted to write a story they could sell.

By Viertel's account, Brecht pledged to help them write a conventional formula story. "Why shouldn't we be able to do as well as any Hollywood hack?" Brecht asked, to which Viertel replied that Hollywood producers wanted something "original but unfamiliar, unusual but popular, moralistic but sexy, true but improbable, tender but violent, slick but a highbrow masterpiece."[14] Brecht did not accept that he was constitutionally incapable of that kind of writing. According to her, he "bit into his cigar and assured me that we could write our story in such a way that they would not notice what a highbrow masterpiece it was."[15]

After agreeing not to consider anything from an ideological or "artistic" viewpoint, they surveyed the Hollywood market. Realizing that everyone in Hollywood was writing war stories, and knowing that consequently there was little material available for women stars, they decided to write a "woman's story." If we assume that here, as in every collaboration, Brecht's ideas and personality dominated, a glance at his plot reveals a fatal mistake that disqualified it from serious consideration in Hollywood.

When Jean Riviere, a lawyer who was wounded at Dunkirk and who fought with the French resistance, returns with Allied occupation troops to his home in Normandy as the head of a commission to locate and punish Nazi collaborators, he finds his wife Toinette with a bandaged head. When he learns that her head was shorn for her association with the Nazi commandant of the city, he realizes that, because she has collaborated, their marriage is destroyed and her testimony against other alleged collaborators, including her brother-in-law, is meaningless. Toinette flees in the direction of the retreating German troops. Riviere finds her again as a prisoner of the Americans, who are interrogating her. She now claims that, on orders from a certain abbé who was working for the underground, she was assigned to extract information from the Nazi commandant that could save French lives, and that she fled in order to reach the abbé. Meanwhile German troops have murdered the abbé, and she has no other witnesses. But at the abbé's funeral, Riviere notices a new stained glass window of Joan of Arc in the abbé's church. The face is clearly that of his wife Toinette. The church sexton recalls how the artist who painted the window sketched Toinette during one of her visits to the abbé, whereupon Toinette recalls that the abbé pointed to her and instructed the painter, "That's how I would like our Joan of Arc to look." The stained glass portrait, her silent witness, has vindicated her.[16]

In many ways this story might have qualified as a first-rate Hollywood picture—the topicality of events in recently liberated France; the suspense of a detective story that sustains audience interest until the final moments; and the happy ending in which misunderstandings and suspicion are overcome and two lovers are reunited. But Brecht seriously miscalculated one element in an otherwise excellent plot reminiscent of the nineteenth-century writer Heinrich von Kleist—his insistence that the star appear with her head shaven. Viertel pleaded that the actress at least be allowed to wear a scarf, but, in her words, "the more we discussed it, the more stubborn Brecht became about the clean-shaven scalp of the leading lady."[17] Needless to say, Hollywood agents knew that no star could be induced to shave her head, and the story was not sold. Brecht's sovereign thinking as a writer had produced a fatal error that prevented a potentially interesting film from being made.

In addition to wanting to help Viertel, Brecht was motivated by another consideration to work on "Silent Witness." He saw the chance to make a film that would serve another interest—re-educating his German countrymen after the war on the proper anti-fascist attitudes. While working on *Hangmen* he had written specific scenes with this in mind; "The Fugitive Venus" and "Children's Crusade, 1939" were also suitable for postwar indoctrination. In May 1945 his journal mentions a discussion with Dieterle about two potential film stories to be used in postwar Germany.[18] The first, "Dr. Ley," never materialized, but the second gave rise to the short story "The Two Sons" (GW XI, 363) sometime that year. In it a German peasant mother wants to save her son, a member of the *Waffen-SS* who is home temporarily, from the sure death that faces him if he returns to battle. Her son, however, is determined to fight the Russians who are advancing on the town. Finally the mother knocks him unconscious, binds him, and delivers him as a prisoner of war to the Russian commandant who has just occupied the town.

Common to these and nearly all of Brecht's ideas for film stories written between 1943 and the end of the war was a strong didactic element. Like his dramas, his films stories were designed primarily to instruct his audiences and, if possible, to change their thinking. A didactic strain in his makeup explains, in part, his continued incursions into film-writing in the face of repeated failure. Brecht, whose convictions of his ideological correctness were matched by his unswerving confidence in his own genius, seldom passed up a chance to teach. Film-writing, whether in Hollywood or in postwar Germany, offered him the prospect of reaching and influencing live audiences, even if he made little money doing it.

In an ironic footnote to this general lack of success, Brecht unexpectedly won in the Hollywood lottery for a work he never wrote for the film world and from a source he despised—Samuel Goldwyn, one of Hollywood's most powerful producers. In 1942 Feuchtwanger had collaborated with Brecht in writing a drama entitled *The Visions of Simone Machard*. At the time they agreed that, while Brecht held rights to the drama, Feuchtwanger could write a novel using the same material, and that they would share royalties from whichever work was sold or published. In 1943 Feuchtwanger arranged for the writer Jo Swerling to give Goldwyn a copy of the drama. Goldwyn returned it with the comment that he could not understand it.[19] Feuchtwanger also tried to sell it to a story editor at Columbia Pictures who seemed interested and wanted to adapt it for Hollywood.[20] Nothing came of it, but a short time later he gave a copy of his own novel based on the same material (entitled *Simone*) to Swerling, who showed it to Goldwyn. Goldwyn read the novel, understood it, liked it, and, early in 1944, purchased film rights to it.[21]

The number of stories for which Hollywood in this era secured the rights exceeded by many times those that reached the screen. *Simone* was one which earned money for its writers without ever being filmed. Movies portraying anti-Nazi resistance at that time normally drew good box-offices, and Goldwyn wanted to capitalize on the trend. Sensing that the lead required an innocent-looking actress capable of playing a teenage girl, he selected Theresa Wright, whose youthful features made her the only one he would consider for the role.[22] But it turned out she was expecting a child. Goldwyn, who could have sold the story to several other interested studios, refused to release it and postponed shooting until Wright was available. By the time she could act again and shooting could be scheduled, France had been liberated, and topical interest in the French Resistance had passed.

Legally, Feuchtwanger had no obligation to share his earnings with Brecht, but Feuchtwanger was not one for legalisms. The final contract with Goldwyn called for $50,000, of which Brecht received $20,000 for his collaboration on the original idea.[23] Notified of the sale while in New York, Brecht celebrated, according to his journal, by "buying a new pair of trousers." For the second and last time in American exile, Brecht had "won big" in Hollywood. With his earnings he paid off his home; otherwise he continued the same Spartan existence that made Hollywood acquaintances think he and his family subsisted on the brink of poverty.

After the war ended, Brecht turned away from war-related topical subjects, but he did not abandon film-writing altogether. In September 1945 he interrupted work on *Galileo* to join his friend Reyher, who was visiting Los Angeles, in writing a "Macbeth-copy for the movies." His journal states that "Shakespeare's grand motif, the fallibility of instinct (indistinctness of the inner voice), cannot be renewed. I'm emphasizing the defenselessness of the little people against the prevailing moral codex, their limited capacity for criminal potential."[1] Originally Brecht and Reyher conceived of it as a vehicle for Lorre, which they hoped to sell on the strength of his reputation. Lorre worked on it briefly, and his name remained on at least the first outline-length version entitled "Lady Macbeth of the Yards," but he withdrew after one or two sessions. The story Brecht and Reyher finished under the name "All Our Yesterdays"[2] began the procession of classical dramas Brecht revised in socially "relevant" terms, an activity that represented the chief dramatic production of the last decade of his life.

Brecht locates his modern *Macbeth* in the Chicago stockyards and transforms it into a clash between Slavic immigrant workers named Mr. and Mrs. Machacek (the husband works as a "steercutter" in the stockyards) and the wealthy cattle dealer Duncan. Early in the story, Machacek saves Duncan from death by trampling in a cattle pen; later, at the insistence of his ambitious wife, he murders Duncan, only to be exposed in the end by Inspector Duffy. Except for occasional sentences in Brecht's hand, Reyher wrote down most of the story. But all twenty-five subsections of the eighteen-page printed version bear Brecht's unmistakable signature. This might account for the lack of success in selling it; Hollywood studios in the fall of 1945 had no more interest in films depicting class conflict than they had in Brecht.

Apparently Brecht persisted in having Lorre try to sell the story. In July 1946 he mentions in a letter to Reyher that Lorre has not yet been able to place it and adds ironically that their friend is "probably having difficulties getting the starring role." After he had spoken with Lorre in New York City early in the spring of 1947, Reyher wrote asking if Brecht knew of Columbia Pictures' "offering a pretty fair sum for the Lady Macbeth, which was turned down by Lorre's agent because of additional stipulations which made it too expensive."[3] Brecht replied in an undated letter early in April that he has heard nothing of it, but that he would like to sell if possible. He had already shown it to the director Lewis Milestone, but Milestone, he claimed, "ran into resistance from his box office."

Lewis Milestone, a noted Hollywood director, had engaged Brecht briefly for his only formal stint as a film-writer with an American director. In the summer and fall of 1946 Charles Laughton, with whom he had been collaborating on his American version of *Galileo*, was playing the role of a Nazi in the *Arch of Triumph*, which Milestone was directing. Because of difficulties in doing the part to his satisfaction, and in order to understand the Nazi mentality, Laughton began to read *Mein Kampf*. Moreover, Laughton was dissatisfied with the script and wanted certain scenes rewritten. When David Lewis, the producer, asked if he knew anyone who might help with additional writing, he suggested Brecht, who was promptly brought in as a "script doctor."[4] Norman Lloyd, an assistant to Milestone who became acquainted with the dramatist at this time, remembers how Milestone had Brecht look at the rough cut of one sequence that was causing difficulty. Immediately Brecht protested what he considered to be an unrealistic, glamorized portrayal of Nazi-occupied southern France and suggested that it be changed. "You can't convince anyone that these people are suffering refugees if you place them in a colorful area in the south of France," he reportedly said.[5] One of the leads, Charles Boyer, sustained Brecht in what he considered to be a misrepresentation. But Ingrid Bergman, another of the leads, allegedly wanted to have bright bathing suits and the bright color of southern France contrast with this otherwise dark picture. As a result, Brecht's re-write of this scene was rejected. Lloyd reports that Brecht worked for a short time on other scenes and bits of dialogue. He was paid a modest sum for his work, but none of it was used.

Early in 1947 Brecht again ventured into film-writing. A journal notation on March 24th states that he has completed "a film outline for Lorre of *The Overcoat* (after Gogol). No prospects for it in Hollywood; I'm thinking of Switzerland." That film story, on which Elisabeth Hauptmann collaborated with him, was not the only one Brecht wrote for the actor at this time. He also began a story called "The Great Clown Emaël" in which Lorre was to play the lead. It, too, was completed the next year in Switzerland. On May 18th a note by Brecht records his efforts to "sell" a story he had written to Milestone, who seemed interested in, or at least sympathetic to Brecht's writings.[6] It was to be an original new version of Offenbach's *Tales of Hoffmann*. Soon after this conversation, Brecht produced a story outline of his idea in which he argued that, in spite of abandoning Offenbach's operatic form, his version would lend itself to a "realistic" film in which he would have music and singing occur at those points where one could realistically expect them. His plot summary and notes gave the story an inevitable social message that he felt every modern revision of a classic work needed. There is no record of Milestone's response to the proposed story, but a note in Brecht's hand at the end of his manuscript stating that he has deposited a copy with the Screen Writers Guild to protect the story idea signaled his firm hope that Milestone or someone else would buy it.

Sometime in the spring of 1947, Brecht met Rod Geiger at Anna Harrington's house at the "Uplifters." This newcomer to Hollywood, who had worked as an assistant to Roberto Rossellini on the quasi-documentaries *Open City* and *Paisa* in 1946, arrived with rave notices about his brilliance, and a personality to enhance his billing. Harrington recalls that Brecht, who spent hours talking with Geiger about films, was fascinated by him.[7] In one of their conversations it came out that Geiger, who was directing a film at the time called *Christ in Concrete* (released in 1949 as *Salt to the Devil*), had a large amount of lire blocked in Italy. Brecht, who was impressed with Geiger's reputed talents, saw an opportunity to get financial backing for a film of *Galileo* with Geiger as producer/director. In August 1947 he wrote Reyher that, based on his conversations, there is "a good chance that Rod Geiger, who was involved with *Open City* and *Paisa*, will produce *Galileo* with Laughton and English actors in Italy in the summer of '48." But Geiger's star in Hollywood faded almost as quickly as it had risen. Again Brecht had lost in Hollywood roulette.

In an undated letter written in 1947 to George Pfanzelt, a boyhood friend in Europe, Brecht reveals that his attitudes toward the film world had not changed since arriving nearly six years earlier: "Everything is available here except dollars, without which nothing is available. Hollywood, currently without a doubt the cultural center of four-fifths of the world, is only 15 kilometers away, but you can smell it from here."

Given this outlook and his record of failures, one might ask why Brecht persisted in writing for films until the end of his American exile. One might as well ask why a race horse runs. Winning a prize, i.e., money, was clearly a prime motivation. In addition, film-writing allowed him to indulge his pedagogical inclination, for Brecht recognized that film was the art form which potentially reaches the widest audience. Further, a strong and genuine interest in the medium of film as a form of expression never abandoned him in America, his negative comments notwithstanding. Had he been successful, or had his talent been recognized, he probably would have sung quite a different song. Most important, however, by constitution and temperament Brecht could not stop writing. It appears that for him, film-writing was an extension of, or an experiment with, another mode of dramatic expression. In this connection, Joseph Losey has said of the dramas that "It always seemed to me that Brecht is very close to film,"[8] while

George Tabori believes that Brecht's epic theater consisted, among other things, of "movie techniques applied to the stage."[9] If these observations are valid, one must conclude that film-writing for Brecht was not an altogether unserious endeavor, in spite of a sardonic prescription for success found in his journal: "One must write as well as one can, and that must be just bad enough."[10] A strong dose of envy is mixed with the gall in that statement. Brecht had no compunctions about writing film stories to make money if it gave him the leisure to write dramas, and he considered anyone who thought otherwise to be foolish. When one of his collaborators in 1946 refused to consider any job writing for Hollywood because it might corrupt her, Brecht's rejoinder was, "It doesn't need to."[11] But he objected to the bad or mediocre writing that he felt succeeded in Hollywood, and he demanded far more of himself and others, regardless of what one earned for it.

Geography also motivated Brecht to write film stories. Had he not lived in American exile, it is doubtful he would have written so many. Throughout Brecht's life, virtually everything he wrote was done in response to or in reaction against his immediate environment. In Southern California, no single environmental factor was as pervasive as the film industry. The fact that he worked on material for more than fifty film stories while there[12] suggests that he was more aware of this world than has generally been realized.

The impression is sometimes given that between 1941-1947 Brecht remained relatively isolated from important Hollywood writers, producers, directors, and actors.[13] Rather the opposite seems to have been the case. For a man who never really broke into film-writing, his circle of contact reads like an abridged *Who's Who in Hollywood*. Letters, journals, and the testimony of friends establish that between 1941 and 1947 he had frequent contact, and in some cases became very well-acquainted, with the writers Clifford Odets, Ben Hecht, Arch Oboler, Aben Kandel, John Wexley, Don Ogden Stewart, Lester Cole, Henry Mankewicz, George Froeschel, Herbert Kline, Robert Thoeren, Vladimir Pozner, Ferdinand Reyher, and Joris Ivens. And the Hollywood producers and directors he knew included George Auerbach, William Dieterle, Lewis Milestone, Orson Welles, Mike Todd, Jed Harris, Jean Renoir, Fritz Lang, Elia Kazan, Joseph Losey, Rod Geiger, John Huston, Billy Wilder, and Ernest Pascal.

Film actors and actresses he knew personally included Elsa Lanchester, Lupe Velez (the so-called "Mexican spit-fire"), Peter Lorre, Groucho Marx, Shelley Winters, Freddie Bartholemew, Paul Henreid, Charles Laughton, and Charlie Chaplin. To a degree his acquaintance with Chaplin summarizes his relationship to many Hollywood personalities. Though they saw each other frequently at Eisler's home, at Salka Viertel's salon, in Chaplin's own home, and at Hollywood gatherings, they failed to "connect."[14] In his autobiography, Chaplin, who declined to answer inquiries about their relationship, summarizes his acquaintance with Brecht in three sentences: "At the Hanns Eisler's we used to meet Bertolt Brecht, who looked decidedly vigorous with his cropped head and, as I remember, was always smoking a cigar. Months later I showed him the script of *Monsieur Verdoux*, which he thumbed through. His only comment: 'Oh, you write a script Chinese fashion.' "[15] Berlau remembers being present when Chaplin related to Brecht his first impressions of arriving in New York,[16] and they undoubtedly discussed more of their own works.

Brecht's own comments about a man whose films and style of acting had exerted a profound impact on his dramatic theories and techniques of epic theater are equally terse. One journal entry reports on a dinner party at Ernest Pascal's with Laughton, Groucho Marx, and Chaplin. The radio was broadcasting presidential election returns: "Helli, Chaplin and I were the only ones listening," he notes.[17] A later entry describes a party at Eisler's where Chaplin imitated Paul Muni's recent role of Chopin in the film *A Song to Remember*. Brecht also notes the actor's remarks about his planned "Bluebeard" film (*Monsieur Verdoux*), in which Chaplin would abandon his classic role as the little tramp.[18] Otherwise, nothing of the two is known beyond the few recollections recorded by Hanns Eisler.

Eisler perceived Brecht's attitude toward Chaplin as somewhat analogous to his own toward his teacher Arnold Schönberg—one of attentive, cordial respect.[19] Whenever they spent evenings together, he or Brecht would start Chaplin talking by relating details they remembered from a scene in one of the actor's films—"that was enough for three hours' entertainment," he stated of a man whose performances off-stage were reportedly as good as they were on. He claimed that their Marxist political orientation radicalized Chaplin, who heard them laugh primarily at jokes that had a strong social thrust. In March 1947, for example, Chaplin invited them to a pre-release screening of *Monsieur Verdoux*. In the presence of 200 Hollywood celebrities, including the bankers who had financed the film, Brecht and Eisler laughed in the wrong places, e.g., when bankers jumped out of skyscraper windows during the Depression.[20] Brecht's journal speaks of the "powerful impression" this Chaplin film made on him,[21] and he recommends it later that month to Reyher under an ironic new title that he felt would be more appropriate—*The Provider*.[22] That summer Chaplin also went with Eisler to see Brecht's *Galileo* performed in Hollywood. But his remarks confirm Eisler's evaluation—he did not understand Brecht's theater enough to respond intelligently to it, and he likewise did not understand the exile as a person.

Today, many film directors, among them Joseph Losey and Jean-Luc Godard, admit their debt to Brecht.[23] The ultimate sign of his "arrival" in the film world exists in a prominent film reference work which claims that Brecht's "alienation method influenced films from *Citizen Kane* to *Alfie*."[24] This is an exaggeration, not to say a misunderstanding. During his years in American exile, Brecht was not understood, and his influence on Hollywood was almost non-existent.

III. THE DIFFICULT BRECHT

As someone who knew his way around the theater world, Brecht should have found more open doors to Broadway than to Hollywood. To a limited degree this was true. In spite of it, he never enjoyed significant success in the American theater during his exile. More than anything else, the limiting factor was the obdurate nature of his genius.

In recent years, a number of oral and written recollections of Brecht by those who knew him in America characterize him as a "dictator" or "tyrant." Variations on this leitmotif include the terms "megalomaniac," "egomaniac," "a field marshal," a "militaristic German," "an amusing tyrant," "a learning dictator," "a difficult man," "dictatorial," and "arrogant." One collaborator who characterizes him as a "real Hitler" echoes the observations of several others. This collaborator recalls that "he was a sensitive poet who reacted against the combination of pedantic schoolmasters and ferocious drill sergeants who represented German popular culture when he was growing up. As often happens in such cases, he reflected that culture just the same."

These perceptions need to be weighed with caution, for they tend to reveal more about the relationship between Brecht and the person with whom they originated than about the complexity of Brecht's personality. The actor John Houseman, who saw a similar trait through friendlier eyes, adds an element missing from these one-dimensional characterizations. Houseman met the playwright in 1935, worked with him in 1942, and was instrumental in staging *Galileo* in 1947.

Basing his opinion on his observations of Brecht during *Galileo* rehearsals and on reports of his earlier work in the theater, Houseman states that "he was notorious for being a fiend incarnate *in the theater* (italics mine). . . . He was an absolute devil at rehearsals. . . . It was not personal malice. It was simply tremendous impatience when anything was less than he wanted it to be."[1] Almost without exception, those who perceived Brecht to be dictatorial experienced these traits in connection with his political ideology or his theatrical ideas. It was his uncompromising position in the latter area which ruined many of his chances for success on the American stage.

Reasons for a mode of behavior which antagonized others are not hard to find. Non-recognition and frustration over Brecht's inability to get his plays performed certainly played a role. But the overwhelming causes were an unshakable belief in his own greatness and a principled stubbornness about his views and his works. This combination made him appear doctrinaire. Houseman correctly perceives how he kept intact what some might call "artistic integrity" or "principle." In terms more compatible with Brecht's vocabulary, he states that the play-wright "was very positive and very firm about what he wanted."[2] What many perceived to be the dictatorial side of Brecht was the external manifestation of a self-assured genius who tenaciously demanded that the American theater world conform to his views and do things on his terms, rather than the other way around. The word "compromise" was not in the vocabulary of a dramatist determined to change the existing theatrical world.

Christopher Isherwood relates an anecdote Brecht told him which illustrates the immense self-confidence of a man who seems to have been unacquainted with self-doubt. At one point, a dinner conversation turned to the Soviet Union. Isherwood pointed to the low intellectual level of many bureaucrats there who passed on acceptable literature for the people and asked what Brecht would do if the local Soviet peasant communes did not like his writings. Brecht's self-assured reply was: "I'd talk them into liking it." Isherwood also recalls hearing Brecht boast how his father in Nazi Germany had received a visit from the local police. They pointed out that his son's books in his possession were subversive, and that as a loyal citizen he should burn them. When they returned, the father claimed the bindings had been too beautiful to burn, so he had sent them out of the country. He did not tell the police that they went to the dramatist himself, who was living in Danish exile. While this story may be an example of Brechtian leg-pulling (shortly after Hitler came to power, Brecht wrote a letter to his father renouncing any claim on an estate),[3] Isherwood saw it as a sign of the fundamental independence of mind which ran in the family.

Many theater people who knew Brecht in America felt that he scorned the notion of legitimate differences of opinion. Gorelik, one of his strongest disciples after 1936, did not share his contempt for the "well-made" play, elements of suspense, climax, and motivation, etc., which Gorelik considered indispensable, but which Brecht considered a swindle of the audience's emotions. Strong disagreement did not surface until they saw each other in America, but, when it did, it appeared as though there was no hope of reconciliation. In 1944, for example, Brecht described to Gorelik, to an émigré journalist named John Winge, and to George Auerbach, a producer from Republic pictures, *The Caucasian Chalk Circle* on which he was currently working. Gorelik questioned the missing elements necessary for a well-made play. Brecht cited *Hamlet* in defense of a non-traditional structure, but Auerbach and Gorelik remained skeptical. After they left, Brecht's journal notes that Winge reported how one of them said afterward: "He'll never be successful. He can't evoke emotions, he can't even bring about identification, and he makes a theory out of it. He's crazy, and he's getting worse." Instead of responding to the substance of their disagreement, Brecht in his journal attributes it to their having "sold out" to prevailing Broadway norms. "The prostitution of these artists is complete," he writes.[4]

A few days later, when Gorelik again insisted on what he held to be basic virtues of drama, the "flesh and blood" of empathy, suspense, and climax, a bitter quarrel ensued. An enraged Brecht threatened to throw him out the window (and might have if Eisler had not intervened). Gorelik assumed their friendship was over, but a short time later Brecht phoned and asked when he was coming again to visit. Gorelik returned to be greeted by Brecht with the observation that "You've changed,"[5] whereupon he was given a set of eleven theses entitled "A Little Private Lesson for My Friend Max Gorelik" (GW xv, 467-71). Gorelik was disappointed that there was not more about their disputed topics of suspense and climax, but he had provoked Brecht into making a further, more refined explanation of his dramatic theories. Characteristically, Brecht had overstated them in an attempt to set them apart from those prevailing in American drama, while ignoring Gorelik's arguments altogether.

The two continued their discussion during this visit (Brecht's journal states that "I was talking to a wall when I explained how little one can understand by 'identification' with a character"), and again when Charles Laughton read them three acts of King Lear. His journal notes how it astonishes him to hear Gorelik raise objections to the poorly motivated, illogical structure of Lear, objections similar to the ones he had raised earlier about Chalk Circle. He approvingly cites the American-Chinese actor Chang's description of Gorelik as "an American bookkeeper who wants to see nothing but American bookkeepers on the stage," a reference to Gorelik's insistence on sense and logic in drama. Brecht also observes how Gorelik's commitments to the prevailing norms of the well-made drama shows "that the pillars on which masterpieces are based are rotting away."[6]

At a dinner in Brecht's home early in 1947 Gorelik again brought up their differences. Among other things, he insisted that in the chronicle form employed by some of Brecht's "epic" plays, each scene was structured to include some suspense and climax. Brecht, he claims, responded: "Is *that* what you mean? Of course I believe that. It's so elementary it isn't worth discussing." They dropped the matter and never argued it again.

This single-minded advocacy of his own ideas in the face of those who thought differently often led Brecht to classify anyone not solidly for him as being against him. Inevitably this created the impression of a close-minded, opinionated, not to say ungenerous, individual.

Harold Clurman became a victim of this hastiness to stereotype those who were unreceptive to his ideas. Brecht knew of Clurman's pioneering efforts on the American stage with his Group Theatre in the thirties, but his fixation that Clurman was beholden to another type of theater reinforced his image as someone inclined to classify those with moderately different views as enemies. While he applauded this gifted director's leftist political orientation, he rejected the style of "method acting" the Group Theatre cultivated under Clurman. For him, the Group Theatre was in thrall to the acting style proclaimed by Konstantin Stanislavsky, which meant naturalism, psychologically motivated characters, and overplayed emotionalism—in short, the theater of almost total hypnosis. Clurman insists that Brecht misjudged him, and to some extent Clurman's biography bears this out. Travels to Russia had made him receptive to equally strong influences from the so-called "formalists" Meyerhold, Eisenstein, and Okhlopkov;[7] he had in fact assimilated some of Meyerhold's anti-naturalist methods that seemed to foreshadow Brecht's. Brecht either did not know or ignored these finer points; he knew only that Clurman was a powerful spokesman for a mode of theater which was at odds with his own, and he categorically cast Clurman in the role of the opposition.

Two encounters illustrate Brecht's reactions to this American theater man who might have helped his career immensely. In October 1944 Brecht had seen Spencer Tracy in the film "The Seventh Cross." A journal entry praises Tracy's acting in somewhat vague terms for certain "sublime expressions that are unusual here in America."[8] When Clurman did not share this enthusiasm for the actor, Brecht flatly told him, "You lack sufficient understanding," to which Clurman retorted that his answer was "typical German arrogance."[9]

An even warmer dispute developed over *Galileo*. Clurman knew of Brecht's collaboration with Laughton on it, and he admired the play. In 1946 he had learned through Audrey Wood, Laughton's agent, that Brecht was looking for someone to produce and direct it. Clurman, who wanted to bring it to New York, felt he was that man. But what looked like obstinacy, which again was Brecht's insistence on doing things his own way, interfered with his success. Not knowing the exile's reputation for leaving even urgent letters and telegrams unanswered, Clurman wrote asking permission to direct the play on Broadway. When he received no reply, he turned to Reyher, who transmitted his request and recommended him warmly to the playwright. Clurman, he wrote, possessed first-rate qualifications—intelligence, understanding, long Broadway experience with the Group Theatre and Theatre Guild, credit as the producer of *Johnny Johnson*, enthusiasm, and a sensible view of *Galileo*.[10] Brecht replied to Reyher a few days later in a letter that revealed his own self-confidence, his unwillingness to allow a production except on his own terms, and his view of Clurman as a representative of the type of theater he opposed:

"Now to Clurman. It's a delicate matter. He's a Stanislavsky man. Among the many things he wrote and said to me (on the telephone), the concept of cooperation on the stage is completely lacking. He appears not to have heard at all, for example, that I have staged more than he has himself, and that this is a new style of theater that he cannot grasp by listening within his own breast. In other words, he first would have to understand that half his activity would consist of learning, of carefully assisting at first—and how will he eliminate psychologizing when my theater will not tolerate this approach? . . . If he could grasp these methodological considerations and accept them, he would be a good prospect because he's an intelligent critic and is interested in theoretical matters. Could you determine what he thinks of all this? Does he know that I arrange and carefully control the groupings and movements, etc.? . . . His job would be to help the actors learn this unfamilar acting method. In brief, if he wants to study and produce while studying, he has the opportunity here. We do not need an 'artistic conception,' a 'personality as director,' or a 'creative center.' "[11]

Because Brecht's letter spoke for itself, Reyher let Clurman read it.[12] Apparently it failed to dissuade him. Through other sources Clurman learned that Brecht would accept him as the producer of *Galileo*, but that he wanted Elia Kazan to direct it. Kazan was not enthusiastic, so Clurman resolved to try again. Soon after Brecht came to New York in late September 1946, he and Kazan visited him in the Chelsea Hotel on West Twenty-Third Street (where Reyher lived). He hoped to persuade the dramatist to allow him to produce and direct the play, with Kazan as co-producer. Clurman recalls the ensuing conversation and how Brecht flatly turned him down: "I assured Brecht of my enthusiasm for the play and fortified what was to be my plea by saying that whatever I failed to understand about its staging I would be happy to learn from him.

"Brecht's response was a categorical 'No!'

" 'I'd rather a circus director do it,' he went on. 'You are a Stanislavsky man and cannot possibly understand how to approach my play.'

"At this I roared, 'My name is Clurman!'

"But he roared back, if possible even louder, 'You don't understand, no one understands, even Piscator doesn't understand. . . . You will try to get "atmosphere"; I don't want atmosphere. You will establish a "mood"; I don't want a mood.'

"I began to scream at the top of my voice. . . . 'Tell me what you're after, and I will follow your instructions.' . . . Kazan never uttered a word. I think Brecht and I had a good time. But the Kazan-Clurman combine never acquired the play."[13]

This was not the first time Brecht's insistence on total control over performance or publication of his works would prevent production. In 1942, after seeing Brecht again at Salka Viertel's, Clurman and his wife, Stella Adler, offered to help to get a New York production of *Master Race*, with Max Reinhardt directing. But Brecht was not interested, since he could not be present during production.[14] Clurman's Broadway connections would have helped to insure excellent publicity and reasonably receptive critics for *Galileo*, a play which, as Brecht knew, departed from conventional American theater norms. But he saw this successful theater director as a symbol of the American theater "Establishment" which he felt compelled to attack from the day his exile began. Clurman later admitted that at the time he did not fully understand what Brecht was after with his theater practice. But understanding may not have helped. Because of Clurman's reputation, Brecht's mind was made up.

Clurman shared something found in most of Brecht's associates—a clear recognition of his talent. This awareness remained intact despite Brecht's rejection of his offers to help. Clurman not only became an advocate of Brecht's drama; next to Eric Bentley, he became probably his most eloquent, and certainly the most influential spokesman in America after Brecht left. When he visited the dramatist in Berlin in 1953 and again in 1956, he met a far more generous person than the seemingly arrogant exile he had known in America. These visits to Berlin at a time when Brecht was no longer struggling for acceptance of his own kind of theater helped one of the important drama critics of our age to achieve an awareness he could never have gained in America—that in addition to being a great playwright, Brecht "was one of the world's outstanding directors (I use the word advisedly: there have been precious few in theater history)."[15]

One of the few acquaintances from American exile to see more than outright cussedness in Brecht's behavior was Eric Bentley. From close collaboration on writing projects and in the theater, he perceived some of the complexities of Brecht's makeup which escaped others. Though he first met Brecht in 1942, it was not until working with him on a production of *Mother Courage* in Munich (1950) that he heard Brecht admit that his temper tantrums in the theater were calculated, and that he permitted himself two major ones in the course of a production. Earlier Bentley had noted some of the peculiarities of this enigmatic exile. His essay on *Master Race*, printed with the play in 1944, de-

scribes "a face no longer young" that "bears the imprint of suffering.
. . . He has not sought to maintain here the reputation he made for
himself in Germany. He waits. He broods. He hopes. . . . He leaves
business matters to others. He almost never replies to letters, even to
those that offer contracts and money. . . . He can be quiet, embarrassed, somber, but suddenly the dark eyes flash, he jumps up from the
chair and paces the room waving his cheap cigar. At such times he
talks in tirades. Metaphors and anecdotes of Brechtian concreteness
flow freely from his lips. His laugh is sharp and staccato. His slight
body and gnome head become important." And he attempts to catch
the contradictions in the man with the words: "Brecht, said a friend,
thinks with his heart and feels with his head. He is an engaging blend
of introvert and extrovert, never, like American writers of the tough
school, so tender-minded that the tough exterior is obvious pose."[16]

Bentley also remembers a quickness to damn, a penchant for calling
those who disagreed with him on theatrical matters a "criminal" (ein
Verbrecher) or a "Nazi," and Brecht's tendency to simplify or reduce
people and issues to categories of good and evil. In a sense, Bentley
thinks, this corresponded to a tendency in his dramas to draw many
characters in black or white.

With a certain admiration, Bentley also calls him a "great careerist,"
and notes the singleness of purpose with which he worked and used
people to promote himself. Resistant to anything which did not square
with his own theories, Bentley recalls, Brecht simply insisted on his
own way. And though Bentley saw what looked like petulance when
Brecht started with his "Hitler-type voice" and "sergeant-major
boom," he also recalls Brecht as one of the coolest, most controlled
individuals he ever knew.

Subsequent chapters will show how insistence on his own way in the
theater and on control over his own works led to several missed opportunities for productions. Had Brecht been more willing to let
others stage his works or to translate his writings on terms he did not
dictate, his name probably would have reached a wider audience fast-
er. And had his manner of informing others that he was the "Einstein
of the new stage form" not been attended by such strong self-certainty,
chances are that he might have had more success during his stay in
America. But ultimately he was right in his insistence on his way of
doing things. Brecht felt he had to meet Broadway and the American
theater on his own terms, or not at all. Unfortunately for him, those
terms seldom corresponded to the prevailing climate in the American
theater.

IV. BRECHT AND THE AMERICAN THEATER

11 BUILDING UP TO BROADWAY

In an interview with the German-language newspaper *New Yorker Staats-Zeitung und Herold* given less than a month after he had arrived in New York City, Brecht states that in view of completely different theatrical conditions in America, he sees "no possibility for performance of his plays, which, with all their revolutionary innovations, arose in the soil of a tradition that simply does not exist (here)."[1] He was not speaking from ignorance. Seven frustrating years of trying to place his plays in America between the *Mother* debacle of 1935 and his arrival in New York in 1943 had prepared him for the worst. His repeated failures confirm how alien his dramas were to the established American theater.

Late in 1938 he had sent Reyher manuscripts of *Galileo* and *The Private Life of the Master Race*, two plays he thought to be more conventional than some of his "epic" ones, and asked him to try for New York productions. Reyher translated and adapted *Master Race* for American audiences under the title *The Devil's Sunday*, but Broadway in 1939-1940 was even less eager to show anti-fascist works than Hollywood was, much less a loosely structured series of scenes that hardly qualified as a play. Reyher's efforts to market the play failed,[2] and he never translated *Galileo*, in part because he was unsuccessful with *Master Race*, but in large measure because Brecht, who was dissatisfied with Reyher's adaptation of that work, demanded tight control over a translation or adaptation of *Galileo*.

European émigré friends told Brecht candidly his plays would not fit Broadway. In response to a manuscript of *Galileo* Brecht had asked him to place, Piscator had written in 1939 that he, Eisler, and Kortner had all read it and agreed that it was a great play, but unsuitable for Broadway.[3]

Days after reaching California, Brecht inquired if Piscator would like to perform his works at the Dramatic Workshop which Piscator had established in 1940. He also contacted H. R. Hays, who had tried unsuccessfully the previous spring to get his own translation of *Mother Courage* produced in New York.[4] Brecht wanted Hays and Piscator to consider *The Private Life of the Master Race*, a play that in his opinion would be "enormously contemporary."[5] A few days later he suggested to Piscator an adaptation of Shakespeare's *Troilus and Cressida*. Piscator replied that he wanted to do *The Good Woman of Setzuan*. Brecht then countered with an offer of his most recent play written especially for America—*The Resistible Rise of Arturo Ui*. Having tailored it to the actor Oskar Homolka, Brecht inquired if Piscator wanted to use Homolka for it. Piscator apparently accepted Brecht's suggestion. He not only applauded the choice of Homolka; he also obtained a copy of the play from Elisabeth Hauptmann, Brecht's former collaborator who was living in Greenwich, Connecticut, and circulated Hays's translation in New York theater circles during September and October of 1941. Weighed in American balances by several readers, it was found sadly wanting.

Piscator's knowledge of Hays was based on what he told Brecht was a very good translation of *Mother Courage*. Playing on Hays's admiration for Brecht and his friendship with Eisler, Piscator and Eisler now pressed him into translating *Arturo Ui* without a contract. The prospect of trade-union backing for an immediate production in Piscator's Dramatic Workshop helped to win him over, and, after one week of intensive work, he delivered a translated script to Piscator in September 1941. Piscator showed it to Louis Shaffer, the director of the Labor Stage, who had expressed interest in underwriting a production. Shaffer's terse reply several weeks later read: "I gave the play to several people to read, and the opinion is, including my own, that it is not advisable to produce it."[6] In all likelihood the basis for this judgment was the unsuitability of Brecht's play itself rather than Hays's translation.

Had Brecht responded to the invitation to let Piscator stage *The Good Woman of Setzuan*, his first New York production might have taken place without delay.[7] In addition to wanting to do it in his own Dramatic Workshop, Piscator had spoken to the Theatre Guild about it. Hays, however, reinforced Brecht's desire to have his works produced in New York solely on his own terms by a letter in the fall of 1941 which stated that "I don't think you should agree to it [a Piscator production] unless you are here in New York and make sure you get a decent cast. As I told you once before, I don't have much faith in Piscator's judgment. He has had three bad productions already, which were received very unkindly by the critics. If he makes mistakes with *Caesar Ui* [Hays's rendering of the title], it can do your work a lot of harm and also ruin your chances with the Theatre Guild or any other producer here."[8] This was all Brecht needed to hear. He had already stipulated that the New School pay his expenses for a trip to New York. Now he stipulated that he be allowed to "collaborate" on every aspect of production from the translation to the staging and directing, which Piscator knew meant ultimate control for Brecht. Brecht's insistence on personal control effectively killed this first real chance for a production of one of his plays in New York, and every other chance for the duration of his American exile.

Hays's pejorative report on Piscator's first three productions in the Dramatic Workshop underscored the frequent mutual lack of sym-

pathy between German and American theater in New York City during these years. New York critics had mauled Piscator's productions
rather severely. In effect, they considered what he did too experimental, too alien to established dramatic and acting practices, and too
"European." Piscator in turn had written Brecht in 1941 that American theatrical thinking was "antiquated" and that theaters wanted
only the "good old drama."[9] The large New York German refugee
colony (including Piscator) never overcame its unmitigated contempt
for American theater based in part on valid complaints, in part on ignorance or lack of sophistication, and in part on an unabashed cultural superiority complex.[10] These refugees scorned the commercial
demands of Broadway, where to them all producers were financial
speculators and serious drama was "show business."[11] They saw nothing comparable to European repertory theaters, and they faulted
Broadway theaters for their lack of continuity and their minimal influence on American cultural life. Though better informed than many
European friends, Brecht not only shared most of these views; he
magnified them because his own plays were so out of step with prevailing Broadway norms.

    Brecht did, however, find a few Americans who seemed to recognize
his ability. In addition to Hays, he mentioned in a letter to Piscator of
August 1941 that Archibald MacLeish and John Latouche would be
glad to give the New School references if the School would renew his
teaching appointment. Latouche, whom Brecht had met in New York
in 1935, was known for his texts of *Ballad for Americans* and *Beggar's
Holiday*. Piscator replied that Latouche, who had a good name in New
York theater circles, is "a great devotee of yours" and would gladly
translate *The Good Woman of Setzuan*.[12] A Black American movie
actor who had heard of Brecht also got in touch with him late in 1941
and asked to perform his best-known work somewhere in California.
A journal entry mentions that "the Negro Clarence Muse has done an
adaptation of *The Threepenny Opera* and wants to put on an all-
Negro production."[13] Brecht's letters and journals give no information on personal contact or collaboration with this Hollywood character actor, but his interest in mounting all-Black productions of his
plays in America, which he first expressed to John Houseman in 1935,
suggests that they may have seen each other in Hollywood. Muse himself states unequivocally that "I was a friend of Bertolt Brecht and associated with him in preparing a Black production of *The Threepenny
Opera* in 1942."[14] No further details of their association are known,
but Brecht clearly wanted the production to take place.

    Ironically, Brecht's relationship to a successful refugee who did not
share the common European view on American theater probably cost

him this production. Kurt Weill, composer for *The Threepenny Opera*, had to give approval for all performance rights in America. More than a decade earlier he had broken with Brecht over political differences. Now he objected to a performance in California. For some time, he stated in response to a letter from Brecht, he himself had been trying for a first-rate American production of their work on Broadway, and this might hurt his chances.[15] Though he asked Brecht to send Muse's version for his perusal, he clearly did not want to approve the proposed production.

Brecht then asked a mutual acquaintance, the exiled musician-sociologist-philosopher Theodor Wiesengrund-Adorno, to intercede with Weill. According to Brecht's journal, Weill's reply to Adorno attacked him and praised Broadway.[16] In reaction Brecht could not resist the temptation to call Weill's latest musical, *Lady in the Dark*, an "amusing thriller" and to mock Weill's total acceptance of Broadway thinking. The collapse of this production of *The Threepenny Opera* added to the long list of his abortive enterprises for the American stage.

An exception to Brecht's bad luck that scarcely counted as an incursion into American theater occurred in New York during May and June 1942—a German-language production of several scenes from *The Private Life of the Master Race*. This time Brecht uncharacteristically trusted a refugee director, the poet and film-maker Berthold Viertel, without demanding final control. Viertel, whom Brecht liked, had assembled a number of well-known refugee actors and actresses under the aegis of one of several German-language cultural coteries that thrived in New York at the time. On May 28, 1942, the "Tribune for Free German Literature and Art in America" backed a German-language performance of four scenes from this play, with Viertel directing: "In Search of Justice," "The Chalk Cross," "The Jewish Wife," and "The Informer." A fifth scene listed in the program, "The Box," was not performed that evening.[17]

From reports by Berlau, by Viertel himself, and by New York German-language newspapers, Brecht concluded that the performance must have been good. Consequently he wrote to Viertel that Max Reinhardt, who was visiting New York, had proposed an English-language production in New York if he could raise the money (this was the same production on which Harold Clurman and Stella Adler had offered to help).[18] Brecht then outlined his concept for a performance—white-faced German soldiers wearing helmets were to be shown in what he called "Hitler's typical Blitzkrieg-truck" as it rolled across Europe with Hitler's "New Order." For the first time he also formulated the English title he wanted—*The Private Life of the Master*

Race, which he apparently borrowed either from Noel Coward's popular *Private Lives*, or from Charles Laughton's academy-award winning film *The Private Life of Henry VIII*, which he had seen in Europe.

New York critics ignored this obscure foreign-language play, but a sell-out crowd at the May 28th evening brought a repeat performance on June 14th. All five scenes were played, though "The Jewish Wife," which has emerged since as a small theatrical gem, nearly flopped. On Brecht's instructions, Berlau had invited Reinhardt to see it as an inducement for him to produce it. Eleonore von Mendelsohn, who played "The Jewish Wife," recognized the famous director in the small audience and froze. The results were predictably catastrophic.[19]

During the first year of American exile, Brecht generally neglected his dramatic writing. By mid-1942, however, there were signs that he was recovering from the effects of "culture shock."

On August 12th his journal mentions his family's move to a two-story, white frame, ranch-style house at 1063-26th Street in Santa Monica. This four-bedroom house, considerably larger than those in the surrounding neighborhood, offered something Brecht had sorely missed in his previous residence—a large working room. "We promptly painted it white and put four tables in it," he writes. Something else appealed to him—in contrast to homes thrown up to meet the housing shortage created by Southern California's burgeoning war industries, this one, he noted, was thirty years old. Two days later his journal states: "For the first time today I feel half-way well here," while later in the month he writes that "the house is very nice. In this garden, Lucretius is readable again."[20]

Only a few weeks after Brecht complained that rent on the new home was $60 a month, "$12.50 more than in 25th Street,"[21] the earnings he received from *Hangmen Also Die* put a temporary end to his financial difficulties. Almost overnight the Brechts enjoyed a middle-class standard of living. With this money they arranged to buy their home for $4500 (they paid it off within five years); he purchased a used Buick with a rumble seat, the only car he would own in Southern California; and with the wife of the actor Paul Henreid, Weigel bought old pieces of furniture which would probably be antiques today.[22] Brecht himself, who elaborated on his love of well-crafted objects reflecting age and human use in a poem written at this time (*GW* x, 857), commented on his wife's detective instinct and good taste in finding this furniture. Praising the "splendid old tables with remarkable wood working and copper spittoons that have been remade into lamps," he used these artifacts to report a discovery: "It seems evident that America once *was* a cultured nation. . . ."[23]

Financially secure and settled in more congenial surroundings, Brecht in late October 1942 started to write his first full-length drama since coming to America—*The Visions of Simone Machard*. One of the least known, most un-epic plays he wrote, it returned to a favorite figure of earlier works, Joan of Arc, and transported her legend to France in 1940 as German armies overran France and thousands of refugees fled to the south.

Less than two weeks after finishing work on *Hangmen*, Brecht noted in his journal a conversation with Lion Feuchtwanger about possibilities for plays.[24] They settled on this idea, which Brecht first conceived of in Finland shortly after the fall of France,[25] and for which he wrote an outline in December 1941 while reading the manuscript of Feuchtwanger's *The Devil in France*, an account of his friend's internment in a French refugee camp at the time of the German invasion.

Brecht needed others as a catalyst to his writing, and Feuchtwanger played the role well. One journal entry, which calls their efforts "recreation after the work on the film," says of Feuchtwanger: "He has a sense of construction, knows how to appreciate nuances of language, also has good poetic and dramaturgical ideas, knows a great deal about literature, respects arguments, and is personally agreeable, a good friend."[26] But their collaboration contributed to the vagueness that makes this one of Brecht's least distinguished, critically problematical plays, for their personal congeniality did not include compatible views on drama. When Brecht liked someone as well as he did this successful novelist, who first befriended him in Munich in 1919, he sometimes let his critical faculties lapse and made surprising concessions.

Feuchtwanger, for example, insisted on a non-epic approach, which emphasized psychological motivation and probability of action. Normally Brecht would have avoided these artifacts of "naturalistic" drama. In one case he claims, he did settle a disagreement by autocratic decree;[27] more often, he seems to have given in. Eisler, who knew the dramatist's propensity for endlessly revising whatever he wrote, speculates after hearing Brecht talk of the play that he left it in less satisfactory condition with an eye to later revisions when he would not need to argue with Feuchtwanger.[28]

The two men enjoyed each other's company. Feuchtwanger characterized their work as "the happiest in a life rich in fortunate experiences."[29] He patiently endured what others considered to be Brecht's irrational arguments and dictatorial pronouncements, not to say his digressions, his zig-zag logic, and the discourses on epic theory, for he knew this was the way Brecht sought to clarify an idea. At one point, according to Eisler, Brecht's exposition of his epic principle moved the decorous Dr. Feuchtwanger to say, "You know Brecht, you can kiss my --- with your theories. I can't hear any more of it. Let's go on."[30] And in a relationship Eisler characterized as "contentious cooperation," Brecht in turn humored Feuchtwanger's rejection of political and economic motivations and accepted suggestions otherwise associated with the "naturalistic" drama he loathed.

Between November 1942 and February 1943 they completed a play in four acts with four visions or "dream sequences." Originally called *The Voices*, they later retitled it *Jeanne d'Arc of Vichy*. Invoking the Joan of Arc legend, the drama turns on the betrayal of a deformed adolescent servant girl named Odette[31] by her fellow Frenchmen who find collaboration with the German invaders economically more convenient than resistance. Simone, as they later call her, is employed in a hostelry in central France. While reading a book on the life of Joan of Arc given to her by her employer, M. Soupeau, the owner of the hostelry, a gas station, and a trucking firm, she is overcome with intense patriotism. At this point, her seventeen-year-old brother André, the only one from their town to volunteer for the French army, appears in the first of four dreams or visions and calls her to save France. Others appear in these dreams as characters from the Joan of Arc legend—the mayor as King Charles, M. Soupeau as the high constable, his mother as the queen mother Isabel, a wealthy vineyard owner as the Duke of Burgundy, a German captain as the English army commander, etc.

In the panic of France's collapse, Simone tries to help starving refugees by smuggling them food hoarded in the hostelry. Everyone else in the city collaborates with the Germans, but her brother has told her in a vision to scorch the earth and to deprive the invaders of supplies. When Simone hears Mme. Soupeau arranging to sell their cache of hoarded gasoline to the German panzer captain, she sets fire to it. In a vision, she is condemned to death just as St. Joan was; in reality, her countrymen commit her to a mental institution. While she is being taken away, the town gymnasium, where fleeing refugees are housed, bursts into flames. The refugees, it seems, have learned something about resistance from Simone.

In many regards this play is highly un-Brechtian. Visions, especially visions with angels, do not lend themselves to easy dramatization in the twentieth century. Further, no epic elements or devices interrupt the straightforward plot. And, while Simone slightly resembles those Brechtian female personifications of innocence whose innate impulse to help others often leads to their own destruction, she appears too fanatical to be a naive child. Eisler observed that she becomes a victim of false patriotism. This type of zeal by a teenage girl on a national scale looks more like mental imbalance than the warmth of pure instinct.

Brecht himself struggled unsuccessfully with his concept of this figure. In 1941 he had abandoned the project because he felt unable to conceptualize things clearly. After two weeks of work with Feuchtwanger in 1942, he confessed that he felt obliged to make Simone "a child" because otherwise he could not justify her rabid patriotism.[32] In early December his journal states the plot is two-thirds completed, but he cannot write a single sentence spoken by Simone—she is still too vague as a character.[33] A few days later he mentions his difficulty in writing one scene "without having a (clear) idea of the main role. Originally I saw a clumsy, mentally retarded, inhibited person; then it appeared more practical to take a child. Now I have only the naked functions and no counterbalance from an individual perspective."[34]

Feuchtwanger reports that they agreed on everything but the age of the heroine.[35] In the course of writing, she grew steadily older for him and increasingly younger for Brecht, who at one point in his journal describes her as thirteen years old.[36] Shortly before his death, Brecht even insisted that an eleven-year-old child must play the role.[37] In the final version the heroine mirrors Brecht's own uncertainty about her age and motivation. Rather than losing control of her, as some say he did with Galileo, Mother Courage, and other characters who outgrew their author's intentions, Brecht never developed Simone Machard clearly enough for this danger to exist. Usually he tailored roles in his plays to specific actors and actresses he knew. Here he was writing without a known model in mind. This, and his isolation from the stage, where he could experiment with unfinished roles like this, no doubt contributed to the blurred outline of this character.

A difference in artistic outlook also kept *Simone* from crystallizing. Brecht believed his main justification as a writer at the time was as an anti-fascist. Yet, with the exception of certain scenes from *The Private Life of the Master Race*, the farther he removed his exile plays from a direct confrontation with facism, the more effective they seemed to be dramatically. *The Good Woman of Setzuan* had employed the parable form. *Galileo, Mother Courage*, and *Lucullus* took the mask of distant history for their statements, while *Puntila and His Servant Matti* sought the comic mode for a tale of feudal conditions in modern Finland. Feuchtwanger reports that Brecht wanted to emphasize parable elements in *Simone*. Had he succeeded, the play might have gained the necessary distance from topical history to make Simone's visions and patriotism credible, for *Simone* has a parabolic core which places it in the tradition of certain types of morality plays. Unambiguous and direct, its personification of the vices and virtues of Everyman in France, and its call for a return to the principles that could save a people from the Evil One (personified by the German invader), are not unlike Jesuit counter-Reformation drama.

But Brecht did not succeed, and the result was a work for which he showed no particular fondness. In contrast to every other drama he wrote in American exile, he never tried to have it produced there; he never asked anyone to translate it for him into English; and he made no effort to include it in a tentative volume of his collected works that he hoped to publish in New York during 1946-1947.

Whatever its weaknesses as a drama, *Simone* brought other benefits. Brecht had not undertaken a new drama for nearly two years. Film-writing and the depression of the first year in America had left him especially out of practice for dramatic writing. With *Simone*, he began to return to form for two major dramas he would write in the next two years. More important, the play gave him the momentum he needed as he set out to conquer the New York theater world.

Late in November 1942 Brecht wrote asking Berlau to solicit an invitation from Piscator's Dramatic Workshop for him to visit New York (as an enemy alien he needed an invitation in order to secure travel permission from the Los Angeles United States attorney's office). Piscator sent a cordial invitation saying the Studio Theatre of his Dramatic Workshop was considering a performance of his *Setzuan* in January 1943, and they needed Brecht there to discuss changes and to help with the translation. He added: "The Dramatic Workshop is also preparing a lecture for you. . . . The title is 'What Is the Theatre Doing To Help Win the War.' "[38] Using Piscator's letter, but with no intention of staging *Setzuan*, Brecht set out for what he called the only street on the continent with theaters, "a branch of the world narcotics trade run by actors."[39] On February 8, 1943, he boarded the Southern Pacific railroad for the first of five cross-country trips to New York City and Broadway.

After a four-day trip which took Brecht through the Chicago stock-yards he had described in his play *St. Joan of the Stockyards*, he arrived in New York City on February 12th. Then, and on each subsequent visit, he stayed with Ruth Berlau in her fourth-floor walk-up apartment at 124 E. 57th St.

Renewed contacts with refugee friends and acquaintances had two purposes—to indulge Brecht's interests in politics and the theater, and to make connections that would help him on his exploratory venture into the New York theater world. With Karl August Wittfogel and Heinz Langerhans, this playwright who openly acknowledged his debt to Chinese theater went to see performances of the Cantonese Players in New York's Chinatown.[1] Brecht also hunted up Elisabeth Hauptmann, his former collaborator from the Berlin years, and asked her to work. His journal notes that, while she was willing, her current living situation with an émigré named Horst Bärensprung left her very little time. Another former collaborator, the brilliant caricaturist George Grosz, whose savage cartoons kept him in repeated legal trouble in Germany of the Weimar Republic, now had an exhibit of his drawings that Brecht visited. Undoubtedly the playwright tried to engage him in some kind of collaboration, but Grosz was far from well-off and could not help Brecht without remuneration.

Soon after he arrived, the émigré publisher Wieland Herzfelde, who in 1941 had established the "Tribune for Free German Literature and Art in America," persuaded Brecht that this group should sponsor a "Brecht evening." Characteristically Brecht, after approving it, selected the program and rehearsed the performers himself. On March 6, 1943 in the Studio Theater of the New School for Social Research, the film stars Peter Lorre and Elisabeth Bergner joined obscure refugees in a German-language program devoted to Brecht's works. Herzfelde spoke on Brecht's writings; Marjory Hess sang Eisler/Brecht songs from *Roundheads and Peak Heads*; four speakers read two scenes from *The Private Life of the Master Race*—"The Sermon on the Mount" and "Plebiscite"; Lorre read a number of Brecht's poems, including "Difficulties of Governing," "On the Designation 'Emigrants' "; "Legend of the Origin of the Book Taoteking on Lao-tse's Journey into Emigration," and the famous "To Posterity"; the composer Paul Dessau, accompanying himself on the piano, sang his own composition of "Ballad of the Black Straw Hats" from *St. Joan of the Stockyards*; and Bergner concluded by reading the poem "Children's Crusade 1939."[2]

Brecht enjoyed the applause that brought him back on stage with Lorre and Bergner several times after the final number. At the cocktail party given by Piscator following the performance, he not only authorized a repeat performance on April 24th; according to later advertisements, he also read from his own unpublished poems at this second performance. In addition to numbers from the first program, the performance included Brecht songs sung by Hertha Glaz and Grete Wittels and slide projections accompanied by Herbert Berghof's reading Brecht's epigrams written for his *Primer of War*.

Brecht often tried to recruit composers to set his works to music. In New York, one offered to work with him. By his own account, Paul Dessau had asked the chief promoter of the Brecht evening on March 6th, George Alexan, to introduce him to the dramatist. Their meeting, which consisted of Dessau's playing one of his compositions for Brecht, launched a collaboration that lasted until the playwright's death. Brecht then offered his services in rehearsing the numbers planned for the program so that Dessau and the singer, Julia Charol, would understand what he meant by "epic singing." At this time, the plan meant rehearsing every word and sentence with them. When Charol withdrew the day before the performance, Brecht asked Dessau to sing alone, which he then did.[3]

Henry Marx, a refugee journalist in the audience on March 6th who admired Brecht's pre-1933 work, was able to interview him and publish the results in the *New Yorker Staats-Zeitung und Herold* on March 7th. This revealing documentation of Brecht's views on playwriting and on American theater in 1943 is singular in its contents. Marx states that the exile wants to develop his ideas of epic theater in films. Reviewing American drama, Brecht optimistically discerns progress in putting on epic-like plays and mentions specifically Thornton Wilder's *Our Town* and *The Skin of Our Teeth* as examples that consciously or unconsciously follow his own principles—they make the viewer an observer, they demand a stance, they instruct, they appeal to reason, and they make each scene independent of the next. Privately Brecht had told Berlau that Wilder stole all this from him; publicly he was more charitable.[4] Answering Marx's comment that William Saroyan followed a similar trend, Brecht disqualified himself—he had not yet seen the recent film of *The Human Comedy*.

At a time when he was reading difficult English texts, Brecht further states that he probably never will write in English—only refugee scholars and journalists have that possibility, he says. He is aware of the difficulty of his position—novels, he states, can be translated into English, but lyric poetry is almost excluded (he specifically notes that many English poets never had good translations in German), and national and cultural considerations make it impossible for many dramas

to be transferred. Acknowledging that he sees no prospects for performances in America, where his plays are still unknown, he surprises
Marx by emphasizing that, in contrast to most refugees, his writing is
strongly oriented toward postwar Germany. He feels that those elements of German theater that were progressive before 1933 will pick
up where they had left off. He says he knows his ideas remained alive
among actors and directors in Berlin and other cities long after Hitler
came to power, and that they will come to life again. Marx is surprised
at the optimism of this realist and concludes with a statement describing the strong personal charisma that emanates from this ascetic
cigar-smoker who scarcely raises his voice to make a point.

If Brecht meant what he said about his chances on the American
stage, his actions belied it, for he set about immediately to write a
work for Broadway. After meeting H. R. Hays in person, Brecht persuaded him to collaborate on the adaptation of an Elizabethan drama
for Elisabeth Bergner, who was currently playing on the New York
stage. That play was John Webster's *The Duchess of Malfi*, which
Bergner wanted to use as a vehicle, and which Bergner's husband, the
producer Paul Czinner, engaged Brecht and Hays to adapt for a production he would back.

After having received Hays's unsolicited *Lucullus* translation in Finland early in 1941, Brecht had responded with a complimentary, albeit
inaccurate, statement: "Many thanks for the fine *Lucullus* translation
and for the magazines. I'm happy about it. This is the first thing that
has been done for my works in the USA."[5] Brecht's reply fired Hays's
enthusiasm. In addition to publishing his translations of *Mother
Courage* and *The Trial of Lucullus* in New Directions, Hays rendered
The Resistible Rise of Arturo Ui into English without compensation.
Charitably he attributed the dramatist's failure to sign a Dramatists
Guild contract for its use to Brecht's "correspondence neurosis,"
which he and other collaborators in America came to know well. An
apology from Brecht in January 1942 smoothed things over.[6] Excusing his long silence, Brecht wrote: "The relocation, together with the
loss of my closest collaborator and the unusual calm and isolation
from world affairs into which I was thrust, have paralyzed me to such
a degree that in six months I have written only a few letters to Eisler,
Miss Hauptmann, and Piscator, as well as two or three poems. I could
not even bring myself to thank those who helped me come over, and it
weighs heavily on me." From this point on, Hays, who seemed to have
adopted Brecht's affairs-in-translation as his own, bombarded James
Laughlin, the publisher of New Directions, with his ideas for promoting Brecht's works.

Hays's and Brecht's collaboration on *Malfi* in the spring of 1943 was apparently a happy one at the outset. After meeting with Czinner and Ann Elmo, a New York agent Brecht had retained a short time before, they signed a Dramatists Guild contract and received a small advance (probably $250-350 each). During the next month, they worked intermittently in Berlau's apartment. Hays remembers how they felt it necessary to eliminate what Brecht considered to be the series of anticlimactic deaths at the end of *Malfi* and to tighten up the sprawling play. In their adaptation, Brecht wanted to highlight two new aspects—the duke's incestuous desire for his sister the duchess as a motivation for his actions, and the cardinal's economic motivation to destroy her and gain her properties.

Hays recalls that "I did all the writing, in the style of Webster, though Brecht and I discussed the scenes to be eliminated or added, the content of scenes, and he sometimes contributed images. Brecht was very much at home in English literature and could speak English quite well (when he wasn't facing a senatorial [sic] committee)."[7] According to a subsequent letter to Hays, Brecht contributed a considerable amount of German material to the script, which he asked Hays to translate and insert.[8] Before Brecht returned to California late in May, they had finished two extensive preliminary versions and a final one[9] which Hays copyrighted, using the title *The Duchess of Malfy. An Adaptation for The Modern Stage.*[10] In June 1943 he received a letter from Brecht reporting that Eisler liked it and would compose the music for it.[11]

When Brecht returned to New York in November 1943, he enlisted Hays in a new round of work on the adaptation which Hays, who was unaware that Brecht never considered anything finished, thought they had completed the previous spring. Unbeknownst to Hays, Brecht had also invited the poet W. H. Auden to join him in yet another adaptation of *Malfi*.[12] Brecht, who was candid about his desire to use prominent names to help to get his works produced, felt Auden's carried more prestige that Hays's. It was also his *modus operandi* to use translations by one collaborator as a means of flattering or challenging another into outdoing the first. Hence Brecht mentions in a letter to Auden an adaptation of *Malfi* "that I wrote you about last summer and which now exists in an English version. . . . I told Bergner that no one could do it as well as you."[13]

In December 1943 Czinner met with Brecht and Hays in the office of Hays's agent, where Czinner broke the news of the change Brecht had instigated by announcement of plans to bring in a "British poet" to "liven up the script." Hays exploded, and, though he was legally bound by a Dramatists Guild collaboration contract that he and Brecht had signed the previous summer,[14] he withdrew. Auden in the meantime had agreed to collaborate, and the version of *Malfi* which reached Broadway in 1946 was an indirect outgrowth of their collaboration in subsequent months, one of which virtually nothing is known.

By most standards, Hays had reason to sever all relations with Brecht. Yet, like so many collaborators who admired or were fascinated by Brecht, he continued to promote that writer's works and reputation until the end of Brecht's American exile. Even after learning that a translation of *Master Race* which he had undertaken at Brecht's request in late 1943 without fee or contract was being duplicated simultaneously by Eric Bentley (also at Brecht's request), Hays came back for more.

Hays experienced something which outside observers might consider exploitation or, at the very least, thoughtlessness on Brecht's part. Joseph Losey, who collaborated with Brecht in 1947, remembers that he "used people like mad, as most artists do."[15] Yet Losey, Hays, and virtually all other collaborators had no sense of being "used" by Brecht. Theirs was rather a sense of unironic privilege for stimulating collaboration with a man they greatly admired. Perhaps the reason was that Brecht treated them as equals when his own genius was so obvious. Hays remembers how they showed each other their poems as they worked on *Malfi*. Brecht gave him "The Mask of Evil," which Hays translated on the spot. Brecht in turn honored Hays by translating into German his poem "Supply and Demand,"[16] which, based on a statement from a magazine or newspaper that the sales of pulp literature declined on days when bombings were reported in the press, condemned the war being fought. Brecht's own free rendering of the poem into German improved on a poem that clearly appealed to him.

Whatever the reasons, Hays was only one of many collaborators who patiently endured a brand of single-minded behavior devoted to the proposition that the name and works of Bertolt Brecht were to be heard and recognized in America.

On May 10, 1943, Brecht's name had appeared on a German-language anti-fascist program billed as an "International Commemoration of the 10th Anniversary of the Burning of the Books, May 10, 1933." No record verifies that Brecht attended, but through this or some other activity he became acquainted in New York with the chairman of the event, a man who figured strongly in the next drama he wrote in America. That was the poet Alfred Kreymborg, and the drama was *Schweyk in the Second World War*.

Since Brecht's work in Piscator's theater in 1927-1928 helping to adapt Jaroslav Hašek's monumental novel *The Good Soldier Schweik* for a memorable stage production, he and Piscator had exchanged ideas about updating this comic prototype of passive resistance, either as a film or as a drama.[17] The idea for Brecht's own version finally crystallized in New York during the spring of 1943. At least three distinct impulses converged to cause it—a visit with Weill, whom he continued to cultivate in hopes of using his name for a production; conversations with Piscator; and a comedy act by two Czech comedians Brecht had seen as part of a mammoth anti-fascist war rally entitled "We Fight Back," which he attended on April 3rd. The final impulse, probably the first in chronological order and the most important, was a skit by Voskovec and Werich, two refugee actors from Prague's "Liberated Theater." They called their comedy number "Schweyk's Spirit Lives On," which was the quintessential idea Brecht later dramatized. One can only speculate how he reacted to it (a review called it "a delightful, humorous portrayal of the courageous Czech spirit of sabotage"),[18] but it was probably as a result of this performance that Brecht began talking with Piscator and Weill about plans to do a play on *Schweyk*.

Brecht's journal remarks that Ernst Josef Aufricht, who in 1928 financed the original *The Threepenny Opera* production in Berlin and now hoped this team could produce a similar spectacular success, brought them together in New York for the first time in nearly a decade. Brecht's cryptic journal entry notes that "Weill wants to produce the *Setzuan* play, and we plan a *Schweyk*."[19] Aufricht and Weill wanted to use the *Schweyk* material for a musical comedy, a concept that eventually caused irreconcilable differences with Brecht.[20]

Sometime in mid-May, Weill invited Brecht to spend a week with him at his country home in New City on the Hudson (Rockland County, New York), where they worked to adapt or write two plays for the American stage—*The Good Woman of Setzuan*, and *Schweyk*. Brecht's terse journal notation summarizing his stay in New City says only "I turned out a *Setzuan* version for here [i.e., for America]." A remark in a letter to Berlau of June 24th that he does not consider this "Americanized version of *Setzuan*" to be his own further implies that Brecht planned to allow Weill to adapt it in whatever form seemed best for the American stage. But apparently they had no plans to push for an immediate production.

Schweyk, however, appealed to Weill as a promising vehicle for Broadway. He and Brecht not only began work on it during the week in New City; they talked of mounting a production in the fall. Lotte Lenya, Kurt Weill's wife, recalls that Weill composed some songs during their working sessions, and a typescript containing a complete story outline in prose with the holograph notation "May 1943/New City (N.Y.)" confirms that Brecht wrote it there.[21] Weill's name and connections to Broadway seemed to augur well for a production of *Schweyk*. But Brecht's stay in New City produced a sour note more characteristic of his relationship to Broadway. Weill held a party at which the guests included Maxwell Anderson, who had collaborated with him on *Knickerbocker Holiday* in 1938, and Elmer Rice. Had Brecht sought to cultivate these two prominent American dramatists, it might have opened some doors on Broadway. But ideological differences often incited his nastiest behavior, and after he and Anderson locked horns over politics, Anderson was later heard to call him a "big Communist," while Brecht concluded that one of America's leading dramatists was hopelessly reactionary.[22]

Piscator also had a role in energizing Brecht to write *Schweyk*. They saw each other in New York several times between February and May, and the old topic came up. Piscator reported on positive discussions with the Theatre Guild about reviving and updating his successful 1928 adaptation, and Brecht asked to collaborate on it.[23] They signed no contract, but Piscator went ahead with preparations on the understanding that Brecht would help him adapt it as he had done in Berlin. In Brecht's mind, the Theatre Guild's interest in the material offered real promise for a Broadway production, or rather productions, for he had two separate productions in mind—the one a revival (in English) of Piscator's 1928 version based on the novel, the other a separate and new Brecht-Weill comedy which he planned to write alone, but which he also hoped to have Piscator direct.[24] After discussing possible actors, Piscator, who was ignorant of plans for a separate Brecht-Weill production, introduced Brecht to Zero Mostel and perhaps to Sam Jaffe, both of whom they thought might play the title role.[25] Before Brecht left, Piscator also asked him to write what he referred to as a "musical play for a pro-Jewish cause."[26] But *Schweyk* was uppermost in Brecht's mind. For the first time since 1935, he thought he had a solid prospect for a Broadway production.

Arriving in Santa Monica on May 26, 1943, Brecht launched into writing *Schweyk* with the characteristic vigor that produced first drafts of plays in a matter of weeks. Three days after his return, he related the plot line to Peter Lorre and tried to recruit him for the main role. The two had been friends since Lorre played Galy Gay in a 1931 Berlin production of *A Man's a Man* that Brecht had directed. Like many of Brecht's European friends, Lorre had achieved the type of commercial success in Hollywood that the playwright hoped to use to his own advantage. The dramatist notes two interesting reactions from this film star, whose acceptance would have made it easier to get a production. Lorre liked the story ("he really went for it")[27], but he ob-

jected to the scene where the dognapper Schweyk killed a dog and
brought the meat to be made into goulash for his gluttonous but starving friend Baloun. Brecht's journal analyzes Lorre's responses with
ironic sympathy: "Of course he has to live down a hair-raising past as
actor in horror movies, and everyone who saw him coming with the
small package would imagine the flayed cadaver, the 'skeleton in
wrapping paper,' as he says."[28] By the last week in June, Brecht states
that Schweyk is "generally finished."[29] "Finished" for Brecht meant a
complete first draft in German that would be subject to weeks and
months of revision before he was satisfied.

About this time Weill came to Los Angeles to help to cast one of his
own musicals. In his journal, Brecht records their discussion of a fall
production and praises Weill's good "dramaturgical judgment."[30] But
differences surfaced over terms of collaboration which eventually
aborted the project. Brecht sensed that Weill wanted to make it a musical comedy. Emphatically he stated that he did not want to be Weill's
librettist: "I need a half-way 'influential' position, not just one where I
fetch beer. Besides, there are political questions involved in this play,
and I need to have a voice in it."[31]

Sometime in July Brecht finished revising the first draft sufficiently
to send copies to Weill and Aufricht via Berlau. He also emended and
returned the Schweyk contract that Weill's attorneys, the law firm
Maurice J. and Herbert A. Speiser, had drawn up, saying he would
sign it any time in the present form. Finally, he urged Berlau to engage
Kreymborg immediately to translate the play: "I'd like to try Kreymborg," he wrote on July 2nd, "he is, after all, a poet . . . if not Kreymborg, then Reyher, but let's not spend a year looking."[32] He overrode
Berlau's objections that Kreymborg was not a dramatist, that he could
not capture the Schweykian humor, and that his name was not prominent enough. Brecht urgently wanted a production in the fall. With a
$100 advance from Lorre, who had shown interest in playing the lead,
Brecht, Berlau, and Aufricht persuaded Kreymborg to begin a translation in August.

The playwright sensed that, because of other interests, Weill was
somewhat reluctant to work on Schweyk. Sometime in August, Weill,
who by now had seen the final German script, wrote Brecht that
American authors with whom he has spoken told him Schweyk was
very "un-American" for a Broadway production. Among others, Weill
was referring to his friend (and Brecht's "enemy") Maxwell Anderson,
who reinforced his own instinct for what would succeed on Broadway.
In addition, Weill noted, Aufricht no longer believed in the play. Later
he returned to his backers the $85,000 he had raised for the produc-

tion.[33] Since Weill had not categorically withdrawn, Brecht pushed ahead with plans of his own by instructing Berlau to secure exclusive rights to the play from the Czech government in exile.

In four weeks, Kreymborg turned out an English version of *Schweyk* that, as Brecht wrote to Berlau, had "more errors than a dog has fleas . . . nevertheless, I have the impression that he has struck the right tone and proved that it can be done."[34] He also wrote Kreymborg two undated letters in September, saying how happy he was with the translation, how much he had enjoyed reading it, and how well it had captured the tone he wanted. But a second look changed his mind. Brecht's English was good enough from this point on that almost every translation of his works he saw failed to pass muster. His son Stefan, Hans Viertel, and Berlau fired his dissatisfaction with this translation. In addition, friends to whom Lorre showed it were "disappointed" when they learned he was seriously considering the role. They claimed it would be impossible to get a production of it,[35] apparently because they could not conceive of Lorre, who in the minds of many film people had become typecast in horror films as a mild-mannered but sinister embodiment of brutality, in a truly comic role.[36] Brecht pressed Gorelik into retranslating a few pages under his own supervision,[37] and, despite his dissatisfaction with Kreymborg's translation, he wrote conciliatory letters asking him to redo it. Brecht returned a text with suggested changes to Kreymborg, who retranslated it with Berlau's assistance. This second translation left Brecht reasonably satisfied, in part because the quality was improved, but more because he had had the final say on it.

The previous spring in New York, Brecht had learned that Piscator planned to have Kreymborg adapt his 1928 script into an English *Schweyk* for a Theatre Guild production, and a note in the *New York Times* on June 22, 1943, announced that they were preparing it for Broadway. Unperturbed, Brecht had lured Kreymborg away by sending him a copy of his own *Schweyk*. On August 8th, Kreymborg wrote Piscator that Brecht and Aufricht had asked him to translate Brecht's *Schweyk*, and that he found it "not only first rate, but decidedly better than anything I could have done in an original form. . . . I have therefore decided to go ahead with Brecht, Weill, and Aufricht."[38] Piscator, who knew nothing of Kreymborg's involvement before this, drafted an angry letter to Brecht, calling his actions a "swinish Brechtian trick" (*Brecht'sche Schweinerei*) and threatened to knock him off his "amoral Olympus."[39] But he waited and sent a more restrained letter in English with copies to Aufricht, Kreymborg, and Weill, stating that he owned the rights to *Schweyk* in the United States, that he was deeply disappointed to read an announcement of the Brecht/Weill production, and that he was giving notice of his rights and of his intention to take legal action if he were obliged to protect them.[40]

Brecht, no stranger to disputes over literary property rights, did as he had always done—disregarded them and went ahead. Realizing that Weill was not eager to collaborate, he asked Eisler to compose songs for a production. Further, he had Berlau contact Zero Mostel, again pre-empting Piscator, who had Mostel in mind for his production. As he states in a letter to her, "an American, especially a comedian, would be more secure in questions of what is intelligible and what is not. Also more productive. Less fearful."[41] He admits that if Mostel were interested, it would be easier to maneuver Lorre into either playing the part or backing a production himself. Again Brecht's touchiness in promoting this work, which may smack of manipulation and disregard for others, sprang directly from the conviction that it was essential that his genius be recognized, regardless of the cost.

In November Brecht again asked Weill to reconsider his negative view of *Schweyk*, but the composer would not budge. Just as Brecht refused to be his librettist, Weill had no desire to write incidental music to a Brechtian play. In a letter of December 5th, Weill insisted on a "musical play with more musical possibilities than the present version." Aware of the play's splendid humor, he also demanded that a leading American author (he named Ben Hecht) be commissioned to rework the text in an attempt to catch the humor of the original. Finally, in this and later correspondence Weill raised the problem of unsettled legal rights to the play and mentioned how possible backers, among them Moss Hart, had lost interest because of Broadway's unwritten agreement not to touch property on which someone else had a claim.[42]

Though this effectively ended hopes for a Broadway production, Brecht refused to give up. In February 1944 he sent a copy of *Schweyk* to Reyher, asking if the play interested him, and if he would translate one scene. With typical conviction about his own works, he stated that "the figure is classical and absolutely must be given over to the stage. Weill wanted to write the music, but now doubts that a good adaptation and translation are possible. If I could show him a single scene, perhaps he'd take the bait again, and with his name it would be easier to get a production."[43] But Reyher declined on the grounds that he thought this play was "unfinished."

Shortly after meeting the actor Charles Laughton in Los Angeles in the spring of 1944, Brecht gave him a copy of *Schweyk*, with the idea of recruiting him for the lead and of using Laughton's name to get a production. Laughton read it the same night. His response the next day was, in Brecht's words, "really enthusiastic."[44] A few days later,

Laughton read aloud two acts of Kreymborg's *Schweyk* translation to Brecht, Eisler, and Hans Winge. In his report to Berlau, Brecht stated with unusual enthusiasm that in Laughton's opinion, "98% of the play came through, and the translation is much better than we thought. We laughed raucously, he understood *all* the jokes."[45] But Laughton never played the role, and one of Brecht's delightful comedies, which was written in America and performed for the first time in Europe long after the war, did not receive its first major American performance until 1977.[46]

The play *Schweyk in the Second World War* is symptomatic of Brecht's troubled relationship to Broadway and of the difficulties of German exile writers in America generally. Knowing that wartime audiences did not like to be burdened with tragedies, Brecht consciously chose the comedy form with an eye on Broadway. A recapitulation of *Schweyk*'s relatively simple plot, however, illustrates how alien the material was to the American mentality of the time.

In a "Prologue in the Higher Regions," Hitler, Himmler, and Göring (all as outsize figures) and Goebbels (an undersized figure) discuss the Führer's question: "What does the 'little man' think of me?" Schweyk, the dognapper who steals mongrels and purebreds and forges pedigrees without compunction, represents that "little man," and through him the answer is obvious. Set in Nazi-occupied Prague, the story follows this unheroic protagonist through a series of episodes that pit him against the Occupation authorities. Much of the action occurs in the tavern "The Goblet," whose patriotic owner, the attractive widow Kopecka, is being courted by the butcher's son, Prochaszka. The suffering of the Czech people is concentrated in this microcosm. For example, the audience sees drunken Nazi officers abusing tavern guests; the agonies of Schweyk's gluttonous friend Baloun, who is about to join the Germany army to get a square meal; and a Gestapo raid.

After Schweyk is picked up, his diabolical imbecilities (he claims he has been officially declared an idiot) secure his release from S.S. headquarters. They also help to sabotage German efforts when he is put to forced labor. But he is arrested again with a package of black-market meat (the flesh of a dog he had originally stolen for the S.S. commandant) as he brings it to "The Goblet" to save his friend Baloun from his own stomach. He is pressed into the German army, where he is last seen lost in a blinding snowstorm fifty kilometers from Stalingrad. As he wanders, he meets a starving dog and, shortly thereafter, Hitler, who is also lost in the Russian snow and cannot return to Germany. But Schweyk and his dog go on, symbols of the "little man's" capacity to survive their rulers' excesses.

Aside from the play's loose and episodic structure, the character of Schweyk himself was foreign to anything American audiences knew. The comic obverse of the mythical idiot-saint like Parsifal or Prince Myshkin, as one critic has called him,[47] his half-intentional, half-innocent idiocies did not even make him an anti-hero—just a petty one. As an embodiment of folk wisdom dealing with elemental survival, his feigned or real imbecilities, his slovenliness, incompetence, and carelessness, not to mention his rank opportunism, were traits that Americans did not easily associate with known comic or tragic figures. Brecht spoke of him as the "opportunist of the few opportunities left to him,"[48] but Schweyk also looked very much like an imbecilic saboteur in the ways he resisted Nazi power.

Whether or not he wanted to, Brecht had written for the American stage a part that was peculiarly European. Like virtually all the plays he wrote in exile, he tailored the leads to specific European actors he had in mind—in this case Peter Lorre as Schweyk, and Lotte Lenya as the widow Kopecka (this was one of Weill's demands to which Brecht readily agreed, since Lenya had performed well in his productions in Berlin before Hitler). Neither Lorre nor Lenya, for all their ability, came close to qualifying as the typical Broadway leading man or lady, and the roles showed it.

The language, especially the humor, had such a distinctly central European ring that it is questionable if any native American could have rendered it better than Kreymborg. There was a 25-cent paperback abridgment of *Schweyk* circulating in America at the time in a translation by Paul Selver which Brecht, in separate letters to Weill and Berlau, had alternately praised and called "lousy."[49] But it had expurgated the most ribald humor and watered down the rest. Brecht himself wrote to Weill and Berlau that the vulgarity would have to be deleted, and that in its present form *Schweyk* could be played only at their old theater on Schiffbauerdamm in Berlin.[50] Realizing that humor is one of the last aspects of national culture that can be transported into an alien country, Brecht and Weill felt that it, like the poetry of the text, had been lost in Kreymborg's translation. Had it been conveyed, American producers and dramatists who read the text might have overlooked the other departures from American theater norms; as it was, there was little to view favorably.

The conflict of writing on American soil for European audiences did not afflict Brecht acutely, since he acknowledged that he was not writing the play for America alone, but primarily for Europe.[51] Yet his environment left its mark on the play.

Brecht's work on *Hangmen* the previous year, and the information obtained from the Czech government-in-exile, gave him useful background material on Prague under Nazi rule that he might not have had—location of Gestapo headquarters, food rationing, the use of forced labor, as well as place and street names and bits of local color. And the visual impact of a color cartoon by Arthur Szyk that he saw in *Look* magazine on September 8, 1942 (originally it appeared on the cover of *Collier's* on January 17, 1942) inspired the entire frame of the drama[52]—Hitler and his satraps in the "higher regions" discussing the little people of Europe. The cartoon, entitled "madness," shows out-sized figures of Hitler, Himmler, and Göring, and a midget-sized Goebbels surveying a large globe decorated with swastika flags to designate Nazi holdings. From it, Brecht conceived of tableau-like scenes using the same characters in similar dimensions for the prologue and interludes of *Schweyk*.

Being in exile, whether in America or elsewhere, affected virtually everything Brecht wrote, and *Schweyk* was no exception. Of two dominant themes that permeated his works in exile, viz., flight from oppressors, and displacement from one's homeland, *Schweyk* takes up the second by showing how the protagonist is pressed into the German army and transported to Russia. And, like most characters in his exile dramas, Schweyk is also a non-heroic individual with no power over the course of events, who struggles only to survive.

In a display of special fondness for *Schweyk*, Brecht's journal says: "Compared with the *Schweyk* I wrote for Piscator around '27 (a pure montage based on the novel), the present Second World War version is a lot sharper, corresponding to the shift from the Hapsburgs' well-ensconced tyranny to the invasion of the Nazis."[53] Critics claim that Schweyk's cunning in matters of survival in many ways resembles Brecht himself, which may be another reason he liked it.[54] In a limited sense this may have been true, for the same journal entry speaks of *Schweyk* as a counterpoise to the sly but villainous Mother Courage, i.e., he was swept up in war, but he resisted instead of battening on it. In most ways, however, the ideologically indifferent, half-anarchistic Schweyk is the opposite of this deeply committed, tough-minded Marxist exile, whose goal in America was far more than simple survival.

If one can accept at face value a poem Brecht wrote shortly after reaching New York City, his first impression of Broadway was one of disappointment. Entitled "The Son's Report" (*GW* x, 876), it describes how, upon reaching the city his father had characterized as the "most beautiful," the son sets out from the train station in search of this famous street. Finally asking someone where that street is, he is told he is standing on it.

Just as the sight of Broadway failed to overwhelm him, so Brecht failed to overwhelm Broadway, though it was not for lack of trying. A single journal entry summarizing his stay in New York between November 1943 and March 1944 concentrates almost exclusively on one topic: staging his plays. It mentions four that have a chance: *Galileo*, *Setzuan*, *The Caucasian Chalk Circle*, and *The Duchess of Malfi*. Three others which he attempted to promote — *Schweyk*, *Master Race*, and *The Threepenny Opera*—remained unmentioned.

Renewed negotiations with Weill over *Schweyk* resulted in Weill's attorney returning Brecht's manuscript with a firm "no." But Weill was still interested in *Setzuan*. For reasons not totally clear, Brecht was reluctant to sign a collaboration contract that Weill had given him in 1943. The agreement Brecht finally signed in January 1944, which was not a Dramatists Guild contract but one drawn up by Weill's attorney,[1] gave Weill sole rights to select an author and writer of lyrics to adapt Brecht's play as a "musical drama" or a "dramatico-musical composition." Both agreed that Lotte Lenya was to play the lead, and Weill received exclusive rights to contract for productions in the following thirty months. Somewhere in the proceedings Brecht must have become unpleasant, perhaps in order to extract an advance on royalties from Weill's attorney. In a letter written from Los Angeles after receiving word of the contract, Weill states he does not want to give up the play because of whatever this "unfortunate incident" is.[2] Further, he says that he has written his attorney suggesting that Brecht receive "financial assistance." But Weill never arranged a production, and his exclusive hold on the play killed it for Broadway.

In the same letter, Weill tried to encourage Brecht by noting that recently he had tried unsuccessfully to sell their opera *Mahagonny* to the movie industry. His attempt to promote their earlier hits might have motivated Brecht at this time to arrange for an American translation of another play—*The Threepenny Opera*. Probably through Weill, Brecht met Elinor Rice and asked her to translate it. A contract authorizing her to do the *The Threepenny Opera* was signed by Brecht on February 19, 1944. From a letter to Berlau in April 1944 saying that an English version of *The Threepenny Opera* had just arrived from Weill,[3] it appears she finished at least one draft. A letter that summer also instructs Berlau to have *The Caucasian Chalk Circle* rendered in English.[4] Perhaps it could be done, Brecht said, "by the woman who translated *The Threepenny Opera*." Today nothing remains of this translation, and Brecht's most popular work never came close to a New York production until years after he left the country.

Late in 1943, H. R. Hays had written James Laughlin, saying that "there is some talk of doing *Mother Courage* in an experimental production at Columbia University."[5] Hays was seeing Brecht at the time and might have told him of these plans, but Brecht's silence suggests that, if he knew of it, he showed little interest. With prestigious Broadway names, it was another matter. His journal praises a "very good" and "progressive" production he saw of Thornton Wilder's *Our Town* directed by Jed Harris. Brecht met Harris, one of the leading directors in America, some time that winter, and Harris expressed interest in staging *Galileo*.[6] Their discussions, and later correspondence, made Brecht genuinely hopeful. More than a month after leaving New York, he wrote Berlau that "The *Galileo* matter looks as if it will work. Not bad, right?"[7] But nothing more was heard from Harris, and the matter lapsed as quickly as it had come up.

Brecht tried to become acquainted with the New York theater world. His journal mentions seeing three productions while there—Wilder's *Our Town*; an unnamed musical that his journal rates "good"; and Shakespeare's *Othello*, with Paul Robeson playing a role that won the 1943 Donaldson Award for the "Best Performance of the Year" on Broadway. Brecht took issue with first-nighters who earlier had given Robeson a twenty-minute standing ovation and ten curtain calls to make the play one of the highlights of the 1943 Broadway season.[8] He cryptically notes that he saw "Robeson as Othello, poor, in a terrible performance."[9] In all probability it was Robeson's gentle, almost glamorized, portrayal of the main character that evoked this negative assessment. One can assume from available evidence that Brecht also saw other musicals and serious dramas, not to mention performances in New York's Chinese theater.

At a time of especially undistinguished theatrical offerings (no Pulitzer Prizes for drama were awarded in 1942 or 1944),[10] the predominance of musicals and comedies on Broadway reflected the escapist nostalgia of a war-weary country. By temperament Brecht rejected Broadway's heavy emphasis on "entertainment," since, in his view, theater should also change its audiences so they would change the world. He bridled at a concept of "show business" that accented the second word so strongly. But, according to his own statements, he held a begrudging respect for several kinds of American theatrical entertainment—burlesque/vaudeville shows, and Broadway musicals.

Writing about his play *The Caucasian Chalk Circle* in Berlin a decade later, Brecht states that "its structure is conditioned in part by a revulsion against the commercialized dramaturgy of Broadway. At the same time, it incorporates certain elements of the older American theater which excelled in burlesque and shows."[11] A note about the New York production of *The Duchess of Malfi* written after Brecht returned to Europe also criticizes Bergner and the actors in the play for their failure to understand how to employ "the technique of the American musical, which, while basically dishonest and offering only empty entertainment . . . nevertheless has developed certain primitive 'epic' devices."[12] The same note adds that the play should have taken the Broadway musical as a model, because the dancing and scenery and, to a lesser extent, the action in these shows employ elements of "epic theater," a phrase that was lavish praise for him.

Except for an anecdote about a remark that Brecht intended as cultural commentary, there is no evidence that he saw burlesque/ vaudeville shows, though he doubtless did. In the words of Florence Homolka, he claimed that "only in America could one see whole families—mother and father and children—yelling in joyous unity at a stripper in a burlesque house 'take it off,' "[13] Features of burlesque/ vaudeville shows and musicals were in fact compatible with Brecht's views on theater. They made no attempt to imitate the conventional Broadway theater of illusion, with its missing fourth wall; they made no pretenses at being tight, "well-made" plays, but moved freely from song to dance to text and back again; they often involved the audience instead of hypnotizing it; and the style of those on stage was appealing because, in Brecht's view, they were "performing" and not trying to act. In 1946 he approached Elsa Lanchester about playing the title role in *Mother Courage* because she billed herself as a "performer," not an actress, and he liked this vaudeville-style playing when he saw her at the Turnabout Theater in Los Angeles.[14] Lanchester recalls that, after reading it, she declined because she did not understand it.

By all odds the most important result to come from this 1943-1944 visit to New York was *The Caucasian Chalk Circle*, which Brecht wrote after Luise Rainer helped him to secure a contract to have it produced on Broadway.

This Austrian-born actress, who came to Hollywood during the thirties and won two successive Academy Awards in 1937 and 1938 for her roles in the films *The Great Ziegfeld* and *The Good Earth*, was at the height of her fame. Brecht met her sometime after he arrived in America and, according to her account, saw her several times at her home in the Brentwood section of Los Angeles. Though she did not, as she claims, sign affidavits for him and for his family to come to the United States, she knew him by reputation.[15] By her account it was during a walk on the beach with Brecht (probably in the late summer or fall of 1943) that he asked what stage role she would prefer to play. She replied that Joan of Arc appealed to her, but that she disliked Brecht's St. Joan play. She then mentioned Klabund's *Chalk Circle*. Brecht, who had taken up the theme several times since Klabund's successful 1925 play, now agreed to write it as a vehicle that Rainer could use for a Broadway production. She in turn got in touch with a New York backer named Jules J. Leventhal, who had wanted to sponsor her in a suitable Broadway play, and arranged for him to commission Brecht to write it.

Some time after arriving in New York that winter, Brecht met with Leventhal. Rainer, meanwhile, had gone on tour of the Mediterranean with a USO camp show. Writing to Brecht, she told him that "your doings are very much on my mind. . . . I hope from [sic] all my heart that the play is developing satisfactorily. It is the thing I want to do right after we return," which, she went on, would be the middle of February.[16] On consecutive days, February 4th and 5th, 1944, Brecht, Leventhal, and a partner, Robert Reud, signed two agreements wherein Brecht contracted to write a play for them to be called *The Caucasian Chalk Circle*. In conjunction with the second agreement, all three signed a standard Dramatic Production Contract of the Dramatists Guild of the Authors League of America, and Leventhal agreed to pay Brecht $800 in advance royalty payments, allegedly because Rainer had told him Brecht needed the money.[17]

What happened next is unclear. Rainer indicates that, after she returned from the Mediterranean with malaria and jaundice in February 1944, Leventhal complained that Brecht had not delivered a single page of script. She states that she met him in New York, and he let her see a single page of blank verse (which probably contained a sketchy plot synopsis). When she visited him somewhat later, perhaps in New York, but probably in California, she remarked on the inadequacy of this single page. She recalls that Brecht sat her down and rehearsed her in his method of acting by having her read it aloud. She resented it, Brecht became indignant, and a quarrel ensued with a dialogue that Rainer remembers went:

> *Brecht* (roaring): Do you know who I am?
> *Rainer* (calmly): Yes. You are Bertolt Brecht. And do you
>   know who I am?
> *Brecht*: Yes. You are nothing. Nothing, I say!

When the exiled dramatist told the famous film star that any actress would jump at the chance to play this role, Rainer decided on the spot to withdraw, since she did not consider herself to be just any actress.[18]

This clash might have involved more than professional pride. Rainer, who was unsympathetic to what she called the "harem" she always found when she visited Brecht, notes that "he had a reputation as a lady's man, (but) he seemed to sense that I was apathetic to him." Brecht evidently made no attempt to treat her as the star she was, and she in turn judged him to be "cruel, selfish, vain—an awful man." For her, the play ended before it was written. She planned to drop the part, and, without her, Leventhal would not back a production.

Brecht, who had a fiendish reputation for run-ins with actors and actresses, normally went back to work with them the next day as though nothing had happened. Apparently he failed to realize how deeply he had hurt Rainer, or he assumed it did not matter. The security of a firm contract which said nothing about her playing the lead seemed to have given him the confidence to ignore or defy her. After he completed the first draft of the play in June 1944 and mailed it to her, he wrote Berlau saying that he had seen Rainer only once. According to him, she complained so loudly about the play's not being finished months ago that it disgusted him. He added that he would not mind if she rejected it.[19] Unbeknownst to him, she had already resolved to do just that. But Brecht's first Broadway contract not only kept alive hopes of a production long after Rainer withdrew; it decisively influenced the kind of play he wrote for an American theater audience.

In the winter of 1944, not long after he signed the contract with Leventhal, Brecht began working on preliminary sketches of the play with Berlau. Notwithstanding Rainer's claims that she saw only a single page in New York, he had developed a full plot outline and done work on a number of scenes before he left for Santa Monica in March. Berlau, whom he acknowledges on the play's title-page as his sole collaborator, recalls working sessions and discussions in her New York apartment while Brecht was writing it. Further, less than a week after arriving back in Santa Monica, Brecht wrote that "I'm still deep in the play,"[20] which suggests he had begun writing before his return.

As Brecht revised old scenes or completed new ones, he mailed them to Berlau with instructions to incorporate them into a master text, or to rewrite parts. On first drafts, Brecht normally worked rapidly. *Chalk Circle* was an exception only because it took him nine or ten weeks rather than the normal three or four. As usual, he neglected his journal somewhat during the writing. Two entries do reveal the reasons for this relatively long gestation period. In one he laments being caught between the demands of "art" (a word he seldom used) and a "contract." He also complains of another problem that plagued him throughout exile—the lack of a stage. To write effectively for the theater, he needed a stage to help to visualize what he wanted to write.[21]

A second note claims it cost him two weeks to establish the social forces that motivated his character Azdak.[22] Because Brecht believed that human behavior arose from social rather than psychological or physiological forces, he needed to resolve this as much as the writer of a well-made play would need to establish plausible psychological motivation. Rainer insists that the character Azdak, which Brecht wrote with Oskar Homolka in mind, was not in the original story that she knew, and that Brecht added it.[23] This may or may not have been so, but, by the time Brecht completed the play in June, it was an integral part of the drama.

While working in Santa Monica, Brecht phoned Christopher Isherwood and asked him to translate the play. The British writer declined. A short time later Brecht visited Isherwood in the Vedanta Center in Hollywood where he was living. Again Isherwood resisted Brecht's arm-twisting, at the same time noting in his diary how ruthless Brecht was where his own projects were concerned.[24] Soon afterwards the dramatist asked a mutual friend (probably Berthold Viertel) to work on Isherwood again. The result was a more unpleasant reaction by Brecht than a normal refusal would have brought. The lead sentence of a journal entry reads: "When a bad person becomes good too quickly, often he only drives the badness underground." Isherwood, he notes, refused to translate *Chalk Circle* because of other translation commitments, a book of his own, film stories, his work with Huxley, etc. "At the conclusion he offered me $100 or $200 if I needed money for a production of the work. A lot, because I know he doesn't have anything. My crime was to bribe a friend of his to work on him again."[25] Apparently Brecht interpreted Isherwood's gesture as one of malicious kindness rising out of a desire to be rid of him.

Unable to work without collaborators, Brecht sought help from Eisler, Hans Viertel, and Winge, his Austrian Socialist friend. With their suggestions and criticisms, he completed the fifth act on June 5, 1944, and sent one copy to Rainer in New York, with a telegram to Leventhal promising another the following week. Rainer, who in her own mind had already abandoned the project, does not recall receiving or looking at the manuscript. But Brecht's work in the coming weeks and months suggested that if he knew of her withdrawal, he paid no attention and went ahead with production plans.

Ten days after completing that version, a journal notation begins: "Suddenly I'm no longer satisfied with Grusha in *The Caucasian Chalk Circle*. She needs to be ingenuous, to look like Brueghel's Dulle

Griet, a beast of burden."[26] Almost as though he sensed that Rainer had abandoned the part, Brecht broke loose from her model and set about revising it after the image of Brueghel's painting.

Like Shakespeare, Molière, and other dramatists, Brecht from his earliest days had written his major plays with specific actors and actresses in mind. He had created Polly in *The Threepenny Opera* and Joan Dark in *St. Joan of the Stockyards* for Carola Neher; he had tailored the roles of Señora Carrar in the play of that name, Peleagea Vlassova in *Mother*, and the dumb Kattrin in *Mother Courage* especially to his wife Helene Weigel; Elisabeth Bergner claims he told her that he patterned the role of Shen-te in *The Good Woman of Setzuan* to her style in the hope she would play it; in America he contracted to write the role of Mrs. Kopecka in *Schweyk* for Lotte Lenya, and he conceived the title figure in the play for Peter Lorre.

How much Rainer, or for that matter any of the actors or actresses for whom he wrote, influenced the roles Brecht created for them is a matter of speculation. But once he liberated himself from the notion that Rainer would play a character he originally called Katja, it underwent a transformation that improved it in Brecht's eyes and simultaneously made it less suitable for Broadway. According to one journal entry, three weeks of hard work went into re-casting the figure.[27] The original Katja, Brecht noted, was much "nicer" than the later Grusha, and, as he concluded, more effective for American audiences. Now he made her less saccharine and more obtuse, a character "that bore the stamp of the retarded development of her class."[28] Elsewhere Brecht had used the English word "sucker" to describe how he wanted her to appear,[29] a concept scarcely designed to make her attractive as the leading lady in a Broadway production.

In their Dramatists Guild contract, Leventhal had agreed to pay for having both a direct English translation and an adaptation made of *Chalk Circle*. Characteristically, Brecht wanted nothing left to chance in the matter of a translation. In New York, Berlau received instructions to try for a rough translation by Elinor Rice.[30] Leventhal, he said, must pay for it. After reporting that Isherwood had refused to make an English adaptation, Brecht suggested that Berlau arrange for W. H. Auden to make an adaptation suitable for the American stage. In the meantime, he looked for another solution.

Between May and July 1944 Brecht engaged Homolka and Hans Viertel to help him on what he envisaged to be a "model translation" of part of *Chalk Circle*. In theory, it was to be a guide for all his future translators working in English. As their source, they took the beginning of the fifth act, where soldiers mistreat Azdak. Viertel was to be the expert on English; the actor Homolka, who had appeared in important roles on Broadway, was to help to provide the theatrical dimension by speaking and acting out various lines; the playwright would direct the translation while interpreting and explaining his wishes. Viertel recalls that they worked several weeks on this "model translation" from the *Chalk Circle* before giving up in despair. Their failure only hardened Brecht's resolve to exercise control over future translations of his works.

Meanwhile, Leventhal and Robert Reud solved the translation problem to their satisfaction by engaging James and Tania Stern to do a rough translation and W. H. Auden, Brecht's choice for the task, to make an American adaptation from it. After the rough translation was finished, Leventhal and Reud mailed a contract to Santa Monica, designating Auden as Brecht's "collaborator" on the drama.[31] In it, Auden agreed to revise and adapt the play for "presentation in a first-class theater" and to deliver his adaptation to Leventhal and Reud by February 1, 1945. Nor was Brecht ignorant of Stern's role in preparing the text. He wrote Auden how pleased he was with their collaboration and how eagerly he looked forward to seeing Auden's adaptation. He also inquired (in English) if Auden had done the lyrics first and added: "Perhaps Mr. Stern told you I made some changes. I send them to you."[32] The playwright, it seems, had already begun correcting Stern's translation.

When Brecht wrote this letter, the Sterns were working with Auden in a house they shared on Fire Island, New York, to prepare an American adaptation of *Chalk Circle*. After they finished, Auden delivered it to Leventhal. On the strength of Auden's name Brecht, who had not seen the translation, authorized the Samuel French agency to negotiate a contract for him. On March 12, 1945, he and Auden signed a Dramatic Production Contract giving Leventhal and Reud exclusive rights to perform *The Caucasian Chalk Circle* in Auden's English adaptation. It called for a production no later than one year from that date. Leventhal and Reud agreed to pay Samuel French, who represented Brecht, and Curtis Brown, Auden's agent, advances on royalties of $100 a month for the first six months, and $150 a month for the six following months.

When he saw the adaptation sometime after signing the contract, Brecht made the inevitable discovery—the translation did not satisfy him. He found too much Stern and too little Auden in it. Writing to Berlau, he claimed Auden had reworked only the lyrics, which he liked, but that all the prose sections were still Stern's, and they needed improvement.[33] He sent a list of changes and assigned Berlau to have Berthold Viertel tactfully raise them with Stern without showing him the list—he did not want to offend. Further, he urged her to solicit other judgments of the adaptation, and, if possible, to have Auden rework the entire prose text before he left for England. But Auden would have nothing more to do with it. Stern, however, completely revised it once again and incorporated the suggested changes, and Brecht later seemed satisfied enough to consider this version for an American edition of his works scheduled to be published in 1947.

The Caucasian Chalk Circle never reached Broadway during Brecht's American years, and its non-performance remains one of the puzzles of his exile. Leventhal evidently wanted a performance even after Rainer withdrew, or he would not have paid for the translation and the adaptation or entered into a new contract. Brecht, who was still hoping for a production, asked Berlau in a letter in the spring of 1945 what she thought of using Elsa Lanchester as Grusha.[34] In another letter to her in the summer of 1946, he asked why Samuel French had not been forwarding royalty payments from Leventhal.[35] At this point a production was still on Brecht's mind. But his letters and journal say nothing further about the drama, and hopes for a Broadway performance of one of Brecht's finest plays died inexplicably without a sound of alarm or regret.

Perhaps it was just as well. By most standards, *Chalk Circle* was hopelessly at odds with the American theater of the day. The settings, the suggestions for dance, and the use of music have some affinity to vaudeville and musicals, forms Brecht admired. The ballad-singing narrator also faintly resembles characters in musicals who interrupt the action to relate in song what otherwise might be acted out. But in other ways Brecht expresses his admitted "revulsion" against Broadway drama by instinctively going against the grain. His attempt, for example, to make Grusha less sympathetic, thereby reducing the possibility of identification, or his constantly intruding narrator make it alien to anything American theatergoers knew. Gorelik recalls that the abrupt interruption of the Grusha story to introduce the seemingly unrelated Azdak story was an affront to the whole method of play construction at that time.[36] Other examples could be added. Yet on at least one count Brecht apparently tried to conform. He well knew that the open or durative endings characteristic of many of his own plays after 1928 violated what he mordantly called "the eternal laws of drama" in America, which, he claimed, were "the very contemporary laws enacted by L. B. Mayer and the Theatre Guild."[37] Normally he rejected the mindless happy endings that dominated contemporary Broadway fare. With *Chalk Circle*, however, he seems to have made a concession in this direction. Its optimistic conclusion was to some extent inherent in his material; Brecht's reworking, however, made it unique among his mature dramas, both for its unmitigated victory of the audience's and the writer's favorite, and for its distinct resolution of dramatic events. Here Brecht undoubtedly geared his writing to Broadway.

In spite of this concession to a bourgeois audience, Brecht again proved himself incapable of writing the kind of drama that Broadway norms of the day required. In addition to entertaining his audiences, he had a didactic strain in his makeup that compelled him to propagandize or to instruct them. The prologue and epilogue, for example, which he considered organic to the play, illustrate the heavy-handed didacticism that would have limited the play's appeal in America. Hans Viertel argued with Brecht from the outset that they were aesthetically and dramatically poor. The language, Viertel insisted, was on a different level from the rest of the play. Further, he maintained that the passages were too blatantly political, not to say journalistic, and that the portrayal of life in Russia had nothing to do with the realities of Soviet life. Brecht may have thought he could capitalize on the wave of Soviet-American friendship being promoted during World War II by the American government and by segments of the press and film industry. But American audiences no doubt would have found his utopian portrayal of two Soviet collective farms settling their dispute over a valley as implausible as a director in Russia did years later when he deleted it as being unplayable for Soviet audiences.[38]

In an interesting footnote to *Chalk Circle*, life came close to imitating art. Near the time Brecht contracted to write the play in New York during the winter of 1944, Berlau became pregnant. She claimed that Brecht learned of it before leaving, and that they discussed the forthcoming birth in her New York apartment and again while working together on *Chalk Circle* that summer in Santa Monica (she had arrived sometime late in June after Peter Lorre paid her way). By her account, the anticipated birth sparked conversations on themes that Brecht was treating in the play, such as the conflict inherent in the claims on a child of blood versus a child of love, or the question of whether one can love someone else's child as much as one's own.

On September 3, 1944, two days after Brecht's last entry reporting that his work on the play was essentially complete, his journal carries a cryptic note: "Ruth is operated on in 'Cedars of Lebanon.'" Berlau, who was probably in her seventh month of pregnancy, submitted to a hysterectomy for removal of a tumor. The male child that was taken lived only a short time, long enough to receive the name "Michel" after the child in the play. In later years, Berlau inverted the chronology by telling visitors that Brecht named the child in the play after hers, whereas the child in the play was "born" some months earlier.

In spite of his complaint about the pressures of writing *Chalk Circle* under contract for the commercial stage, Brecht seems to have created precisely what he wanted here with greater surety than he exhibited with any play he wrote in America. Some of his earlier dramas exist in up to a dozen versions that reflect his endless rethinking and rewriting. *Chalk Circle* escaped this patchwork fate. At the end it still looked much like the whole cloth from which it had first been cut. There are fewer variants than with many of his less elaborately developed plays, and the two separate versions he did make, though filled with minor changes, do not deviate from each other significantly except in one or two points. In contrast to other plays that Brecht compulsively rewrote every few years, he left this one essentially untouched for a decade.

Of the plays he wrote in America, *The Caucasian Chalk Circle* is generally considered the best, and one that ranks among his most popular today. Before it achieved that recognition, however, Brecht had to return to Europe and establish an international reputation. New York theatergoers meanwhile would wait more than two decades to see the one play performed which he had written especially for Broadway.

14 OFF-BROADWAY, 1945:
THE PRIVATE LIFE OF THE MASTER RACE

In May 1945 Brecht travelled with Hanns Eisler to New York to
supervise the English-language production of a play he considered
conventional enough for American audiences to understand. Nearly
four years after he arrived in the United States, *The Private Life of the
Master Race*, his first play to reach New York, flopped badly. And it
flopped because Brecht insisted on doing it on his own terms under
circumstances which did not allow it.

Master Race holds a unique place among the works Brecht tried to
stage in America. Because he supervised its translation, it was the first
work in English to receive his unqualified imprimatur. Between mid-
December 1943 and mid-January 1944 Eric Bentley, on Christmas
break from Black Mountain College, translated it under the dramatist's personal tutelage at Elisabeth Hauptmann's Riverside Drive
apartment. Brecht had brought in this former collaborator to assist
Bentley on political and linguistic nuances that he wanted stressed.
The dramatist and Hauptmann carefully controlled the selection of
scenes that were to comprise the English stage version, at the same
time instructing Bentley on Brecht's dramatic theories.

Master Race illustrates how Brecht tried to exercise control over
every detail of a drama as it moved from translation to production in
the theater. In preparation for publication, he instructed Bentley to
write an introduction based on his own explication of his work. "I
shall explain his dramatic theories—more or less as he has explained
them to me," Bentley notes in a letter to Laughlin.[1] "Brecht complains
that everything written about him is wrong. I shall try to do something
right." Clearly, Brecht intended to approve every detail before it
reached print.

Though Laughlin was eager to publish *Master Race* in New Directions, Brecht, who tended to look endlessly and negotiate with as
many competing groups as possible before committing himself, was in
no hurry to agree. After several months, the persuasive powers of
Bentley, Laughlin, and Berthold Viertel, who was to direct any stage
version, prevailed, and Brecht signed a contract in May 1944, calling
for himself and Bentley to share equally in the 10 percent royalties on
all printed copies sold.[2] In September that year, after unsuccessful
negotiations with George Grosz to produce some drawings to accompany the text, New Directions published seventeen scenes from
Brecht's original play under the title *The Private Life of the Master
Race*.

Generally favorable reviews gave it the first broad exposure of any of Brecht's works since he arrived in America. Writing in the influential *Saturday Review of Literature*, Brecht's friend F. C. Weiskopf told readers that this "powerful author-experimentator is still almost unknown in this country" and that this "latest and most mature work" supplied a long-neglected want for those interested in literature "which is modern yet not modernistic at any price, experimental yet not *l'art pour l'artistic*, documentary yet full of poetic imagination."[3] Marjorie Farber, in *The New York Times* (December 17, 1944), began by stating that this "original documentary play offers plausible hints for the resuscitation of Broadway." Calling the play "nearly perfect in form," her review showed understanding of Brecht's intentions with a work that was "intensely dramatic, even though addressed to the critical intelligence—rather than the emotions—of the average audience."

Praising the play in *Tomorrow* magazine (February 1945, No. 5) H. R. Hays called Brecht "one of the few geniuses of our time. Perhaps if his work is published and discussed it will eventually find its way to Broadway. When it does, it should have a stimulating influence on the drama, for Brecht is a playwright of tomorrow."

These and other reviews in newspapers, magazines, and theater journals aroused the interest of at least one potential backer. Early in 1945 Ernest Roberts, a young producer who knew Piscator, wrote Bentley about using his translation for an off-Broadway production by his experimental group, "The Theatre of All Nations." Roberts planned to have Piscator direct, who in turn was to furnish actors from his Dramatic Workshop for the cast. Eager to have Brecht produced in New York, Bentley urged the playwright to give approval. After repeated letters to Brecht drew no response, Bentley forced the issue and authorized a production on his own.

When Berlau learned what Bentley had done, she alerted Brecht. His suspicion of commercialized Broadway theater was exceeded only by his reluctance to have experimental or off-Broadway troupes perform his works, for Brecht shared Berlau's fears that he might get a mediocre, low-budget performance from inexperienced actors.

A letter to Berlau in late March 1945 expresses his reservations: "I also believe that we cannot afford a slipshod, cheap performance of *Master Race*. Bentley only has the right to deny use of his translation. I am the only one who grants performance rights." A postscript adds "In regard to *Master Race*—be diplomatic. I require a very good cast, etc.; can only approve an excellent production."

At the same time that he was not answering Bentley's letters, Brecht wired an option to perform the play to the émigré Wolfgang Roth, a scene designer in New York. When Bentley learned this, he wrote Laughlin at New Directions that, as usual, "Our friend Brecht has created a god-awful mess. Just after I had given Roberts an option, he wired another to somebody else in New York. I am now hectically trying to straighten things out. What a man!"[4] About the same time, Bentley sent an undated letter to Berthold Viertel, complaining of difficulties in dealing with Brecht, which concludes: "He has neither good manners nor elementary decency. He lives out his own theory that it is impossible to behave well in this society. . . . He is like Dubedat in *The Doctor's Dilemma*—a scoundrel but an artist." Correspondence throughout April speaks of ongoing negotiations. Finally Bentley notified Laughlin that "there will definitely be a New York production of the Brecht beginning June 12."[5] Brecht had agreed to a production by Roberts and by the "Theatre of All Nations," with Piscator as director.

In a letter to Berlau written around mid-April, Brecht enclosed a note that spelled out his conditions for a production: "You should give the enclosed letter to Piscator. Tell him that of course I would not take a 'position,' but would accept an invitation in order to get a visa [i.e., travel permission] and transportation for a little inspection trip." The enclosed letter to Piscator, which is lost, touched on at least two points—Brecht's desire for a first-rate performance with the best available actors, and the provision that he himself oversee certain aspects of the production. Piscator apparently acceded in principle to both requests.

From the moment he arrived in New York, Brecht found his worst fears substantiated. The production, scheduled to open in three weeks, was billed as an experimental undertaking. Roberts had announced to the press that it had "no aspirations to invade Broadway";[6] and, if one believes Brecht's journal entry summarizing the trip, it was mounted on a $6,000 budget. He took an immediate disliking to the young producer Roberts, whom he called "a criminal—not a big criminal, but a petty criminal."[7] When Brecht learned that the group called itself the "Theatre of All Nations," he caustically replied "It's too many."[8] He soon grasped the irony of the name, for ten of twenty-four cast members were German or Austrian émigrés. Three of them—Theo Goetz, Elisabeth Neumann, and Ludwig Roth—had played in Viertel's 1942 German-language production of scenes from *Master Race* and knew something of Brecht. But it did not bode well for an American production that nearly half the actors did not speak English as their native tongue, and that several of the younger American actors had had little or no experience in major theater productions. Brecht was furious. He referred to these players, several of whom came from Piscator's New

School Dramatic Workshop, as "schoolchildren," and he felt betrayed by this second-rate cast.

Had he been given absolute control to stage the play on his own terms, Brecht might have accepted the actors and the low-budget production. But Piscator, a director he recognized as one of the great theatrical innovators of the century, had different dramaturgical ideas, and the two clashed immediately. Their differences centered on, but were not limited to, the frame scenes of the play.

In discussions with Max Reinhardt in 1942, Brecht had conceived of a frame for the play that showed twelve German soldiers riding in a half-track somewhere on the eastern front. The various scenes of daily life under the Nazi dictatorship that followed were, in effect, flashbacks depicting the circumstances that turned these ordinary men into Hitler's henchmen. Piscator's extensive notes and sketches show that Brecht planned to have the action begin informally with actors and stagehands preparing the stage. After a pianist had played "The Star-Spangled Banner," a giant S.S. man with a revolver would force the pianist to switch to the Horst-Wessel song. Following a discussion of democracy and dictatorship and comments about epic theater and Brecht himself, the frame scene would begin.[9]

Brecht's general dissatisfaction boiled over at this tampering with his play, and he quarreled with Piscator. Elisabeth Neumann recalls that their heated discussions virtually stopped all rehearsals. On May 29th, six days after the dramatist arrived in New York, Piscator withdrew as director and suggested that Brecht himself take over. His letter of that date (in English) to "Dear Mr. Brecht" told of approaching the whole production hesitantly and, wherever possible, waiting for Brecht's arrival before making final decisions—especially in the casting—simply to get the performance together. But "you came late, not to say too late, and your presence didn't help to achieve results and to simplify the complications. . . . Unfortunately I can't permit myself the luxury of an artistic failure. On the other hand, when I direct, I need the time for myself without your co-directing—and when you direct you need the time without me. For my part, I have conceived a different physical performance from yours, and I have greater difficulties in following your version—enough so that I suggest that you take over the directing, and I withdraw."[10]

In spite of this breach, Brecht did not want to alienate Piscator. In a letter of June 2nd, he wrote Piscator saying: "The disgusting thing is that for lack of time there is no opportunity really to think through theoretical disputes. Of course it is possible that the present balladesque frame alone is not sufficient. You simply must believe me—even if I were convinced that a radical artistic change were necessary (and the one you suggested was radical and would have to be examined carefully and then portrayed in a totally new way), I would not be in a position to make it. I am grateful that you are continuing to help by letting us use your people and other things to make our work easier. That way the impression cannot arise (which might be welcome to others) that we have become bitter enemies."

Less than two weeks before the opening, Brecht engaged Berthold Viertel to direct. In addition to other great gifts, Viertel possessed one qualification necessary to direct a Brechtian play—a willingness to do exactly what Brecht told him. In effect, the playwright directed Viertel, and Viertel directed the actors. Viertel's main contribution was to pressure Brecht into meeting a curtain deadline, for he realized the playwright normally spent months in rehearsals and experimented with every detail a half-dozen times on stage before deciding it. But generally he had difficulty controlling Brecht.

Bentley recalls that almost as soon as Brecht arrived in New York, he had wanted to cancel the play. When he learned he was bound by a production contract, his fear of a second-rate performance made him consider another ploy—excluding the press from any performances. This, too, he discovered, was not feasible. Frustrated, he soon conveyed the impression that, with a grand triumph out of reach, he preferred a disaster. Actors and outside observers felt that, intentionally or not, Brecht ruined his own play.

This was true of Naomi Replansky, a young poet Brecht met and engaged to help to translate some of his poems on a previous trip, after she attended one rehearsal.[11] Laughlin, who observed the rehearsal disputes between Brecht and certain actors and actresses, states unequivocally that "he destroyed his own work."[12] They and others observed how protracted discussions with Viertel about Brecht's theories of acting consumed precious rehearsal time, and they as well as the players gained the impression that he did not care how little they rehearsed. They watched, too, how Brecht insulted some of the actors or actresses as he ruthlessly cut their lines.

Brecht's behavior toward the young Austrian actress Vilma Kurer, whose ability he regarded with open contempt, destroyed what should have been the *tour de force* of the play—"The Jewish Wife," in which Kurer played the title role. Brainerd Duffield, who played Kurer's Aryan husband in this scene, relates that Kurer resented Brecht's repeated corrections, whereas the playwright, who considered her inexperienced and mediocre, wanted to get rid of her by whatever means. Bentley recalls that Brecht cut this scene until there was almost nothing left of it, and Duffield states that they did not have a single run-through until the dress rehearsal. By that time it was too late. New

York critics failed to sense the potential impact of this mutilated scene, and it was dropped after opening night,[13] allegedly to save time, but probably to eliminate Kurer.

When Brecht first heard Albert Bassermann speak what resembled English during rehearsals, he reportedly laughed.[14] This prominent German actor had come to America in 1939 at the age of 72 without knowing a word of English. After playing a number of character parts in films, the first of which he memorized phonetically without understanding what he was saying, he appeared successfully in 1944 as the Pope in a Broadway dramatization of Werfel's *Embezzled Heaven*. Because of his great respect for the 78-year-old actor, Brecht rehearsed him privately in "epic acting."[15] But in less than two weeks neither Bassermann nor his wife Else, nor any other cast member, seemed able to grasp Brecht's style of playing. Viertel tried to convey these concepts to the players,[16] but Brecht's response to the actors' difficulties was to complicate matters by further revising their parts.

Critics knew nothing of these behind-the-scenes problems, and the play and its author received several favorable pre-production notices. One of them originated with the columnist Dorothy Norman, whom Brecht knew from his visit in 1943-1944. In her column "A World To Live In," which appeared in the *New York Post* magazine section on June 11, 1945, she talked of the play's interesting relationship between politics and art and called it "a burning indictment of Hitler Germany by one of the most talented anti-Nazi writers to escape from its barbaric rule."

When *The Private Life of the Master Race* opened on June 12, 1945 (a preview was held on June 11th) in the huge and poorly ventilated auditorium of City College of New York known as the Pauline Edwards Theatre (23rd St. and Lexington Ave.), the cast was not much better prepared for Brecht's play than New York critics were. Semi-intelligible German accents, poor acoustics, and minor mishaps (the wig Bassermann wore to make him look younger kept slipping) added to a confused picture of a play not ready for performance. First-nighters saw a total of nine scenes performed in groups of three that corresponded roughly to acts, but any resemblance to a well-made Broadway play based on suspense, pity, or illusion ended there.

Representative adjectives reflect the tone of generally devastating reviews the next day: "dull and repetitious,"[17] "perfectly awful,"[18] "dated by the times and defeated by its own defects,"[19] "a dull and muddled experimental production,"[20] "painfully slow,"[21] "incredibly dull,"[22] "ponderous," and "undistinguished,"[23] to quote only a few. One reviewer sensed what had happened, though he wrongly blamed the director when he pointed out that "if the Theatre of All Nations had set out deliberately to destroy a play which had been interesting and occasionally exciting in the reading, they couldn't have done a better job than in the butchering of Bertold [sic] Brecht's *The Private Life of the Master Race*."[24] Virtually every reviewer faulted the play for its length and its slow gait. *The New York Post*'s critic noted that "the pacing was painfully slow, and much of the dialogue was either difficult to hear or to understand without considerable strain."[25] *The New York Times* review, by far the most moderate, charitably observed that "some of its incidents are too long; they would be more pointed if cut in half,"[26] while the *Journal-American* carped that in spite of only nine episodes being played, "they're as interminable as they are uncalled for . . . these continue from close onto 9 until closer onto midnight."[27] In 1939 Reyher had warned Brecht that his adaptations for the American stage needed to be given a sharpened drive, "simply because our mode of thinking and our interests are gaited to a more nervous tempo, and what induces us to think in this country is not ideas, but actions."[28] The same criticism would be heard of *Galileo* again in 1947. American audiences were not prepared for the tempo or style of an approach to theater that placed ideas above action. "Was it a play or was it propaganda?"[29] asked one reviewer, who summarized the opinion of many others.

The term "experimental" which turned up in several reviews also demonstrated that one of Brecht's most conventional dramas was still unconventional for the American stage. Burton Rascoe, who left the theater with the impression that "it was perfectly awful," asked: "And just why Dwight Marfield (a good actor) should have to wear two burnt-cork smudges on his cheeks to indicate that he is a worker, or that Clarence Derwent should have to wear putty eyebrows to indicate he is a judge, or that Maurice Ellis, the narrator (a Negro) should have to wear white calcium on his brow and cheeks (leaving the natural dark of his skin otherwise exposed) to indicate that he is an Aryan, Nordic, nasty Nazi—these are things I can't figure out."[30] Brecht intentionally used these techniques to remind viewers that they were seeing a theatrical piece. There also must have been some involuntary "alienation" or "distanciation" in Albert Bassermann's playing, which critics panned. In addition to mentioning his unintelligible speech, two reviews compared his playing with domestic comedy in the New York Yiddish theater: "He works harder than Sam Bernard ever did in "Potash and Perlmutter" to get laughs in situations which the author intended to be tragic," said Burton Rascoe in the *New York World Telegram* about an effect Brecht had not intended.[31]

With the exception of kudos for the acting of Dwight Marfield, who played the part of a worker in "The Chalk Cross" and a dying man in

"The Sermon on the Mount," and for Eisler's incidental music, opening night critics gave the production uniformly low marks. Even a friendly critic who saw it later in the week and spoke of Brecht's "genius as a playwright" concluded that "if this vehicle represents, as claimed, the ultimate in Brecht's purpose as a dramatist, then he seems destined certainly for the mechanical arts—for television particularly—rather than for the stage."[32] This evaluation alludes to Bentley's hyperbolic promotional statement in his introductory essay to the play that "no single work of Brecht's is more important" than this one.[33] But New York critics lacked a basis of comparison. They had witnessed an alien kind of production at a time when, in their view, Germany's recent capitulation had robbed the material of much of its timeliness.

Among other things, *Master Race* was a victim of poor timing. Early in 1945 Laughlin had written Hallie Flanagan, a dominant force in American theater of the thirties, asking if the play merited a production. Her response anticipated the reactions of several critics who saw it. The work, she wrote, "is of historical interest rather than of topical interest . . . five years ago it would have been very strong—ten years from now it would have great historical significance, but definitely the moment is not now."[34] The collapse of Nazi Germany the previous month had put a sudden end to any topical interest it might have had. Several reviewers found *Master Race* reminiscent of the Federal Theatre's "Living Newspaper" productions, which was as close as they could come to categorizing what looked like a string of loosely connected episodes. Their perplexed comments on the unconventional staging, lighting, props, use of an off-stage narrator, a projection screen, and similar devices also reflected a lack of understanding of what are now standard trademarks of "epic theater."

Brecht's journal notation that critics "attacked the production but left the work itself unscathed" means that they did not discuss its politics in his terms.[35] Bentley reports that the playwright spread out reviews of the production on the floor of Berlau's apartment and announced his intention of printing them in his collected works. He had been humiliated in the one American city that mattered most in the theater, and he wanted to preserve that record, too.

Five days before its New York premiere, another production of *Master Race* opened in the Wheeler auditorium of the University of California, Berkeley, and played four performances in three days. Under the auspices of the Department of Dramatic Arts and its Little Theatre, Henry Schnitzler, son of the Austrian writer Arthur Schnitzler, had directed a cast in all seventeen scenes of Bentley's translation. The play was done as part of the official program for delegates to the

United Nations Conference taking place in San Francisco. After the opening, Schnitzler sent Brecht an enthusiastic telegram saying that the "audience followed every scene with profound attention."[36] A review in the student daily singling out "The Jewish Wife" and "The Informer" as two of the strongest scenes[37] suggests that this production achieved its author's intentions better than the New York one. Bentley recalls how much this success pleased Brecht. But Berkeley was not New York City. A journal note about the New York production, with parenthetical comments on the prevailing conditions on Broadway ("Broadway amply mirrors the intellectual life of the States"), bespeaks angry frustration.[38]

In a letter written after *Master Race* opened, Piscator blames Brecht for the production's failure. He scolds him for directing "like every amateur. At different moments the other evening I wanted to jump over the footlights, come backstage, and beat you. Not because I personally felt insulted when I saw the results of this work, but as the more objective harm you have done to yourself."[39] But Piscator was not altogether right, for Brecht had scarcely harmed a nonexistent reputation. In the final analysis, his behavior was consistent with his conviction about representing himself and his style of theater on his own terms or not at all, and he was probably more "right" than Piscator. Had Brecht allowed others to stage this work, he might have gained more recognition, but it would have been recognition based on distortion or misunderstanding. His uncompromising determination to go ahead in his own way represented the only course he knew. It was a risk, and he lost. But in losing he kept intact his own vision, his own theoretical principles, and what, for want of a better word, one must call his "artistic integrity."

The memory of the *Master Race* production, in combination with this desire to make a name on Broadway, stayed with Brecht long after he left America. In 1948 he authorized Reyher and Bentley to grant permission for American productions of his works everywhere except in New York City, where he alone would decide.[39] And, in 1949, when Bentley tried to have Brecht approve a New York City production of *The Good Woman of Setzuan* (Bentley was to direct) by a group called "The Interplayers," the dramatist mildly reproved him for it. No matter that a successful production in the 300-seat Carnegie Recital Hall might have moved to Broadway. Brecht wanted a professional show on Broadway or nothing. In a letter to Reyher in 1949, he wrote: "As I've often told Bentley, I do not want any more small experimental productions in New York. I've had too many of them already. Furthermore, the lead in *Good Woman must* be played by a first-rate artist; good will is not enough in this case." In spite of this ambition, for the next two decades the best Brechtian productions in America would be done largely by university theaters or experimental troupes not tied to Broadway.

Brecht attended to other dramatic affairs during his 1945 visit to New York: "In an idiotic play I see a completely modern actress, Taylor. She plays in epic fashion."[41] This surprising tribute went to Laurette Taylor, whom Brecht had seen play the role of the mother in Tennessee Williams's *Glass Menagerie*, a piece whose psychological probings irritated him. During his visit to New York the following year, Brecht paid Taylor the ultimate compliment by telling Wolfgang Roth that he would like her for the title role in his *Mother Courage*.[42]

Another sentence in the same journal entry which reads: "I complete a rough draft of *Malfi* with Bergner (at the conclusion in Vermont)" alludes to the most obscure collaboration of his American exile—his work on *Malfi*. There is no record that Brecht saw Auden during this visit to New York, and if he did complete a version of *Malfi*, existing texts offer no evidence of it. Following *Master Race*, however, Brecht accompanied Bergner and Czinner to a rented summer home near Woodstock, Vermont, where they worked on the text. Other activities occupied him there. Several times he went to see Berthold Viertel and the actress Elisabeth Neumann at their summer home fifteen minutes away, where he helped Viertel on poems to be included in that writer's autobiography.[43] He also hunted up Carl Zuckmayer, one of the leading dramatists of the Weimar Republic, who lived on a small farm nearby, writing and raising chickens that he named after Nazi big-wigs.[44] And he visited the political journalist and Marxist Hermann Budzislawski, a ghost writer for Dorothy Thompson's syndicated columns, who was working with her in a nearby summer home. There he met the influential American journalist, gained a bad impression of her, and conducted a Marxist discussion of world politics on this staunch Republican's front porch.[45]

While he was rehearsing *Master Race*, a letter written in Newtonville, Mass. addressed to "Dear Eugen" reached Brecht. It came from a relative named "Rosalie," who was probably his first cousin and the daughter of his paternal aunt. In addition to transmitting bits of family news, she invited him to see her parents in Katonah, New York.[46] Brecht left no record of traveling to Westchester county to see them, and his other activities probably precluded it. But a long period would elapse before his relatives read about him again in any New York newspapers. By the time he left on July 15, 1945, his name, like that of dozens of other dramatists who fail to make Broadway each year, had vanished as quickly as it had appeared. To the New York theater world, Brecht was still another unknown playwright.

15 BROADWAY AND BUST, 1946:
THE DUCHESS OF MALFI

After H. R. Hays withdrew from the *Malfi* collaboration in December 1943, Brecht set to work on it with W. H. Auden, with whom he met during January and February 1944. Their most intense collaborative efforts, however, fell between February and March 1946 during Brecht's fourth stay in New York. In a letter at the time to Bergner, to whom he was sending completed portions of the latest adaptation, Brecht reported that "the discussions are interesting, Auden very amiable and open. Let me know if you have any objections."[1] A version they completed at this time bears each of their names and the copyright date April 4, 1946.[2] Independently of Auden, Brecht went on revising *Malfi* and discussing production details with Bergner and Czinner. Roth remembers that Brecht and Czinner had him build a stage model for *Malfi* during this period, and that the three of them discussed details relating to sets. Amid talk of a director and a composer for the incidental music, firm plans were made before Brecht returned to California in early May for a production in the fall.

In mid-September 1946 Brecht, accompanied by Berlau, drove from Santa Monica to New York in Laughton's car to watch the production of this, the first play with his name on it scheduled for performance on Broadway. But a pre-production debacle induced him to withdraw his name shortly before the premiere, and, when it opened, not only was his name missing from the playbill; the play itself closed after a cool reception by New York critics.

Malfi was already in rehearsal when Brecht and Auden signed the final Dramatists Guild contract on September 19, 1946, calling for Czinner to use their version in his forthcoming production.[3] The play that opened in New York's Ethel Barrymore Theatre on October 15th, however, was not their joint work at all, but a conscious rejection of their version and a return to the Webster original, with minor emendations by Auden. For Brecht, it was another miss, but a near miss of some importance. Until the last minute it appeared that his adaptation of this play would reach American audiences on Broadway.

The existence of five complete or near-complete versions of *Malfi* written between 1943-1946 reflects some of the problems that led to a last-minute substitution of the original for Brecht's and Auden's adaptation. Bergner and Czinner appear to have exerted considerable influence on the evolution of the various texts. She, for example, suggested that Brecht and Auden incorporate material from Webster's other tragedy, *The White Devil*, in the first adaptation.[4] And it was she who encouraged, or at least approved, the interpolation of passages from Webster's *The Devil's Law Case*[5] into later versions, not to mention a prologue for one draft written to reinforce the incest motif that appropriated almost verbatim passages from John Ford's *'Tis Pity She's a Whore*. Bergner's knowledge of Elizabethan drama and her own style made her quick with suggestions and difficult to satisfy on a play that was to be a vehicle for her.

In 1945 Brecht wrote Berlau that he felt the version he had completed at the Bergner and Czinner summer house in Vermont was ready for production, but that Bergner insisted it was only a "basis" for further work.[6] Consequently he agreed to revise it again. A letter to Bergner a few months later describing changes he and Auden are making says: "Let me know if you have objections; I'm hoping that the love tragedy, one of the most beautiful in literature, is slowly coming out."[7] Bergner's influence on the text may be gauged by Berlau's assertion (she claims she heard it from Brecht) that Bergner refused to die in a recumbent position because one of her recent plays with a similar death scene had flopped, and she feared a repetition.[8] Bergner denies it,[9] but this anecdote rings true, for in the draft where Brecht's hand is most noticeable, the scene was rewritten to achieve precisely that effect.[10] He has the Duchess herself take an oath, by kissing the cover of a poisoned prayer book, never to remarry. Walking about to work off the effects of the poison, she finally succumbs, leaning on her lady-in-waiting.

In a description of the evolution of *Malfi* written some years later, Brecht mentions his collaborator in a single ironic sentence that describes how Auden "saw to it that the original was not unduly maltreated."[11] This remark half conceals what must have been major differences in perception and execution of the play. Probably they existed before and after a letter to Bergner of February 1946 in which Brecht reported that their main difficulty arose from their differing interpretation of the play.[12] Auden considered it "decadent" and saw the Duchess's love for Antonio as a lark, while Brecht felt that her husband was more than a gigolo in this love tragedy caused by economic and incestuous motives. Further, Auden wanted to have Ferdinand receive news of the Duchess's pregnancy after he was captured in battle, while Brecht insisted it must come before he was taken prisoner. Brecht also spoke of a "compromise" with Auden on the matter of whether the Cardinal's excommunication of Malfi should be in English or Latin—they finally agreed that only the opening lines were to be Latin.

Those sections in which Brecht followed his own head depart significantly from Webster. Among other things, he introduces an economic motive, i.e., greed to acquire the Duchess's property, as the moving force behind the behavior of her older brother, the Cardinal. Further, he develops another motive implicit in Webster, but not spelled out—Ferdinand's jealousy arising from an incestuous desire for his sister. In a totally new scene, Brecht has Ferdinand kill his brother, the Cardinal, as the first in a crescendo of deaths that eliminate the Duchess, Ferdinand, and Bosola. Other significant changes in various versions include a large role for Delio; the reduction of the role of the villainous Bosola (Brecht, who did not care for Webster's extensive psychological portrayal of the character, saw him as a "librarian, a frustrated scholar");[13] the elimination of the subplot dealing with the Cardinal's mistress Julia; the disappearance of two minor characters; and the restructuring of the work in three acts instead of five.[14]

Brecht made much of Duke Ferdinand's foreign wars alluded to but not shown by Webster. He wrote a battle scene in one version to explain the delay between the moment the Duke receives news that his widowed sister has remarried and become pregnant, and his return more than two years later. In his version, this news so confuses the Duke that he fights badly and is taken prisoner. As a by-product of this scene, Brecht wrote one of three poems connected with *Malfi*—"When We Came Before Milan" (*GW* x, 879), a soldier's poem as relevant to the twentieth as to the seventeenth century, which in Auden's translation received the title "I Wrote My Love a Letter." Two other poems written in America, "Once Among Many Times" and "Lightly as Though Never Touching the Floor" (*GW* x, 880-81), refer specifically to the *Malfi* plot, though they are not intended for use in the play.[15]

Brecht's remark that Auden wanted to protect the original text should also be read as a veiled reference to the ultimate fate of their adaptation. The events which caused that version to be abandoned occurred in late August 1946, and they happened largely without Brecht's knowledge.

In 1945, a production of *The Duchess of Malfi* that opened in London at the Haymarket Theatre, with Peggy Ashcroft as the Duchess and John Gielgud as Ferdinand, went on to become one of the most successful plays of the season. On the theory that success is transferable, the financial backers of the play urged Czinner to model the New York production after the London hit.[16] Unbeknownst to Brecht, Czinner not only arranged for the set and costume designs to be copied; he also brought over the director of the London *Malfi* to take charge of his production. This director, George Rylands, a Cambridge Elizabethan scholar and friend of Auden's, represented everything in the theater that Brecht opposed (the dramatist later noted that Rylands's staging "involved old-style declamation in accordance with that so-called Shakespearean tradition whose style derives from the nineteenth century and has, of course, nothing to do with the Elizabethan theater").[17]

Rylands assumed that he would be directing the original Webster play. But, he recalls, "when I arrived [in late August 1946] Elisabeth Bergner informed me that she wished to use a Brecht-Auden version or versions (one of them if I remember right was a conflation of *The Duchess* and *The White Devil*)! I said that in that case I would take the next plane back to England."[18] In an act that she later called her "shame,"[19] Bergner gave in to the British director and, indirectly, to the financial backers. In doing so, she allowed to be scuttled a work she had commissioned as a vehicle for herself by a dramatist she admired. Rylands remembers that he reluctantly retained a brief soliloquy in Act I, where Ferdinand hinted that his motive was incestuous jealousy (probably the scene that Brecht and Auden took from Ford's *'Tis Pity She's a Whore*); an emendation where the corpses of the Duchess' children were discovered in a great wardrobe (Act III, scene 3);[20] and a few textual changes in the last act.[21] Otherwise he reinstated Webster's original text.

After three weeks of rehearsals, *Malfi* opened on September 20, 1946, in the Providence, Rhode Island, Metropolitan Theatre, as the first stop on the out-of-town tryout circuit. According to *Variety*, it was done at Providence in an "adaptation by W. H. Auden and Bertold [sic] Brecht."[22] Brecht, in the meantime, who was ignorant of Rylands' changes, was travelling eastward to see and influence what he thought would be a performance of his adaptation. By September 22nd he was in New York,[23] and on September 25th he drove to Boston to see the production there. Newspaper advertisements for the Boston opening still carried the notation "Adapted by W. H. Auden and Bertold Brecht."[24] But what the dramatist saw in the Schubert Theatre disabused him of that fiction. Within hours, he launched a counter-offensive.

On September 26th Brecht wrote a letter to Czinner containing objections that he probably transmitted orally to the producer after the final curtain. Reduced to their simplest terms, his modest proposals were that Czinner fire the director; that he reinstate the adaptation Brecht and Auden had made; that he hire a new actor to play Ferdinand; and that he leave details of lighting, grouping, and casting to Brecht. In defense of his adaptation which, Brecht said, "the present director has ignored . . . and seems quite incapable of directing in such a way as to allow the audience to follow the plot," he asserts that the text he and Auden have prepared "consists in a series of carefully considered cuts which were thoroughly and frequently discussed with

Elisabeth Bergner, who approved them." In a gentle ultimatum, he closes by asking Czinner: "Would you let me know by Monday, September 30th, what you propose to do about these points?"[25]

Czinner's response must have given Brecht reason to believe that he still had a voice in the production. Back in New York, the dramatist contacted Brainerd Duffield, the actor who had played in *Master Race*, about assuming the role of Ferdinand in *Malfi*. Duffield remembers how Brecht, who acted as if he had authority to employ him, kept him up late, rehearsing in Berlau's apartment because he wanted Duffield to replace the actor he had seen play the role in Boston.

Meanwhile the play had run six days in Boston. When it opened in Hartford, Connecticut, on September 30th for a two-night stand, the credit line "Adapted by W. H. Auden and Berthold Brecht" still appeared in advertisements. By the time it moved to New Haven, Connecticut, for a four-day stand (October 3-6), and to Princeton, New Jersey, for its final out-of-town performances (October 7-8), Brecht was considering legal action. He seems to have realized that Rylands and Czinner would not use his text, but he maintained that the Dramatists Guild contract that he and Auden signed clearly required this. Consequently, he asked his agent for this play, Ann Elmo, to get him a copy of the contract from the Dramatists Guild to verify it. In addition to trying through Auden's agent and Czinner's attorney, Elmo called the Dramatists Guild daily for ten days before the opening, but her attempts to get a copy of the contract failed. As a consequence, in Elmo's words, her client, who "had attended an out-of-town performance [of *Malfi*] and was not at all satisfied with it . . . decided to withdraw his name from the billing."[26]

The forthcoming Broadway production of his own *Galileo* must have figured strongly in Brecht's decision. After the treatment his *Master Race* production received from New York critics the previous year, he may have felt he did not want to risk another failure with his name attached to it if *Galileo* were to receive a favorable press in New York. With customary self-confidence, he was convinced that his own *Malfi* adaptation would have appealed to Broadway playgoers; he had no such faith either in Rylands or in the original Webster text. As Brecht had pointed out to Czinner in a letter, his revisions made the plot intelligible to the audience; by contrast, he said, "I understand that the London critics likewise complained of the 'obscure plot' in his [Rylands's] directing of the original Webster version."[27]

Withdrawing his name from the program and withdrawing from the production were two different matters. Brecht was still speaking to Czinner and Bergner, for, according to Bergner, when Rylands left for England after the first week of performances in New York, they brought Brecht back to assist with the play.[28] Thus Rylands's statement that "Brecht had nothing to do with my production in America"[29] applies only until the point in time when Rylands departed for England. After that, Bergner insists, she had Brecht rehearse the actors and rearrange parts of the performance; she even thinks he might have re-introduced some of his original text. She states that his changes strengthened the play considerably, though it was too late to affect the bad press it received when it opened. Wolfgang Roth confirms that Brecht again became involved in the production after Rylands's departure, for he remembers how the playwright rehearsed Bergner in her part during this period.

There is no documentary evidence supporting Bergner's and Roth's claims of Brecht's participation in the play after Rylands left, but at some point early in the production he must have made his voice heard indirectly, probably through Bergner. Shortly before *Malfi* opened, the actor McKay Morris, who was to have played Bosola, walked out. Rylands and Bergner replaced him with the black actor Canada Lee, who arrived when the play was in Boston. While Lee was learning his lines, Rylands played the part himself in a few performances. By the time Lee played the role on Broadway, he was wearing white-face. In his New York production of *Master Race* the previous year, Brecht had also used a black actor in white-face playing a symbolically evil part. It would be a remarkable coincidence if an unorthodox stage technique that appeared in two plays with which Brecht was connected did not originate on his recommendation, just as it seems unlikely that a classical-style director like Rylands would have tried something so clearly experimental unless someone else (like Bergner) had suggested it. New York critics unanimously panned it, and it became one of those elements that, in Rylands's view, doomed the production from the start.[30]

There is no certainty that the unadulterated Brecht/Auden version would have succeeded on Broadway. In spite of illustrious names like Benjamin Britten as composer and Ignatz Strasfogel as arranger of the incidental music, Auden as adaptor (his name remained on the playbill), and Elisabeth Bergner, John Carradine, and Canada Lee in the cast, *The Duchess of Malfi* drew little more than hostile yawns from New York critics. A review in the *New York Daily News* of October 17th carried the headline "*Duchess of Malfi* a Slow, Long, and Unimportant Theatre Relic," while Howard Barnes, in the *New York Herald Tribune*, summarized the prevailing views on the same date when he called it "a preposterous bore . . . dull and unpalatable diversion." After thirty-nine performances in a thirty-one-day run, the play closed on November 16, 1946.[31]

The royalties that Brecht received for *Malfi* constitute circumstantial evidence that the missing Dramatists Guild contract called for his adaptation to be used in production. In November 1946 his New York attorney, Maurice J. Speiser, wrote Brecht at Berlau's apartment regarding the first of these payments: "As I explained to you over the telephone the check for $1500 came for the week of October 19th. The accountant has promised he will have the other check sent without any definite sum or week being mentioned."[32] But even with remuneration from *Malfi* Brecht experienced problems. Czinner, it seems, had paid the medical bills for the treatment and hospitalization of Berlau, following a breakdown she had the previous winter. To recover his expenses, he had the Dramatists Guild block Brecht's royalty account after this first payment on *Malfi*. The following summer the matter was still not settled; at that time James A. Stabile of the Dramatists Guild wrote Brecht about "the money we are holding in your Special Account pending receipt of your advice about the doctor's bills that Dr. Czinner sent to us."[33] There is no record that Brecht responded to Stabile's request for disposition of the matter. His normal attitude toward such matters suggests that he probably left the money unclaimed rather than repay a man whom he felt had betrayed him.

A postscript to *Malfi* alludes to yet another of the many unknowns surrounding Brecht's involvement. The exile not only withdrew his name from the production; in late November or early December 1946 he instructed his attorney to initiate arbitration proceedings against Czinner for violation of their contract. On December 9, 1946, Speiser wrote Brecht that "I have this day notified the Dramatists Guild of our desire to join in the arbitration against Dr. Czinner."[34] But the Dramatists Guild today cannot locate the production contract signed by Brecht, Auden, and Czinner in 1946 nor any correspondence pertaining to *Malfi*,[35] and it is not known if the arbitration hearing took place.

Sometime in the fall of 1946 Brecht wrote a fragmentary treatise on "How *The Duchess of Malfi* Ought To Be Performed." In it, he insists that "the model to be followed is the Broadway musical which, thanks to certain fiercely competing groups composed of speculators, popular stars, good scene designers, bad composers, witty if second-rate song writers, inspired costumers, and truly modern dance directors, has become the authentic expression of all that is American."[36] Praising the musical as a theatrical form for its use of distanciation effects and gestic elements found in his epic theater, he wanted it to serve as the model for the production of this Elizabethan play.

Among other things, a performance Brecht saw with Reyher on September 30, 1946 of *Oklahoma!* one of the all-time favorite American musicals, triggered these surprisingly positive observations.[37] The disappointment friends heard him express over his failure to make a name on Broadway with *Malfi* no doubt caused some bitterness and jealousy in a man whose ambition it was to conquer and change the establishment that excluded him. Yet this born theater man could not resist the lure of New York plays and musicals. Bentley reports that Brecht attended a performance of Eugene O'Neill's *The Iceman Cometh* in the Martin Beck Theater, and Wolfgang Roth remembers taking him to the American Repertory Theater on Columbia Circle. According to Roth, they saw Eva Le Gallienne perform in one of two roles she was playing at the time, either in Barrie's *What Every Woman Knows* (November 8th) or in Ibsen's *John Gabriel Borkman* (November 12th). Somehow Le Gallienne, the guiding spirit of the American Repertory Theater and one of the best-known American actresses of the day, had become acquainted with Brecht's *Mother Courage* and had told Roth that she wanted to play the lead. After seeing her perform in one or both of these plays, Brecht replied to Roth in English: "Over my dead body."[38] Le Gallienne's "method-acting" obviously did not pass muster with the playwright whose name has become synonymous with "epic" acting.

From testimony of friends and acquaintances it may be assumed that, on every trip to New York, Brecht went with friends to see Chinese theater; this trip was no exception. In his diary on October 3, 1946, Reyher records going with Brecht and Berlau to a Chinese theater that he called a "big barn, over 1,000 nightly." A discussion must have ensued with Brecht, for nearly three years later, Reyher wrote to his friend, who had since returned to Europe: "I can't get our continuous (Chinese) theater out of mind. There is the absolute duty of at least trying it. There is no reason we can't go through the world's preceding day's events from 9 to 11, indicate the day's play from 11 to 1, rehearse from 3 to 5, and go on at 8. This of course includes fresh sets, lyrics, and music."[39] In their conversations they must have talked of dramatizing the day's events much as the "Living Newspaper" had done, but apparently in the narrative style of Chinese theater, where a performance might last several hours and repeat the same or similar scenes as viewers come and go at will.

In taking *Malfi* and revising it, Brecht signaled the direction he would follow in nearly all his dramatic works after this point—genial adaptations of older plays that he revitalized without doing violence to the original framework. In April 1948 he wrote to Reyher about his recent adaptation of *Antigone* in words that might have applied equally to *Malfi*. It was, he said, "an experiment in the direction of which we spoke—to examine what we can do for the old plays, and what they can do for us." But an unsympathetic director and backers who were more interested in a successful production than in what the play could do for audiences frustrated those intentions on Broadway in October 1946.

Since his youth, Brecht had been grooming himself for posterity. If anything, lack of success in American exile intensified these efforts. Careless about letter-writing and conventional sources of document-ing his life, he devoted his attention to preserving what he considered more significant—a record of his thought, and his works themselves. One such record is his "working journal." This unusual work, which contains more entries between 1941-1947 than from any period of his life, makes no attempt to document his daily activities in detail. Long periods elapse without an entry; incorrect dates show that Brecht sometimes recorded events days or weeks after they happened. It is less an account of the physical man and his private life than of his mind and his writings. Hence, he called it a "working journal," not a diary, since he defined "work" in terms of his writings, and of the intellecutal and ideological workings of the mind.

The journal does mention dates and events, and Brecht includes many newspaper clippings, magazine photos, charts, advertisements, poems, snapshots, telegrams, and other material that gives it the semblance of a documentary work. But the material is seldom about himself, and often the accompanying text expected by the reader is non-existent. When text does appear, it often seems to have little bear-ing on the pasted-in material. As if reading a literary work, the reader is left to interpret for himself what the author intends. Sometimes Brecht veils essentially subjective reactions in forms that resemble a collection of aphorisms or Oriental Wisdom Literature. Written in lapidary form, the tone of the writing is often so detached that a reader unfamiliar with Brecht's thought wonders where he stands. As a col-lection of reflections and maxims in combination with a chronicle of selected events from his external life, this journal underscores Brecht's tendency to turn attention away from his private life and toward his thought and works.

In order to preserve these works for posterity, Brecht had Ruth Berlau set up a microfilm archive of all his published and unpublished writings. Berlau had learned to produce microfilms with the Leica camera Brecht had brought from Germany. After she returned to Santa Monica in June 1944, she began photographing copies of his works as the basis for the archive. Brecht soon found opportunities to use these microfilms; in 1945 two institutions acquired them at a time when his name meant nothing to most Americans.

Shortly after she returned to the east coast in late March 1945, Berlau offered a microfilm copy of all of Brecht's work to the New York Public Library. The offer was accepted, and on August 1, 1945, Brecht wrote the library, granting it permission "to make and deliver photographic or other reproductions of said material" for research purposes, "regardless of copyright privileges."

Materials from this archive had a long-range impact for Brecht at Harvard University. In 1945 Gerhard Nellhaus, a senior at Harvard College, approached the chairman of the German department, Professor Taylor Starck, and asked for a senior honors thesis topic. Starck suggested that Nellhaus write on a German author living in American exile. Through other émigrés Starck, who had met Brecht in Berlin in 1932, located his address and wrote requesting a list of his unpublished works after 1933.[1] Surprisingly, Brecht replied with a cordial letter and sent a microfilm copy of his published and unpublished works. From these, Nellhaus wrote the first scholarly investigation of Brecht's works in America—a senior honors thesis at Harvard completed in the spring of 1946 entitled "Berthold [sic] Brecht. The Development of a Dialectical Poet-Dramatist." As with many others, Nellhaus's exposure to Brecht infected him, and, he too, became an enthusiastic translator and promoter of Brecht's works. In 1959, this initial link to Harvard was renewed when the Brecht family chose it as the only repository in America for microfilmed copies of the holdings of the Brecht Archives in East Berlin.

Preserving his name for posterity likewise meant promoting publications of his works. This Brecht did with an intensity mitigated only by reluctance if things were not precisely as he liked. Had he not exercised such close control over publication of his works, and had he allowed enthusiastic supporters to promote him as they wanted to, a substantial number of his plays and poems might have been published before he returned to Europe. As it was, there appeared only a single play (*Master Race*, 1944) and a slender volume of collected poems (1947).

Two collaborators figured prominently in his publication efforts in America—Bentley and Hays. Almost from the moment Bentley, a young English instructor at UCLA with a recent doctorate from Yale, appeared at his door in search of someone to help him translate Stefan George, the self-styled prophet and high priest of early-twentieth-century German poetry (Brecht was not interested), he channeled great energy into publishing works by and about Brecht.

Early in 1943, his articles touting Brecht's works began to appear in journals, magazines, and newspapers. The prestigious anti-Communist *Partisan Review* had rejected Bentley's translation of "To the German Soldiers in the East" on the grounds that its contents were politically outrageous,[2] but Bentley's articles on Brecht's published works appeared in *The Nation, Books Abroad, Theatre Arts*, and *The Rocky Mountain Review*. In 1943, after taking a teaching position at Black Mountain College in North Carolina, Bentley opened negotiations with Laughlin that led to publication of Brecht's *Private Life of the Master Race* by New Directions in 1944.

Brecht's collaborators endured much in attempting to publish him. His refusal to answer letters, and what seemed like erratic behavior when it came to promoting his own affairs, plagued Bentley, his publishers, and everyone who worked with him. During negotiations for publication of *Master Race*, Bentley wrote dozens of letters to Laughlin at New Directions; Brecht never wrote one, but transmitted instructions to Bentley orally, or not at all. Bentley was left to negotiate the contract, write to Brecht's friends for publicity statements to accompany the book, and attend to dozens of details. Brecht waited until everything had been settled before he voiced objections.

While in New York during June 1945 in connection with the production of *Master Race*, Bentley met with Walter Pistole of Reynal and Hitchcock publishers, who wanted to publish one volume of Brecht's collected plays in English. Brecht vetoed these plans and instructed Bentley to offer it to New Directions instead. In a letter to Laughlin, Bentley states: "What Brecht would like best is that you should bring out his collected works over the next five years or so, beginning with a volume of plays." Commenting on their mutual irritation at Brecht's unbusinesslike ways and his refusal to answer letters, Bentley continues: "Both you and I have a right to be out of patience with Brecht. But he is still important as an artist."[3]

Whenever he intervened in business matters, Brecht usually left a trail of confusion. After telling Bentley in mid-June 1945 that he wanted him to act as general editor of his collected works for New Directions, he met personally with Laughlin and told him that he would act as editor himself. Bentley then wrote Laughlin saying that "your news cancels Brecht's instructions to me, which were that *I* was to deal with you and Reynal. . . . Brecht said I was editor and should take charge, and then he takes charge himself. What a man!"[4] Later, Bentley notified Laughlin that he was holding on to several English translations of Brecht's plays for the putative edition: "I won't send any of these to Brecht, or they'll never be heard of again."[5] But Laughlin was unable to publish the edition, whereupon Reynal and Hitchcock wrote Brecht offering specific terms for his complete dramatic works to appear over the next five years. The matter lingered until a visit to New York in February 1946, when Brecht personally signed a preliminary agreement with the publishers for a multi-volume edition on which he received an advance of $500.[6] Had the project materialized, the history of Brecht publishing in America would have been happier and simpler. But the writer's tight reign delayed publication long enough for circumstances to terminate the project.

In February 1946 Brecht wrote Bentley, stressing the importance to him of seeing his works published in America. His distaste for letter-writing, he confessed, forced him to engage strong assistants to take care of details. Hence he selected Bentley to function as general editor. The other assistant would be Hauptmann, a longtime collaborator who had helped him write every major work between 1925-1933 and who understood his theatrical wishes. Because she knew his works in detail and enjoyed his total confidence, he was giving her *plein pouvoir* to rewrite, correct, or edit anything she wished without consulting him. Bentley understood this from working with her on the *Master Race* translation in 1943-1944, at which time she had rewritten the ending of one scene and changed a number of other lines on her own authority.

Brecht describes how he visualized their collaboration. Bentley, whose name would appear as the sole general editor, is to deal directly with all translators, adaptors, the press, and his publishers. But Hauptmann, who is to select the plays for each volume, will transmit to Bentley suggestions for textual emendations, which he would pass on to the translators. Brecht emphasizes that the plays for the first volume must be selected on the basis of their chance of being performed, and the translators on their ability to solve theater problems in the text. He insists that *Galileo* and *Caucasian Chalk Circle* must appear in the first volume because he has contracts for productions of each— "I must be able to use my theater connections" he observes. And to mollify Bentley, he adds in a conciliatory tone: "Please don't regard this . . . as a matter of competence. I simply see no other way to organize a long-standing collaboration between us (i.e., Hauptmann). After all, I'm not dead like Ibsen or Sophocles, and the theater is an extremely vital and many-faceted thing, as you of all people understand so well."[7]

Initially Bentley was irritated. In a letter to Laughlin, he wrote: "Brecht has now signed a contract with R. & H. He suggests me as his general editor, but upon impossible terms: I'm to do all the dirty work, and Brecht is to boss everything. Unless he withdraws his demand to supervise the whole show, I must be counted out. I've had enough of Brecht and his female followers. He even asks that my introductions contain no criticism of his work!"[8]

But Bentley finally succumbed to a man whose work he greatly admired, whereupon Brecht wrote to him and Hauptmann in mid-1946, outlining what he wanted Bentley's introduction to say. Among other things, he is to stress that these plays are written in an age of revolutions and world wars; that Brecht writes lyric poetry, dramas, and theoretical works; that his work picks up forgotten traditional forms, just as Stravinsky and Picasso did in their art; that the new aspect they introduce might be called "dialectic realism"; that he is a realist; that his plays aim to instruct *and* entertain; and that ideological considerations should not dominate. He wants Bentley to translate his theoretical remarks on *The Threepenny Opera* before writing the introduction, presumably as a supplementary statement to the introduction, and he promises to prepare a small collection of his own theoretical writings to assist in explaining his ideas. In his letter to Hauptmann, he expresses appreciation for Bentley's collaboration: "I'm happy that I have Bentley for the editorial work, and I hope he takes the unique opportunity to do a scholarly, i.e., a careful piece of work; there is scarcely anything [about me] now but feuilletons."

In this edition Brecht envisaged three volumes of his plays and additional volumes of his prose and theoretical writings. Between May and August 1946 he sent translations of at least eight of his plays to Bentley and compiled an index of seventeen plays in all that he hoped to include. He had specific translations in mind: Laughton's *Galileo*; either Bentley's or Auden/Stern's *Good Woman of Setzuan*; Bentley's *Master Race*; Hays's *Mother Courage*; Auden and Stern's *Caucasian Chalk Circle*; Desmond Vesey's *Threepenny Opera*; Frank Jones's *St. Joan of the Stockyards*; and V. J. Jerome's *Mother*.[9] But Brecht's obsession with having a hand in each of these, and his dissatisfaction, fired by his own grasp of English and by collaborators who pointed out all the inadequacies and none of the strengths, counterbalanced his passion to put his name before American readers.

Writing to Hauptmann in early June 1946, Brecht asserts that *Galileo* is the only translation ready for the first volume, no doubt because he had spent eighteen months personally rewriting and translating it with Laughton. Hauptmann's reply perceptively notes that Brecht's knowledge of English made him far more critical than he would have been in languages he did not know: "It's true that with the exception of *Galileo*, nothing is ready for volume one. What's bad is that we're here in this country and in a position to judge the translations. But it would be a crime to be here and not to do it. In Italy the whole thing would appear without [your] critique. Or do you know that much Italian?"[10] As it was, this fastidiousness caused a protracted delay. By July 1947, nearly eighteen months after Brecht had signed a contract, he had still failed to deliver enough material for a single volume. At that point Reynal and Hitchcock reduced its proposed edition to one volume of his "selected works." Later that year the firm was sold, and Harcourt-Brace, the new owners, dropped the project completely.

Bentley's translations of *The Good Woman of Setzuan* and *The Caucasian Chalk Circle*, which Brecht had encouraged him to do for the edition and which he later approved, were the only concrete results of this ambitious undertaking. In subsequent years, and with the playwright's permission, Bentley tried to have individual dramas published wherever possible. But the prospect for introducing Brecht to the American public on a broader scale slipped away because Brecht's critical awareness that came from living in the country and knowing the language conflicted with his self-promotional instinct. Had Brecht spent his exile in South America or Mexico with other German friends, chances are that his translated works would have been introduced to American audiences by advocates like Bentley more quickly, and certainly with fewer difficulties than they were.

As early as 1942, Hays had proposed to Laughlin that New Directions issue a volume of Brecht's poems in translation. While Brecht was in New York in 1943, Hays managed to extract an agreement from him to have Hays translate and prepare this edition, but Laughlin failed to respond to Hays's urgings that they sign before Brecht was out of reach.[11]

In mid-1944 Hays again hammered away at Laughlin. Late in the year the publisher backed off. Bentley's *Master Race* translation, which had appeared in September 1944, was not selling well, and Brecht was still not answering letters or telegrams. Sometime in 1944, Joseph Losey also approached Hays about using his *Lucullus* translation on the "Words of War" radio program he was producing. This project, too, foundered when Brecht refused to answer letters.

With Laughlin no longer interested in the poems, Hays spoke with Reynal and Hitchcock, who had published his second novel, *Lie Down in Darkness*, in 1944. They were interested, and once again he tried to stir Brecht. He did it through a letter to Eisler asking him to be a go-between. The letter reported that the publisher wanted a bilingual volume of about one hundred pages, with exclusive publication rights for two years and an option to do a volume of his selected plays, for which he would receive a $300 advance.[12] Brecht answered early in March with an enthusiastic letter approving the terms in general, asking which of his poems Hays had, and outlining his ideas on selection. He also sent a list of poems he wanted included, tactfully implying that he needed to approve all translations. "I'd also like to have an opportunity to write you comments about your 'imitations' [i.e., English renderings]. I know one cannot 'correct' imitations, but often verses contain implications that escape the most ingenious connoisseur of languages; above all, there are political implications we will need to discuss at various points (lack of clarity in my verse, ambiguities, etc.). I would answer quickly each time—when working, I can easily overcome my aversion to writing. Again, *many* thanks for your efforts." Through Ann Elmo, his New York agent, Brecht signed a contract on April 18, 1945, for Hays to translate and Reynal and Hitchcock to publish a selection of his poems.[13]

When he visited New York in June 1945, the dramatist talked with an editor at Reynal and Hitchcock and, with Hays's help, began to select the poems he wanted published. Hays recalls the exile's reluctance to include his early non-Marxist verse, but Hays's insistence on their high quality overcame this objection. Brecht did stipulate that his "Grand Chorale of Thanksgiving" must appear at the end of the section of early poems because its uncompromising atheism provided the ideological basis for the verse that followed.

With Hays's permission, Bentley published some of his translations in the spring 1945 issue of *The Kenyon Review*. When Brecht saw these and others which appeared that year in *Accent* and *Poetry* magazines, he solicited evaluations from friends, with predictable results. When it came to rendering Brecht in English, each of his collaborators prided himself on sole possession of the truth. Typically, suggested emendations seldom improved, but only changed. Morton Wurtele, a graduate student in physics at UCLA who lived in Brecht's home during 1945-1946, recorded some of the corrections Brecht entered on a copy of Hays's renderings in *The Kenyon Review* which represented no improvement over Hays's translations. Without unanimous assurance (which he never got) that his poems or plays were as good in translation as they had been in the German original, Brecht seems to have been dissatisfied with every rendering in which he did not personally have a hand. Complaining to Hauptmann about the inadequacy of the translations for the forthcoming edition of his works, he observes that Hays's *Mother Courage* needs considerable revision because Hays has not understood everything. And this, Brecht adds, in the wake of the "catastrophe with the poems."[14]

Because of this dissatisfaction, Brecht, who was in New York at the time (1946) working with Hays to put the final touches on the poems, approached Albert Erskine, an editor at Reynal and Hitchcock, while the poems were in the proof stage and asked about engaging a well-known American poet to translate them. When Erskine parried with the observation that the interest would then be in the translator and not in him, Brecht dropped the matter.[15]

Reynal and Hitchcock published fifty of Brecht's *Selected Poems* in

September 1947. Had Brecht not been bound by a contract, there is a chance that his fetish about absolute control over his translations might have blocked this publication, too. Because Hays persisted, this would be the only edition of Brecht's poems available in English for nearly two decades to follow.

Nor did this represent the full scope of Brecht's publishing opportunities. In June 1945 Bentley's *Master Race* translation caught the eye of Joyce Hartmann, an editor at Houghton-Mifflin, who wrote the dramatist, saying she had seen the play on the stage, and she and others were enthusiastic about his works. Was he writing (or had he written) a novel or non-fiction? If so, they would be eager to consider it if he would call or write.[16] Brecht apparently never responded. Another opportunity to introduce himself to an American audience presented itself in the person of Dorothy Norman, whom he had met through Berlau in the fall of 1944. Again his dissatisfaction with a translation almost prevented publication. Norman, a journalist, millionaire, and publisher, was active in a variety of liberal and literary causes. She and Brecht met together a number of times in Berlau's 57th St. apartment and Norman's Lescaze house at 124 E. 70th Street. "We talked a lot about politics and his work" remembers Norman, an avid anti-fascist herself.[17] Ironically, the Marxist Brecht and this plutocratic Grande Dame seem to have gotten along well. Normally Brecht would have been on his worst behavior with such a person; Norman, however, states that she refused to be shocked by what he said, but rather laughed at his provocative remarks. The consequence was a fine relationship.

A visit in the spring of 1946 resulted in an invitation to publish in Norman's literary journal *Twice a Year*.[18] Perhaps with readers of his forthcoming edition of plays in mind, Brecht selected a piece that explained to American readers why he wrote as he did in exile: "Writing the Truth: Five Difficulties." After Richard Winston finished translating the first two sections, he sent them to Norman with a request to print some remarks on its "vicious anti-art and anti-cultural tendency. This is how it strikes me, at any rate. . . . I dislike intensely this deceptive simplicity of style and content that Brecht affects: 'Come, children, gather round me and it will all be explained to you. The fascists are wicked, we all know that so let's not talk about it. Your real enemies are the bourgeois writers who get paid for their work and don't believe that truth is only what serves your cause.' The other sections are in a similar vein."[19] Sensing that Brecht was referring to bourgeois writers like Thomas Mann, whom he admired, Winston later remarked that "I dislike almost everything Brecht says, but he is a very clever writer and a cunning teacher."[20]

Without mentioning Winston's ideological objections, Norman sent his translation to Brecht for what she assumed would be routine approval. The dramatist may not have sensed that his work had fallen into hostile hands, but he found other reasons to be dissatisfied. Writing to Norman, Berlau reported that Isherwood, whom Brecht had asked to look the translation over, had found it to be "a rather bad and unelegant translation and not good enough for your book *Twice a Year*. So Brecht thought Bentley could do a job on it."[21] After Bentley revised it, Brecht entered his own corrections, but apparently he was still dissatisfied.

. For more than a year, Norman worked to secure Brecht's approval to publish the translation. In 1947 he agreed to let Bentley rework it again and to accept his corrections. Norman had it re-set and sent him printer's proofs—but again Brecht stalled. Finally in 1947 she delivered an ultimatum:

"I shall go ahead and use your piece on the 'Difficulties of Writing' unless I receive the corrected copy from you within the next week. I think the piece should be seen. You said you would stand by Bentley's corrections. The corrections were incorporated. I can see no further reason to delay. Even if the piece is not perfect, unless you cooperate, I do think that you should stand by your original agreement. If I did not love you so dearly, I would not have been so patient about waiting."[22]

In 1948 Norman published a double number of *Twice a Year*. It included a laudatory essay entitled "Bertold Brecht and Writing the Truth," which Norman had commissioned Berthold Viertel to write two years earlier; Brecht's own piece, with Richard Winston named as sole translator; and translations of four Brecht poems done (under Brecht's supervision) by Naomi Replansky.

Writing for a refugee audience, Brecht also published a number of shorter pieces in his native language. Here, too, he exercised the same strict control that he did with translations of his works. Late in 1943 Berthold Viertel persuaded him to contribute to *Freiheit für Österreich*, an Austrian refugee newspaper. On January 15, 1944, the paper published a four-stanza version of Brecht's "Song of a German Mother" and, on June 29, 1946, an early version of his poem "Children's Crusade, 1939." Viertel also introduced Brecht to Elisabeth Freundlich, an Austrian exile who edited the cultural section of the monthly *Austro-American Tribune*, another German language newspaper. Knowing Brecht's reputation, she hoped to solicit contributions from him in German. Freundlich remembers how Brecht demanded to know her political views (she was a leftist, but not a Communist), asked for information on Austrian resistance to Hitler, and inquired about her newspaper.[23] Perhaps to test the climate of the parent publication, Brecht allowed Freundlich to arrange an interview with a correspondent from *The Young Austro-American* that appeared in the February 1944 issue.

Lydia Infeld's interview could have carried the caption, "Difficulties in Talking with Bertolt Brecht," for the poet's reluctance to discuss private matters led her to comment: "I learned very little about Brecht from Brecht himself. He revealed only that, at the moment, his play *Private Life of the Master Race* was being translated into English, and that, to quote Brecht, 'I like a good murder mystery better than mediocre poetry.' " Brecht made this remark when asked about German literature written in exile, which he dubbed "preserved literature" that had to be "preserved" for use in postwar Germany. He observed that traditionally, Chinese poets in exile retained contact with the indigenous forms of Chinese poetry, whereas German poets-in-exile of this age were obliged to find new forms for themselves. He urged young people to read as much German prose and poetry as possible to increase their vocabularies. To sharpen their literary skills, he suggested that they read, discuss, and criticize their works among small groups of listeners as he had done in taverns when he was young. He was not interested, according to the interviewer, in hearing why someone failed because of great obstacles, but why someone succeeded in spite of them. Finally, Brecht encouraged his young readers to be "reporters" of their circumstances, whether in schools or factories.

The *Austro-American Tribune* must have passed muster with him, for he invited Freundlich to meet several times in Berlau's apartment and select pictures and poems for publication. Since the late thirties Brecht had been collecting newspaper and magazine photos dealing with Nazi Germany and Hitler's war and writing anti-war epigrammatic quatrains to accompany them. The first of these in print appeared in the February 1944 issue of *The Austro-American Tribune*. It shows Ukrainian women and children returning to their ravaged homesites after German invaders had been driven off. The accompanying epigram expresses the poet's guilt at seeing his German countrymen destroy the homes of innocent women and children, and his joy at hearing that the Germans have been repulsed.

In an introductory paragraph, Freundlich designated these as "documents of our times" with captions based on the classical epigram, and compared them with Goya's paintings on "Los Desastres de la Guerra." In the next four months, her paper published two more of these "photograms," as Brecht called them. The March 1944 *Austro-American Tribune* carried a photo showing dazed, half-frozen German soldiers stumbling along (probably toward a Russian POW camp), with an epigram by Brecht comparing "these, our sons" with the wolf that needs a warm place to hide. The June 1944 issue, with a photo of a white American soldier rescuing a black from a white mob during the 1943 Detroit racial riots, printed a caption stating that this soldier needed more courage than those who fought in Bataan, Kiska, and El Guettar.

Years later in East Berlin, Brecht selected sixty-nine of these "photograms" from a much larger number and published them under the title *Primer of War*. The first two of the three that appeared in the *Austro-American Tribune* were among those he included. While he neither began nor ended this anti-war collection in America, Brecht wrote well over half the epigrams and collected the majority of his photos for it during his American exile. *Life* magazine, with its documentary photography of the war, served as a particularly rich source of material. In many cases, Brecht borrowed words or descriptive phrases from the accompanying articles or picture captions for his epigrams. Brecht classified these "photograms" as part of a "literary report" of his exile.[24]

This unique literary experiment reveals how a vivid visual event could often trigger a poem or an entire scene in Brecht's imagination. As with so much he did, Brecht had created nothing new here, but, as Reinhold Grimm has demonstrated, only re-created an old form in modern garb—the "emblems" popular in Renaissance and Baroque times consisting of allegorical pictures with moralistic inscriptions accompanying them.[25] As modern-day emblems that combined topical visual history with the precision and brevity of an epigram, these rose far above most of the agit-prop lyrics Brecht had written for the Communist cause in the thirties. Even without the accompanying photos, many of these little-known Brechtian poems demonstrate that his exile experience in no way diminished his splendid lyrical gifts.

Each time he returned to New York, Brecht arranged with Freundlich for publication of more material. The song "The Calves' March" from *Schweyk* appeared in September 1944, while a poem from *Master Race* was printed in July 1945, not to mention a lengthy review of the New York production of that work and a tribute to Brecht by Berthold Viertel in the same issue. The *Austro-American Tribune* also counts as the first source anywhere to print a scene from his unpublished play *Galileo*. Through Freundlich's efforts, its January 1947 issue carried the scene between Galileo and the Little Monk that, in the American version, became Scene 7. And using the pen name Elisabeth Lanzer, Freundlich wrote what she claims was the first review in any German-language newspaper of that work's New York premiere in 1947.[26]

Throughout his American exile, Brecht discussed, rethought, and refined his theories of so-called "epic theater." While none was published at the time, he probably wrote a preliminary version of his most important single exposition of these mature theories—his *Short Organum for the Theater*—sometime during 1946. Evidence of this comes from Hans Viertel, who claims that Brecht personally gave him a manuscript copy of the *Short Organum* to read. If, as he insists, Viertel saw this work in manuscript form, it could have been no later than the summer of 1946, since Viertel was never with the playwright after that. No extant documents confirm his claim (Brecht kept no journal in 1946, save a single entry on January 5th), but circumstantial evidence suggests that Viertel, a reliable informant on Brecht's American exile, might be right. That evidence relates to a theoretical discussion about his concept of epic theater which Brecht was carrying on with Bentley at this time.

In 1946, Bentley's book *The Playwright as Thinker* appeared with Reynal and Hitchcock. Like a figure in Brecht's poem "Legend of the Origin of the Book of Taoteking on Lao-tse's Journey into Emigration," Bentley used it to imitate the lowly customs official there who compelled the sage to record his wisdom. Seeing a chance to make Brecht explain his own theories, Bentley sent him a copy and invited him to respond to its treatment of modern drama by expounding on his own theories, which Bentley had attempted to outline there. From Brecht's response, he hoped to engage the dramatist in an exchange of letters he could publish. In an undated letter written sometime in July, 1946, Brecht agreed: "Your invitation to use your book as a point of departure is legitimate. I am reading it slowly, and with great enjoyment. . . . Give me a little time for reading. This kind of thing should not be done hastily."

After reading Bentley's book, Brecht replied in a letter dated August 1946 that responds to specific categories Bentley uses. "Bourgeois" theater, i.e., Ibsenesque theater, which attempts to create an illusion of reality, is bankrupt, and what looks like today's transitional period is really a period of total decline, he says. Though he lays no claim to his own theater's being "great," Brecht rejects as too neutral Bentley's descriptions which call his epic theater "temporary," "provisional," or "experimental." For him it is already the theater of the future. The definitive function of theater is not to establish binding forms, but to make dramatic experimentation a binding principle. He goes on to disagree mildly with Bentley's explanation of "epic theater":

"I am only defending myself against the customary neutral treatment which even you on occasion do not oppose strongly enough, viz. the mollifying claims that it is a matter of something tentative, provisional, non-binding, in short experiments, when in fact it is an attempt to establish the experimental method as a definitive function of the theater. It was not Francis Bacon's experiments that were decisive, but the definitive introduction of experimentation in science. My very different theatrical forms are by no means attempts to arrive at a definitive form; only the variety of forms should be definitive. And the introduction of the experimental method in dramatics is not only a matter of form. If the critique of the reality portrayed is to be revealed as a main source of artistic enjoyment, the spectators should actually be transformed into social experimentors."[27]

In response, Bentley challenged him to elaborate on his conception of art: "The explanation you gave in 'Telling the Truth: Five Difficulties' was not enough. I felt that you brushed aside all modern art except your own kind . . . you did not really cope with it. I would welcome two things: a brief account of your philosophy of art, and . . . an account of Epic Theatre that deals with some of the difficulties raised by Edmund Fuller some years ago and, more recently, by myself." Though he recognized Brecht's genius, Bentley was no blind disciple of his theories, but a perceptive critic who, as Brecht told him later, was almost the only person who would raise issues that really challenged his ideas.

In the same letter, Bentley had shown the courage to say something that might have estranged others from him: "Like Shaw, you are more eager to explain your politics and your morality than your art. This is your privilege. But I warn you that you will never make any further advance in America unless you can dispel the illusions and doubts that at present surround your kind of enterprise."[28]

The discovery that a sympathetic collaborator and promoter of his works like Bentley did not understand his theories well enough to explain them to Brecht's satisfaction seems to have been the catalyst in Brecht's writing this early version of the *Short Organum*. The reference in his letter to Francis Bacon, the title of whose famous work Brecht consciously imitated in the title of his own treatise, connects that work with this discussion Bentley triggered. If Viertel's memory is accurate and Brecht did write a first draft of *The Short Organum* that summer, it arose, not as a random project, but in response to specific circumstances: the reading of Bentley's book *The Playwright as Thinker*, and the wish to have his theories explained satisfactorily to American readers in a forthcoming edition of his own plays.

A little-known piece of playwriting took place in 1945 when Brecht invited Gorelik to collaborate on a play designed for American audiences. Gorelik remembers that the dramatist agreed to his proposed title *Nothing But the Best* (originally Brecht planned to call it *The Vin-*

egar Sponge)[29] because it was about the desire of every American worker for the best in material comfort.

They intended to portray American workers' middle-class aspirations and their "dog-eat-dog" efforts to get ahead. Brecht supplied the notes and some of the ideas while Gorelik did the writing. Gorelik claims Brecht stopped work after a few sessions, saying he did not know enough about the American working class. But a difference in playwriting styles doubtless contributed to the plan's demise. Brecht's journal records his surprise at the warning not to mention money in the play (though money was its central theme), since, as Gorelik informed him, "It's anathema on Broadway." He adds his own observation that "in fact, in commercial theaters no one talks about money any more than one talks about cancer in front of cancer patients." Gorelik also remembers Brecht's saying in this context that "money is so seldom the subject of plays by American playwrights that maybe it's their object." Almost instinctively, he had discovered a taboo by violating it.

Gorelik's discussions defending Stanislavsky-inspired acting continued to provoke Brecht. Early in 1947, he tried to persuade the exiled writer to come to the Actors Laboratory Theatre in Hollywood, where he had designed the sets for several productions, and to explain his views to the young actors there. After strong resistance, Brecht finally agreed. But when Gorelik approached Mary Tarcai, the director of the Lab at the time, she knew enough about Brecht to realize that having him visit would be like inviting a wolf into a sheep pen. She firmly declined on the grounds that "our actors use the Stanislavsky system. Brecht would only confuse them."[30]

Brecht did attend at least one performance of Gorelik's one-act play *Paul Thompson Forever* put on by the Actors Lab in the first half of 1947. He complimented a play that, according to his standards, counted as unmitigated Aristotelian drama by sending Berlau to photograph a performance of it.[31] If Brecht had not already seen productions at the Actors Lab before 1947, he knew about them from his wife and Laughton. The program notes to *Galileo* that same summer state that William Phipps, who played the role of Andrea, "was spotted by Charles Laughton and Mrs. Brecht and offered his current role in *Galileo*" while playing in an Actors Lab production of *Men in White*.

Several other actors in the *Galileo* premiere, among them William Cottrel, Ken Jones, and Stephen Brown, were likewise recruited from the Actors Lab. Brecht's abortive lecture on epic acting was given belatedly that same year to at least some pupils from the Actors Lab— during rehearsals for his own *Galileo*.

Brecht's association with a writer in Hollywood early in 1947, Don Ogden Stewart, had a direct impact on a drama which reached Broadway the following September. Stewart, past president of the League of American Writers and a prominent writer of the American left, had known Brecht since 1942. He remembers showing Brecht his play *How I Wonder* early in 1947 and asking for suggestions. They came in an undated letter that Brecht wrote him that spring. Stewart's play (Brecht calls it a "comedy") deals with a professor of astronomy, Lemuel Stevenson, who has discovered a new star inhabited by human beings on which political institutions and scientific progress have reached approximately the same stage of development they have on earth. The professor's "mind" or conscience, which assumes the role of a visitor from this new planet, tells him that scientists who do not protest the abuses of science are culpable (specific reference is made to atomic scientists).

Brecht's letter praises Stewart's concept of the scientist's moral dilemma as "very useful," but his subsequent remarks tend to damn with faint praise. He thinks the theme of a bourgeois intellectual whose conscience is pricked and who finds himself at odds with society demands a more rigorous treatment than Stewart has given it. Conscience pangs and protest alone do not change the world, says Brecht, since the professor remains a member of the bourgeois class and seeks a solution within traditional class boundaries. Comparing Ibsen's dramas with Chekhov's, Brecht notes that Ibsen saw solutions within the existing social system, while Chekhov saw none. He points to the present-day regimentation of atomic scientists which, he says, makes the Holy Inquisition look harmless, and gently chides Stewart for his optimism and hope. "The audience cannot be activated with consoling references to the 'continued existence of human decency.' We have fraternized too long with ignorant decency." In effect, Brecht was exhorting Stewart to radicalize a play which he considered too mild.

During his last nine months in America, Brecht's name began to impress itself on a few important people. One of these was the composer Roger Sessions, who had joined the music faculty at the University of California, Berkeley, in 1945. Sessions had read some of Brecht's works in the original and was drawn to them. Discussions between Sessions and Henry Schnitzler, who had staged *Master Race* at the University of California, Berkeley, in June 1945, led to a plan whereby Sessions would compose an opera using a libretto by Brecht. In September 1946 Schnitzler wrote Brecht inviting him to collaborate with "one of the leading modern composers of the United States" in a short opera similar to the *Yea-Sayer* and *Nay-Sayer* that he had done with

Kurt Weill.[32] Sessions, too, wrote Brecht saying "I feel confident that anything you would be interested in writing would certainly appeal strongly to me, and that I would be able to find your dramatic conceptions congenial." Eager to collaborate with this prominent composer, Brecht sent two copies of his *Lucullus* in the H. R. Hays translation. Though the text was nearly twice as long as Sessions had envisaged it, he went ahead with the composition. The result, a 75-minute opera which was performed in Berkeley on April 18, 1947, received positive reviews throughout the country, though more on the strength of Sessions's music than on Brecht's text.[33]

In 1947, Brecht's name also came to the attention of John Gassner, who had met him in New York in the winter of 1935-1936. Gassner, an important drama critic and theater figure, was employed at the time in the play department at Columbia Pictures. The Experimental Theater in New York had sent Gassner a copy they had acquired of *The Caucasian Chalk Circle* in Bentley's recent translation, and they requested an opinion. Gassner found it delightful. Writing to Bentley, he calls the play "an utterly fascinating achievement" and says he will recommend it enthusiastically to the Experimental Theater. He continues: "I should like to take a stab at getting the play on Broadway, come what may, by beating the drums in the offices of the producers who work closely with me, although the expensiveness of a production is certain to impede the effort. May I try?"[34] But the story broke off without a satisfactory ending. Brecht knew nothing of his name's having reached Gassner, or of Gassner's positive evaluation, and no *Chalk Circle* production was mounted. But Gassner's enthusiasm for Brecht doubtless influenced the decision of the Experimental Theater three months later to write to Brecht about staging another play of his that was about to go into rehearsal when they first wrote Gassner—the American version of *Galileo*.

In late March 1944, Brecht met at Salka Viertel's salon the single most important person for him in his American exile—the actor Charles Laughton. Their meeting inaugurated a three-and-one-half-year collaboration which culminated in what a critic calls "one of the most successful jobs of translation and adaptation ever done for the American stage"[1]—*Galileo*.

Before coming to America, Brecht knew Laughton from several of the British-born actor's films, among them *Rembrandt* and the Academy-Award winning *The Private Life of Henry VIII*,[2] a performance Brecht reputedly liked because of the way Laughton tore a chicken apart while eating it. No doubt he also knew of Laughton's famous film roles as Quasimodo in *The Hunchback of Notre Dame* or as Captain Bligh in *Mutiny on the Bounty*. But it was more than celebrity consciousness that drew him to Laughton, though Brecht unquestionably believed that the actor's connections might aid his own career. He admired the actor, and Laughton reciprocated with unreserved acceptance of Brecht as a gifted, important writer.

Vast differences in personality and outlook suggest that to some extent it was a case of opposites' being attracted. Laughton suffered agonizing guilt at his own homosexuality. To judge by his writings and statements, Brecht, whose early poems rejected the domination of a Christian conscience, seldom experienced a pang of guilt in his life. That Laughton was apolitical to the point of cowardice initially disturbed the Marxist Brecht, who saw repeated evidence of Laughton's indifference or trepidation.[3] Brecht's politics, in turn, made Laughton uneasy; he was fearful that their association might jeopardize his career or his chance of getting United States citizenship.[4]

Despite his enormous talent, Laughton suffered from lack of confidence that led to debilitating bouts of depression. Only once in his journal does Brecht's conviction of his own greatness allow him to understand such self-doubt. A passage notes that "now and then I catch a glimmer of the agony of the ungifted."[5] But he himself never experienced it. Guilt at fleeing England when World War II broke out also plagued Laughton. To Brecht's good fortune, he tried to assuage it by consorting in Hollywood with European émigrés.[6] Few refugees, on the other hand, viewed flight from their homeland and the impending war as a more honorable badge of distinction than Brecht did.

In spite of these extremes, they "connected" almost immediately. Brecht's initial interest in Laughton sprang from his desire for prominent names to help him to get productions and for compatible collaborators who understood him. Laughton was both, and a brilliant actor as well. Several lines Brecht wrote in his journal about actors generally illuminate why Laughton must have appealed to him: "For me, an actor is often something entirely outside of morality; he derives his morality simply from his attitude toward what he produces as an actor. Egocentricity is fun for me if it is expressed vividly; essentially asocial traits such as cowardice, obsequiousness, brutality, when reduced to an aesthetic formula, even enrich me."[7]

Laughton's attraction to the exiled writer sprang from complex personal reasons. His widow recalls that this great interpreter of English literature never became what he most wanted to be—a writer. "His writing was the only thing he was vain about," she states.[8] In Brecht, Laughton recognized a writer who could help him, one who could also understand how writing might develop as an extension of acting.

Brecht appeared at the right moment in Laughton's life. The noted actor believed, with some justification, that his film career was slipping. A friend at MGM recalls how that studio at this time regarded him as "tantramental and box office poison and kept offering him roles in support of Wallace Beery and Marjorie Main."[9] Collaboration with Brecht soon changed that. The dramatist made Laughton feel like the only important actor of his era. More important, he reinforced Laughton's ego as a frustrated writer. The actor later told Hollywood friends that he was never so happy as he had been helping Brecht with the English adaptation of *Galileo*.[10]

Each had the ability to bully people, and each had an explosive temper. Yet they treated each other with almost courtly deference. Both were also born pedagogues who delighted in attracting and teaching disciples, and they were not content to let their art simply entertain. When Brecht once asked Laughton why he acted, the answer might have come from a Brechtian essay on the purpose of epic theater: "Because people don't know what they are like, and I think I can show them."[11] Laughton's acting, as his widow points out, had a strong element of wanting to help others—one of the chief impulses behind Brecht's own political commitment. Laughton's iconoclastic views and behavior delighted the playwright. The actor shared with him a strong dislike for authority figures and a certain sympathy for common people. His mocking irreverence of social institutions and pompous people also delighted the maverick Brecht, who came to exercise unusual forbearance with Laughton's squeamishness in political matters.

Kreymborg's English translation of *Schweyk* and Brecht's willingness to hear Laughton read it aloud on April 17, 1944, were the bait that snared the actor. His interpretation of the humor entertained Brecht immensely. From then on they saw each other often—sometimes at Brecht's home in Santa Monica; sometimes at Laughton's Pacific Palisades home on 14954 Corona Del Mar in a garden filled with pre-Columbian statuary that Brecht admired; and sometimes on the Hollywood cocktail circuit.

While working on *Chalk Circle* in the summer of 1944, Brecht always found time to hear Laughton read. His journal notes that once the actor visited him at their home in Santa Monica and recited *Measure for Measure* and *The Tempest* for them.[12] Later Laughton read aloud the first three acts of *King Lear* for Brecht, his son Stefan, Feuchtwanger, Gorelik, Winge, Tsiang, and Dessau.[13] Other readings in ensuing months ranged from Walt Whitman to the Bible, with Shakespeare as the staple. Hans Viertel recalls an evening at Laughton's where Brecht listened with delight to passages read from the Old Testament which, in Laughton's renderings, depicted unmistakable homosexual relationships.[14] There is no evidence that Brecht ever had such a relationship with Laughton, but he was clearly aware of Laughton's homosexuality. Because of his enthusiasm over Laughton's rendition of the Biblical account of the creation, Brecht encouraged him to record it and had him prepare accounts of the creation in different dialects (Brecht viewed them as class perspectives on God) to break his habit of speaking in what Brecht called "the well-known international clerical tone."[15]

In the summer of 1944 Brecht began a long poem about the impressive garden behind Laughton's home on the bluffs above the ocean at Pacific Palisades. "Garden in Progress" (he uses the English title in *GW* x, 883) is a statement of admiration for the wisdom and creative hand that had arranged it. But it is also intended as a social commentary. Brecht extols the efforts that have created a subtle balance among the diverse forms of flora in a garden which reflects his idea of what the ideal society should be. But the same garden, according to the poem, suggests the inevitable decay that will overtake present-day society. The pre-Columbian statues in it seem to be waiting patiently for the present age to pass into dust, just as their civilizations had. Brecht's poem was still unfinished when a subterranean stream beneath the bluffs undermined a section of Laughton's garden, causing eight or ten feet of one corner to slip off. Now Brecht found an appropriate ending to his poem—the pensive observation that little time remains to complete the task of beautifying this garden.

As a Hollywood celebrity and not a poet, Laughton reacted differently to this loss. Sensing deep shame when stories of it appeared in the newspapers, he interpreted it as a confirmation that his life and career were "slipping." Loss of confidence had caused him to turn down the few film roles offered him recently, and the word had gone out in Hollywood studios that he was a "ham."[16] The day after his garden slipped, Laughton called Brecht and asked if he might visit them. Weigel recalls that he entered their house with a coat over his head out of embarrassment at being recognized. Brecht's journal expands on Laughton's desolation: "When he came, he excused himself for coming with his troubles to people who have not really had a roof over their heads for a decade."[17] After Laughton read aloud some material Brecht had urged him to record, his wife Elsa Lanchester joined him. Brecht's journal records their lament:

" 'It's only the beginning,' he says, 'more will go, I've been told that there's a subterranean stream. In all honesty, I don't want to see anyone now, I'm so ashamed. It's in all the newspapers.' I show him the two large pages of my description to cheer him up and say: 'Your garden will become a myth, consisting of an illustrious rumor. They say transience is an essential element of beauty that intensifies the pleasure.' But he knows that the misfortune will hurt him, also in his profession. Not to mention that the property is damaged. And because he has had limited success lately and is often accused of being a 'ham' (which means little more here than an 'actor,' but which is fatal), he probably fears that he can't acquire anything like it again."

Within days after this visit, and perhaps as an attempt at therapy, the dramatist introduced Laughton to his play *Galileo*. In addition to Laughton's talent as an actor, his physical appearance struck Brecht as ideal for the part. One journal entry describes Laughton sitting cross-legged on a white sofa "so that only his Buddha-like belly is visible."[18] That summer Brecht memorialized this anatomical feature in one of the most unusual poems he ever wrote. He entitled it "Laughton's Belly" (*GW* x, 875). He does not drag his belly around like illicit plunder, says Brecht, but presents it like a poem written for his own edification, carefully cultivated with foods selected in leisure, and splendidly executed according to a fine plan.

Brecht's poem, and his admiration for Laughton's physical appetite and appearance, explain another facet of this complex friendship. To some extent he saw Laughton as the idealization of his own desires. Never a vigorous eater, Brecht admitted in an undated note around 1930 that he often wanted to eat something, but after consuming only a small portion his stomach would hold no more, and desire gave way to discomfort. He admired people with great appetites, he said: "It seemed to me a natural advantage if people could eat heartily and with enjoyment, or generally wished to derive as much as possible from things, etc."[19] Laughton was the incarnation of a character type who enjoyed the pleasures of the flesh to the fullest. His well-made belly symbolized the physical enjoyment Brecht associated with intellectual achievement.

Ever since Goethe's *Faust*, Germans had made what Brecht viewed as a fateful separation between the sensuous and the rational in man. He rejected this dualism, and Laughton strengthened his conviction that, in great persons, thought and passion had a common origin. When he first conceived *Galileo*, he had in mind a man for whom thinking was a physical pleasure ("He indulges in thinking-bouts," says the Pope of Galileo; "He cannot say no to an old wine or a new thought"[20]). In Laughton, he met the perfect embodiment of this combination of intellect and sensory pleasure. Had the play not predated their friendship, Brecht probably would have had to write it for or about him.

Because Laughton knew no German, Brecht showed him the only English version he had—a rendering he claimed had been done by a "secretary."[21] It was almost certainly the work of Elisabeth Hauptmann, since no native speaker of English would have produced a translation so full of literally rendered German idioms and constructions. Furthermore, it resembles other translations she did for him.[22] Out of admiration for the work or for Brecht, Laughton hired two young writers he knew from MGM, Brainerd Duffield and Emerson Crocker, to produce a readable English version. Because of their limitations in the German language, they did not try to be slavishly literal. Crocker had never learned German, and Duffield knew it only from some courses at UCLA and from his work with refugee writers at MGM. With the secretary's version, they retired to Laughton's mountain cabin at Idyllwild, California in October 1944, where they largely ignored that rendering and, with the aid of dictionaries, worked instead from Brecht's original.

By late November they had finished a literate, competent translation.[23] Duffield claims that "Helli Brecht, Salka Viertel, and others read the completed translation and said we had done an excellent job of catching Brecht's flavor, even to the puns and slang."[24] A telegram from Laughton to Duffield soon after it was completed stated: "Can only say that most of the play reads as if it were originally written in English. Brecht as you know is delighted."[25] The two writers continued to revise their translation until shortly before Christmas, when Laughton paid them for their work and had their version mimeographed.[26]

Typically, Brecht's enthusiasm for this English translation faded quickly. Among other reasons, he apparently sensed an opportunity to have Laughton play the lead by engaging him personally as the writer and adaptor of *Galileo*. The temptation was more than an aspiring writer like Laughton could resist. Somewhat over two weeks after Laughton's telegram praising the Duffield/Crocker version, Brecht's journal notes: "Working now systematically with Laughton on the translation and stage version of *The Life of the Physicist Galileo*."[27]

A later journal entry underscores some of the problems in their earlier collaborations: "He [Laughton] translates sentence by sentence, initially writing down by hand my awkward translation, then his own. At the same time we make changes [in the text]. Galileo's speech in the first scene about this age causes the greatest difficulty, especially the sentence 'because it's that way, it doesn't stay that way.' Making associations in English is so very different, as is the mode of arguing and the humor. We attempt to replace the Biblical quality of 'For where Faith has dwelt 1000 years, now Doubt assumes its place,' with the blank verse 'blind placed faith deposed by healthy doubt!' which at least gives it a scholastic quality."[28]

To judge by this passage, Brecht's later claim that he scarcely knew a word of English (Laughton definitely knew no German) should not be taken at face value.[29] He knew a considerable amount by this time, but he called his own translations "awkward" because he had little confidence in them. By this time he could and did translate virtually every line for Laughton. From the same journal entry it appears that Laughton's English tended to be more florid than his own glass-and-steel German diction. Extant manuscripts from various stages of their collaboration show that Laughton, a proponent of the mighty phrase, tended to inflate or elevate the text, while Brecht attempted to reduce the language to its leanest form. Only gradually were they able to calibrate their linguistic sensitivities to a common mode of speech. The innocuous comment that they made "changes" in the text as they worked intimates what ultimately happened—in adapting the play for the American stage, they created a work quite different from the earlier German version.

Initially, and throughout much of their collaboration, they translated by acting out the lines on which they were working. First Brecht would speak a line in his own English, and sometimes even in German, to demonstrate how he wanted it played. Laughton would then imitate it by acting out in his own words what Brecht called the basic *gestus* implicit in each sentence. This process continued, with each taking turns acting and recording the words, until Brecht approved the results.[30] This method also helped them to avoid psychological probings of their text and its speakers, something which each detested. They were interested only in how lines "played," i.e., how they sounded and what they suggested by way of action. Brecht reports that Laughton was often brutally indifferent toward anything beyond a performing script, and that he refused to work on sections that Brecht hoped to translate and publish for their literary qualities.[31]

Laughton influenced more than the language; his physical presence defined the contours of the leading character in this version. Brecht praised the realist in Laughton that liked to "show things as they are,"[32] meaning the mass of contradictions in this complex character. He had discovered a flesh-and-blood Galileo who possessed the same enormous vitality, the same physical and moral cowardice, the same extreme sensuousness, and the same instinct for survival he originally envisioned for his character. Now he tried to have his art imitate life. To his new *Galileo* he gave a sharply delineated profile which the 1938-1939 version had lacked. Consistent with his normal practice, he undoubtedly had a specific actor in mind when he created the part. In 1942 or 1943 he told Oskar Homolka that he had written the role for him.[33] When the program announcing the Hollywood premiere of *Galileo* appeared in 1947, it claimed that "Brecht reveals that he fashioned his leading character with the English actor in mind." Both statements are probably valid, for they refer to different *Galileos*.

In Hollywood parlance, Brecht's play became a "vehicle" for Laughton. More accurately, Laughton became a vehicle for Brecht to use in re-structuring his play. The actor's known tendency in film studios to "construct" or "build up" his film roles as they were shot drove film directors to desperation. But precisely this "building up" of a role gave Brecht a far stronger and more effective character than he had first created.

In February 1945 Laughton interrupted their work to spend eight weeks making the film *Captain Kidd*.[34] This was to be the first of many hiatuses during more than three-and-one-half years of work on *Galileo*.

From late 1945 until 1947, American occupational officials and theater directors in Germany and Austria eager to stage Brecht's plays wrote him repeatedly for permission to perform them. Without exception, he refused; he had chosen to defer almost certain success in Europe for a more immediate goal expressed in a letter to Berlau dated August 1945: "I still hope to get *Galileo* on its legs in New York, which is important in many regards." Before leaving America, Brecht was determined to conquer Broadway, and *Galileo* was to be his weapon.

After Laughton completed *Captain Kidd*, they worked together briefly in May 1945.[1] The next extensive round of collaboration, however, began soon after Brecht returned from New York in July. The intensity of their work was evident from something that happened to Brecht's English. For the first time in four years, he appears to have broken through the language barrier. Letters to Berlau complain how strenuous his work with Laughton is, for it compels him to speak English all day.[2] More and more English phrases in Brecht's own hand that begin to appear in extant manuscripts reflect his growing confidence in using the written language. Monolingual Americans who met Brecht after 1945, usually in connection with *Galileo*, give convincing testimony of his increased facility with English. Without exception, the interview question as to how well Brecht spoke the language caused them to ponder—it never occurred to them that he had a problem.

Letters in July and August 1945 report daily work on *Galileo*. When Laughton stopped in late August to make the film *Because of Him*, Brecht wrote Berlau that "Laughton worked until Friday night on *Galileo*. His movie began Saturday morning." Another letter written while Laughton was shooting the film speaks of "a great deal of work. Laughton is continuing work on the play, in spite of his movie."[3]

A compulsive reviser like Brecht constantly looked for new materials to support his works in progress. A letter to Berlau in late July 1945 asks her to send him a copy of the "book of scientists that we bought" [in New York]. He was probably referring to *The Autobiography of Science*, a collection of biographical sketches and excerpts from the writings of great scientists that had appeared earlier that year.[4] When he left America in 1947, Brecht gave his personal copy of that book to Egon Breiner, who understood that he had consulted it in connection with *Galileo*. Contemporary history likewise furnished new material on August 6 and 9, 1945, when atomic bombs were dropped on Hiroshima and Nagasaki. Oddly, neither date merited an entry in Brecht's journal. The following month, however, he noted the reactions of the American people to the introduction of the atomic age and recorded Laughton's personal fears that it could harm their play on the birth of modern science by discrediting it: "The wrong kind of publicity, old man," he quotes Laughton as saying.[5]

In September Brecht wrote Berlau advising that he was sending a completed English version of *Galileo*. This would be one of several times he "finished" the play in the next two years, for the advent of the atomic age touched off another round of work.

Writing in 1947, Brecht insists that the debut of the atomic age changed the biography of the founder of modern physics overnight by putting his conflict with the authorities in sharper relief. Though he claims it did not necessitate a single change in the play's structure,[6] Brecht undertook a complete rewrite in order to sharpen the contours and condemn Galileo more explicitly as a traitor.

The 1938 version of the play had stopped short of condemnation by balancing Galileo's apparent betrayal of science against his cunning in outsmarting the Inquisition. Brecht had created what Bentley calls a "winning rogue."[7] The confrontation between Galileo and Andrea toward the end of the play is perhaps one of the most ironic Brecht ever wrote. At the same time Galileo seems to be condemning himself for recanting, he is also condemning his deeply ingrained "vice" of conducting scientific inquiry and writing down the results in secret. Showing Andrea his concealed manuscript of the *Discorsi*, he claims to live in "constant fear that these notes of mine might fall into the wrong hands and be read abroad in countries where sinful people are unable to appreciate the more convincing arguments of the Inquisition and . . . who might totally misunderstand the conclusions I've come to." This is typical of passages that expose Galileo's actions as an exercise in duplicity. The same double meaning underlies his words before he entrusts the manuscript to Andrea: "Any man with any sense would disown me. He would say no new science could spring from muddy waters of this kind—this man once had a reputation in the world . . . but he became a liar out of fear. Therefore, any words that he has written must be examined very carefully . . . the only proof is in the words themselves." Thereupon he gives Andrea the manuscript with the admonition: "Take care when you travel through Germany with the truth under your coat."[8]

In terms of dramatic effectiveness, Galileo's self-condemnation in this scene is not only ironic; his renewal of friendship with Andrea confirms that the former pupil understands and accepts his recantation as a means to dupe the Inquisition and go on producing. In late 1945 Brecht began to change this scene and eliminate what might be construed as a vindication of Galileo's actions. To make the connection between the seventeenth-century physicist and atomic scientists who participated in the Manhattan Project of the 1940's, he rewrote it in a tone void of irony. In the process, he encountered unexpected resistance from Laughton which helped to make the protagonist a far more complex dramatic figure than Brecht alone might have created.

Laughton's depression over his film career caused him to lean heavily on Brecht. Duffield claims he idolized the exile dramatist,[9] whom by now he called an "original genius" and "the greatest playwright of the century."[10] It appears that he depended increasingly on the *Galileo* collaboration for his own sense of survival as an actor and human being. But, contrary to Brecht, who wanted to condemn the cowardice behind Galileo's recantation, Laughton was in no mood to damn. To the dramatist's consternation, he tried to shape the role with an almost perverse sense of pride in Galileo's physical weakness. A journal entry reveals this conflict in their perceptions of the character:

"Laughton is perfectly ready to throw his figure to the wolves. He has a kind of devil in his head that has transformed scorn for himself into empty pride—pride in the greatness of his crime, etc. He insists on the complete portrayal of the decadence resulting from the crime that caused Galileo's negative traits to unfold. The only thing intact is the excellent brain, which functions emptily. . . . He underscores his concept clearly one evening when he crosses a picket line in front of the studio and is called a 'scab,' which hurts him deeply—he did not receive any applause. . . ."[11]

During a ten-day strike at Warner Brothers studios early in October, Laughton, who was still filming *Because of Him*, lived the role of an intellectual coward in Brecht's eyes by crossing the picket lines there. He saw his declining career in further jeopardy if he did not finish the film. According to Morton Wurtele, Brecht scolded him for it, though he soon dropped the matter and resumed work.

This unresolved conflict was not the only one to enrich the play's main character. Politics, or rather Laughton's indifference to them, moved the normally uncompromising Brecht to unaccustomed deference vis-à-vis his actor friend. The journal entry describing the actor's justification of Galileo's weaknesses mentions that "Laughton, driven by his theatrical instinct, constantly expunges the political elements in *Galileo*."

Among other things, Laughton deleted obvious references to contemporary history and politics. An allusion to this in Brecht's writings on *Galileo* suggests that it must have pained him: "Laughton, in a conspicuous and sometimes brutal manner, showed an indifference toward the 'book' that the playwright did not always have."[12] For example, the line "Take care when you travel through Germany with the truth under your coat," with its clear allusion to Nazi Germany, became simply "take care of yourself." The only references to contemporary history Laughton left intact were veiled hints of Brecht's own exile experience—Galileo's loss of certain privileges in exile; his retreat to a "country house" (Brecht spent more than five years of his exile in a Danish farm house); and parallels between dates three centuries apart, e.g., Galileo's popularity among the people in the carnival scene of 1632 that forces truth to go into exile.[13] Brecht accepted Laughton's "brutality" toward his text with surprising equanimity; in the end he acknowledged that this "stubborn sensitivity" had improved the play. A journal notation summarizing their most recent version praises Laughton's cuts: "often the changes made for aesthetic reasons strengthened it politically, and each time Laughton was very satisfied with them."[14]

The same entry describes a conflict within Laughton that affected the play's development. Although strongly anti-clerical, the actor feared public reaction if audiences construed the play as a statement against the Catholic Church. Observing this, Brecht wrote: "Laughton's fear at offending the public (usually in religious matters) often was at odds with his desire to correct the erroneous thinking of his viewers. Usually the latter wish triumphed." The version they did between late September and early December 1945 also shows this tension in at least one episode Laughton contributed which is not in earlier versions—the verbal duel in scene 6 where Cardinal Barberini and Galileo both quote Biblical proverbs to make their point. Here Laughton drew on the King James Bible both to defend the Church and to question its authority.

For the first time in their collaboration Brecht began to solicit help from others. Hans Reichenbach, a fellow émigré and professor of the philosophy of science at UCLA, devoted hours to advising him on scientific aspects of the work. Morton Wurtele, a graduate student in physics at UCLA who spent much of 1945-1946 living with the Brechts, recalls being asked to make suggestions on the text whenever Laughton came to the house. At Brecht's request, Wurtele also read certain scenes and wrote a brief essay in response to them.[15] Laughton, meanwhile, was testing audience response by reading it to anyone who would listen—soldiers in army hospitals, Hollywood friends, agents, and prospective backers. Their reactions also influenced what went into the text.

On December 1, 1945, a few friends of the two collaborators gathered to hear Laughton read what Brecht's journal calls the "complete American version of *Galileo*." A German poem in his journal of that date is labelled as the prologue to the play. Its opening line, which addresses the public as "Ladies and Gentlemen of Broadway," bares his undisguised determination to reach The Great White Way with *Galileo*. No one knew better than Brecht that it would be subject to further revisions. But for the first time he had a semi-finished product that seemed to have satisfied him.

An incident which occurred at this time betrays Brecht's firm conviction of his own greatness. After Brecht had enlisted him as an adviser to the play, Wurtele checked references to Galileo's life in the UCLA library. To his surprise, he discovered a five-act tragedy on the life of Galileo written by a German playwright named Arthur Trebitsch and published in Berlin in 1920. Certain that his discovery of *Galileo Galilei. Ein Trauerspiel in fünf Akten* done completely in blank verse would upset Brecht when he learned he had been anticipated, he checked it out in early December 1945 and gave it to him to read.[16] Brecht returned it unperturbed and without significant comment.[17] He was, after all, Bertolt Brecht.

A few days later the dramatist's journal states that Laughton had read the play to Orson Welles, who immediately agreed to direct it: "His attitude is pleasant, his remarks intelligent," Brecht observes.[18] Laughton now sent Brecht a contract calling for the actor to receive two-thirds of the royalties and Brecht one-third.[19] Brecht demurred, and, after discussions with the actor, signed a preliminary contract reversing the ratio[20] and agreeing that credit should read "*Galileo* by Bertolt Brecht, English Version by Charles Laughton." On January 7, 1946 they signed a final contract, and what had essentially become a new play began the long road toward a production Laughton's agent planned for that fall by Welles's Mercury Theatre.[21]

Early in 1946 *The New York Times* carried a theater column announcing that Laughton, along with Welles, was in New York. He would return, it said, to begin rehearsals of *Galileo* on August 1st for a fall production in "a translation arrived at between the actor and the author after eighteen months of struggle."[22] Laughton, however, was unaware of Brecht's penchant for complicating the simplest arrangements until he got his own way. It would be a year and a half and several rewrites later before *Galileo* reached the stage.

Among the arrangements he began to make for a fall production, Laughton telephoned Audrey Wood, a New York agent who represented Tennessee Williams, and asked her to listen to him read *Galileo*. Because she also represented a client named Barrie Stavis who had written a Galileo play entitled *Lamp at Midnight*, and because she knew Laughton wanted her to take Brecht's *Galileo*, Wood declined. But a long-distance scolding from Orson Welles changed her mind, and, after listening to Laughton give a midnight reading of the text, she wearily accepted it and dropped the Stavis play.[23] Laughton's attempts to locate a director in New York produced a compliment typical of the way he touted Brecht to American theater people. In a note to Alfred Lunt written in New York City sometime in early 1946, he asked him to read the play in manuscript and consider directing it: "The nearer the hour to rehearsal, the more scared I become of being directed in the play by anyone but an actor. It seems that Brecht is our man and is launching the theater back to us on the old Elizabethan terms."

Before he returned to the West Coast in mid-February 1946, Laughton completed arrangements for rehearsals to begin on August 1st. Shortly thereafter Orson Welles wrote Brecht. He agreed to direct the play if his own Mercury Productions presented it, and he asked for negotiation of a Dramatists Guild contract.[24] Brecht, however, wanted Laughton as co-producer. Laughton's agent then wrote Brecht that Welles was agreeable, though Welles would direct it himself.[25] Brecht, who was in New York, seemed satisfied, but, to gain assurance, he decided to visit Welles in Boston and see his production of Cole Porter's *Around the World*, which Welles had given as the reason he could not produce *Galileo* that spring. What he saw on stage convinced him that Welles was his man.

For a circus scene in this musical extravaganza, Welles had hired circus performers to train the chorus and the cast. Richard A. Wilson, Welles's partner in Mercury Productions, remembers being with Welles in the dressing room after a disastrous opening night in April 1946. A knock came, and a man entered. In a German accent he introduced himself as Bertolt Brecht and said concerning the circus scene: "This is the greatest thing I have seen in American theater. This is wonderful. This is what theater should be." With his sense of what constituted theater, Brecht realized that he was watching actors perform instead of act, which is one way of defining his style of epic acting. He told Welles he wanted him to direct *Galileo*, and that he was the only one he wanted.

In the course of several meetings Welles found that working with the dramatist was not easy. Writing to Laughton he complained that "Brecht was very, very tiresome today until (I'm sorry to say) I was stern and a trifle shitty. Then he behaved. I hate working like that."[26] Their last recorded meeting occurred in New York on May 5, 1946. In a diary entry two days later Reyher relates that Brecht "told me of Sunday lunch with Welles, now ready to direct *Galileo*."

Without Laughton's knowledge, Brecht persuaded Reyher to help him rewrite the text of *Galileo* which Laughton considered finished. A notation in Reyher's diary describes one session during the period of several weeks they worked on it: "last scene of *Galileo* continued. Jacked up Andrea, restored some of old version, and sharpened dialog. But particularly motivated the long delay of Andrea getting out with the book and made theater of the scene. Big speech still ahead."[27] Inevitably, much of their work involved discarding or reworking Laughton's English. Another of Reyher's diary entries speaks of his last working session with Brecht: "Tired, but at windup of Galileo. Smacked the final scene into good shape and fixed ending to cut out his original bad final scene. Rewrote the big speech and others so that they say his meaning clearly for the first time. Really did a job of work on the play, and repaired it greatly."[28]

After his return to California, Brecht began to have misgivings about Welles, who was still involved with *Around the World* and would not be available immediately. Among other things, there was disagreement over terms of the contract. Though Welles and his partner still wanted to produce *Galileo*,[29] Brecht began negotiating elsewhere. With Meta Reis, a young woman who handled literary matters for Berg-Allenberg, Laughton's agent, he tried to arrange a pre-production sale of the play to a studio.[30] This meant a film studio would advance the money for a stage production by purchasing the movie rights to it. Suddenly, and without warning, Brecht and Laughton culminated several weeks of negotiations with the film producer Mike Todd by signing an agreement which gave him an option to produce *Galileo* because he offered more attractive financial terms than Welles. Offended at Brecht's and Laughton's new offer to co-produce with Todd, Welles felt betrayed at losing a chance to produce what he believed could have been "one of the greatest productions in contemporary theater."[31]

In the meantime, Brecht embarked on another re-write of *Galileo* with Laughton prompted by Reyher's hand in the text. Writing to Reyher in mid-July, he alludes to the extensive changes they have made:

"The notes with your objections and improvements have plunged me into new work with Laughton, which we just finished today. As soon as copies are made, the first one will go to you. Laughton considered every comma-suggestion thoroughly and was stimulated by them, with increasing respect. He's a great worker, so he knew how to appreciate your help. It proved to be tremendous. In the meantime we've signed with Mike Todd for the production. 'That's protection,' Laughton said, 'that's what you need.' We still don't have a director. [Elia] Kazan would like to do it and spoke intelligently about it (what pleases me most of all was his assertion that he did not know how to do such a play), but he cannot before November because of film commitments."

Because of his involvement in *Galileo* since its inception in Denmark in 1938, not to mention his collaboration a few months earlier, the version that reached Reyher early in August disturbed him. Failing to understand that everything Brecht wrote was tentative, he saw only that little remained of his own contributions. Writing to his dramatist friend, he reacts to the radical changes he has discovered:

"I think you and Laughton have gone mad with overwork and the California climate. . . . I feel the presence of another influence. I pass over our efforts here, because virtually nothing of them is left. . . . Much wit, splendor, modernity, characterization, magnificent ease of its flow have dribbled out of it. I can't understand it. . . . I can only say, refer to the German, refer to Laughton's earlier drafts. But really I don't know what to say."[32]

Reyher was at least partially right about the presence of "another influence." Brecht and Laughton had been testing *Galileo* on audiences and individual listeners and readers, and whatever did not read well, they changed. Brecht, too, was consulting others on the text when Laughton was not available. Wurtele and Replansky assisted him in the summer of 1946, and in the following twelve months the list of collaborators grew.

Brecht's letters to Reyher in the summer of 1946 tell of his search for a director. After mentioning Elia Kazan and Vincent Sherman, he asks for Reyher's opinion of Michael Gordon and Alfred Lunt. Finally, in a letter written in response to Reyher's critique, he announces that he thinks he has found his man: Joseph Losey.[33] Further, several meetings with Mike Todd convinced him that Todd lacked the understanding to produce *Galileo* as he wanted it done. Todd, for example, told him that he planned to use Renaissance furniture and sets from a Hollywood studio for it.[34] By the end of the summer Todd, whose interest diminished further after he read the play, dropped all plans for a production, and Laughton and Brecht were again without a producer.

In New York during September, Laughton searched for someone to replace Todd while Brecht tried to placate Reyher's resentment over what that writer construed as Laughton's negative influence on *Galileo*. According to Reyher's journal of September 29th, Brecht brought the three of them together in Reyher's apartment in the Chelsea Hotel, where they struck a truce. Friends and relatives remember seeing the three of them, or sometimes only Brecht and Reyher, working on *Galileo* during the next two months.[35]

The frequency of meetings indicates that they revised extensively. Several of Reyher's texts survived this period of collaboration. One is a long speech from the final scene of the 1939 version which Brecht asked him to render in English, though the playwright had dropped it once before. A second is Reyher's own adaptation of the carnival scene (Scene 9), which Brecht asked him to write in his own style after giving him the basic idea. The playwright had no intention of using this rendition. In his eyes, Reyher and other collaborators were furnishing him material to which he could react, not finished copy. Reyher did not understand that this compulsive reviser viewed whatever others wrote as building blocks in a structure he would tear down and rebuild again in a different shape.

Work on *Galileo* in New York that autumn extended beyond textual revision. Looking forward to a performance, Brecht and Laughton began to gather materials for costumes, scenes, and the slide projections that often accompanied his stagings. Duffield, whom Laughton tried to enlist at this time for the role of Ludovico, reports that Brecht fixed on a painting they saw in New York's Metropolitan Museum of Art as the model for this character—Bronzino's "Portrait of a Young Man," an arrogant figure typical of young noblemen at the court of the Medici. Laughton, he states, gave him a color print of this picture as an inducement to take the part. Brecht's strong visual orientation often influenced his writings; it is not unreasonable to assume that Ludovico's emergence in the American version of the play as a stronger, more distasteful character sprang in part from Brecht's confrontation with this Renaissance painting.

Brecht and Laughton also worked in the New York Public Library, poring over books on costumes and Renaissance or late medieval art. Losey remembers that the boy playing the young Medici prince in their production was dressed in a costume "copied from a Renaissance portrait of a tailor," while "many of the other costumes were Brueghel, particularly in the Carnival scene."[36] Most of these, as well as slide projections of original drawings by Michelangelo, Leonardo da Vinci, Jacques Callot, and Galileo himself that they used in the Hollywood and New York productions came from books they saw in the New York Public Library during autumn 1946.

By now Brecht had settled on Losey to direct *Galileo*. Losey, who had met Brecht in Russia in 1935 and again in New York in 1936, had good left-wing political credentials, which were reinforced by affinities in their views on theater evident from Losey's productions of The Federal Theater Project's "Living Newspaper" in 1936.

In addition to discussing plans for *Galileo* during these months, Brecht, Laughton, and Losey, who was also in New York, began some preliminary casting. Eda Reiss Merin, who would play Mrs. Sarti in the Hollywood production the following summer, recalls being summoned to Laughton's hotel by Brecht. The dramatist knew her from a role she had played in his production of *Master Race* the previous year. Brecht, Losey, and Laughton interviewed her about the play, which she had read the night before, and Brecht concluded by saying he wanted her for the part.[37]

In the latter half of October, Brecht received a letter from Laughton's agent announcing that because of nebulous prospects for an immediate performance of *Galileo*, Laughton had accepted an offer to appear in a forthcoming Hitchcock-Selznick film, *The Paradine Case*.[38] In Laughton's name, he offered Brecht $5,000 "which he would like to give you to defray part of the cost to you which the possible delay may occasion." There is no record whether Brecht accepted the money, but the delay apparently did not diminish his hopes. In New York, and later in Los Angeles, they continued revising *Galileo* until Laughton began work on the film.

A. PREPARATION FOR PRODUCTION: APRIL-JULY 1947

Writing to Reyher about *Galileo* in mid-March 1947, Brecht states that "Laughton will finish shooting [*The Big Clock*] in mid-April. It's unclear what will happen then. Perhaps you should call Losey (in Ruth's apartment). He knows more than I do." Losey, who was in New York directing Arnold Sundgaard's *The Great Campaign*, deserves almost sole credit for arranging the circumstances and bringing together the people who made possible an American production of this play which absorbed Brecht completely from mid-April to early August.

While directing *The Great Campaign*, Losey told its producer T. Edward Hambleton, a philanthropic young man with the means and the interest to finance good theatrical productions, about *Galileo* and encouraged him to back it. In Hollywood that spring, John Houseman and Norman Lloyd had announced their intention to open "Pelican Productions," a small company designed to give Los Angeles its own legitimate theater fare. Hambleton knew Houseman, and, when he heard this, he agreed, at Losey's urging, to finance half the production costs of *Galileo* in the small, recently renovated Coronet Theater on La Cienega Boulevard in Hollywood if Laughton would put up the other half.

After Laughton finished shooting *The Big Clock* in mid-April 1947, he went back to work on *Galileo*. In the meantime Losey had flown to the West Coast with Hambleton to begin production arrangements. On April 27th he wrote Reyher, stating that Brecht and Laughton were again revising the script, and that a production was now scheduled for the summer: "*Galileo* proceeds pretty well. Brecht in fine spirits. They seem to have been doing some constructive work on the script for a change. The stairway scene is back in and improved. The Ludovico-Galileo conflict scene (Sc. 8) is greatly bettered. . . . I'd like very much if you could see it before it was entirely finished. We start preparations now . . . and start rehearsals end of May, open July 1."

When Hambleton began negotiating a contract with Brecht sometime late in April, he discovered how obdurate the playwright could be. Not knowing Brecht's thinking, he had his lawyers ask for exclusive world production rights. Brecht declined with a statement that impressed Hambleton with its finality: "I've held out against Hitler, and I'm not going to give in to you."[1] Hambleton, whom Brecht came to admire greatly in the ensuing months, wisely compromised. The

Dramatists Guild production contract he finally signed with Brecht and Laughton was limited to American productions only.[2]

With the attention to detail that marked their efforts throughout the production, Brecht and Laughton began casting sometime in May. Except for the major roles, they selected young, relatively inexperienced actors and actresses in a cast that ultimately reached fifty persons. Several came from the Actors Lab in Hollywood, which had recently been forced to close; others came from the film world; still others were Laughton's acquaintances. Brecht's preference for unspoiled, teachable younger people who had not achieved stardom dictated the selection of so many unknown names; but so did financial considerations. Losey reports that Laughton and Hambleton each put up $25,000 for the production. Given the huge cast, a projected four-week run, and a 260-seat theater, it was impossible to pay high salaries. Five seasoned actors, among them Laughton, received $40 a week for rehearsals and performance. Three other younger principals received $20 a week,[3] while other actors received even less.

When Losey wrote Reyher that the play would open on July 1st, he and Hambleton had assumed it would inaugurate the Pelican Productions season. Because Houseman and his associates realized that *Galileo* was somewhat bold, non-conventional theater fare for American audiences, they selected instead Thornton Wilder's *The Skin of Our Teeth* for their opener, with *Galileo* to follow.[4] In each play they allowed the playwright to recommend staging or to stage it according to his wishes.

When rehearsals officially began on June 24th, Losey was the director in name, but it soon became apparent to the cast and the producers that Brecht, with assistance from Laughton, was really directing, and that Losey functioned as his mouthpiece. One cast member, Stephen Brown, recalls that "Brecht and Charles were the real directors, and everybody in the cast knew it," while Houseman confirms that "Joe was to be the director of this, which really meant . . . that actually Brecht would produce and direct himself with aid from Charles Laughton."[5] When asked if he did not feel redundant in this role, Losey replied, "I'm learning."[6] Because he was willing to learn, Losey qualified as Brecht's kind of director. He seems to have been one of the rare theater and film people in America who recognized Brecht's genius at once and at least partially understood him.

Brecht in turn had confidence in Losey. This director knew American theater, and Brecht generally accepted his counsel on the possibilities and limitations of that institution. He also listened to Losey's personnel recommendations. He agreed, for example, to use Robert Davison, who had done the sets and costumes for Losey in *The Great*

Campaign, and Anna Sokolow, his choreographer for the same show. Davison quickly passed muster by recognizing that Brecht was the *de facto* producer/director and by raising no objection when Weigel was given a dominant hand in making the costumes. Sokolow, however, exhibited too much independence and too little willingness to do things Brecht's way. Norman Lloyd remembers how Brecht stopped her and said: "We want none of your tawdry Broadway dances in the production." Unwilling to submit to his iron rule, she quit, and Brecht replaced her with Lotte Goslar, a talented émigré mime-dancer whose dance pantomimes he had seen at the Turnabout Theater a few blocks away. In part because Goslar and Brecht agreed on the matter of avoiding excessive emotion in narrative technique, and in part because of her European background, Brecht seemed satisfied and seldom interfered with her work.

Considering the playwright's normal behavior in rehearsals, he and Losey worked together with unusual harmony. Whether premeditated or not, Brecht had only two rows with Losey during rehearsals, the number he claims he allowed himself in a production. In the first, Brecht provoked the director to a point where Losey threw his script at him and announced he was quitting. Losey recalls going home and doing some gardening: "then the phone rang. It was Charles Laughton saying 'Please come back.' 'I will,' I said, 'if Brecht apologizes to me.' Laughton hung up, and after a while he called back saying, 'Brecht says please come back, and he also says you should know Brecht never apologizes.' I went back, and nothing more was ever said about the row."[7] The second altercation occurred at 4 o'clock in the morning shortly before the opening when they disagreed over painting the scenery a certain color. This, too, was quickly forgotten. In general, according to Losey, Brecht behaved himself better during *Galileo* than he normally did, in large degree because of Losey's forbearance and willingness to tolerate his demands.

"Better," however, was far from model behavior. Hambleton recalls how Brecht "would snap back in his usual fashion at people involved in the production end of the play. For instance, he would shout about the primitive, ill-painted stage properties." Hambleton erroneously attributed this to the exile's frustration over his failure in Hollywood. Houseman perceived another reason—his insistence on excellence. He recalls that Brecht "did a great deal of screaming throughout rehearsals about the costumes, about the scenery, and about everything . . . but it was all for the good of the show. It was not personal malice. It was simply tremendous impatience when anything was less than he wanted it to be."[8]

Most of Brecht's criticism was directed toward those involved with production matters. Members of the cast, who in large measure were spared his anger, remember him as a perfectionist at work. Stephen Brown reports that Brecht "never criticized, but he demanded perfection. He always felt things could be better." They soon realized that Brechtian direction meant constant experimentation, and that he was trying to do something vastly different from what they were accustomed to in American theater. Frances Heflin, the sister of the film star Van Heflin, remembers that most of the cast did not understand the play, nor did they grasp Brecht's style of acting. Repeatedly Brecht explained he did not want sentimentality in the play, but intelligent playing, and he stated repeatedly that the actors were not to impose private or personal feelings on the character they were representing. This ran counter to the Stanislavsky-oriented "method acting," which called for "living" the character. Generally Brecht exercised restraint when lecturing the players on his own method of "epic" acting, but periodically he lost his patience. In scene 5, a group of monks gathered at the Collegium Romanum, awaiting the Church's verdict on Galileo, mock his teachings by feigning dizziness and pretending to fall off the rapidly moving globe. Losey remembers how the players in this scene asked him a question basic to their style of playing: "What's our motivation?" Brecht had Losey caustically ask them: "What's the motivation of a tightrope walker not to fall off the high wire?" Repeatedly he had to steer his cast members away from understanding their roles in psychological terms and toward a type of presentation that eschewed psychology and stressed "demonstration" of the character.

At least one actress profitted from Brecht's instruction and was grateful to him for it. Eda Reiss Merin, who played Mrs. Sarti, walked out after Losey continued to find fault with the way she played her part. Brecht followed and asked her to stay, saying his wife would help her to understand how to play it. Merin recalls how Weigel asked if she could speak a foreign language or knew any dialects. Hearing that she could do a Brooklyn Jewish accent, she had her speak the part that way. For the first time, Merin claims, she understood the meaning of "estrangement" and was able to get a fresh look at the part. Brecht heard and approved her after this episode, and she stayed.[9] She is typical of actors and actresses in the production who, retrospectively, felt privileged to have worked with Brecht and Laughton. Their dedication to the two and to the production was also evident in the time they spent rehearsing. Actors Equity allowed only four weeks of rehearsals; many of them began to rehearse without pay much earlier.[10]

Early in production, Brecht reverted to a habit he had acquired in Europe that helped him to visualize how he wanted various scenes to be staged. He convinced Laughton that they needed an artist to make

sketches portraying the action. Laughton agreed, and on Losey's recommendation they engaged John Hubley, an artist who had worked at
Walt Disney studios and whom Losey had already used on one of his
productions. Brecht's visually oriented imagination demanded the
kind of sketches that Hubley later characterized as "book illustrations."[11] The playwright would explain each scene and designate a decisive moment that he wanted crystallized in a sketch. From these
sketches, which were inspired by what Hubley called Brecht's "tableau
sense," the playwright would move to staging. If he did not like one,
he asked Hubley to redo it. Generally Brecht was satisfied with Hubley's drawings, but Laughton had reservations. The actor, Hubley recalls, did not understand them, and it led to conflict with Brecht. The
playwright himself later admitted that they "turned out rather wick-
edly; Laughton used them, but cautiously."[12]

The production profited directly in another way from Hubley's visual sensibilities. Scene 11 depicts Galileo's old friend Barberini, now
Pope Urban VIII, being robed for a conclave while the Inquisitor tries
to persuade him that Galileo must be shown the Inquisition's instru-
ments of torture. As Barberini the man disappears beneath the robes of
the office, he gradually acquiesces. In discussing how to stage this
scene, Hubley insisted that it needed to be played "straight out" to the
audience. His suggestion for placing the characters was also followed,
and the result was one of the most effective scenes in the play.

Throughout exile Brecht had complained of how it handicapped
him to write without seeing his plays performed on a stage. Because
his imagination responded strongly to visual stimuli, he traditionally
used rehearsals as an opportunity to rewrite his plays, much to the
dismay of actors who found themselves memorizing new lines for
a given scene a half dozen times before a play opened. *Galileo* was
no exception, and the actors experienced considerable frustration.
Stephen Brown, who played the street singer in scene 9, recalls that
Brecht went on changing the lyrics in this scene up to the day before
they opened. This was an extreme case, but it was not an exception.
Losey was assisting Brecht and Laughton in re-writing efforts that
continued throughout rehearsals. Some of their changes were minor,
and Laughton, who spoke most of these new lines, appeared quite
willing to make them. But problems with two scenes, the ninth and the
thirteenth, demonstrated that Brecht's theories of epic theater were
not so much a fixed set of rules as an ongoing experimental search for
what worked to make effective theater.

The Carnival scene (scene 9), which had been inspired by paintings
of Pieter Brueghel the Elder, had plagued the dramatist since its inception. In 1947, Brecht was still struggling to find an adequate version of

what had been a very brief scene in the original. Because of his dissatisfaction with it in 1944, Brecht instructed Laughton not to have
Duffield and Crocker translate it at all in their version. Brecht himself
revised it several times, and he had had Reyher do an original re-write
sometime in 1946. But the dramatist knew what was "right" for his
play, and he had still not found it.

Sometime in early 1947, Laughton introduced Brecht to Abe Burrows, a writer known for his nationwide weekly radio show "Duffy's
Tavern." When Brecht learned from Laughton that Burrows had a
knack for writing catchy song texts, he enlisted him to do a version of
the street singer's ballad that comprises the bulk of the scene. After
Brecht explained what he wanted, Burrows asked about the singer's
motivation, a question that stamped him as a Stanislavsky disciple.
The ensuing dialogue, as Burrows reconstructs it, says little about the
scene and much about Brecht's opposition to conventional theater:

> *Burrows*: Tell me, Bert, how does this street singer feel about
> Galileo?
> *Brecht*: He feels nothing.
> *Burrows*: (hesitantly) I mean . . . is he praising Galileo?
> *Brecht*: No.
> *Burrows*: Is he against Galileo?
> *Brecht*: No.
> *Burrows*: What do the pamphlets that he's selling say about
> Galileo?
> *Brecht*: They just tell about him.
> *Burrows*: (puzzled) Are they for him or against him?
> *Brecht*: It doesn't matter.
> *Burrows*: Well, just tell me one thing, Bert. Why is the man
> singing a song?
> *Brecht*: Because I want him to.[13]

Despite getting nowhere with his questions, Burrows went to work
with Hanns Eisler, who was composing the music, and wrote several
versions of the street singer's ballad. But, for whatever reasons, Brecht
never used them.

Sometime during rehearsal, Laughton introduced Brecht to a young
friend and poet named Albert Brush, whom they also engaged to write
the ballad for this ninth scene and to translate the lyric passages preceding other scenes. Losey considered Brush a "terrible poet," but apparently Brush distinguished himself by his willingness to listen to and
to do exactly what Brecht said. The playwright later told Bentley that
he himself had written the doggerel verse preceding each scene, which
suggests that Brush had worked under his close supervision. The

printed program contains a notation that the lyrics were "adapted by Albert Brush," a statement that fails to acknowledge Brecht's hand, the unused lyrics by Burrows and Reyher, the closing lines that Barbara Brecht and Naomi Replansky contributed to the play, or others written by Joseph Losey and George Tabori. The final version, and to some degree nearly every play Brecht wrote, was like a tapestry created by one master who allowed several assistants to weave in threads and even small scenes, but who controlled the overall design himself.

Just as he had struggled to find the right lyrics, Brecht found that his attempts to stage the street singer's scene also caused him unusual difficulties. His friend Walter Benjamin, who read the play shortly after it was first written in 1938, had observed that in *Galileo* the hero was the people. More than any single scene, this one showing the popular effect of Galileo's teachings in the marketplace illustrates the correctness of that dictum. But Brecht seemed unable to find a satisfactory concept for staging the scene. According to rehearsal schedules for the last three-and-one-half weeks before the play opened, this scene was rehearsed twice as much as any other. Goslar, who worked closely with Brecht on the dancing in it, claims that he was critical of his own solutions and unsuccessfully changed the scene so often that he finally turned much of it over to Laughton for staging. His own remarks in his essay "Building Up of a Role" corroborate her recollection, for Brecht admits that "Laughton participated most strongly in this scene," and as an example cites Laughton's idea to have the various guilds toss an effigy of the cardinal in the air.[14] Laughton himself, in an interview published in the *Los Angeles Times* ten days before the opening, singled out this scene as one of his favorites when he remarked that this All Fools' Day Carnival "made fun of things as they are," which he felt was the chief function of theater.[15] But Brecht did not surrender control over the scene. Among other things, he got rid of the trained tenor who had been cast as the street singer and substituted Stephen Brown, who had once sung in vaudeville. Through Laughton, Brecht communicated that he wanted a "ragged quality" about the singing, and that it made no difference if the ballad was out of Brown's range.[16]

Losey reports that during rehearsals the final scene (scene 13) in which Galileo figuratively tears open his breast to his pupil Andrea came to be called "the pelican scene" after that bird's fabled manner of nourishing its young. This scene created enough problems so that Brecht, Laughton, and Losey all felt the scene was unsatisfactory when the play opened. Though they continued to rewrite it up to the opening, the difficulty was not their ability to write, but a discrepancy be-

tween Brecht's intentions and Laughton's perceptions. The playwright
wanted an unequivocal damnation of Galileo that exposed the mag-
nitude of his criminality in having recanted when he knew his discoveries were true. Brecht kept rewriting to adjust the text accordingly. He was banking on Laughton's sense of guilt as well as his lack
of physical and moral courage generally to lend realism to his portrayal of Galileo. But Laughton seemed unable to play the role that
way, perhaps because portraying someone else's guilt on the stage
would have come too close to tearing open his own breast, or perhaps
because he realized that, in dramatic terms, nothing in the play justified the savage condemnation that Brecht now wanted.

The result was a psychological tug-of-war between Brecht and this
fearful, vain actor. During rehearsals, Laughton had agreed on almost
every aspect of the play and on the character of Galileo, sometimes
outdoing Brecht in vehemence of portrayal. Repeatedly the dramatist
had to tone down his tendency to overemphasize anti-clerical elements
implicit in the play. Generally, Brecht applauded the way Laughton in
the early scenes built up the role to make Galileo an iconoclast, and he
admired the actor's instinct for intensifying the social criticism inherent in the play. Brecht's later essay on this drama sounds as though
they intuitively understood each other's purposes and worked in complete harmony until the end. But when they reached the point in
Galileo's self-denunciation in scene 13 where he says to Andrea:
"Then welcome to my gutter, dear colleague in science and brother in
treason," they parted company.

Brecht comments that "this was one of the few passages with which
Laughton had difficulty. He doubted that the viewer would grasp the
sense, not to mention that the words here are inconsistent with
Galileo's otherwise purely logical vocabulary."[17] But Laughton's difficulty had little to do with vocabulary. Up to this point he had taken
almost malicious delight in exposing Galileo's physical cowardice. To
damn that cowardice would have been to destroy a monument he had
built up, a monument to a great man and to his weaknesses. Apparently Laughton wanted to create sympathy, or at the very least understanding, for the protagonist's frailties. This was the way he played his
role in this crucial scene, and quite certainly it was the way he perceived it. When Laughton appeared in scene 12 after the recantation,
Brecht remarks that he made Galileo seem infantile, like a grinning
boy who had wet his pants.[18] But the embarrassed grin of such a boy
could also be interpreted as a plea for sympathy. Laughton, in any
case, did not see it as grounds for damnation, and he refused to play
the following scene that way.

A *Los Angeles Times* story on Laughton published on July 20,

1947, cites the actor's views: "What we are doing in this play," he
states, "is to bring that mysterious personage who works in labora-
tories out into the spotlight. . . . Our play is historical of course, but it
is still the impression of the physicist at work. Galileo is responsible
for many inventions in his time. He even forecast the atomic age in
some of his discoveries and pronouncements—his theory that all
things moved in the celestial and terrestrial sphere. Carried to the ultimate, this defines atomic action, and while he had no glimmer of
what we know now in the age in which he lived, there is still a relationship." But Laughton mentions nothing about an indictment of
modern atomic scientists or a condemnation of the man Brecht viewed
as the father of modern physics. Basically he did not share Brecht's
post-1945 perception of the play's protagonist as a traitor. Brecht
himself ascribed Laughton's interpretation and portrayal of Galileo to
a lack of ideological understanding. In his own view, Galileo was an
opportunist. Laughton, he wrote, was unable to grasp the concept that
when one condemns those who accept the fruits of opportunism, one
must likewise condemn the opportunist.[19]

The fact that Laughton could play the part as he did suggests that
the text itself allows an anti-Brechtian interpretation. The dramatist
had created a drama and a protagonist too complex for the relatively
simple ideological message that he wished to send. Laughton might
have contravened Brecht's wishes, but he did not subvert his text. He
played the part as he saw it emerge there. Had he wanted to change the
role significantly, Brecht would have to have written an altogether
different play. Several years later, Brecht tried to preclude the kind of
misinterpretation he thought Laughton had given *Galileo* by reworking the play for a production in East Berlin. Again he failed. There,
too, the burden to demonstrate Galileo's culpability fell on the actor
who portrayed him, for, in spite of Brecht's revisions, the text was still
richly ambiguous. Ernst Busch, a politically conscious Marxist chosen
for the role, also resisted Brecht's urgings to have him condemn
Galileo. In spite of, or perhaps because of, his ideological understanding, Busch viewed Galileo's recantation as a positive accomplishment
and played the role accordingly.[20] An East German critic who saw him
in that production shared Busch's perceptions of the role in Brecht's
play. He asked how we are supposed to hate or condemn a man who
had weakened his eyes at the telescope and who had now almost gone
blind working illegally to copy a book extremely useful to mankind;
one whose quest for truth had driven him into increasingly dangerous
situations; and one who was now being held prisoner while being
spied upon by a stupid and shrewish daughter.[21] Unwittingly, Brecht

had created a character that liberated itself from his ideological intentions. Both Laughton and Busch had sensed something the playwright refused to accept.

A handsome playbill announcing the "world premiere" of *Galileo* on July 24, 1947, erred on two counts. Technically it was a world premiere of only this English version, since a German language production of the 1938-1939 *Galileo* had taken place in the Zürich Schauspielhaus in September 1943. Nor did the play open on July 24th. A printed note clipped to the playbill a week before opening announced a postponement until July 30th because of "tremendous detail . . . involved in preparing *Galileo* with its cast of 50; 13 scenes; 90 costumes; and so forth." The final three words euphemistically conceal Brecht's involvement in details of the production.

On July 15th, Kate Drain Lawson, Houseman's executive director in the Coronet Theater, sent Houseman a memo saying that Brecht's continuous alterations of costumes, culminating in fourteen changes on July 9th, had caused an immense amount of extra work in the costume shop, and that two extra people had had to be hired to keep up. Further, Brecht had made twenty additions to the props and one addition to and one major alteration in the set during this time. Now Lawson had received plans for the ballad singer's wife's costume, and she was distressed to hear that there also might be an additional child. Brecht was experimenting and changing without regard for deadlines or expenses.

Brecht's essay on *Galileo* describes in detail how meticulously he and Laughton worked out the sets. One reviewer of the premiere associated them with the Constructivist stage of Soviet Russia in the twenties.[22] For American audiences the scenery appeared somewhat sparse. Each scene was to have its own basic color transmitted through the sets and the costumes. Galileo's social ascent, for example, was to be reflected by making the colors of each scene progressively brighter, culminating in the carnival scene on All Fools' Day, which was to be an explosion of color. The following ones were to show Galileo descending into dull or gray colors symbolic of his fall. The young Ludovico's peacock-blue costume in the first scene, which Herbert Anderson remembers as the most elaborate in the production, was made of a heavy fabric by Laughton's personal tailor. It contrasted starkly with the basic white, gray, and yellow of the first scene that highlighted Galileo's modest scholarly surroundings.

Brecht was dictatorial on these details. In the matter of props he took similar pains. Wurtele, the production's "scientific adviser," attended many rehearsals to insure that the scientific experiments were plausible. It was also his task to instruct Laughton on the use of the props, which, Wurtele reports, the actor did with remarkable ease for someone without training.

Opening-night audiences never would have guessed from the relative simplicity of the costumes how carefully they had been selected and designed from Renaissance prints. Not only were they to give the appearance of having been worn; they were designed to emphasize class differences that otherwise might not be obvious to modern viewers. Weigel personally sewed many of the costumes and generally oversaw the numerous changes in them that threatened to run far over the alloted budget. But 90 costumes were still beyond the capacity of all the hired costume makers and Weigel's volunteer efforts. Brecht's attention to detail had shortened by eight days a production that was scheduled to play only until August 17th.

The collaboration of two personalities like Brecht and Laughton generated an inevitable amount of theater lore. *The Hollywood Reporter* informed its readers that Brecht had been toiling on the play for ten years,[23] an exaggeration in the same category with newspaper statements that this was Laughton's first appearance in the theater in fifteen years (actually it was thirteen years).[24] But an anecdote related in 1967 by the actress Shelley Winters has the faint ring of truth to it, though there is nothing to confirm it. A fan and pupil of Charles Laughton, this young actress had wanted to play in *Galileo*, but her studio would not allow it. Because she was under the impression that Laughton had written *Galileo*, she attended several rehearsals. At one of them she noticed a "funny little man" in the theater who seemed lonely, and they struck up a conversation. Not knowing who Brecht was, Winters invited him home to meet her parents (she remembers it was a Jewish holiday), and he came. Her father took him to the park to play cards with his friends, and when she finally returned to the theater alone, everyone was looking for the playwright. At home that evening, her mother commented, "That Mr. Brecht is a very nice man." "Did you ask him what he does?" questioned Winters, who still had no idea that he was the dramatist. Her mother answered, "Yes, he makes costume jewelry. He said that back in Germany he made 'jewels for the poor people.' " Winters claims it was years later, after seeing pictures of Brecht in newspapers, that she recognized him as the little "jewel-maker" she had taken home.[25]

Brainerd Duffield also recalls an anecdote dealing with Orson Welles, with whom he was working on a screenplay for *Macbeth* at the time *Galileo* opened. Welles, who had not forgotten Laughton's nasty letter when he withdrew production rights to the play in 1946, read the *Los Angeles Times* interview with Laughton published just before the play opened. In it, Laughton indicated that he himself had done the English adaptation of the play. Welles knew of the Brainerd Duffield translation, and he was furious that Duffield was not mentioned. After a few drinks, he composed a telegram berating Laughton's integrity. Knowing of the actor's severe fright before going on stage, he calculated to have it arrive on opening night a few minutes before curtain time. Whether the telegram was ever sent is not known, but Duffield says he avoided the Coronet Theater and Laughton for a long time afterward.

Despite Brecht's heavy involvement in *Galileo*, he took time during the last weeks of rehearsal to write a brief piece for a member of the production staff that was unusual in its concept and contents—a story outline for a pantomime. Lotte Goslar recalls that one day at rehearsal Brecht handed her a single typewritten sheet and said, "Here's something you might be able to use." Beneath Brecht's handwritten notation, "subject for a pantomime," follows a story outline entitled "From Circus Life." It describes a "terrible scene" in a circus when a clown inadvertently finds himself trapped in a lion's cage. The clown attempts to frighten the lion, but soon something curious happens— the lion hypnotizes him with its gaze and gradually induces him to perform the very tricks the trained lion had once done. The transformation of man into beast is so complete that when the lion turns its gaze from the clown for a moment, the clown springs on it. Disregarding attempts by attendants to divert him with pistol shots and iron hooks, he proceeds to bite the lion to death.

Exactly what moved Brecht to write this is not clear. One is reminded of his early fascination with the transmutability of human personality that he explored in *A Man's a Man* and certain short stories. In later years, he was fond of saying that in a capitalistic society, if one fights a tiger, one becomes a tiger, i.e., that one assumes the characteristics of one's oppressors.[26] Goslar, who was flattered by Brecht's unpretentious kindness in writing this for her, viewed the outline as a "silent script" comparable to Beckett's "Scenes Without Words." In 1973 she staged a 15-minute production of the pantomime, but Brecht's text that inspired it is still unpublished today.

B. The Performance

When *Galileo* opened on July 30, 1947, in what the *Los Angeles News* called a "gala premiere," it was the talk of Hollywood. Laughton's return to the legitimate stage had attracted a wide circle of film personalities who had heard him read a play he had touted as one of the great dramas of the century. Brecht, too, had a following. Houseman recalls that "the town was filled with European émigrés at that time who had a cult of Brecht and had had no chance to see any recent Brecht plays, so that we were completely sold out even before we opened."[27] The playbill advertising *Galileo* announced that after its premiere at the Coronet Theater, T. Edward Hambleton "will bring the play to Broadway in the fall, thus making one of the rare instances when important theatrical fare has originated in this cinema community." These and other factors transformed the opening into an artistic and social event for Hollywood's glamour set.

The list of first-nighters alone insured the play of celebrity success. Gossip columns reported the names of Charlie Chaplin, Charles Boyer, Ingrid Bergman, Anthony Quinn, Van Heflin, John Garfield, Gene Kelly, Sydney Greenstreet, Richard Conte, Howard da Silva, Sam Wanamaker, David Loew, Lewis Milestone, and Frank Lloyd Wright among those attending. *Variety* caught the play's snob appeal in a note on August 1st that began "Turn out for the Theatah: Cinema Intelligentsia and just plain folks flocked to the Coronet theater Wednesday night to see Charles Laughton do his stuff as Galileo." In the course of seventeen performances many of the seats, which ranged in price from $1.20 to $3.60, were occupied by names prominent in the screen world, and every performance played to standing room only crowds. Worry over his return to the theater made Laughton almost hysterical with fear. Norman Lloyd recalls how, on opening night, the actor agonized over the possibility of a terrible setback to his career if the play failed. Brecht later reported that to make the illustrious first-night audience comfortable in the summer heat, Laughton "insisted that trucks full of ice blocks should be parked against the theater and the fans turned on 'so that the audience can think' " (*GW* XVII, 1126).

Galileo opened to reviews that ranged from intelligent and/or enthusiastic to vicious and obtuse. Contrary to Brecht's later recollection,[28] all the important reviewers did not attack the play. Several were unusually sympathetic and positive. A sensitive review by Virginia Wright in the *Los Angeles Daily News* of July 31st understood precisely the critique of contemporary science inherent in the play and remarked that it was made more effective by "lack of emphasis on period trappings." She acclaims Laughton's acting as honest and intelligent, and she comments on a stage that contained "mere suggestions of the times." Edwin Schallert in the *Los Angeles Times* of the same date speaks of the play's "pioneering character and the fact that the subject itself will unquestionably arouse marked controversial interest." Praising *Galileo* as a revolutionary production, he hails the unconventional staging and mode of presentation as something that will "capture the imagination of those who want to see drama put on a technically freer basis." Though he correctly perceives the parallel between Galileo and modern atomic scientists, he also sees something Brecht tried to downplay—the anti-clericalism inherent in the clash between Galileo and the Church. "*Galileo* in its dramatic content is nothing that would easily pass by the Johnston office as a regulation cinema production," he says. "The clash between the scientist and the Church is not treated with a gloved approach."

On the negative side, the *Los Angeles Examiner's* sarcastic review by Patterson Greene on August 1st ignores most of the production to attack the play's ideology. Calling *Galileo* a "fussy, juvenile harangue," Greene faults it for its anti-clericalism, its misrepresentation of history, and what he views as propaganda. "Mr. Brecht's corn is red," he carps, adding that Laughton, who he claims played the role without makeup, portrays the brilliant scientist as a porcine boor.

East Coast reviewers who attended the premiere also submitted unfriendly accounts. A review in the New York edition of *Variety* on August 6th begins: "There is a symbolic bit of business in the final scene of Bertolt Brecht's new play. Galileo, investigating the laws of motion, rolls a small metal ball down an incline and measures its ability to roll up the other side of the u-shaped chute. The ball doesn't quite make the grade. Neither, unfortunately, does the script." After lauding Laughton's performance as a "personal triumph," it adds that "the overall impression is one of dullness." The review concedes that "it is a somewhat interesting treatment of an intriguing theme, but the script itself is too heavy to be digested easily by the majority of ticket buyers. Slated for Broadway after its local run, the financial success of *Galileo* rests upon the shoulders of Laughton. He, not the play, will make the draw." It closes with the remark that Pelican Productions might well change its name to "Provocative Productions."

In an even-handed review in the *New York Times* of August 1st, Gladwin Hill describes the play's theme as "the topical one of science's conflict with the public mind." After a careful description of its action, Hill gives high marks to the technical aspects of the production ("artistic settings by Robert Davison are in the abbreviated, implicit Shakespeare mode and are altogether pleasing") and Laughton's acting ("Laughton . . . makes the scientist an appealing human figure. He is devoid of pretension, amiably contemptuous of the fetters that bind the popular mind, devoted to pure science, and, altogether, heroic while professing to be a coward"). But Hill also summarizes the difficulties that caused many critics to bridle at this play. To them, it was experimental theater outside the mainstream of American drama, and it bore little resemblance to the conventional "well-made play." "The production . . . seems barren of climaxes and even sparse in stirring moments. Hardly a sign of sympathy is inspired when Galileo's scientific determination cuts off his daughter's romance. His recantation comes out cut-and-dried. Overly zealous underplaying by Mr. Laughton and the entire cast . . . and the script itself may have been responsible in part. But it also seems questionable whether the episodic technique is as facile a vehicle for a theme that is less expository than emotional."

Critics understood at least some of the theatrical practices in *Galileo* and tried to accept what to them were unfamiliar, experimental staging methods. The *New York Times* review mentions the "episodic living-newspaper technique" in the context of Losey's background with the New York Federal Theater. Writing in the *New York Sun* on July 31st, Bob Thomas likewise observes that the play is "skillfully written and artfully presented," but that it is "more a chronicle than a drama." The West Coast edition of *Variety* on August 1st reports that "staging techniques new to Los Angeles, based on that of epic theater in Europe, heighten the presentation." Along with most other reviewers, *Variety* notices and praises the single, changeable set, the authentic slide projections, and the three choir boys from St. Paul's cathedral who sang the doggerel verses introducing each scene which, as Patterson Greene observes, "forecast what is to happen next." Almost all of them call attention to the gauze sub-curtain pulled by a little boy to indicate a change of scene. *The Hollywood Reporter* of August 1st comments on another aspect that was unfamiliar to American theatergoers at the time: "both in staging and in the dialogue the play approaches the old English Shakespearean style of presentation, wherein scenery is but illusionary and the actors move the props around themselves." Only the unusual dance sequences, especially those in scene 9, failed to gain approval or understanding. The New York *Variety* article of August 6th speaks of the "rather dubious choreography of a market place scene that would be better eliminated," while *The Hollywood Reporter* (August 1st) faults the "so called choreography" for its incoherence.

Critics generally praised Hugo Haas in his role as Cardinal Barbarini, and later as Pope Urban VIII; Peter Brocco, who played the aged cardinal in scene 5 and the informer in scene 12; Frances Heflin in the role of Virginia; and Stephen Brown, who doubled as a cardinal and the street singer. But essentially *Galileo* was a one-man show by Laughton. With few exceptions, critics found that show satisfactory. "A practical realist," "accomplished and intelligent," "a personal triumph," "an etched and nigh flawless performance," "the greatest and most restrained performance of his career," were a few of the accolades given, though critics also mentioned signs of opening-night nervousness. But they were puzzled by a script they did not quite understand. Had Laughton obscured a great text, or had he strengthened an obscure one? The East Coast *Variety* review conjectures that "the script itself may well be hailed by the intelligentsia as great theater," an idea seconded (with reservations) by *The Hollywood Reporter* in a review entitled "*Galileo* Erudite but Dubious Drama." Pursuing the theme of a highly intellectual script, the review predicts that "there will, too, be discussions as to whether the script is actually great theater or simply a disappointing play. The latter seems to be the case."

Those discussions began immediately, and they were not always friendly. Both the production and the script of *Galileo* became a source of minor controversy in the Hollywood community. In a letter to Reyher, Frank (Spig) Wead, a minor screen writer, conveyed his impressions of one performance that he had seen. His critique of the play was representative of many in Hollywood who did not know how to deal with this unconventional drama. After erroneously stating that *Galileo* had been withdrawn from production after about ten days, he reported: "I caught the show on the fourth night. Most of the people stuck it out, but quite a few dribbled away during the performance, and the comment was mostly bad. The reason is entirely due to Laughton. The thing is now just a monologue for him. Other people have nothing to do or say, and nobody wants to listen to Laughton make a two-hour speech. Also the show has no direction or control, and the result is that Laughton mugs, hams, leers, and postures around the stage to the point where it's ludicrous and disgusting."[29]

Losey remembers that there were also voices in Hollywood which called the play "amateurish and unreadable."[30] They led an assault on Pelican Productions for including *Galileo* in its repertory. On August 25th Houseman wrote a column in the *Los Angeles Daily News* explaining the background and philosophy of Pelican Productions in its selections of plays. Much of it was a response to the controversy created by *Galileo*: "Certain very capable members of our acting and writing community have taken Pelican Productions to task for its presentation of *Galileo*. They have been in the main exponents of the naturalistic theater—the stage of realistic detail which Brecht sought to escape when he founded his Epic Theater in Germany in the late 1920's. We of Pelican have no quarrel with these critics. We appreciate their interest, and we are grateful for their passion. As a matter of fact, some members of the Pelican organization esteem the theater of Odets and of O'Casey above that of Brecht or Wilder. Nevertheless they will support, to the death, the thesis that the Coronet stage must be a platform for all that is exciting and important, no mat-

ter how it rates in their personal catalogue of dramatic values."
Houseman had pinpointed the type of traditional perception of drama
that denied the majority of theatergoers easy access to *Galileo*.
Though Brecht himself considered it one of his most conventional
dramas, and though he attempted to conform to certain American
theater norms in writing some of it, he was learning from American
audiences how his staging and acting methods affected the reception
of even his relatively conventional works.

T. Edward Hambleton was one of many who felt that the production itself never quite captured the excitement that was generated
when Laughton read the script aloud to friends. The "estrangement"
Brecht's stage version had created did more than produce the distance
and sense of unfamiliarity that he felt were necessary for viewers to
exercise their rational faculties in the theater; it actually alienated audiences who were unprepared for this type of theater. One of the actors claims that, after opening night, the architect Frank Lloyd Wright
came backstage and commented that the stage looked like "a lighted
sepulchre,"[31] something alien to his experience in the theater and to
the experience of many viewers. This was a result of the unusual brilliant white stage lighting intended to destroy excessive illusion.

In spite of the controversy the play provoked, Brecht himself was
unusually pleased with the production. Writing to Reyher about the
Hollywood *Galileo*, he paid it the highest compliment possible by
comparing it favorably with his productions in Berlin: "The stage and
the production were strongly reminiscent of the Schiffbauerdamm
Theater in Berlin, as was the intellectual part of the audience."[32] In
large measure this was a consequence of Brecht's being able for the
first time on American soil to stage a production completely on his
own terms. Laughton, too, figured prominently in his satisfaction. He
considered Laughton to be the perfect Galileo, and Bentley agrees that
"it is unlikely anyone again will combine as he did every appearance of
intellectual brilliance with every appearance of physical self-in-
dulgence."[33] This second trait also caused mild problems for Brecht.

One of Laughton's mannerisms threatened to distract from the production in a serious way. In three preview performances before opening night, Laughton had become so nervous during the opening scene
that he put his hands in his pants pockets and began playing with his
genitals. Stripped to the waist as he was after having washed himself
on stage, he gave a reinforcement of his reputation as a homosexual
which did not bode well for the play's reception by audiences or
critics. Later Brecht detachedly observed that Laughton's "comfortable manner of going back and forth, and the play with his hands in his

trouser pockets while planning new research, reached the limits of the obscene."[34] At the time, the unwelcome distraction worried him.

According to Norman Lloyd, Brecht did not want to correct Laughton for fear of damaging their relationship, so he asked Lloyd to speak to Laughton. Lloyd declined, and finally Weigel intervened. The next night, an angry Laughton was seen chasing a wardrobe girl across the stage shouting "who sewed up these pockets?" What Mrs. Brecht had instigated, the unhappy wardrobe girl had to undo stitch by stitch.[35] Three weeks later, this incident found its way in slightly varied form into a Hollywood gossip column. Writing in *Variety* on August 18th, Florabel Muir included a note that "Charles Laughton was fit to be tied that night they sewed up the pockets of the trousers he wears in *Galileo* at the Coronet theater. A backstage prankster gave him a bad time until he managed to get the stitching out."

When *Galileo* closed on August 17, 1947, approximately 4500 people had seen its seventeen performances. T. Edward Hambleton was still negotiating for a New York production. If this did not materialize, he planned to capitalize on its drawing power by bringing it back to the Coronet Theater after Sartre's *No Exit* had finished a four-week run. Los Angeles and Hollywood papers speculated whether Hambleton would get the financial backing to take the production to New York. The Theatre Guild was interested, and so was the American National Theatre and Academy (ANTA). On August 28th, Hambleton sent a telegram to Houseman stating: "Definite decision not to return Galileo Coronet. New York or bust." ANTA had tentatively agreed to do the play late that fall, and the Hollywood production eliminated the need for a try-out performance outside New York. In its September edition, *Vogue* magazine reported that the play would appear in New York and conjectured that there might be some reaction to its anti-clericalism.[36] The Hollywood sets were to be shipped to New York, and Laughton would again play the lead. But by the time it opened on December 7, 1947, Brecht would no longer be in America. Before he experienced a Broadway production on his own terms, his "exile in paradise" would end.

V. BRECHT AND FEELINGS

In his life of Samuel Johnson, Boswell attempts to show the existence of "humanity and real kindness in a man represented as having been harsh and destitute of tenderness."[1] The same case needs to be made for Brecht. When one discounts biographical reminiscences by friends, most of them Eastern European Marxists from the last years of his life who wished to "canonize" him,[2] what remains appears to some critics as "coldness of character" and a "sleazy, nasty opportunistic life."[3] Both extremes overlook the complexity of this difficult man and ignore a tough tenderness evident throughout his life, especially in his American exile. Brecht was made of highly contradictory stuff, and few were able to perceive or experience the many facets of his makeup. To state it another way, there were almost as many Brechts as there were people who knew him.

Reflecting on years of association and collaboration with Brecht, Bentley remembers a cordial impersonalness about him. In Bentley's view human feelings were secondary to actions or ideas. A deliberate tendency to depersonalize human relationships stands out in his mind as the single strongest trait of this unusual human being. Writing in 1948 of their first meeting in 1942, Bentley recalls that "he did not try to find out much about me. He did not invite me to find out much about him. As in his plays, two people would encounter each other for the sake of what they have to do together."[4]

The Brecht he knew, says Bentley, was, in a fundamental sense, not interested in individuals. Not given to sympathetic or psychological intuition about people, Brecht tended to view them much as a caricaturist might when sketching a person's striking features in line drawings without filling in the human details. In a word, Bentley says, most people seemed to bore him, and he appeared unable to respond to their feelings. Further, he lacked the objective and many-sided interest in human beings that makes great novelists capable of exploring people's minds and hearts and habits. Bentley also claims that, with the exception of a prodigious amount of sexual experience, Brecht was incapable of the small encounters that constitute ordinary human intercourse. Working sessions with him were committee meetings. There was no small talk or banter, and there was little exchange that recognized the other person's mood or feelings.

The Brecht whom Eric Bentley knew was not the whole Brecht, but his observations seem to square with some of Brecht's dramatic theories and the way he drew characters in his plays. From remarks Brecht made about Chekhov, Bentley gathered that he was uninterested in the human details that Chekhov presents so masterfully. For

him, someone's humanity consisted of deeds, like Kattrin's warning
the city of Halle in *Mother Courage*, or Grusha's saving the abandoned baby in *Chalk Circle*. Stated another way, one might say that
Brecht respected people for the direction of their thought and actions
rather than for the quality of their feelings. Bentley maintains that
Brecht would have had no interest in knowing what kind of human
being someone was. Certainly this applies to his dramas, which es-
chew character probing and motivation. Only a few love scenes occur
in his dramas; those which do tend to depersonalize love.

Bentley concludes that the dramatist consciously structured his
highly specialized, unusual existence to minimize or exclude the subjective element. His mode of life mirrored and inspired a unique type
of drama that attempts to objectify and depersonalize most human relations. That Brecht's intentions often failed, but sometimes achieved
greatness in failing, is another matter.

Bentley lacked the intimacy needed to see a tender or compassionate
side of Brecht, not to mention the fun-loving side a few friends like
Reyher, or his wife Weigel, recall. All these traits existed. Nor does
Bentley's observation that Brecht attempted to minimize or exclude
private emotions from his life and works mean they did not exist. The
fact that Brecht chose to downplay them and to depersonalize human
relationships generally could be construed to mean the very opposite.
He felt deeply about many things and people, but his style was, where-
ever possible, to exclude the private sphere and to guard against excessive revelations of his person.

Much evidence for this fact exists. During his American exile Brecht
was ill several times, as letters from those who knew him confirm. But
he mentions it only once, and that not in his journal, but in a letter to
Reyher.[5] It was almost as if his private life did not interest him. The
strongest evidence for this mode of thought is found in his works. In
later years Berlau claimed that she wrote the love scenes in *Chalk
Circle* because Brecht was incapable of it. This is not true, but it illustrates the point that this was not something he took to easily. But even
if Berlau did provide some material which Brecht revised to fit his own
tastes, the final product is undeniably what he wanted, i.e., two of the
most understated yet memorable love scenes in modern drama, whose
strength lies in the indirection with which they express obvious passion. In the first act the soldier Simon becomes engaged to the servant
girl Grusha without directly asking her to marry him, and they say
goodby without so much as a kiss. Their poignant meeting after his
return in act IV shows them symbolically separated by a stream as they
address each other in the impersonal third person.[6] In the process of
avoiding too direct portrayal of emotion, Brecht intensifies that emo-

tion in viewers who cannot help filling in what remains unstated or understated.

Many occasional poems Brecht wrote in America, especially those on the death of his collaborator Margarete Steffin, likewise express strong emotion. Yet the choice of lyric poetry as his vehicle, and his impersonal mode of expression in many poems, allowed him to avoid revealing too much of himself by assuming the mask of an anonymous speaker or by interjecting a poetic voice between him and the emotion expressed. For Brecht as for T. S. Eliot, writing poetry represented an escape from emotion. This habit of dealing with tenderness through indirection, understatement, and concealment occurs repeatedly in Brecht's writings and in his biography.

In the fall of 1941 his journal mentions attending a reading of his poems in German by émigré actors in a "Jewish club."[7] Either on New Year's Eve 1941, or the following day, Alexander Granach took Brecht to a party of the "Los Angeles Jewish Collective" in what might have been the same "club," the Soto Jewish Center in East Los Angeles. There the poet Martin Birnbaum recited a Yiddish version he had prepared of Brecht's poem "And What Did The Soldier's Wife Receive?" and sang his text of the poem "To the German Soldiers in the East" in Yiddish to Eisler's music. They impressed at least one listener, Samuel Bernstein, a tailor who operated a dry-cleaning establishment in Los Angeles. When a friend pointed out Brecht in the audience, Bernstein took pity on the poorly dressed refugee and had Granach inquire if he might send him a suit. In 1935 in New York Gorelik's brother, distressed by Brecht's intentionally shabby dress at a dinner party, had made a similar offer that was declined.[8] Brecht now accepted, though he turned down an optometrist in the audience who offered to make him new glasses.[9] A few days later Brecht received in the mail, with an offer to alter it to fit, the dark suit Bernstein had worn at his own wedding.

This gesture touched Brecht, and in March 1942 he responded with a poem that contrasted the hardships of his recent exile with such kindness:

"Friends Everywhere"
The Finnish workers
Gave him beds and a desk
The writers of the Soviet Union brought him to the ship
And a Jewish tailor in Los Angeles
Sent him a suit: The enemy of the butchers
Found friends.
(GW x, 844)

He wrote Bernstein a gracious thank-you letter saying that, since his poems generally make enemies, it was gratifying to know they can also make friends.[10] The suit, he said, fit as if it were made for him and needed no alterations. A note that Ruth Berlau appended to a copy of the letter claims that Brecht wrote this one "at a time when he didn't answer telegrams."

This is not an isolated example of Brecht's ability to feel deeply and to respond warmly, however obliquely. In the midst of *Galileo* rehearsals, Brecht's close friends Egon and Leopoldine Breiner had their first son, a boy named Peter, born on July 4, 1947. As a gift, Brecht asked Paul Dessau to compose a musical setting for one of his poems (*GW* IX, 432) and to take it to the hospital for the Breiners. Given the new title "Lullaby for Peter Breiner" and dated "Independence Day, 1947," it is the kind of lullaby a proletarian mother in one of Brecht's plays might sing to her son, i.e., one that expresses emotion by avoiding it. Addressing the child, the text states that the mother has neither money nor prayer for the child, but only hope. Though the child might possess no special qualities, still the mother is not raising it to fight wars for others or to die in some barbed-wire entanglement. It closes with an admonition to remain loyal to his own, i.e., to the working class, and to help insure that there will no longer be two kinds of people on earth. While not a particularly distinguished poem, it shows among other things that for all the importance of *Galileo* Brecht did not permit the birth of his first major production on American soil to make him oblivious to the birth of a human being.

A direct and somewhat atypical expression in Brecht's journal of a private response deals with his satisfaction in keeping a corner of arid California green: "What I enjoy is watering the garden. Otherwise why the concern that a spot of lawn might be overlooked, that the little plant there might not get anything, or less so, that the old tree there might be neglected because it looks so strong? And weeds or not, everything green needs water. . . ."[11] A poem Brecht wrote a short time later illustrates how he was able to depersonalize even the most private experience and give it broader ideological implications. Entitled "On Sprinkling the Garden" (*GW* X, 861), it is not a celebration of nature at all, but reverse Social Darwinism calling for survival of the unfittest, for each according to its need and not its function. Even weeds and unproductive plants deserve to survive and need to be nurtured, it says. Nature in the poem is a metaphor for living things known as people, while the poem itself is an expression of sympathy for the underprivileged and those less able to care for themselves. The gardener looking out for them is the Marxist revolutionary and world-changer Bertolt Brecht at his private best, a writer who, since his early play

Baal, had been on the side of those outside the pale of social accepta-
bility.[12]

When the financial stress of the first year abated, a generosity of
spirit fundamental to Brecht's character manifested itself again. After
receiving a paycheck for *Hangmen* in September or early October
1942, he no longer needed the European Film Fund to support him.
Instead he began to repay the Fund by assisting another refugee writer,
Alfred Döblin, whose health and financial means were dwindling.
With characteristic modesty in such matters, Brecht fails to mention it
in letters or in his journal. Only Döblin's letter to a friend[13] documents
this action.

Between 1942-1944 Hans Viertel assisted Brecht on a number of his
writing projects. Viertel recalls an act in which Brecht disguised great
sensitivity behind a facade of objectivity. Viertel was about to leave for
the East Coast and needed money. Without comment, Brecht, who
knew this, handed him a sizeable check with the remark: "This is in
payment for your work." Viertel, of course, was not working for
money, but he appreciated this impersonal, unpretentious generosity
that left no sense of obligation.

Elisabeth Freundlich relates an incident typical of Brecht's style of
showing kindness without displaying feeling. In the fall of 1946, he
used Laughton's car to drive Freundlich's sister-in-law and her husband to the New York pier, where they embarked for Europe. When
Freundlich attempted to thank him, he brushed it off with a statement
which, while not necessarily relevant, was typical of the indirection he
used. He said simply: "It's practical."[14]

Florence Homolka, who, with her husband, saw Brecht frequently
and liked him, observed that "in his human relationships he was a
fighter for people's rights without being overly concerned with the
happiness of persons close to him."[15] This observation fails to recognize the deep concern Brecht felt and showed for a number of friends.
After the war, he was vitally interested in boyhood friends in Augsburg and wrote them, inquiring whether CARE packages or packages
sent through normal postal channels arrived more quickly. From this
time until they departed for Europe in 1947, he and his wife sent many
packages of food and clothing to friends and acquaintances in Europe.

Among examples of his ability to care deeply about others are his
relationships to two of the closest friends he had in the USA—Peter
Lorre and Ferdinand Reyher.

Bentley has observed that Brecht tended to be possessive about people
he liked. Peter Lorre was one of those. Ever since his appearance in a
1931 production of *A Man's a Man* in Berlin, Lorre had been one of
Brecht's favorite actors. Lorre reciprocated with a dedication to Brecht
that verged on adulation. Abe Burrows recalls hearing Lorre speak of
Brecht as the greatest director of all,[1] and, according to Lorre's biographer, the actor proclaimed that Brecht was a genius, "one of the
greatest writers of our time."[2]

In addition to admiring Lorre's keen intellect and broad reading,
Brecht saw in him a natural talent that acted instinctively on the stage.
He sensed that beneath Lorre's mild exterior lay an angry non-
conformist, a dissenter with limited courage. Bentley postulates that
the "psychotic split" evident in Lorre's films—i.e., the discrepancy between the surface innocence of a naive voice that expressed few or no
emotions, and the horrifying deeds that manifested menacing pas-
sions—fitted Brecht's style of acting perfectly. This ability to be at a
distance from his own emotions while acting would have made Lorre,
among other things, a perfect Galy Gay, the character in *A Man's a
Man* who loses his identity by being cut off from his own feelings. It is
also no accident that Brecht's first choice to play the role of Schweyk
when he wrote it in 1943 was Lorre. The actor himself seems to have
sensed a strong affinity for this role, for he already had played a
Schweykian role in the film *Crack-Up* in 1936. One might speculate
that, in his manner of speech and behavior, Brecht recognized him as
the prototypical Schweyk.

In contrast to most other émigrés who succeeded in Hollywood,
Lorre did not arouse Brecht's jealousy, though Brecht apparently did
let him know that he thought Lorre had debased himself in the film
world. But Lorre was too useful for Brecht to be jealous. In a letter to
George Pfanzelt in the spring of 1946, Brecht asked him to cable his
address to Peter Lorre, "who is known to almost every American." He
recognized and tried to take advantage of Lorre's excellent connections to Hollywood, but without success. Lorre's contacts were not
sufficient to sell Brecht's film stories for "Children's Crusade 1939"
and "The Crouching Venus" during the three days Lorre and Brecht
spent with the screenwriter Ernest Pascal at Lake Arrowhead in July
1943; his attempts to find financial backing for a *Schweyk* production
the same year also ended woefully; and Lorre's initial involvement in
writing the film story "All Our Yesterdays" in 1945 was not enough to
help Brecht to place it. In his efforts to use Lorre, Brecht never misused
or abused him. His admiration for the actor is documented in a film

1. The Swedish freighter "Annie Johnson" on which Brecht sailed from Vladivostok to America, June-July, 1941.

2. View of Brecht's home at 1063-26th Street, Santa Monica, California, taken from adjoining vacant lot.

3. A relaxed Brecht at home of Oskar Homolka, Bel Air, California, 1942.

4. Brecht and Oskar Homolka, Bel Air, California, 1942.

5. Brecht and Florence Homolka at Homolka's Bel Air home, 1942.

6. Peter Lorre, one of Brecht's close friends during American exile, reading a copy of Brecht's poetry collection *Svendborger Gedichte.*

7. Fritz Lang checking the street model for the film "Hangmen Also Die," which he produced and directed from a screenplay co-authored by Brecht, Hollywood, 1942.

8. The composer Hanns Eisler, friend and collaborator of Brecht's, at his home in Malibu, California, probably summer of 1946.

9. Brecht and Lion Feuchtwanger.

10. Brecht and W. H. Auden, in New York City, probably 1944.

11. Brecht and Charlie Chaplin in Hollywood, probably 1946-1947.

12. Brecht and Ferdinand Reyher resting during an excursion into the New Jersey countryside, October 1946.

13. Brecht and Eric Bentley, Zurich, 1948.

14. Brecht and Charles Laughton, Pacific Palisades (Laughton's home), probably 1946.

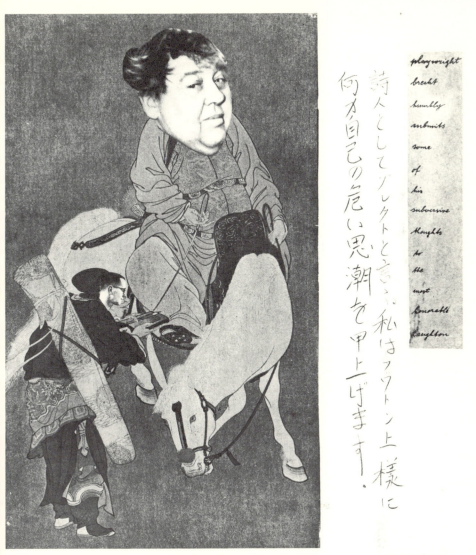

詩人としてブレクトと言ふ私はフワトン上様に何才自己の危い思潮を甲上げます。

playwright brecht humbly submits some of his subversive thoughts to the most honorable laughton

15. Photo of a collage Brecht made to serve as the cover of a collection of his unpublished poems which he gave to Charles Laughton for Christmas, 1945 or 1946. It appears to be modeled after the situation in Brecht's poem "Legend of the Origin of the Book Taoteking." The inscription in Brecht's hand reads: "Playwright Brecht Humbly Submits Some of His Subversive Thoughts to the Most Honorable Laughton." Characters at the left in Japanese correspond to the English meaning.

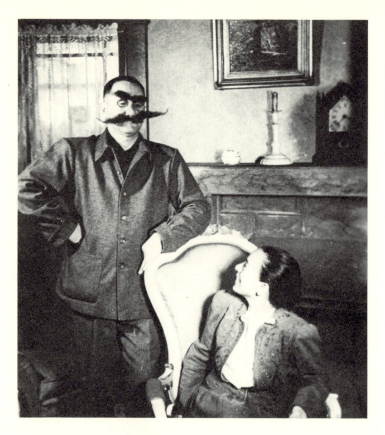

16. (*Above*) Brecht and his wife Helene Weigel in their 26th St. home, Santa Monica, probably 1945-1946. Brecht appears to be doing an imitation of Stalin.

17. (*Left*) Helene Weigel, Brecht's wife, Santa Monica, 1946.

18. Brecht in New York City, probably 1946.

19. (*Above*) Ruth Berlau, Brecht's friend and collaborator, in New York City, 1944 or 1945.

20. (*Left*) Brecht and Ruth Berlau, probably 1942.

21. Brecht before unidentified motel somewhere in New Mexico or Arizona during cross-country trip by car, December 1946. In his journal he compares this part of America to Siberia.

22. Brecht at desk in Ruth Berlau's apartment, New York City, 1943 or 1944.

23. Brecht and his son Stefan, a graduate student at Harvard, in New York City, 1946.

24. Scene "In Search of Justice" from 1945 New York production of *Private Life of the Master Race*. Actors: Harry Simberg, Paul Andor.

25. Charles Laughton in Scene Eight of American version of *Galileo*, produced in Hollywood, summer of 1947. Characters L. to R. are: Federzoni (David Clarke); Galileo (Laughton); Andrea (William Phipps), and the Little Monk (Mickey Knox).

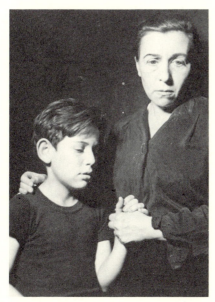

26. Scenes from 1942 New York production of *Furcht und Elend. Left*: Elisabeth Neumann and unidentified boy in "Die Kiste." *Right*: Ludwig Roth and Elisabeth Neumann in "Das Kreidekreuz."

27. Brecht being sworn in as the eleventh of the "Unfriendly Nineteen" witnesses before the House Un-American Activities Committee on October 30, 1947.

story entitled "Rich Man's Friend," a biographical account of how a Hollywood producer "discovered" the impoverished Lorre in London during the 1930's and brought him to America.[3] Early in his American exile, after hearing Lorre tell this bizarre tale, Brecht wrote a German version of it as an outline for a film story. He failed to sell it, but it stands as a tribute to this actor over whom Brecht seems to have cast an unusual spell.

Several times Lorre assisted Brecht and his friends financially. He advanced the money for Kreymborg to translate *Schweyk* in 1943. The following year he paid to have Berlau brought to Los Angeles to deliver her baby. Again in 1946 Lorre apparently contributed some money to assist Hauptmann in coming from New York to Los Angeles. Brecht reciprocated with the kind of attention that Lorre found flattering. As a result, the actor felt Brecht was one of the few who truly appreciated his talent. This highly literate actor wanted to be a writer himself, and there are unconfirmed reports that he and Brecht worked together on a number of poems which have since been destroyed.[4] Brecht did in fact give him a copy of his *Svendborg Poems* (see illustration no. 6) and encouraged the actor to cultivate the more serious art of poetry reading. Brecht told friends that he considered Lorre to be the best reader of German poetry alive. Lorre's reading of Brechtian poems on an obscure German language program in New York City at the height of his career in March 1943 reflected his devotion to Brecht as a person as well as his admiration for poetry. The fact that Brecht rehearsed the readings with him also gave his ego a lift. In addition to being a frequent guest at the Sunday night gatherings in his friend's Santa Monica home, Lorre, according to one of Brecht's journal entries,[5] enjoyed the status of being one of the few from whom Brecht cheerfully tolerated criticism of his acting theories. Because he disliked many of his own type-cast roles in Hollywood films, Lorre responded warmly to Brecht's treatment of him as an intelligent human being and as a gifted actor.

Had Brecht been interested in Lorre only for his usefulness in the film community, that interest would have waned when Lorre was no longer in a position to help him. It is a measure of Brecht's ability to care deeply that, when this happened, he showed his strongest interest in his friend. In 1946 Warner Brothers studios allowed Lorre's contract to expire without renewing it. The actor's career began to decline immediately. Hurt and depressed, Lorre grew increasingly insecure, and a long-time problem with morphine addiction began to plague him severely. Convinced that his physical appearance was a detriment to his career, he was doubly pained to gain the reputation in Hollywood of a pathetic clown. Yet economic necessity forced him to go on accepting roles that cast him as an unwitting fool, such as a part in *My Favorite Brunette* (1947) with Bob Hope and Lon Chaney, Jr.

Brecht's ability to show deep but unobtrusive concern for someone, which had restored Charles Laughton's confidence in himself as an actor when Hollywood considered the actor to be "box-office poison," now drew Lorre closer to him. Friendship became therapy, with Brecht as the therapist. Mutual acquaintances remember the salutary effect on Lorre of long discussions in 1946-1947 about postwar Germany, actors in American exile, national and world politics, and the theater. A dependency relationship developed that took on proportions of near worship. The knowledge that this good friend and dramatic genius believed in him as an actor sustained Lorre and helped him to regain some of his self-confidence.

During 1946 Lorre had established his own independent production company, "Lorre, Incorporated," a subdivision of Rooney, Incorporated. That company, and Lorre's ongoing need for therapy, may have prompted Brecht to venture into film writing again in 1947. On March 24th his journal contains a notation that he had completed "a film outline for Lorre of *The Overcoat* (after Gogol)." That film story was not the only vehicle he had in mind for the actor. He began to write another called "The Great Clown Emaël" in which Lorre was to play the lead. One wonders to what extent it arose from hearing Lorre talk about his pitiful new image as a clown. Brecht did not finish this story until the next year in Switzerland. Perhaps it is only coincidence, but he must have completed it soon after receiving a letter from Losey reminding him of Lorre's Hollywood reputation. It stated that the actor was not acceptable for a remake of the film *M* because "he is now regarded by the American movie public as a clown."[6] In Brecht's story one reads of a clown reminiscent in some ways of the split person he knew in Lorre. Publicly Emaël was known for his brilliance as a clown; privately he was a totally different person who lived in great comfort and loved literature, especially Shakespeare. Lorre himself was probably not directly involved in developing these stories with Brecht, but he was on Brecht's mind for personal reasons, and these stories represented Brecht's way to assist him or to bolster his confidence.

In late February 1947, while on a nightclub theater tour in New York City, Lorre encountered serious problems with local authorities over his drug habit. How or when Brecht learned of his difficulties is unclear, but a letter to Reyher in mid-March suggests that Brecht phoned Reyher in New York several times for assistance while trying to settle Lorre's West Coast affairs. It also illustrates how Brecht cites objective reasons for needing Lorre to obscure his urgent concern for his person: "Again many thanks for your rapid help in the Lorre matter. It's not only that I like him; I urgently need him in Germany to assemble my theater. Writing plays has become a complicated and comprehensive profession; now I'm here trying to untangle Lorre's confused affairs. Naturally he's entirely in the hands of a racket. Like Laughton, Lorre lives in shameful poverty with four horses and his own Japanese gardeners in a $50,000 villa." In the same letter that speaks of his conversation with Lorre about "All Our Yesterdays," Reyher writes that "Lorre may straighten out." Yet, except for this exchange of letters, Brecht concealed his involvement and assistance as discreetly as he did the nature of Lorre's problems.

Bentley recalls hearing Brecht talk in 1947 about the corrupting influence that Hollywood had had on Lorre. Big money had ruined him by making life easy and morphine readily available. Sometime early in 1947, Brecht asked Naomi Replansky to translate a poem he had just written about a friend's sinking into the swamp of Hollywood. She recalls asking during one of their working sessions if the poem were about Lorre, whose drug habit and declining reputation were common knowledge. Brecht shrugged and answered, "It might be." Friends and relatives of Lorre who read the poem also heard Brecht or someone else say that it was about Lorre; years later they recall the same impression that Replansky gained. The fact that the German original of the poem, which had previously been lost, turned up in mid-1977 among some of Lorre's posthumous papers, seems to confirm the fact that Brecht gave it to him for therapeutic purposes. The complete text, in an English translation by Naomi Replansky done under Brecht's supervision, reads:

I saw many friends
And the friend I loved most
Among them helplessly sunk
Into the swamp.
I pass by daily.
And a drowning was not over in a single morning.
This made it more terrible.
And the memory of our long talks about the swamp
Which already held so many powerless.
Now I watched him leaning back
Covered with leeches in the shimmering, softly moving slime
Upon the sinking face
That ghastly blissful smile.[7]

The closing lines remind readers of the gentle but deadly smile that German and American cinema fans had come to associate with Lorre in many of his film roles. The reference to sinking into the swamp "covered with leeches" likewise has overtones of Brecht's statement that Lorre was "in the hands of a racket," though it might also refer to his drug addiction. Brecht's poem reveals a concern for Lorre that extends far beyond wanting him for his postwar theater ensemble. The poem is for Lorre as a human being whom he wanted to help.

Personal requests to Lorre in 1946 and 1947, repeated invitations from Europe between 1948-1950 to join him there, and messages through friends all failed to recruit someone whom Brecht cared for as a friend. After returning to Europe, Brecht in his journal describes plans for assembling his own theater ensemble in Europe. Among the names of plays and actors he has in mind is Lorre, playing the lead in *Schweyk*. In 1950 Brecht renewed earlier invitations with a touching poem entitled "To the Actor P.L. in Exile." After urging Lorre to return to a homeland in which "milk and honey once flowed," but which is now destroyed, the poem closes with an impersonal phrase which, for Brecht, represents a deep expression of concern—that the other person is "needed":

> And we can offer you nothing more
> Than this: that you are needed.
>
> Poor or rich
> Healthy or sick
> Forget everything
> And come.
> (*GW* x, 967)

But Lorre returned only for visits, and he never visited Brecht. His drug habit and the relative ease of existence in Hollywood would have been impossible to maintain in the austerity of postwar Europe. Brecht's compassion and friendship had not been enough to save one of his dearest friends from what he saw as the Hollywood morass.

Brecht's closest American friend, and perhaps one of the best male friends in his lifetime, was Ferdinand Reyher.[1] From the time they met in Berlin in 1927, they sensed a kinship that persisted for nearly three decades. To the degree that Brecht was able to let his hair down and expose part of his real self, it seems to have happened with Reyher.

During Brecht's first year in America, Reyher came to his home frequently. A welcome friend, he entered into discussions that contrasted sharply with the way Brecht spoke to exile friends—boisterous laughter, loud talk, and perambulating conversations while both men gesticulated to make a point and blew smoke from cheap cigars that might have driven less steadfast companions from the room. This was a special friendship. On occasions such as a Christmas gathering on December 26, 1941, or Christmas Eve 1942, Reyher was the only American present. Especially during the first gloomy year, whenever Reyher announced a visit, Brecht would come alive with anticipation and talk about it for days after.[2]

Like Lorre, Reyher was one of the rare persons from whom Brecht not only tolerated disagreement, but whose opinions he respected. To convince them that American cooking was palatable, Reyher invited the Brechts to a dinner he cooked with food from the Los Angeles Farmer's Market. Brecht's journal entry for the evening describes eating Virginian meat-loaf with macaroni and a soup "with every vegetable in the world in it."[3] It also records their conversation on a number of topics and illustrates how Reyher tried to educate him by challenging his own preconceptions: "For example," writes Brecht, "I make the remark that a large number of American women over sixty, who go around with clothing and makeup looking like flappers, have lost their dignity, forced by cosmetic firms and movies to continue their sexual competition to the grave. Upset, he answers quickly with the argument that America has increased the youth of its women ten to twenty years, and that it doesn't throw its 45-year-olds on the trash heap, etc. Or he defends the office of a judge and describes how attorneys with huge practices ($100,000 a year) accept a position on the bench for $8,000 a year. Again and again he comes back to the American businessman type like Hudson, who only wants to organize and who would do it in any society that could accommodate such strong men." Brecht summarizes the conversation with generous praise: "He's a good cicerone for the states when . . . he explains the humorous idiosyncracies of this giant infant, America."

Brecht accepted at least part of Reyher's analysis that evening, and a short time later a similar idea found its way into a poem entitled "The

Democratic Judge" (*GW* x, 860) written in 1942 or 1943. The poem,
which uses "democracy" to mean sympathy with the disadvantaged,
narrates an episode that Brecht might have heard from Reyher. An
Italian restaurant keeper appears before a judge in Los Angeles to be
examined for American citizenship. Hindered by ignorance of English,
he answers the question "what is the eighth amendment" with
"1492." The judge denies him citizenship. When he appears three
months later and gives the same answer to the question " who was the
victorious general in the Civil War?" he is again turned down. Appearing a third time, he experiences the same results when he answers the
question of the length of an American president's term of office with
"1492." Realizing that the man will never learn English, and discover-
ing that he works hard for a living, the judge asks him at his fourth
appearance when America was discovered. Because of the man's correct answer, the judge grants him citizenship. This was the kind of
offbeat American lore Reyher loved to relate. He may not have inspired the poem directly, but its contents not only typify the side of
American life that he tried to make Brecht see; they depart radically
from more negative observations that Brecht made about the American and German judiciary.

For all his wit, Brecht was seldom given to "small talk." Yet an exchange of banter in 1946 was typical of the humor and verbal horse-
play that marked private conversations and correspondence with this
friend. In July 1946 Reyher sent him a newspaper clipping about the
theft of jewels worth several hundred thousand dollars that an art
museum in Frankfurt had stored during the war in Büdingen. Apparently American occupation troops took them. Büdingen was Reyher's
ancestral home in Germany and a town he had visited in the twenties.
Brecht begins a letter dated August 1946 with an unusual bit of leg-
pulling: "Now I'm convinced that after the First World War you were
in Büdingen to reconnoiter the terrain for your countrymen after the
Second World War . . . an evil town, that Büdingen, with a curious
attraction for shady types." Reyher responded in kind: "Naturally I
was casing the joint in Büdingen. I tried to hint as much to you, and
would have cut you in, but you just wouldn't believe the lay existed."[4]

Brecht's closeness to Reyher is evident from the number of letters in
which he complains that his friend is not with him for discussions, for
instruction on what he calls "American folklore," and for chess
games. Brecht's concern for his friend's health also showed the ability
to care deeply which he normally concealed. Writing early in 1944
after Reyher had broken a leg, Brecht asks about it, observing that
"one should only break a leg once; here, too, moderation is necessary," and urging him to recover so he could come to Germany with

the Brechts.[5] Here Reyher, the only American whom Brecht invited to return to Europe with him as a collaborator for his theater ensemble, is told he is "needed." During American exile this statement became Brecht's encoded way of expressing concern, and it was reserved for those few for whom he cared deeply.

Another example of Brecht's solicitude for Reyher occurred in the spring of 1946. Reyher, who was living as a free-lance writer in the Chelsea Hotel in New York, had been suffering severe nosebleeds in the aftermath of a minor stroke. Sometime in March or April his daughter Faith notified Brecht, who was in New York, of her father's condition. The dramatist went immediately, waited several hours in Reyher's room, and left a note scrawled on the back of Chelsea Hotel stationary which read: "Faith called me, and I came over. Found you sleeping soundly and sat for several hours. Going now because I don't want to leave Ruth alone. *Please* call when you wake up, at the latest tomorrow." Later letters by Brecht damn "the gentlemen of the medical racket" for their inability to stop Reyher's nosebleeds. Repeatedly he invited Reyher back to Europe with him, where, he said, he and his wife will "supervise your convalescence."[6]

This is not to say Brecht was always a thoughtful friend. Because he possessed a stronger personality, a greater conviction of his own genius, and a surer sense of purpose than Reyher, Brecht's actions occasionally hurt this sensitive American. After several weeks of revising *Galileo* together in the spring of 1946, Reyher's diary notes his annoyance when Brecht suddenly announced his departure, "Broke out he's leaving for California at 5 a.m. tomorrow—and 'thought I knew.' He uses the papal legate shift not infrequently."[7] The following day his diary again expresses irritation at this shabby treatment:

"Sticking in my craw, Brecht's departure without a word. Something demoralizing in this. Not the grace or imagination of a word. A cheap view of one; a subconscious wish to make my work on *Galileo* unimportant, even unnecessary. . . . Any place or person where my presence might challenge his credit, out. Never or rarely credits a line, idea, suggestion, correction, etc. Taken, and credit with it. Too bad; I can be had so cheaply, too, if not cheapened. . . ."

Yet the concluding words of the same entry reflect the uncanny "something" which took hold of nearly all Brecht's collaborators and never let go: "Sorry and relieved to see him go, as always, with all. In a few days will miss him much; in a few days not miss him; then, if ever, be happier to see him than almost anyone else I know."

A diary entry by Reyher in 1953 says something of the admiration each had for the other man's abilities and the unselfish help on each other's works which cemented their relationship in America: "In my life I have met two men with objective respect for material, and I have accepted help without sense of obligation or its obverse, resentment, and they equally from me. Brecht and John Huston."[8] Throughout their collaboration there was never a sense that Brecht considered or treated Reyher as anything but an equal, or that Reyher felt inferior to him. Initially, in fact, Reyher's work as an established screenwriter put him in the position of helping Brecht to write film stories that he could sell to Hollywood.

In the course of his life, Brecht called several different people his "teachers." Though Reyher was not one of them, the manner in which Brecht cast him in the role of his mentor for America shows the eagerness to learn from others which helped to captivate them as collaborators. In contrast to most refugees, Brecht was eager to learn about his host country from a brilliant raconteur who has been called "a walking encyclopedia of Americana."[9] Reyher's short stories from the twenties; his collaboration with Sinclair Lewis on that writer's American labor novel; his personal acquaintance with F. Scott Fitzgerald, Hemingway, Wallace Stevens, and other American writers; his own work on at least two panoramic novels dealing with American history, one in the guise of a history of poker, the other as seen through the eyes of a tramp photographer modelled on Mathew Brady; his 1946 novel about the growth of a midwestern town entitled *I Heard Them Sing*; and notes for projects ranging from Puritan law to the history of railroads, scarcely cover the breadth of his interests and information.

A list of conversation topics with Reyher over the years would be sufficient to dispel the myth that Brecht knew little about the realities of America. Only a few tantalizing details are known about one project Reyher suggested which arose from their discussions of the labor movement in America—a series of short plays on American history. In August 1946 Brecht wrote Reyher saying, "I would really like to begin with the short plays on American history which we discussed. This continent is becoming more important each day (and fun more difficult to find)." These were probably the one-act plays Brecht spoke of in another letter as "American stories (40 minutes long, ten of them)."[10] Helene Weigel believed they were to treat the history of American labor and to include figures such as Joe Hill, Eva Pastor, and Molly McGuire, whose names Brecht first heard from Reyher. It is true that Brecht wrote no plays about America after being exposed to American realities; it is not true, however, that he knew nothing about or had no interest in such topics.

Work on an abortive film project serves as an example of Reyher's role in transmitting American culture to Brecht. As early as 1941 he had made Brecht aware of Edgar Lee Masters's *Spoon River Anthology* and had suggested that he read it. They talked of doing a film story based on Masters's American classic, and Brecht jotted down a note: "Lee Masters' epigrams as a film. The persons in the small town recite their poems while walking. Spoon River Anthology."[11]

In 1944 or 1945 Brecht returned to the idea and asked Reyher, who knew Masters, to locate him and to discuss a film version of that work. This was probably just after Masters's convalescence in New York's Bellevue Hospital, where he was taken in 1944, suffering from pneumonia and malnutrition. Reyher wrote or called the American poet either in the Poconos region of western New York or in Charlotte, North Carolina, and invited him to meet them in New York City and discuss the putative project. At the time, Masters was receiving limited support from The Authors' League of America and did not have the money.[12] He agreed to come if they paid his train fare to New York. Silence followed, and the matter lapsed. Somehow Brecht misconstrued Reyher's report and understood that Masters was confined to a home for the aged somewhere in New York State, and that he was destitute. The playwright was indignant, and in subsequent years he repeatedly told this version to demonstrate how capitalist America treated its great writers.[13]

Reyher's work on *Galileo*, their most extensive collaboration, was not done without reciprocation. Brecht spent considerable time discussing or working with him on his own materials. Two major projects reflect Brecht's stance of support and critical encouragement. The first, a mysterious work known as "Hodge Podge," dragged on for years without being published. A handwritten postscript in a letter from Brecht of late May 1946 reads: "Remember Hotch Potch." Three times in the next three years he inquired about it. One letter written in 1949 asks: "How do things stand with Hodge Podge, the fragment? If you could send it to me, I would arrange to have it translated, and then we wouldn't have just Wilder."[14] Since Brecht was assembling plays for his new theater group at this time, the reference to Thornton Wilder intimates that "Hodge Podge" might have been a drama. But the unknown work that sparked his interest never appeared, and today no manuscript can be located.

Brecht's solicitude for a second work produced a written document which remains unpublished. Reyher's research on the history of photography, especially the life of the French photographer Eugene Atget, generated a plan for an ambitious novel with the title *Tin* that was to trace the social, economic, political, and cultural history of America from the 1830's to the Civil War through the eyes of an itinerant tin-type photographer modelled on Mathew B. Brady and known variously as Brady or Burbank. During their meetings in the spring of 1946, Brecht listened to Reyher's plan, discussed how he might treat the material, and left with a synopsis or outline of the novel to read when he returned to Santa Monica.

Despite intense work on *Galileo*, Brecht responded in early August with a seven-page typewritten commentary on various points of Reyher's project. In fourteen numbered paragraphs which interlace incisive remarks and suggestions with questions for Reyher, Brecht displays his gifts as a critic and theoretician as well as his almost reflexive willingness to help friends and collaborators with their own writing. At the end he observes that "your material is so interesting that in my opinion you can afford a new kind of presentation which is not the usual one. In the States you can count on the interest of your fellow citizens in their history; in Europe, which is again becoming significant as a reader's market, on the interest in the new manner of presentation." Brecht concludes with an invitation: "Why don't you make a few models that we could discuss?"[15]

If Reyher's letters are credible, these comments, and Brecht's repeated inquiries over the next four years, motivated Reyher to go on with the novel. By 1950, it had grown into a multi-volume but incomplete work. But in spite of Brecht's repeated urgings and his invitation in 1950 to publish sections of it in the East German literary journal *Sinn und Form*,[16] Reyher failed to finish it.

During Brecht's exile years, Reyher may have caught glimpses of what Bentley saw as an impersonalness in human relations, but it did not affect him. Brecht's writing and everything connected with it were his life, and Reyher knew this. Unless people became intimately involved in that writing and learning process, they remained ignorant of the deep concern that he was capable of showing and feeling toward a select few. Reyher was one of those. As long as they worked together in America, the Brecht he knew was a generous, humorous friend who genuinely cared.

Photographs of Brecht fail to convey the uncanny attraction he held for women. A famous German actress once told a friend he was the most sexually exciting man she had ever met.[1] Losey, who associated closely with Brecht during his last year in America, remembers that he was always accompanied by two or three women, and that "he ate very little, drank very little, and fornicated a great deal."[2] A number of Americans who knew him well noted (or complained) that he was constantly surrounded by women—his "harem," his "female follow-ers," his "lady admirers," and his "coterie of mistresses" are a few of their descriptions. These observations apply mainly to Brecht's last two years of American exile, especially while he was working on *Galileo*. Before that time, personal circumstances restricted his opportunities for such liaisons.

All his life Brecht had entered freely into sexual relationships without a sense of obligation or guilt. He rejected the bourgeois notion of love, which to him was an extension of capitalist notions of property ownership based on the feeling that two people "belonged" to each other. His alliances were motivated by a variety of reasons as simple as relaxation or help on his writing and as complex as fundamental ego needs and the desire for intimate human contact. Almost without exception the women he attracted were not beauties, but writers and artists themselves with highly independent personalities.

The consensus among friends is that Brecht's women were captivated by his genius. But speculation on the sources of his personal attraction is ultimately a futile exercise, just as it would be impossible to document the names of all the women with whom he had sexual liaisons in America. Doubtless there were a number of casual relationships, but they are not significant. In terms of his work, there were only two women in America who mattered—his wife Helene Weigel, and Ruth Berlau. His relationship to them mirrors some of the complexity of his makeup which permitted him to care for people without letting emotional considerations control him.

A. RUTH BERLAU

A day after Laughton read the completed *Galileo* to Brecht's assembled friends in early December 1945, a vague journal entry mentions a long-distance call to New York: "At night I call R. and hear unfavorable things."[3] These "unfavorable things" pertained to Ruth Berlau's deteriorating mental state. A family history of mental illness, and the loss of the child she was expecting by Brecht in 1944, had left her more unbalanced than ever. As Christmas 1945 approached, her behavior became increasingly peculiar. On December 27th she became violent with her roommate Ida Bachmann, who called a doctor.[4] When the doctor arrived, Berlau attacked him, whereupon Bachmann called Brecht's friend Fritz Sternberg. Brecht placed one of his regular long-distance calls to Berlau's apartment while Sternberg was there, and the latter confirmed through "yes-no" answers that she had suffered a breakdown.[5] Brecht then phoned Reyher, whom Berlau liked, and asked for help. The next day Reyher, a Dr. Gruenthal, and the police picked up Berlau and took her to Bellevue Hospital. On December 31st she was transferred to a mental hospital in Amityville, Long Island, where she spent a number of weeks undergoing electric-shock treatment.

Brecht, who was sick with severe flu and a high fever in January, could not come immediately. But sentences from a letter to Reyher reporting a telephone conversation with Berlau following her confinement show that his feeling for her ran deep enough to make an unusual confession: "They must allow her to call me here when she is able. That, too, would help her. . . . The fact that she is so far away and in strange hands naturally upsets me very much."[6]

Brecht's sole purpose for the cross-country trip which brought him to New York on February 10th was to care for Berlau. Hoping to have her released from the hospital, he accompanied Bergner and Czinner to Amityville, only to discover she was still very ill. On one visit he told Berlau he wanted to take her home. She shouted that he would have to get enough cars for the thirty-two other patients there, whereupon she threw him out. Berlau later claimed he muttered something to Bergner about no one being as crazy as a crazy Communist,[7] but he continued to return until some time in March, when Berlau was well enough to be released to his care. In the ensuing weeks Brecht was preoccupied with looking after her in her 57th Street apartment. Only when she stabilized did he resume promoting his own theater projects.

Like Brecht's other female collaborators, Berlau was an alter ego who filled a need in his writing. In America, his need for her became particularly acute. After Margarete Steffin's death in Moscow in 1941, he had no other close female associate. Consequently he began to invest in Berlau the attention he normally shared with several at once. With the exception of Weigel, no person, male or female, played a more significant role in his life and works between 1941-1945 than Berlau, and few relationships at any time were more intense. In Brecht's words, her love "could make five continents happy."[8]

Berlau was a warm, spontaneous, and affectionate person. She was also a scolding, possessive, often hysterical individual who existed only in extremes and who could shift from one mood to the other without warning. Never secure in Brecht's affection, she made such excessive demands on him that at times she became his personal fury. Her insistence that he write her daily forced him to send more letters to her during his American years than to all other friends combined, and more than to any single person in his lifetime.[9] In them he reveals a private side that is seldom seen. One letter thanking her for cigars she sent (he had her buy El Capitan Corona cigars from a shop in New York) contains an uncharacteristically sentimental expression by Brecht, who describes walking in his garden in Santa Monica one evening: "A silver haze filled the evening sky, and no stars were visible. But I knew you were looking up, and I stood, so to speak, next to you."[10] Others show him as a concerned friend and lover who is solicitous of her health (she did not eat properly and drank excessively), reassuring about his feelings for her, and sometimes almost maudlin in expressing them. Brecht seldom apologized, but Berlau managed to extract repeated apologies from him for his irregular letters. Her constant reprimands were no doubt responsible for eliciting from him unusually direct expressions of affection. But it would be inaccurate to claim that Berlau extracted these reassurances from an unwilling subject.

If one can believe his letters, Brecht felt a genuine need for Berlau. Like a leitmotif, the phrase "I need you" recurs throughout them as his means of expressing feeling obliquely. And dozens of letters close with the abbreviation (and sometimes the complete words) of "I love you" in Berlau's native Danish tongue (*je elsker dig*) or with the abbreviation e.p.e.p. for the Latin *et probe et procus* (near and far). Yet these are not conventional love letters. In spite of the strong concern they express for her diet, her health, her writing, her discomfort in the New York heat, and her financial circumstances, they more often resemble business correspondence instructing an agent how to deal with his works, requesting help, or seeking advice on collaborative projects. Brecht tried to structure their relationship that way. To compensate Berlau for losing her job with the Office of War Information in mid-1943 (her employers discovered that she was a Communist), he asked her to become his "New York office" and manage his affairs there. Quickly she assumed the role of his authorized agent. This required that his letters to her deal largely with business matters, thereby keeping emotional and private considerations in the background. Though he sent her money from time to time, he even tried to depersonalize this. In one letter containing two checks, he states that they are in payment for "six months work" and urges her to keep receipts "for tax purposes."[11]

It was also a sign of Brecht's need for and dependence on her that nearly everything he wrote in America, including poems, went to her for criticism and approval. In New York, in Santa Monica, or by mail, Berlau collaborated on *The Primer of War, Chalk Circle*, a long epic poem that includes part of the *Communist Manifesto, Schweyk, Set-zuan*, and a number of lesser works. After the 1942 production of *Master Race*, he assigned her to send clippings and to communicate with the director about possible future performances. At the 1945 English production, she worked in the theater with him as his "production secretary" and photographed the rehearsals and the performances. On July 10, 1945, Brecht wrote out a formal power of attorney for her to act in his behalf.[12]

After becoming pregnant by Brecht early in 1944, Berlau returned to Santa Monica in June of that year. The removal of a tumor on September 3rd, which resulted in the premature birth of a male child, left further evidence of Brecht's concealed tender side. A note in an envelope of the Cedars of Lebanon Hospital addressed to her in room 314 reads: "Love, I am so glad that you are fighting so courageously. Don't think that I do not want to see you when you are ill. You are beautiful then, too. I am coming tomorrow before noon. Yours, Bertolt."[13]

After returning to New York in March 1945 Berlau did odd jobs, ranging from factory work and house cleaning to barkeeping. But jobs were only a means of subsistence; her life was essentially committed to Brecht and his works. Unselfish, generous to a fault, and self-effacing when it came to his works, but also domineering, histrionic, and brazen, she promoted him so zealously that she sometimes hurt his best interests. Laughlin recalls her marching into the New Directions office in the summer of 1945 and, in dramatic fashion, announcing that she was "very important" to Brecht. She then demanded royalty payments for the book version of *Master Race*, which Brecht had asked her to pick up. Luise Rainer, who called her "loony," remembers Berlau's coming to her apartment in New York with a version of *Galileo* and ordering her to get out her recording machine so she could read it aloud for her. In her determination to record Brecht's works for posterity, Berlau also took a three-month photography course from Joseph Breitenbach in the spring of 1944, specifically to learn how to make microfilm copies.[14] After 1947 this skill enabled her to photograph and to produce "model books" showing exemplary scenes from his plays as he staged them himself. Her abrasiveness, however, did not please Brecht, nor did her use of his name in money matters. In promoting his affairs, she felt entitled to use people. She never paid Breitenbach for his instruction, and she generally avoided settling debts by explaining that she and Brecht did not have the money.

For years Weigel had tolerated Brecht's female collaborators and even entertained them in her home. During Brecht's American exile, she explained her forbearance by stoically telling a friend that when one is married to a genius, one tolerates things one would not in a normal marriage.[15] She knew Brecht needed women for his writing, and normally she endured it silently. But she could not abide Berlau. All his life Brecht paid inordinate attention to the opinions of his female alter egos. In the United States, Berlau's role was magnified because he was in a strange land struggling for success, and at the outset she was the lone surviving member of his coterie of ego reinforcers. Friends close to both of them maintain that she was very important to him at this time and that, in contrast to other relationships, their closeness virtually made her Brecht's second wife.[16] Weigel reacted strongly against her because she recognized this unusual intimacy. In her opinion, Berlau's near worship of Brecht was a destructive influence on him.

Berlau's notorious indiscretion angered Weigel. To fellow employees of the OWI in New York, she trumpeted that she was the "whore of a classical writer"; in Santa Monica after her breakdown, she broadcast that she was "Brecht's backstreet wife."[17] Berlau's intimidating aggressiveness in promoting him soured friendships, and more than once Brecht felt obliged to defend her bizarre actions to his own detriment. In dealing with Brecht's translators in New York, this Danish woman, who commanded neither English nor German well, condemned nearly every translation of Brecht into English in which he did not personally have a hand. Overly protective of his works, she was excessively critical of Kreymborg's *Schweyk* translations, of the Stern and Auden *Chalk Circle*, and of lesser translations. Repeatedly Brecht's letters to her rebut her criticisms, gracefully reject bad advice, and generally try to mollify her. In them, one of the few times in his life, he was usually defensive.

In spite of an overbearing manner and a demanding nature, Berlau was blindly devoted to Brecht. She claimed, for example, that she dressed in the puritanical fashion he dictated, which included wearing dark, solid colors and long dresses. Because she had once been an actress at the Danish Royal theater and an aspiring writer herself, in American exile Berlau felt increasingly frustrated at having accomplished nothing of note. Brecht demanded that all his collaborators produce their own works, and he usually assisted them unselfishly. In Denmark he had helped Berlau write several pieces, but in America this almost stopped. She could not or would not write, and this intensified a sense of inadequacy that she compensated for by her work for and with Brecht. In a series of vignettes about his feelings for her which he wrote during his Scandinavian and American exile and appended to the *Me-Ti/Book of Changes*, Brecht characterizes her importance to him in terms that he intends as complimentary. One passage demonstrates how completely she lived for him. Using the mask "Lai-tu" for her, he writes: "Lai-tu has a low regard for herself because she had not produced any great work. . . . Neither as an actress nor as a writer has she accomplished anything special. . . . Me-ti [Brecht] said to her: it is true that you have not delivered any goods, but that does not mean you have not accomplished anything. Your kindness has been noticed and appreciated by its being used. Thus an apple achieves fame by being eaten" (*GW* XII, 585).

Weigel's analysis of Berlau's baleful influence on Brecht may or may not have been correct, but, if Brecht's letters are credible, his devotion to Berlau was undisputable. There the mode of speech is always "we," not "you" or "I." Repeatedly he speaks of wanting her to return to Santa Monica as soon as he can support her. When she returned to New York in 1945, she extracted a promise of complete fidelity from him and agreed on a code phrase that appeared in many subsequent letters reassuring her that he was faithful to her. The phrase was: "Everything is all right." She was apparently the first to violate this promise when she had an affair with a Danish acquaintance shortly before her breakdown. Her infidelity clearly hurt Brecht. In reaction to it he wrote a poem entitled "The Writer Feels Himself Betrayed by a Friend," an unusual expression of personal vulnerability on Brecht's part. Speaking obliquely of his reaction as though it were someone else's experience ("the writer") and being intentionally vague about what is felt, this poem about a faithless beloved uses the title to make six simple comparisons lacking commentary:

> What a child feels when its mother goes away with a strange man.
> What a carpenter feels when overcome by dizziness, a sign of
>   aging.
> What a painter feels when his model does not return and the
>   picture is not finished.
> What a physicist feels when he discovers the error at the
>   beginning of his series of experiments.
> What a flier feels when the oil pressure drops while over the
>   mountains.
> What an airplane, if it could feel, feels when its pilot is drunk.
> (*GW* X, 938)

Berlau reproached herself when Brecht disapproved of her behavior. To a puzzled roommate she quoted a statement she heard him use many times: "Call a dog a bitch, and it turns into a bitch." She appended to it, "Call a woman a whore, and she becomes a whore. I am now a whore."[18]

Berlau's hysterical, sometimes maniacal behavior in the years following her breakdown and convalescence became one of the heaviest burdens that Brecht bore in the last decade of his life. It also stretched Weigel to the limit of her endurance. Rhoda Riker, a friend of the family, remembers receiving a phone call from Weigel in the spring of 1946, saying her husband had just phoned from New York. If she did not take in Berlau, he had said, he would not come home. With her usual sense of realism, Weigel accepted necessity and arranged for Berlau to stay with Anna Harrington in her "Uplifters" apartment in Santa Monica. Her only condition was that Berlau be kept out of her sight.

B. HELENE ("HELLI") WEIGEL

Helene Weigel shared at least one trait with her husband—each put his career ahead of personal feelings. Unusually devoted to him, and as convinced of his genius as he was, her life in American exile displayed the same single-mindedness in promoting Brecht's career that marked his own actions. When she told a friend that Berlau's affection for Brecht inflated his ego in a way harmful to his creativity,[19] she was speaking less from jealousy than from the conviction that emotional pampering was not good for him. She seems to have understood his emotional makeup and, if possible, she was more tough-minded than he was in protecting him against excessive passion, especially if it were for a demanding and difficult woman. Knowing his need to be surrounded by stimulating friends and collaborators, she put on weekly socials for him. Many European and American friends report attending her Sunday night "kindergarten," as it came to be called by some.

On the surface their marriage manifested what appeared to be a depersonalization of feeling by two artists who respected and promoted each other. Brecht, for example, never spoke of her by her first name, but only as "Weigel"; she in turn never referred to him in the presence of close friends or in letters as "my husband" or "Bertolt," but always as "Brecht." Yet beneath this exterior existed genuine admiration and concern for the other. But, in the Brecht household, private affairs were seldom discussed, to say nothing of emotions. Their relationship apparently minimized the emotional or private side of life. As Brecht's dramas prove, concealing them this way can sometimes be the most effective means of expressing them. Elsa Lanchester recalls that "she was loyal to him; they understood each other."[20] Moreover, they learned from each other. Bentley believes that Weigel, along with one or two other actors and actresses who were close to Brecht over the years, did more to shape his conception of acting than all abstract considerations of theatrical theory. A number of his characters and much of his theory of unemotive "epic" acting can be traced directly to this woman who excelled at this type of portrayal.

That is not to say that Weigel lacked emotions. She possessed great sensitivity and deep feelings. She was enormously generous, whether in supporting Salka Viertel financially for a period of five to six months during 1946 when Mrs. Viertel was without funds,[21] or in turning her home after the war into a relief center that dispatched countless packages to relatives and to acquaintances in Europe. Friends and neighbors recount dozens of anecdotes about her thoughtfulness and compassion. Brecht's long absences in 1946 (he spent nearly six months of that year on the East Coast) also moved her to something unusual—this normally very private woman expressed her frustration to a friend.[22] But this was uncharacteristic. She was a lady all her life, albeit a Marxist lady in proletarian garb, and she seldom lost control or surrendered her natural graciousness.

Wurtele recalls overhearing a conversation in their home which illustrates her toughness of mind. Weigel had maintained that women have more physical fortitude than men and had cited menstruation, child-bearing, etc., as evidence. Brecht, who was noted for an ever-present two-day growth of beard, lamely retorted, "Men shave," to which Weigel fired back, "How do you know?" Weigel appears to have been one of the few persons, especially among those closest to Brecht, who could hold her own with him. Tenacity and devotion; unshaken conviction of her husband's greatness; total commitment to a common political ideology; stoic forbearance, charm, and a splendid sense of humor—these made her equal to the difficult demands of consorting with this complex man. She learned English better than Brecht and probably adjusted to daily life in America more readily than he. In refusing to be frustrated by the circumstances of exile, she established surprisingly stable conditions for him and for his writing. It is impossible to estimate how much her sheer presence helped to keep alive his dramatic gifts during a period when he had no stage to write for. As a genius of theater *praxis* who also happened to be a dramatist, Brecht needed contact with actors and actresses in order to write. Throughout his exile, the actress Weigel represented the only uninterrupted connection he had with someone whose ideas on the performability of his works were accompanied by credibility as his kind of performer. In America, Weigel had no chance to display her ability anywhere except in conversations with Brecht.

Speaking of Weigel's lot in American exile, Salka Viertel claims she went through hell for Brecht: "I can't imagine another woman taking all that." Nor did she mean only Brecht's peccadillos. Flight from Germany in 1933 had abruptly ended Weigel's flourishing career as an actress and had cast her in the unaccustomed role of housewife, mother, business manager and support troops for the exiled dramatist. American theater people often expressed disbelief when they learned that this frugal, hard-working German *hausfrau*, whose bobbed hair and plain features made her resemble a Käthe Kollwitz drawing, had been a prominent European actress. They saw only how she furnished their home from junk shops and Good Will, cooked, scrubbed, painted, gardened, sewed, and baked excellent Viennese apple strudel for her Sunday night socials. In addition to housework, she nursed dying trees and a tubercular daughter; exchanged recipes, fruits, and baked goods with her neighbors; and tried to surround Brecht with the stimulating friends he needed for his writing.

Those who had known Weigel as an actress in Europe generally pitied her, and there is no question that she felt frustrated by lack of opportunity. Salka Viertel states that "It is not easy to be a domestic slavey, but Helli never complained."[23] Oskar Homolka called her a "kitchen slave" who did not participate in conversations and who always withdrew voluntarily when Brecht's male friends gathered. Elsa Lanchester claims that Brecht "did not want her—he would not allow her—to appear in Hollywood films in small character parts. Because, of course, she would have had a German accent. . . . And so she was a rather unhappy woman."[24]

Most of these perceptions are not accurate, especially the remark that Brecht did not want Weigel to appear in Hollywood films. His vain attempts to secure roles for her is a token of the admiration he felt. He explicitly wrote what he thought would be a role for her in *Hangmen Also Die* and extracted a promise from Lang to let her play it. A copy of the script at one point shows her name on a tentative cast list for the role of Mrs. Dvorak, the vegetable woman,[25] and Brecht's journal claims that Lang gave her a brief screen test for the role.[26] Lang denies having made such a promise or having given her a screen test,[27] and she did not get the role. In 1944, through the help of refugee friends, Weigel did play a 30-second silent part in the film *The Seventh Cross* starring Spencer Tracy. Weigel later told friends that this represented the highest paid part per second in her acting career.[28] It was her only professional appearance in more than six years of

American exile, a dormant period that left her uncertain about her ability as an actress. As a consequence, the first drama in which she appeared after returning to Europe had to be in a small provincial theater in Chur, Switzerland, since she lacked the confidence to make her debut in a major city.

Claims have been made that Weigel gave acting instruction to aspiring actresses in Hollywood,[29] but reality was less glamourous. Sometime during 1941-1942 she met a Hungarian-born, German-speaking actress who had been studying at Max Reinhardt's Hollywood dramatic school. After hearing her complain of her lack of success, Weigel gave her acting lessons (in English) in their living room.[30] Generally her activities were restricted to this type of behind-the-scenes work to promote someone else's career.

Salka Viertel remembers hearing Brecht say how it upset him that Weigel was not given more parts in Hollywood films. He was as concerned about her career as he was about his own, for he considered her a first-rate actress. In September 1946, after watching Elisabeth Bergner open on Broadway in *The Duchess of Malfi*, Brecht sent a telegram to Weigel succinctly comparing her to this internationally known stage and film star: "As for Bergner, I see what an actress you are."[31] This expression of admiration, referring to her professional rather than personal qualities, is typical of Brecht's tendency to structure even the most intimate human relationships with as much detachment as possible.

Weigel was a silent but significant figure in Brecht's American exile. His journal and reports of friends prove that she was present at far more discussions about the theater and about his works than one might expect of a "kitchen slave," for Brecht esteemed her practical judgment on the theater as highly as he did her political commitment. During preparations for the Hollywood *Galileo* production in 1947, she was also a dominant behind-the-scenes presence, sewing costumes, rehearsing actors and actresses, and helping with hundreds of details. In the American exile she dedicated her great gifts to promoting the works and image of Bertolt Brecht at a time when she had no chance to use her own talent.

When Brecht left Santa Monica for Washington and New York in October 1947 on the way to Europe, Weigel closed up the house, sold their goods, and followed a few days later. In New York for the first time, preparing to embark for Europe and a renewed stage career, she and her daughter Barbara did what they never could do in Santa Monica—went to Broadway musicals. Among others, they saw "Finian's Rainbow" and "Oklahoma!" But it was Ethel Merman in a performance of "Annie Get Your Gun" who proved that the actress in

Weigel was still alive and learning. At one point, Merman responded to seeing the man she loved by standing with her mouth agape. Less than three years later, Weigel borrowed the same gesture for her smash success in *Mother Courage* at the point when Courage met her former lover, the cook.[32] With one exception, this minor addition to her acting career and the wide circle of friends she gained were the only positive results of her years in America. That exception was to help to keep alive Bertolt Brecht's dramatic talent in American exile.

VI. THE CHARISMATIC BRECHT

Working alone on plays had never been Brecht's forte. Before he ever discovered Marxism, he had surrounded himself with associates (often minor writers themselves) who discussed ideas, fed him material, re-wrote his own, and generally helped to "produce" his work. Had the Marxist concept of the collective and collective productivity not existed, Brecht would have invented it.

By buttonholing almost any willing listener and drawing him or her into his current writing project, Brecht attracted willing and talented people who became collaborators, translators, informants, promoters, discussion partners, and catalysts for his writing. Most of them found it flattering to be engaged by him, for whether it was his genius or his force of personality, they recognized something unusual about him. Bentley has observed that even Brecht's detractors will have to explain what took hold of those who knew and worked with him when, like Bentley, they often disagreed with a man who supposedly cherished agreement with his views above all else.[1]

These collaborative relationships, however close, were not necessar-ily built on a sense of deep friendship. With the exception of Reyher, an unusual "brother under the skin," Brecht did not enjoy particular intellectual intimacy with any man. Some who knew him have com-mented on a certain reserve about this self-styled Confucian sage that resembled shyness as much as aloofness.[2] Clearly Brecht's charisma did not lie in his appearance. In different garb, this angular, austere-looking figure with close-cropped hair, piercing, sunken eyes, high cheekbones, a scarred left cheek, and a Roman profile, might have passed for a monk or a Jesuit priest. One friend compared him with Gandhi.[3] Others who have described him as a "Savonarola of the in-dustrial age,"[4] a "cigar-smoking Julius Caesar,"[5] and "a combination of Ignatius Loyola and a Roman consul in Bavaria"[6] referred to his physiognomy rather than to his studied anti-bourgeois appearance.

Brecht's shabby dress and personal habits gave others the false im-pression that he was trying to cultivate a "proletarian" look in order to identify with the working class.[7] Dirty fingernails, an unwashed body, an ill-shaven face, teeth that have been described as "little tombstones sticking out of a black mouth,"[8] an ever-present cigar, baggy trousers, and a high-collared flannel or denim jacket of the style later popularized by Mao Tse-tung did not add up to an attractive ap-pearance. But neither were they proletarian. Workers in Germany or America did not dress or look that way, and Brecht knew it. This was his means of announcing an anti-middle-class stance long before the youth counter-culture of the sixties appropriated similar dress for that purpose. Brecht, however, was no drop-out from society. Beneath this exterior, friends still sensed the quasi-religious intensity of a deeply committed artist, an "El Greco in mufti," as Clurman called him.[9] However one viewed him, Brecht's undeniable attractiveness was evident to virtually every collaborator. In the final analysis, it probably went beyond creative brilliance and intellectual vitality and had to do with an enormously interesting personality. Bentley states unequivocally that he was "the most fascinating man I have ever met."[10]

Whatever the fascination was that caused others to attach themselves to or associate with Brecht, most of them did so willingly, even eagerly. This same "something" motivated them to continue working after serious disagreements with and thoughtless behavior by Brecht. Though detractors may claim he "used" others to promote his own ends, with few exceptions his collaborators expressed no sense of exploitation, but rather appreciation for the association. During a jurisdictional dispute over rights to the *Chalk Circle* in 1948 (Brecht had assigned them to at least three different parties), Bentley wrote Reyher, saying: "Thanks for your notes, and forgive my irritation, which has years of chaotic dealings with Brecht behind it."[11] After many more incidents of frustration caused by Brecht, Bentley wrote a tribute at his death in 1956, acknowledging that "I had the experience of being his political enemy and his personal friend, and I must record that the friendship was given precedence over the enmity."[12]

Hays, too, experienced frustration and personal indignity in his enthusiasm for promoting Brecht's works. Yet something sustained him in this relationship and brought him back for more. That "something" was related to a statement he made in a letter to Laughlin in 1941, in which he wrote that Brecht was "the only poet to really absorb Marxism and use it creatively in the theater."[13]

Reyher's commitment to Brecht and to his works was so profound that for two full years following Brecht's return to Europe he functioned as Brecht's official business manager, authorizing performances of the plays, corresponding with Brecht and with those interested in such performances, forwarding royalty checks, and performing many incidental tasks. For the countless hours he spent, Reyher never received any remuneration.

Gorelik's relationship helps to explain some of Brecht's ability to hold collaborators. In spite of repeated disagreements over everything from dramatic theory to the question of German war guilt, Gorelik returned for more collaboration and discussion. Part of the attraction lay in Brecht's repeated invitations to undertake something new together. More significantly, Brecht understood how to depersonalize the disagreements they had and tried to let Gorelik and other collaborators understand that they should do the same. For him, issues had to be separated from personal feelings. The success of his works was more important than any personal considerations, including hurt feelings. This is one reason Brecht was not inclined to apologize. Apologies pertain to the affective sphere; in collaborative relationships, Brecht wanted to ignore that sphere. In separating the work or the issue involved from his own words or actions, he assumed that his collaborators shared the same conviction of his genius that he possessed. With few exceptions he was correct.

There were, however, a few collaborators or potential collaborators who were not magnetized by him, among them W. H. Auden and Christopher Isherwood. Their relationship emphasizes that those not for Brecht tended to be very much against him. It also illustrates how difficult Brecht could be when someone resisted his attempts to draw them into his orbit.

Two points about Brecht's association with W. H. Auden are clear—that they did not like each other personally, and that each had high regard for the other's work. In Brecht's case, the second statement requires correction—he thought highly of Auden's talent, though not necessarily of all his works. After leafing through volumes of poetry by Auden and T. S. Eliot, Brecht's journal calls them "the veritable verse of augurs. Catholicism (or Marxism) plus intimate matters."[14] And Brecht's mockery of the writings of Isherwood, Aldous Huxley, and Auden during an evening he spent with Isherwood suggests that in Auden's more recent works he missed the political commitment he knew from that author's writings of the thirties.[15]

Letters and the manuscripts of *Chalk Circle* and *Malfi* prove that Brecht and Auden spent weeks and perhaps months working together, but the silence surrounding these sessions conceals what, at the end, was a strained personal relationship, at least for Auden.

Brecht tried to be deferential, even cordial, toward Auden, whom he clearly respected. He knew that many of Auden's plays and poems resembled his own in certain ways. They were aimed at the widest possible audience; they employed the vernacular much as his own works did (both had been strongly influenced by Kipling); and at least some of them were openly didactic in a political sense. But this affinity did not extend to other areas. Berlau and Reyher remember Brecht's complaints about Auden as a person—his personal sloppiness, his working habits, and even the appearance of his desk.[16] Brecht once remarked on the contrast between a container on Reyher's desk with an assortment of neatly sharpened pencils in it, and the disheveled condition of

Auden's table. A strong sense of German bourgeois orderliness and tidiness possessed Brecht all his life. Lack of it in Auden obviously bothered him.

Brecht must have behaved badly toward Auden, for in later years Auden refused to or was unable to recall anything of their collaboration except what he called the exiled playwright's "poor manners." In 1958, while translating Brecht's *Seven Deadly Sins*, Auden's only impressions of Brecht were that he was a "remarkable writer," but "a most unpleasant man."[17] Robert Craft's biography of Stravinsky quotes Auden as saying that Brecht was one of the few people for whom he thought a death sentence might have been justifiable: "In fact, I can imagine doing it to him myself," he stated.[18] In 1971, a quarter of a century after their collaboration, Auden summarized his views of Brecht when he stated: "I think him a great lyric poet, but not as good a playwright. I think there was a split between his natural sensibility, which was pessimistic, even Christian, and the optimistic Marxist philosophy he tried to adapt to."[19] But when asked for details of their work together, Auden repeated that "my memories of the collaboration with Brecht are now nonexistent."[20] He recalled only that Brecht was "an odious person."[21] Some unpleasant personal experiences obviously lay behind this deep-seated antipathy, but what they were remains a mystery.

Paradoxically, in spite of loathing Brecht's person, Auden continued to feel attracted to his works. In the spring of 1946 his translation of a song from the fifth act of *Chalk Circle* had appeared in the *Kenyon Review*, the first of many he would do. And he translated other poems at this time, for a letter from Brecht to Berthold Viertel in June 1946 states that Auden has rendered the "Children's Crusade 1939" into English. In subsequent years, he produced first-rate English versions of a ballet text called *The Seven Deadly Sins*; of the texts for *Mahagonny* and *Mother Courage*; and of a number of poems. But there is no record of personal contact after 1946.

Like Auden, Christopher Isherwood also grew to dislike Brecht as a person. In contrast to Auden, his reasons are well known. Isherwood acknowledges liking Brecht when they first met and admits being influenced by that writer's works.[22] It was not so much Brecht's aggressive attempt to win Isherwood as a collaborator that offended the British-born writer as it was the German exile's effort to catechize him politically. Brecht believed Isherwood had been led astray by religious devotion, and he was determined to save him. In August 1943 Berthold Viertel, who had been Isherwood's pseudonymous hero in *Prater Violet*, took Isherwood to visit Brecht.[23] The British-born writer remarked in his diary how he liked Brecht, and how Brecht immediately tried to engage him to translate some lines for his *Duchess of Malfi* adaptation. Isherwood declined and suggested Auden. They met a number of times at Salka Viertel's salon before an invitation to dinner with the Brechts on September 20, 1943, which Isherwood accepted, ended any chance of collaboration.

Brecht's journal account of the evening admitted that he hoped Isherwood, to whom he had earlier given his *Good Woman of Setzuan*, would translate it for him. Isherwood expressed uneasiness at the three pathetic gods portrayed in it, and, though Brecht's journal records that Isherwood laughed at the playwright's explanation of them as personifications of a dead morality, he "dropped the subject relatively quickly." Then Berthold Viertel arrived and began teasing Isherwood about what Brecht called his "Buddhism" (actually it was Vedanta). "India has conquered you," he said, speaking of Isherwood, Auden, and Huxley; Brecht's journal then relates how he picked up Viertel's theme:

" 'It has infected you with leprosy,' I said, continuing the attack. In fact, Isherwood is a Buddhist (a little ersatz-monk, standing barefoot in his cowl in the incense of a Hollywood monastery that is really a boarding house), Auden an Anglican, and Huxley a hazy kind of deist. Isherwood, a close friend of the other two, allows me to poke fun at his intelligent, finely nuanced, detailed descriptions of the spiritual agonies of these parasites. But when I call him "bought," he looks at his watch and gets up. Such matters cannot be discussed. Waiter, the check! I have the feeling a surgeon must have when his patient stands up during an operation and leaves; I only wounded him."

Brecht had wanted to perform a spiritual lobotomy on Isherwood, who was living at the time in a Vedanta monastery in Hollywood. Anything connected with religion or spiritual matters was a red flag to him, and politically uncommitted artists angered him. Brecht and his wife, who, Isherwood recalls, reminded him of a Salvation Army lass with her strident call to repentance, felt that in the course of this evening they had to save his talent by talking him out of what they considered to be a dalliance with Oriental mysticism. Isherwood's diary for the same evening notes that Brecht and his friends called only Huxley (and not himself) "bought," but the effect was the same—Brecht had hurt him badly, or, as he understated it in retrospect, "Brecht simply had very bad manners." While Isherwood says he did not leave their home immediately, he was angry enough not to prolong the visit. Even Viertel, who agreed with Brecht's position, was upset by the exile's behavior and wrote to Isherwood the next day to apologize.

Several times in subsequent years Brecht approached Isherwood for help on translations—on parts of *Master Race*, on the poem "Children's Crusade 1939," on the entire *Chalk Circle*, and on his essay "Writing the Truth: Five Difficulties." Brecht applied considerable pressure and even visited Isherwood at his Vedanta retreat on Ivar Street in Hollywood. Each time Isherwood declined. In retrospect he states that Brecht was absolutely "ruthless" when his own projects were concerned, and he had no desire to be exploited or to be bullied.

In negative terms Isherwood describes traits which other collaborators who had worked closely with Brecht either did not see or were able to overlook in consideration of his obvious genius and the debt they felt for the assistance he gave them.

In Berlin during the last years of his life, Brecht became a living legend among aspiring young directors and actors who sat at his feet in the Berliner Ensemble and recorded many of his words. But his association with a small group of young people in America illustrates that he was already drawing those of the next generation under his spell.

Throughout the first twelve years of exile, Brecht had associated chiefly with refugees of his own generation. In America he began to draw around him a group of young college-aged men and women from his son Stefan's generation that included Hans Viertel; Rhoda (Ricki) Riker, and Morton Wurtele, student friends of Stefan's at UCLA; Naomi Replansky, a New York poet who came to Los Angeles and joined this youthful coterie; and, to a lesser degree, Peter Kaus, son of the émigré film writer Gina Kaus. They spent many hours with Brecht, discussing his writings and other topics. Each of them lived in his house for various periods or saw Brecht and his family there regularly, and nearly all of them were drawn into collaboration on his works.

The unequivocal admiration this group felt toward Brecht was partly a consequence of age. Collaborators near Brecht's age considered themselves to be equals or near-equals. This inevitably created unconscious tensions. Those tensions were absent in the clear-cut teacher-pupil relationship Brecht had with these adults nearly a generation younger than he was. Consequently they saw Brecht at his best. Without exception they knew him as a thoughtful, supportive person of overwhelming genius. All remember his kindness toward them, and all viewed him as their teacher. In addition to confirming the portrait of him based on perceptions of other contemporaries, they add several unknown nuances.

Each of them experienced Brecht's insistence on absolute control over every aspect of works by and about him. Wurtele reports that, in the summer of 1946, *Vogue* magazine wanted to do a story on Brecht, presumably after Laughton had contacted them in connection with pre-production publicity for *Galileo*. Brecht agreed, but only if Florence Homolka were allowed to photograph him. *Vogue* wanted to use its own photographers, and the matter ended there.

Riker heard a variation on the theme of total control which also had to do with physical survival. Brecht told her that, while in Moscow during his trip across the Soviet Union in 1941, he was offered a position at the Moscow Art Theater, which he declined. In part, theatrical considerations motivated this decision. Knowing that the doctrines of Stanislavsky reigned in Moscow, Brecht realized he would have even

less chance of introducing his ideas and controlling theatrical productions there than he would in America. And he also knew of the fate of
émigré friends who had gone to the Soviet Union and had been liquidated, and he had no desire to risk that.

These young people recall Brecht's deep commitment to a work
ethic—his life was his writing, and he had no time for anything that
did not serve it. They noticed his ascetic life style, characterized, one of
them observes, by taking cold showers in the guest cottage behind his
home,[1] or by drinking nothing stronger than beer.

As an example of the thoughtfulness all remember, Replansky, a
young poet whom Brecht met in New York in 1944 and who moved to
Santa Monica in 1946, recalls how she was without funds. In response, Brecht asked her to copy by hand an entire book that he and
Laughton were using in connection with *Galileo*, for which he had
Laughton pay her $50. Laughton's protests at the price suggest that
the project was not indispensable to *Galileo*, but assistance for Replansky at this point was indispensable for Brecht.

Brecht's limited tolerance for disagreement did not seem to trouble
those young friends who noticed it. Viertel remembers how sharply
they disagreed on political and ideological matters. A member of the
Young People's Socialist League and of the American section of the
Fourth International, Viertel engaged in heated arguments with him,
many of which focused on the writer's Stalinist views. A committed
Trotskyist at the time, he criticized Brecht's stand on a number of issues. He remembers questioning Brecht's uncritical support of what he
called an imperialist war, and how Russia had played down this aspect
to serve its own ends. Brecht reacted strongly against these hostile remarks that to him subverted the solidarity he thought every leftist
should show with the Soviet Union and the Communist Party. Disagreement notwithstanding, Viertel continued to collaborate as cheerfully as he claims Brecht helped him.

When politics impinged on art, however, young Viertel took exception. Differences arose over the frame scenes in the *Chalk Circle*. After
first seeing them, Viertel argued with Brecht that the language was
journalistic, and that the scenes were aesthetically poor and politically
embarrassing. History has proved him correct on at least some of the
matters he argued with the exiled writer, and he was aware of limitations in this fascinating friend. Brecht, he claims, wrote with one grand
illusion—that his audience was the politically sophisticated, culturally
refined working class of Berlin. Viertel realized that this advocate of
the working class had never written a drama using a worker or a
world-historical individual as its protagonist. Yet knowing these limitations did nothing to diminish his respect, and Brecht seems to have

liked this young disciple precisely because of this critical habit of mind.

The amount of disagreement Brecht tolerated from these young associates was more than a matter of feeling at ease around pupils who looked upon him as a master teacher. His pedagogical instincts moved him to invite their criticism and to accept it as freely as he dispensed it, for that was the way he learned. When Replansky objected that an epigram he wrote to be used in his *Primer of War* describing how well Russian soldiers behaved toward German women in occupied Germany in 1945, Replansky objected that it was too sentimental. Brecht dropped it without comment. And when she took issue with a stanza in "Children's Crusade 1939" about a rich Jewish child by pointing out that all Jews are not wealthy, Brecht instructed her to delete it from her translation.

Brecht in turn gave criticism kindly, according to Replansky. While working on his *Primer of War*, she mentioned that she liked Rilke's poetry. Brecht, who could not abide Rilke, pointed to a photo of a welder in a mask and explained how Rilke would have aestheticized it by glorifying one aspect of the man, such as the hands, the head, or the brow. "But I see what a man is doing and show that," he remarked.

Late in his life Brecht acknowledged that, although he was known as a playwright and theater director, he considered himself primarily a teacher. As a teacher, however, he had always been a bit of a director. Just as he attempted to keep close control over production details in the theater, he sometimes tried to direct the careers of his pupils as though he were coaching them in a play. His efforts to mold and promote them illustrate how satisfying he found the role of mentor.

After first meeting Naomi Replansky, Brecht was impressed enough to give her some epigrams from his *Primer of War* to translate. By working with her on translations of his own poems, and by reading her works, he gained such regard for her ability that he went out of his way to help her to establish herself as a writer. Early in 1945 Replansky had applied for a literary award offered by an unidentified American publisher. When she wrote Brecht requesting a letter, he asked that she recite her poems to Berthold Viertel in New York, who apparently confirmed his positive judgment of her. In late March 1945 he wrote an unusual recommendation that Berlau delivered personally to Replansky. It read (in Brecht's own English): "I have re-read your poems, and they impressed me even more than the first time. Curiously sophisticated volkslieder. They have the youth, the verve, and the sensitive vigor of your great cities, virtues one expects of the contemporary American literature (but doesn't very often meet). In my opinion the publisher of this collection will one day be proud of it. Some of these poems I will translate into German; at least I will attempt it." Brecht genuinely meant what he wrote; others remember his speaking of Replansky as one of the three greatest American women poets, though he did not identify the other two.

By entrusting Replansky with the translation of his poems under his supervision, Brecht was honoring her as the only kind of translator he would approve—another poet. He supervised her in translating a number of them, e.g., the "Hollywood Elegies," "O Germany, Pale Mother," "The Swamp," "Children's Crusade 1939," and many epigrams from *The Primer of War*. Brecht would explain the substance of the poem to Replansky in English; she would render it; then he would go over it. Replansky remembers that Brecht wanted to assess the translation's originality as much as its fidelity. She recalls how he made a virtue of her high-school reading knowledge of German by letting errors in meaning stand because they made poetic sense, such as a line from "O Germany, Pale Mother" that read "Wie sitzest du . . ./ . . ./ unter den Befleckten" that she rendered "even among the lepers—untouchable."

In addition to supportive encouragement, Brecht gave concrete help. Through him, Dorothy Norman published a number of Replansky's original poems in the same issue of *Twice a Year* which carried her renderings of Brecht's poetry. One example of his influence on her confidence as a poet was a compliment he paid when he let others know that he preferred her translation of "Children's Crusade 1939" to several others in circulation, including one by W. H. Auden.

For a period between 1945 and 1947, Brecht tried to plan the life and career of Rhoda Riker, an eager follower who was overwhelmed by the dramatist's creative gifts. In a joint teacher-pupil project, Brecht helped this UCLA undergraduate philosophy major to write a paper on the differences between Marx and Engels for one of her courses. Both viewed it as a lark, but the instructor who read their paper laced with long quotations by the two thinkers rewarded it with an "A" and praised it, noting that it had the makings of a great book. More seriously, Brecht tried to do with Riker what he did with everyone around him—make her into a writer. After graduation from UCLA, she began doing social work. Upon listening avidly to her accounts of dealing with welfare recipients, Brecht urged her to make a record of her experiences, both for her own practice and for their value as social commentaries.

In addition to spending hours discussing a career with Riker, Brecht instructed her on topics as diverse as music, film, and politics. In order to help her to sharpen her verbal skills and to overcome her shyness, he made her speak in crowds. Above all, he built her confidence by entrusting her with important assignments, e.g., acting as a contact with Isherwood, whom he had asked to look at a copy of *Master Race*, or consulting her on lines of *Galileo*. Not long before that play opened in Hollywood, he and Weigel ceremoniously presented her with a copy of the final manuscript and announced that she was the first American to receive it. Though Brecht retrieved it later for a member of the cast to use in rehearsals, his action had the same effect on Riker's ego experienced by many others who considered themselves honored to have been singled out for his attention.

Largely because of his esteem for the natural sciences, Brecht did not attempt to influence the career of Wurtele, a graduate student in physics at UCLA. According to friends, he and Weigel expressed high regard for the mind of this friend of Stefan's who lived in the small guest cottage back of Brecht's home from December 1945 until September 1946. Wurtele's study of physics, however, did not exempt him from instruction by Brecht. Wurtele was not a writer, but in his capacity as technical adviser to the *Galileo* production, Brecht had him write an essay critically analyzing several scenes from the play.

Only once did Brecht's penchant for turning those around him into writers meet with frustration. Friends report how it upset him that Viertel failed to become a productive writer, and how he spoke with some agitation about Viertel's waste of considerable gifts. In spite of their periodic collaboration and Brecht's expressions of esteem for him, he seems to have taken it personally that he could not induce Viertel to go on writing.

From their intimate position as frequent visitors in or members of the Brecht household, these collaborators observed a relatively unknown side of the writer—Brecht with his hair down. Viertel and Riker recall attending movies with him (Riker remembers that Brecht's passion for gangster movies took them to see *Dillinger*), and she claims that, while washing dishes in Brecht's kitchen, she taught him the "International" in Yiddish, which Brecht preferred to the German version. Viertel reports on some informal scenes with Brecht which provide insight into how the dramatist's visually oriented mind operated.

Several times Viertel was present at "performances" in which Brecht translated real or imagined events of political life into dramatic reality. Like Charlie Chaplin, whose impromptu parodies in Hollywood living rooms often equalled his screen performances, Brecht would act out vignettes as he thought they might have happened. After newspapers reported the friction between the American commanders at Pearl Harbor in 1941, Brecht played an impromptu one-man skit for Viertel on what might have transpired between them. It included such memorable lines as: *Admiral Kimmel* (in a German accent): "Short, the Japs are coming." *General Short* (likewise in a German accent): "I'm not speaking to you, sir." In a more serious vein, he demonstrated how Roosevelt and Stalin might have spoken together. Brecht saw the world as a *theatrum mundi,* and he tended to think of world events in visual terms related to the stage. Hence these vignettes became a means of clarifying or expressing ideas. Another friend who witnessed the same thing recalls describing to Brecht a decision-making conference between Roosevelt and Churchill. Brecht rejected it, saying, "No, that can't be, I can't show that on the stage." But when he learned that Harry Hopkins entered with a report from Stalin, he exclaimed, "Now I can show it; now it's credible."[2] For Brecht, the truth was always concrete, if only in a dramatist's special sense.

Another relatively obscure side of Brecht emerges from reports by members of this coterie—his interest in learning about America generally, and American English specifically. Viertel provoked his curiosity about the attitudes and conditions of the American worker, for, when Brecht met him in 1941, Viertel was working in a shipyard. His employment there, and later in another shipyard, followed by a job as an aircraft helper for Pan-Am, made him a welcome informant on American labor, and Brecht listened eagerly. Under Brecht's interrogation Wurtele, who had grown up in Kentucky, became an informant on the dialect of that region. Wurtele claims that Brecht not only loved idiomatic American English, but that he questioned anyone who would serve as an informant on regionalisms. As intelligent native speakers he, Viertel, Replansky, and Riker were often enlisted to evaluate English translations of Brecht's works. In conversations about his favorite diversion, Brecht also learned from Wurtele about the murder mysteries of Erle Stanley Gardner, which he now began to read.

After more than five years of acclimatization in America, Brecht's association with these friends made him exhibit greater interest than ever in the language and customs of his host land. Ricki Riker remembers an evening in 1946 or 1947 at the home of Fritz Kortner or Paul Henreid, where Brecht, together with Peter Lorre and others, heard Burl Ives, probably America's best known folk-singer at the time, perform American folk songs. Brecht's reaction was startling. He called Ives a "great man"; his songs represented a totally new and exciting experience for him. For days he talked enthusiastically about his discovery of a New America, a new American idiom. Replansky reports a similar experience that left a trace in Brecht's works. At one point she played a record for him of the famous American Negro singer "Leadbelly" (Huddie Ledbetter) singing "The Gray Goose," a balladesque narrative of a goose that is shot, but, being too tough to eat, flies off.

Thinking that this part of the black cultural heritage would appeal to Brecht, she explained how the toughness of the gray goose symbolized the American Negro's ability to survive whatever had been inflicted on him. When Charles Laughton heard it, he did not share Brecht's enthusiasm for this subtle song of protest, but the exiled poet liked it enough to translate the text into German under the title "The Durable Gray Goose" (GW x, 1081). Brecht's free rendering also gave it a new direction. In the closing lines, he had the gray goose fly off with its six goslings in a symbolic direction missing from the original—toward the east.

Without exception, these young associates today express unqualified appreciation for the privilege of having known and worked with Brecht. Viertel says theirs was never an exploitative relationship for him, but a remarkable learning process. Replansky expresses the same sense of privilege. Brecht's encouragement and help on her own work made her feel that he considered it as important as his own. Consulting her as he did in the smallest detail or problem not only flattered her; it motivated her and others to give him their best. A request to "look over some lines" probably made her the author of the last two lines of the concluding quatrain in the English version of *Galileo* (Barbara Brecht wrote the first two):

> May you now guard science' light.
> Kindle it and use it right.
> Lest it be a flame to fall
> Downward to consume us all.

Riker's devotion can be measured less by the way she helped to close the Brecht household and dispose of a few items when they left for Europe than by an anecdote she relates. She claims that, shortly before leaving, Brecht gave her a large amount of manuscript and photograph material of the type he had used as a basis for the *Primer of War*. Insisting that he did not like it, he instructed her to burn everything. Obediently she did it. To destroy anything he wrote sounds out of character for Brecht, but the anecdote underlines her complete dedication to him. In this as in almost everything else, she and her contemporaries were the devoted disciples of a man they admired without reservation.

VII. BRECHT AND THE GERMANS

26 "WHERE I AM IS GERMANY"— THE REFUGEE GHETTO

In 1939 the German exile philosopher Ernst Bloch described two categories of refugee artists he observed in America. Those in the first group had written off Nazi Germany and severed connections with German life and culture. They scorned their native tongue and became "Americanized" with such fervor that their acquired manners and behavior often made them appear foolish, if not grotesque.

Members of the second group wanted to create a German cultural island in America. Clinging to naive concepts of American life gleaned from European sources, they felt themselves superior to a culturally underdeveloped land that existed as a minor satellite in a Euro-centric universe. With an admixture of contempt and zeal, they set out to cultivate and enlighten the natives, while at the same time resisting the fatal disease called "assimilation."[1]

Brecht defies easy classification in either category. By choice and necessity he associated largely with European refugees during his first two years in America. In most ways he stood closer to the second group, for Europe was unquestionably the center of his universe. "The exile's trade is hoping," he wrote of his intention to return (*GW* xx, 284). On the other hand, his interest in learning about America, and his tendency to assume an oppositional stance in virtually everything, left him at odds with most fellow émigrés.

Brecht's frustration when he realized that his European reputation meant nothing in America explains some of his irascibility in the first two years. At the same time, he refused to fall into the self-pity that many exiles, especially those with European reputations, cultivated with public accounts of their tribulations. When Berthold Viertel wrote in 1941 that a volume of his own German poems (*Fürchte dich nicht*) was about to appear in New York, Brecht congratulated him on being published in an age when books were burned more easily than printed and counseled Viertel to delete anything in the foreword that might suggest self-pity, personal suffering, *inter exilem silent musae*, or "don't be so amazed that I'm still alive."[2] And, in 1946, after reading Naomi Replansky's poem "City of Dreadful Night," Brecht praised all of it but a stanza that he thought sentimentalized and thereby falsified the exile experience:

> The exile moves stiffly through cities of woe,
> Learns a language he never had wished to know.
> His rapid heartbeat
> Fills the foreign street.

At his objection, she deleted it.[3]

Brecht had no illusions about life in exile, but, in contrast to many refugees, he seemed to sense pride in his state and cultivated the image of having been exiled involuntarily. As he wrote in March 1942 to Karen Michaelis, the Danish writer who gave his family asylum in Denmark after they fled Germany: "Our literary history does not boast of as many exiled writers as, for example, the Chinese. We must excuse ourselves on grounds that our literature is still very young and not yet cultivated enough. Chinese lyric poets and philosophers, I hear, were used to going into exile as ours go into the Academy" (*GW* XIX, 478). Unlike many refugees, Brecht viewed exile as a political necessity, especially for writers. He not only accepted its hardships; in the *Refugee Dialogues* he praised exile as "the best school for dialectics" (*GW* XIV, 1462). To him, the experience of forced flight and of exile in a foreign land were inescapable consequences of his fight against fascism.

Nor was this absence of self-pity the only trait that set Brecht apart. He shared neither the cultural arrogance nor the insularity of many European refugees in America. A large number viewed themselves, in the description of one observer, as Athenian teachers in the New Rome.[4] Brecht himself quoted a statement he had heard attributed to Thomas Mann,[5] but also made by others who considered themselves spokesmen for German culture in exile. With slight variations it read: "Where I am is Germany" or, in the version Brecht ascribes to Mann, "German culture is where I am" (*GW* XIX, 480). Brecht refused to consider himself a missionary for what he viewed as a dubious cultural heritage, and he denied having taken Germany into exile with him.[6] His mission was to promote one overriding cause—the theatrical ideas and works of Bertolt Brecht, which, just by chance, arose on German soil.

True, Brecht did resist assimilation into American life and thinking. Friends often heard his rejoinder when confronted with American food: "We didn't have that in Augsburg" (his birthplace). But he also disliked unfamiliar European food set before him by the wife of a refugee friend, which he declined with the comment that he liked experiments in the theater, but not in the kitchen.[7] And, though he claimed he would never master English, Brecht criticized in his journal friends who had been in the States several years without learning a word of the language. His refusal to be philo-Semitic at a time when German refugees with a conscience felt they had no other choice (his own wife was Jewish) illustrates how even among them Brecht remained an outsider. Kortner claims that Brecht considered the whole topic of anti-Semitism unworthy of discussion because of the patronizing attitude it implied.[8] For a variety of reasons, Brecht was out of step with most members of the refugee subculture.

Perhaps the only area of agreement was an admiration for President Franklin Delano Roosevelt. Few Americans can appreciate the extent of Roosevelt-worship among German-speaking refugees.[9] They looked upon the American president, whose liberal policies, springing from his hatred of Hitler, had helped to save the lives of many among them, as a father figure and, in extreme cases, as a savior. Roosevelt's social reforms also appealed to them as the most enlightened aspect of American democracy. The poems and tributes to Roosevelt written in German were often painfully embarrassing, however sincere. Brecht eschewed such expressions, but friends state that he never spoke of FDR with anything but respect. Journal entries and letters document his admiration for the man whom Brecht honored at his death by calling an "enlightened Democrat."[10]

One might expect that the exile experience would have forged closeness among refugees who otherwise had nothing in common. Often this did occur. More often they carried with them to America their European intrigues, jealousies, and political differences. In many cases the hardships of exile, and especially the whimsical way that Fortune passed out her favors, wounded egos and magnified differences far out of proportion. Those who had succeeded in America (and this included many who had modest reputations or none at all in Europe) could afford to be generous and magnanimous, and often were. But those struggling or starving had ample time and opportunity to indulge in petty gossip and back-stabbing. Denunciations were common, and there was a rush to inform on left- or right-wing enemies. In this atmosphere, the FBI had a ready pool of informants on Brecht and many others. From FBI files it is evident that the majority of those who supplied information on Brecht were fellow émigrés.

Brecht found this atmosphere oppressive. A letter to Korsch in October 1941, which insists that in the back woods of Finland he was not as removed from the world as he is here, attempts to describe some of the pettiness in the exile community: "hostilities flourish here like the oranges, and, like them, have no seeds. Jews accuse each other of anti-Semitism, and Germans charge each other with philo-Semitism." Yet Brecht, too, could not resist indulging in the same petty gossip, especially during the difficult early months of exile. One journal entry states that Kortner has heard Fritz Lang making anti-Semitic remarks, and that Rolf Nürnberg hates Lorre;[11] in another, he mentions that Lilli Laté, Lang's female companion of many years, is stepping out with a friend.[12] Also in the category of gossip is Brecht's note saying that Alfred Döblin and Heinrich Mann, two first-rate German novelists, are penniless after completing short-term contracts as film writers. Mann, after the expiration of a $6000-a-year contract with Warner Brothers, was in fact receiving money from his brother

Thomas,[13] while Döblin received assistance from the European Film Fund.[14] That Brecht bothered to record such gossip in his journal indicates how isolated and frustrated he felt during the early months in America. These entries also reflect a habit of mind that originally led him to Marxism—his sympathy with the underdog and his belief in the survival of the unfittest.

Being a "have-not" in a world where the "haves" were successful émigrés who, in his opinion, were superficial or short on talent brought out the worst in Brecht. Privately he was contemptuous of the actors Robert Thoeren and Paul Henreid, both successful in Hollywood, who invited him to their homes and apparently treated him well.[15] Erich Remarque, author of *All Quiet on The Western Front* and now a successful Hollywood writer, became the object of a devastating one-line journal vignette when he dropped in on a New Year's Eve party Brecht was attending in 1941: "Remarque is wearing a tuxedo, looks like [the popular Nazi writer] Hanns Heinz Ewers; something strikes me as missing from his face, probably a monocle."[16] Brecht's journal documents his opinion of Franz Werfel, the Austrian writer whose novel *The Song of Bernadette* and drama *Jacobowsky and the Colonel* scored Hollywood and Broadway successes in the forties. Brecht called him "The Holy Frunz of Hollywood, the Geschwerfel" and reported that he had stolen the story for his *Jacobowsky* drama from a poor emigrant who received nothing for it.[17]

Paul Henreid recalls that the Second World War was an exciting time to be in Hollywood because "everyone who was anyone was there," meaning an international array of intellectuals, artists, and film people. Brecht, who was not part of the "in" group, did not find it so. For him there was a pervasive dreariness about most émigré activities—the endless discussions of Hitler's strength (the majority in 1941-1942 held that he could not be beaten);[18] of the progress of the war (very badly for the Allies); and of the dim prospects of returning to Europe. Then there were the odious comparisons between European and American culture, the second-hand tales of intra-mural battles in the film studios, and the stories of injustices that deprived émigrés of roles they deserved.

With the exception of Egon Breiner, who worked for the Southern Pacific Railroad, his wife Leopoldine, who was a doctor, and Hans Winge, a critic, those with whom Brecht associated most closely in the refugee community were artists in the broadest sense—writers, actors, directors, and musicians who inevitably became collaborators on his projects. Ideologically this group covered a spectrum which reveals that Brecht was able to give personal compatability preference over ideological agreement. The profoundly conservative Döblin was a recent Jewish convert to Catholicism; Lorre was essentially apolitical; Homolka, who by his own admission parted company with Brecht over politics in the late twenties, and Czinner and Bergner were all moderately conservative; Breiner, a Socialist, quarreled with Brecht over Marxism. While other associates, like Winge, Dieterle, Kortner, and Berthold Viertel, were generally liberal, they were far from being radical Marxists. Only Hanns Eisler subscribed to the same brand of Marxism that Brecht did.

The refugee writer Hermann Borchardt, whom Brecht had known in Berlin and whom he had met again in New York during the spring of 1943, was one example of Brecht's subordinating politics to person, especially to a person's talent. He knew that Borchardt, who had lost his fingers and become deaf from maltreatment in the Buchenwald concentration camp, had been converted to Catholicism after his release. But Brecht liked him and admired his writing in spite of it. Before reading Borchardt's 1943 novel *The Conspiracy of the Carpenters*, he devoted an entire journal entry to its defense. Refugees had found it confusing, religious, and reactionary, he says. But Brecht admired this man whom he called a moralist, a satirist, a provocateur, one "whose works rise far above those of Werfel and consorts by depicting the social struggles of our age. In fact, in the bourgeois camp one finds reflections of social struggles almost exclusively in religious soil."[19] Later Brecht formulated his feelings toward Borchardt succinctly, though regretfully: "He's the greatest satirist in the German language, but, unfortunately, reactionary."[20]

Brecht's contact with other refugees showed the same paradox of getting along where it would be least expected. Breiner recalls inviting Brecht to dinner with Paul Hertz, the Reichstag floor leader of the Social Democratic Party in the Weimar Republic. Knowing of the hatred between Socialists and Communists of that era, Breiner expected fireworks. But each man knew the other by reputation, and they took an immediate liking to each other. They not only skillfully avoided a clash over politics;[21] the evening passed with great cordiality.

Eisler recalls introducing Brecht to his teacher Arnold Schönberg, who was also exiled in southern California. Schönberg had no idea who Brecht was, but Brecht, who knew of the composer's reputation, sarcastically rejected the great man's music as "too melodious, too sweet."[22] Eisler respected his aging mentor, in spite of Schönberg's hostile views toward socialism. Knowing that Schönberg's reactionary views might incense Brecht, Eisler warned him to behave himself, or their friendship was over.[23] Brecht agreed, and the meeting with Schönberg went flawlessly. They exchanged courtesies for an hour until Schönberg told an anecdote about learning from a donkey. At that point, Brecht was won over. Though one journal entry calls him an "old tyrant,"[24] later notations reporting contact express respect for this pioneer of modern music. Anecdotes Brecht heard from or about Schönberg and recorded in his journal or letters imply that he could identify with someone else who fought to establish a new mode of artistic expression in this century.

Basically generous by nature, Brecht was magnanimous when surrounded by financial security, artistic recognition, and ego reinforcement. The shortage of these in American exile cramped his innate capacity for generosity, though it did not kill it. Less generous toward successful émigré friends than he might have been during these years, Brecht showed the greatest kindness toward those whom exile had treated unfavorably.

After the reunion with his artist friend George Grosz in New York in the spring of 1943, Brecht notes in his journal that Grosz's works are not selling. When his friend asked about exhibiting his works on the West Coast, Brecht, after returning to California, called Fritz Lang's secretary Lilli Laté and asked for assistance in arranging an exhibit there. Laté found a San Francisco museum which agreed to pay shipping charges.[25] Had Grosz made a big name in America, Brecht probably would not have bothered to help.

In another example of his kindness toward disadvantaged friends, Brecht and his wife organized a celebration in August 1943 for Alfred Döblin's 65th birthday. Before approximately two hundred German-speaking friends in a small theater on Montana Avenue in Hollywood, Heinrich Mann delivered a commemorative address; congratulatory letters from prominent exiles such as Thomas Mann, Feuchtwanger, and Werfel (all of whom were present) were read; Granach, Lorre, and Kortner read from Döblin's works; Blandine Ebinger sang Berlin chansons; Eduard Steuermann played a piano number by Hanns Eisler; and Döblin himself concluded with remarks that were followed by a cold buffet and drinks. "A little bit of Europe" summarized a grateful Döblin in a letter to a friend.[26] The guest of honor's concluding words, however, left part of the audience, including Brecht, squirming. This convert to Catholicism delivered a sermon ascribing guilt for Hitler-Germany to his own failure (and by implication, that of all present) to seek God. Brecht captured his own reaction to the evening in a poem he entitled "Embarrassing Incident." It begins: "When one of my highest gods reached his 10,000th birthday,/ I came with my friends and disciples to celebrate" (*GW* x, 861-62).

Döblin's confession, in the words of Brecht's journal, "offended the irreligious feelings of most of those present. A fatal feeling seized the more rational listeners, something like sympathetic dismay at a fellow prisoner who succumbs to torture and confesses everything."[27] His poem concludes: "For three days/ I have not dared/ to appear among my friends and disciples because/ I'm so ashamed." Yet compassion mitigated Brecht's verdict, and his journal goes on to justify his friend, though not his lapse of taste. Sympathetically he mentions how Döblin has been affected by the loss of two sons in France; his angina pectoris; his inability to find a publisher for his works; and his life with a petty and obtuse woman.

Of those Brecht met in the refugee ghetto, intellectuals impressed him the least. Though he was in contact with some of the best minds of Europe who were living in Southern California at the time, this did nothing to change his life-long contempt for them. His relationship to Theodor Wiesengrund-Adorno, Max Horkheimer, Friedrich Pollock, Herbert Marcuse, and those associated with them (his journal erroneously links Günter Stern [Anders] and Ludwig Marcuse to this group) confirms that Brecht did not get along where one might expect it most.

In 1922 Hermann Weil, a wealthy German-Jewish businessman with large wheat holdings in Argentina, had endowed the establishment of an institute to study Marxism which became loosely associated with the University of Frankfurt. Before Hitler came to power, the Institute of Social Research (also called the "Frankfurt School") deposited its sizable endowment abroad. Eventually most of its members came to America, where they settled first on the East Coast, and later in Los Angeles. In 1929 Brecht met Walter Benjamin, one of the Institute's luminaries. Benjamin admired the dramatist greatly and, to some extent, shared his thinking or, as his colleagues thought, fell under his baleful influence.[28] By 1941 Benjamin was dead, but Brecht and other members of the Institute were well acquainted with each other by reputation when he arrived in America.

Adorno, Horkheimer, and Pollock were developing the now-famous "Critical Theory" of society, a radical critique of bourgeois consciousness and the capitalistic society that produced it. The goal of this "Critical Theory" was to change man's perceptions of himself and of society in order to prepare for revolutionary social change. Using Hegelian thought to reinterpret and go beyond Marx, the group hoped to avoid the dogmatism of orthodox Marxism by the use of dialectical reasoning. In effect, their critique of everything in late capitalist bourgeois society became an "unremitting process of negation."[29] True mandarins, they valued theory above *praxis* and speculative, reflective activity over unmediated facts.

Though they respected Brecht's literary achievements, they considered him the worst sort of "vulgar" Marxist. In their eyes his thinking was crude and simplistic, his materialism "vulgar," and his optimism undialectical. Worse yet, they considered his traditional Marxist commitment to the working class misplaced, for, in their view, the proletariat had become too reactionary to serve as the "motor of history." The time for revolutionary action by the proletariat as Marx defined it had passed, and history demanded a radical critique of the entire superstructure of society and an alignment of all progressive social forces rather than a commitment to the working class alone.

Members of the Institute were not above using petty arguments directed against Brecht's person to discredit his ideas. Adorno maliciously noted that Brecht spent two hours a day pushing dirt under his fingernails to make himself look proletarian.[30] Brecht's habit of attacking their views with sweeping assertions which they took to be doctrinaire pronouncements prompted them to brand him an anti-intellectual. Further, Brecht's support of Stalin and Russian Communism made him, in their eyes, a "petit-bourgeois poseur and apologist for Stalinism."[31] What probably irritated them most was the way Brecht turned their own weapons against them with his radical critique of nearly everything members of the Institute thought and did. He openly despised them as cultural elitists who acted as if they had never left Germany. He rejected their cultural arrogance, their comfortable grand-bourgeois life-style in the world center of capitalism, and their claims of thinking for all humanity.

A section of Brecht's *Refugee Dialogues* written in America takes aim at these members of the Frankfurt Institute. A worker there observes that their claims to be representative social critics would be "like our thinking that we're building cars for the general public. We don't, because we know it's for the auto manufacturers, and the public be damned" (*GW* XIV, 1482). In Brecht's eyes, they were not thinking for humanity at all, but only for themselves, for like-minded intellectuals, and for organizations who supported their research. From their financially secure position, they had been bought, or rather had sold out. Instead of serving specific people or groups of people, their commitment was to serve an abstraction called "spirit," i.e., the spirit of radical inquiry and social critique. Just as Brecht's specific commitment to Marx's working classes made him a "vulgar" Marxist in their eyes, so their total lack of commitment in human terms made them free-floating, irresponsible intellectuals in his.

Reduced to a fundamental level, Brecht's contempt for the "Frankfurtists," as he called these utopian thinkers, sprang more from personal loathing than from ideological differences. Resentment magnified this dislike, for he could not help comparing his poverty with the relative comfort these refugees enjoyed through support from American foundations. Yet in part because he needed bright debating partners to sharpen his own wits, and in part because they were raw material for his writings, Brecht continued to associate with them through most of his American exile. A dozen journal entries report on meetings with them, and there were more. If his comments accurately reflect what he said in their presence, it is a wonder they invited him back.

Writing to Korsch, who was receiving support from the Institute, Brecht mentions in September 1941 that he periodically sees Marcuse, Horkheimer, and Pollock (the last two only at parties), but that their association is not rewarding. Mocking their high seriousness and pontifical manner, he states: "A film about Lourdes is going to be made shortly. I assume they're speculating about [playing] the clerical roles." He was also critical of Herbert Marcuse during the war for going to work for the OSS and later the U.S. State Department.[32] One journal entry describes how Horkheimer had cited with alarm vice-president Henry A. Wallace's demand that, after the war, every child in the world must receive one pint of milk a day.[33] Horkheimer wondered if this did not represent a serious threat to culture, since it might introduce the "century of the common man." The whole matter amused Brecht, who had no use for "culture" when people needed to be fed. He even found himself involuntarily defending American prosperity against the Frankfurt group, since theirs was an implicit argument against a decent standard of living for the masses.

Once or twice Brecht assessed something by Institute members positively, e.g., Adorno's essay on Wagner,[34] though he objected to its Freudian interpretation, or a stimulating conversation with Adorno on technical and aesthetic distinctions between film and live drama.[35] Generally, however, his journal made it sound as though he had great fun baiting them. At one point he confessed that he could not resist shocking them with an attack on Schönberg, whose music, he asserted, raised the body temperature too much to allow clear thought.[36] And after the Institute received a grant from New York Jews in 1944 for what was to become a classic study on the origins of anti-Semitism, Brecht admitted suggesting a malicious question to Adorno for inclusion on the questionnaire that they were using. He had heard the Institute say that Marx's pamphlet on anti-Semitism was outdated and incorrect. Now, Brecht said, they should inquire whether New York Jews would finance a study on anti-Semitism if it proved Marx might have been right after all in his negative attitude toward Jews and their relationship to money.[37] Often his intellectual jousting with Institute members served no purpose other than to amuse himself.

In 1938 Brecht's journal first mentions the idea for a so-called "Tui" novel that had originated as early as 1930-1931. "Tui" was Brecht's

acronym for "tellect-ual-in," which, like the people it designated, was
a corruption. It meant all intellectuals who produced and sold ideas
and opinions on demand. In Brecht's view this was the position of the
Frankfurt Institute, and in America it became the model for an unfinished "Tui" novel. Members of the Institute came to constitute what
his journal called a "treasure trove for my Tui novel."[38] Parodying
what for Brecht were their stilted, abstract language, their elitism,
their isolation from human affairs, and their wrong-headedness, he
used them to supplement the series of anecdotes, vignettes, and stories
that he had begun in the thirties and that he hoped to fuse into one
novel. Brecht never finished it, but traces of his association with the
Frankfurt Institute remain in sketches for a work that was to be located in a fictitious land of "Chima." One section heading even translates the word "Hollywood" into German and comes up with "Die
Tuis von Stechpalmenwald" (The Tuis of Holly-wood, *GW* xii, 673).
How Brecht planned to incorporate this fragment into his novel remains uncertain, but his play *Turnadot, or the Congress of Whitewashers*, which he completed in 1954, owes at least some of its material on the misuse of intellect to his association with these refugee intellectuals in America.

In the exile colony in America, three topics of conversation dominated all others—the progress of the war in Europe (for most German
refugees, including Brecht, the war in the Pacific was less significant);
the state of the German people, including the question of their respon-
sibility for Hitler and the war; and the political future of Germany.
Inevitably, these topics drove former friends and old enemies into
sharply divergent positions. In one such acrimonious dispute, Brecht
squared off against the Nobel prize-winning novelist Thomas Mann,
the most prominent spokesman for German artists and intellectuals in
America, whose word carried great authority with the United States
government.

In the July 21, 1943 issue of *Pravda*, a group of German prisoners of
war and exiled labor leaders, artists, and intellectuals in Moscow issued a full-page manifesto calling on German soldiers to mutiny and
on workers at home to lay down their tools and sabotage the war effort. Insisting that "Germany must not die," the manifesto urged the
people to overthrow its leaders and to sue for peace so that democracy
could be established in a postwar German state cleansed of Nazis and
the Wehrmacht. Printed in both Russian and German, it was signed by
the "Free Germany National Committee."

Brecht brushed aside an account of the manifesto in *The Los
Angeles Examiner* which claimed that the Communist Party was behind it. In fact Wilhelm Pieck, secretary of the recently dissolved Third

Internationale, was among the signatories, but so were trade unionists, writers, and former members of the German Parliament. In the name of anti-fascist unity Brecht seized on this as an opportunity to bring together prominent Germans in American exile who might be induced to respond with a similar proclamation. Since Thomas Mann's name meant national attention, he was among those Brecht invited to meet on the relatively neutral ground of Berthold and Salka Viertel's home on August 1, 1943. Others included Mann's brother Heinrich; Feuchtwanger; Mann's close friend Bruno Frank, whose drama *Storm Over Patsy* had run successfully on Broadway in 1937; the philosopher-physicist Hans Reichenbach; the writer Ludwig Marcuse; Berthold Viertel; and their wives.

Strained feelings existed from the start, with Brecht and his friends in one camp, and Thomas Mann and Bruno Frank in the other. Hans Viertel, who was present, recalls that their wives had coffee downstairs while the men worked in an upstairs bedroom. Frequently Brecht appeared and asked the young Viertel to help him to formulate something in English (for publicity purposes, the proclamation was to appear in German and English). Then he disappeared into the next bedroom and argued further. After four hours of discussion, they agreed on a brief statement which Thomas Mann approvingly read before the assembled women. It announced: "At this moment, as the victory of the allied nations approaches, we, the undersigned writers, scientists, and artists of German origin, consider it our duty to make the following public declaration. We greet the proclamation of the German prisoners-of-war and émigrés in the Soviet Union that calls on the German people to force their oppressors into unconditional surrender and to work for a strong democracy in Germany. We, too, consider it necessary to distinguish clearly between the Hitler regime and the group aligned with it on the one hand, and the German people on the other. We are convinced that there can be no lasting world peace without a strong German democracy."

The next morning, Mann notified Feuchtwanger that he and Bruno Frank were withdrawing their signatures. Brecht's second-hand account in his journal reports the reasons for their objections—they wanted to avoid identification with any cause that the American government might deem pro-Communist.[39] Further, they did not accept a distinction between the German people and Nazi Germany. Brecht's journal note continues with a personal reaction: "The inflexible wretchedness of these 'bearers of culture' crippled even me for a moment . . . they agree with Goebbels's claim (picked up by the Hearst press) that Hitler and Germany are one . . . weren't the Germans militarists before Hitler? Thomas Mann remembers how he himself, along with ninety-one other intellectuals, approved of the invasion of Belgium by the Kaiser's armies in 1914. Such a people must be punished! . . . For a moment, even I pondered how 'the German people' could justify tolerating not only the atrocities of the Hitler regime, but also the novels of Thomas Mann, the latter without twenty to thirty SS divisions over them."

The seemingly innocuous statement which Brecht and Mann signed at the Viertel's home concealed bitter differences that derived from antagonistic views of German culture, the German people, and Germany itself. In capsule form, these outlooks summarized the arguments about Nazi Germany that agitated German refugees in America during World War II. To some degree, they continue to exercise philosophers and historians today. Each of the writers who held these views was great in his own right, was very "German," and was emotionally and ideologically incapable of understanding the other.

27 BRECHT, THOMAS MANN, AND GERMANY

It is one of the ironies of German literary history that a bitter enemy, Thomas Mann, considered by many to be that country's best prose writer in this century, first introduced its greatest dramatist of the century to American readers. As the German literary correspondent for the American magazine *Dial*, Mann's description of the Munich production of Brecht's *Drums in the Night* in the September 1923 issue displays neither sympathy nor hostility toward this rebellious young dramatist.[1] But the opening sentence of another review by Mann in the November 1924 issue, dealing with Brecht's adaptation and performance of Marlowe's *Edward the Second*, which calls him a "strong but somewhat careless talent who has been pampered by the public in Germany,"[2] sounds the discordant note that marked their relationship for three decades.

For reasons more profound than ideology or ideas, Brecht hated Mann and everything he stood for. Nothing tempered his dislike of Mann's genteel background; Mann's role as a literary spokesman of a class and intellectual tradition that Brecht rejected; personal habits that made Mann look too good and talk too wisely; in short, an air that Germans call *Representation*, which, among other things, implies making oneself look very good. To summarize their differences, one might modify Heinrich Mann's observation that his brother Thomas was "born to represent, not reject"[3] and say that Brecht was born to reject, not represent.

America was not the breeding ground for Brecht's antipathy. He had begun to polemicize against Mann in 1920, and he never stopped.[4] In 1926 he stated that Mann's works were among the kind he would pay to have suppressed.[5] Even at that time it would have gratified Brecht to see this Olympian figure dethroned. He elaborated on his "inclination to use terror" against the novelist by stating that "I single out Mann's books solely because he is the most successful type of the bourgeois producer of vain, artistic, useless books."[6] Brecht also ridiculed one of the central problems of Mann's works, viz., the conflict between the artist and bourgeois society. In Brecht's eyes, the problem of man in an unjust society, rather than the conflict of the artist with bourgeois society, demanded the attention of a modern writer.

Brecht's invectives during the twenties and thirties were directed against Mann's person, his family, his views, and his works, notably *The Magic Mountain*, which Brecht had never read, but from which he had heard Mann himself read selections in 1920.[7] A single stanza from

his "Ballad on Approving of the World" (1930) had sounded a leitmotif for their entire relationship—blindness:

> The writer lets us read his Magic Mountain,
> And what he writes (for money) is well described!
> What he conceals (for nothing) might have been the truth.
> I say that Mann is only blind, not bribed.
> (GW IX, 472)

The writer of these lines on Mann's ideological blindness was himself
afflicted with another kind of blindness—that of hatred. In Southern
California, this condition grew worse. Germany was large enough for
the two men to co-exist by avoiding each other; in the narrow confines
of the Los Angeles refugee community, they could not avoid contact.
Contact led to confrontation, and confrontation in America divided
them more bitterly and deeply than at any time in the previous two
decades.

Less than one month after arriving in America, Brecht mentions in a
letter to Korsch that he has already seen Mann. He describes his impression by paraphrasing Napoleon's statement before the pyramids
of Egypt: "I meet Thomas Mann at best by chance, and then 3000
years gaze down upon me."[8] Rumors and half-truths further poisoned
their relationship. While trying to flee Finland in 1941, Brecht had
written friends in America asking for affidavits of support for his family. Someone must have mentioned his plight to Mann, who had been
living in America since 1938. This was reported back to Brecht; his
daughter Barbara remembers hearing in her family that Mann had refused to provide affidavits for them. Even among the worst of refugee
enemies, this would have been tantamount to treason.

One of Brecht's journal entries depicts Mann's alleged callousness
toward his elder brother Heinrich, who had been released from a contract with Warner Brothers studios.[9] It says of Heinrich: "He goes to
the unemployment office and picks up $18.50 a week in support, since
his contract with the film company has expired. He is over 70. His
brother Thomas is building a large villa." Two years later Brecht again
mentions how depressing it is to see Döblin and Heinrich Mann, who
are "more than unsuccessful." Heinrich Mann, he notes, "does not
have the money to call a doctor, and his heart is finished. His brother,
with a house he built for himself and four or five cars, literally lets him
starve."[10]

In each case, Brecht had chosen to believe what he wanted to believe. There is no evidence that anyone approached Mann about assisting the Brecht family with a donation or with affidavits. Further, according to reports from Mann's eldest son, who lived in America at

the time, Heinrich Mann and his wife were receiving a monthly sum from his brother Thomas that exceeded the $120 a month on which the Brecht family had subsisted during the first year.[11] In addition, the European Film Fund was giving him a monthly sum of $150,[12] and he was receiving some royalties from his works published in other countries.[13] This kind of willful ignorance on Brecht's part extended to Mann's works, which Brecht continued to condemn without reading.[14] His friend Eisler, who saw the Manns socially and tried to mediate between the two writers, read and reported to Brecht on the novelist's works.[15] Eisler's negative evaluation of *Tonio Kröger* prompted a journal entry stating that Eisler had tried to read Mann's *Joseph* Tetralogy, "the encyclopedia of the cultured philistine," which in turn triggered the assertion that "basically we just do not have any literature."[16]

To some extent, Mann reciprocated with petty obscurantism by refusing to read the works of Brecht. According to his son Golo, "he never got around to it,"[17] though an intense loathing for Brecht's person had something to do with his lack of time. Both writers reserved some of their choicest formulations for the other. Notable among them was Mann's undocumented but oft-cited description of Brecht: "very gifted, unfortunately," which was already in circulation by 1944.[18] Others included the terms "monster"[19] and "party-liner."[20] Brecht in turn selected epithets like "half-wit"[21] or "reptile"[22] and called Mann's works "clerico-fascist."[23] Possibly the kindest appellation he attached to Mann was "that short story writer."[24] Though his statement was intended to damn with faint praise, Brecht had in fact read a few of Mann's short stories. After the war, when friends forced each writer into a confession of begrudging respect for the other, it was Mann's short stories that Brecht allegedly singled out as laudable.[25]

As the object of Brecht's hatred, Mann was hardly to blame for the reasonably comfortable circumstances that he enjoyed, or for his literary reputation in the English-speaking world. To make matters worse, he had involuntarily been cast in a role which one observer saw as an unwilling "kaiser" among German émigrés.[26] What exacerbated the ill-will between the two men in America more than anything else were Mann's views on Germany, the German people, and their future. As the most prominent refugee and *de facto* spokesman for Germany in America, Mann found himself under attack as Germany's judge and jury by a writer whose antipathy for judges was legendary.

Brecht's motives in signing the declaration of August 1, 1943 calling on the Germans to rise up against Hitler were unequivocal. He rejected the widely accepted thesis proposed early in the war by Robert

Gilbert Lord Vansittart and echoed by the prominent exiled German historian Emil Ludwig that the national character of the German people and Nazism were identical. For Brecht, they were two separate phenomena. Because he believed that Hitler and Nazism could be explained in terms of Marxist economics and class theory, he expected that when the war had progressed enough to weaken Hitler's hold, the German people, especially the working classes, would rise up and overthrow their Nazi oppressors. Further, Brecht opposed a postwar division of Germany[27] or any politically imposed settlement that would destroy the German nation. Not only must the German people be allowed to decide their own postwar destiny; Brecht believed that any attempt to punish a people who already had suffered under the Nazis would be double jeopardy. Signing the declaration at Berthold Viertel's home represented his personal form of political engagement in trying to shape the future of a Germany he hoped to see arise.

Mann's views were more complex and decidedly more ambivalent. Even if Brecht had not heard the widely circulated rumor in refugee circles that President Roosevelt was touting Mann as the head of a government-in-exile to unify anti-Nazi Germans,[28] he at least knew that Mann had the ear of the American president and of the State Department. This made him important to any exile politics which treated Germany's future. But Brecht failed to realize that Mann considered such talk nonsense, for Mann thought postwar Germany would not be politically independent and would not need a head.[29]

Initially Brecht had reason to believe that he and Mann agreed on Germany. When he had seen Mann at a cocktail party in February 1943, the novelist said, "I hope the Russians are in Berlin before the Allies."[30] On June 27th Mann delivered a radio speech that stated almost exactly what Brecht maintained: "the doctrine that one cannot distinguish between it [the German people] and Nazism, and that German and Nazi are one and the same is sometimes disseminated in allied countries, and not unintelligently; but it is untenable and will not prevail. Too many facts contradict it."[31] Brecht urged his listeners in Nazi-occupied European countries to resist the Nazis as many Germans had done at home. As proof that opposition to Hitler existed in Germany, he referred to the two hundred thousand political inmates who were in Nazi concentration camps when the war broke out.

Shortly after American newspapers carried the story of the declaration of the Moscow Free Germany Committee, Mann issued a statement for publication, agreeing with its stated goals and confirming that he, too, had called on the German people to throw off their Nazi rulers.[32] He echoed the Committee's challenge by urging Germans to follow the Italian example and to overthrow their dictator.[33] Both expressions sounded like something Brecht might have written.

No sooner had Mann signed the August 1st declaration than he was overcome by second thoughts. In a letter to Agnes Meyer, Mann describes the evening at the Viertel's and explains that he withdrew his signature out of the conviction that the Moscow Free Germany declaration was not spontaneous, but manipulated by the Communists, and he did not wish to lend his name to their propaganda. Further, he felt that émigrés had no right to dictate to allied governments what should be done with postwar Germany.[34] By implication, if punishment were to be meted out, that was not his concern.

When Mann called and withdrew his signature from the August 1st statement, he disagreed with a brand of refugee patriotism which insisted that Germany should not have to suffer for Hitler's sins. If Brecht's journal entry of August 2, 1943 is correct, Mann told Feuchtwanger that "he would not find it unjust if the allies punished Germany for ten to twenty years." This outraged Brecht. Writing in his journal one week later, he magnified Mann's cruelty by describing him (presumably at the August 1st gathering) with his hands in his lap leaning back and saying, "Yes, a half million people in Germany will have to be killed." Brecht commented: "It sounded out and out bestial, it was the starched collar talking."[35] One month later another journal note fumes over the perfidy of Thomas Mann and his wife, who, according to friends, were spreading rumors that "leftists like Brecht are carrying out orders from Moscow when they try to have him [Mann] sign statements making a distinction between Hitler and Germany."[36] Brecht comments: "The reptile can't imagine anyone doing something for Germany (and against Hitler) without orders, or that anyone, say out of conviction, might see anything else in Germany except a financially sound reading public."

Brecht's judgments were reactions to the August 1st discussion with Mann on whether "Germanness" and Nazism could be equated. No matter that soon after the war Brecht himself wrote a poem that came close to equating them by condemning the German people as a whole and observing that occupation troops had searched in vain for a single German who regretted the Second World War (GW x, 933). Brecht refused to grant this representative of German bourgeois culture the same privilege. Following the August 1st incident, Mann tried to clarify his own ambivalent statements. In his lecture "The War and the Future" (later published as "What is Germany"[37]), which he wrote immediately thereafter, Mann tried to walk the tightrope between both positions, but he fell rather clearly on the side opposite Brecht.

Long before this time, Mann's views of history, philosophy, and art had made "the German nation" almost a mythical entity for him, a people with a collective soul possessing unique spiritual traits.[38] Scrutinizing that people once again in his lecture, Mann concludes that Hitler's attempt to conquer the world represents an aberrant form of the universalism found in every German. Under Nazism, the Faustian urge to know and experience everything, a source of many great cultural and intellectual achievements, has run amuck. Throughout his lecture, leitmotifs of collective guilt and the need for purging a nation's soul occur with such emphasis that the conclusion is inescapable—the German people are responsible for Nazism, a conclusion that in Brecht's eyes was synonymous with the Vansittart theory.

In October 1943 a group of prominent exiles in New York City who hoped to found the equivalent of a Free Germany Committee in America tried to recruit Mann as their nominal head. Foremost among them were the Socialist politician Paul Hertz and the theologian Paul Tillich, whom Brecht met a few weeks later. Mann, who was in New York at the time on a lecture tour, went to Washington. After consultations with Undersecretary of State Adolf A. Berle,[39] he declined their invitation, for, unless the action had the backing of the host country's government, as the Moscow Free Germany Committee obviously had, Mann thought it was imprudent. In this case it did not. In his own words, Mann did not wish to lend his name to the Committee at a time when hatred of everything German in the United States and in Europe would bring it under suspicion as a conspiracy to protect Germany from its Nazi misdeeds. Further, he felt that he and fellow refugees had no right to dictate to the allied powers how they should treat Germany after the war.[40]

In early November Mann delivered his lecture "The War and the Future" at Columbia University.[41] Reports of it infuriated those trying to form the Committee, and they told him when they met with him a few days later. Brecht, who had arrived in New York too late for the lecture, was now present. Tillich, Mann wrote to Agnes Meyer in early December, accused Mann of "having pronounced a death sentence on Germany,"[42] and Brecht's face, he reported, was "mockingly bitter."

The commitment to Marxism by Brecht and other exiles who wanted to use Mann's name in shaping Germany's future made the novelist nervous. Ironically his lecture had warned the bourgeois world against irrational anti-Communism, which he called "superstitious, childish, the basic folly of our epoch."[43] But he entertained real fears over Brecht's political attitudes and what would happen if they were directed against him. A letter to Agnes Meyer calls Brecht a "party-liner who, if the Russians ever helped him to power in Germany, would do me all the harm possible."[44]

Hoping to overcome Mann's reluctance to head a refugee coalition, Brecht shortly thereafter initiated the only exchange of correspondence that ever took place between them. In a courteous letter he admits that his desire to unify all opponents of Hitler in American exile prompted him to write, "since it was the great dissension among the workers' parties in the [Weimar] Republic that contributed so much to Hitler's seizure of power. Because I know how much you can contribute to such unity, I feel obligated to inform you of the painful surprise of all those with whom I spoke after our meeting caused by your emphatic doubts about a strong contrast between the Hitler regime and his satraps, and democratic forces in Germany. The representatives of those former workers' parties and Paul Tillich (evidently out of deep religious conviction) feel it is neither their right nor their duty to be sitting opposite the German people at the bar of judgment. To them, their place would appear to be on the defendant's bench."[45]

Continuing, Brecht cites the very evidence for internal resistance by Germans to Nazism that Mann himself had used in his radio speech. He concludes by asking this man who, "more than any other one of us, has the ear of America," to settle the uneasiness of his friends by taking a position that will not increase doubts about the existence of "significant democratic forces in Germany, since the future of Germany and Europe depends on helping these forces to victory."

Mann, who found what he called Brecht's "harsh, accusatory" letter[46] waiting when he returned to Southern California in early December, replied immediately. After expressing surprise that none of the émigrés who claimed to have valued his name so highly had bothered to come to his lecture, he re-states the essence of his remarks to demonstrate that he has been misjudged. On the one hand, he claims, "a person and a people are somehow responsible for that which they are and do." On the other hand, he vehemently denies that "Nazi" and "German" can be equated, and he says he has listed all the arguments against such a view. He hopes for a genuine and cleansing German "revolution" (a word probably intended as a concession to Brecht) that will be aided by the victorious powers.

In his generally conciliatory reply, Mann carefully skirts the issue of latent "democratic forces of resistance" in Nazi Germany, which was the central point of Brecht's letter. This has nothing to do, Mann says, with the question of timing, which he feels is wrong for establishing a Free Germany Committee. It would create suspicion in America, and especially in the Nazi-occupied lands, where many terrible things could still happen to evoke the horror of the entire world. His closing exhortation, while calculated to appease Brecht, had the opposite effect: "Let the military defeat of Germany come about; let the hour approach that will allow Germans to have their reckoning with destruction, as thoroughly and mercilessly as the world can hardly dare to hope upon our unrevolutionary people. Then for us here, the moment will have come to testify that Germany is free, that Germany has truly purged itself, Germany must live."[47]

Mann avoids the question of whether democratic forces still exist among the people in Nazi Germany because in his view they do not. At that moment he was working on his novel *Doktor Faustus*, a reckoning with the dark side of the German soul that, as he saw it, had prevented a democratic spirit from arising there. Brecht's letter had reproached him for this disbelief, and Mann had confided to his journal that Brecht's reproach was accurate. "How did I let it be noticed, this disbelief?"[48] he asks himself as he weighs a response to Brecht's accusation.

Shortly after receiving Mann's letter in late December 1943 or in early January 1944, Brecht wrote one of the bitterest poems of his life. This versified invective, which summarizes his quarrel with Thomas Mann, carries the baroque title "Upon the Nobel Prize Winner Thomas Mann's Authorizing the Americans and the English to Punish the German People Ten Full Years for the Crimes of the Hitler Regime." It was composed with a pen dipped in gall, as two of eight stanzas illustrate:

> With his hands in his barren lap
> The refugee demands the death of half a million people.
> For their victims he demands
> Ten years of punishment. The sufferers
> Must be chastized.
>
> The prize bearer challenged the cross bearer
> To attack his armed tormentors with bare hands.
> The press did not respond. Now,
> Being offended, he demands that
> The crucified be chastized.
> (*GW* x, 871)

Instead of putting aside old differences, two German writers exiled in America allowed their consuming passion for the fate of the German people under Hitler to inflict deep new wounds in an already bitter relationship.

VIII. THE IDEOLOGICAL BRECHT

When Brecht took out immigration papers in Helsinki in May 1941, he signed a statement required of all applicants which disavowed any intent to overthrow the United States government by force or violence. Having made no such promise about Hitler's Germany, Brecht engaged in a variety of anti-fascist activities in America that had one purpose—to topple Hitler and to establish a new social order in post-war Germany.

Probably the only thing in his life that Brecht took more seriously than his writing was his ideology. His anti-fascism was synonymous with the struggle to help the working classes. Hitler, he thought, served the interests of the industrialists, the generals, and the ruling bourgeois class in Germany, who in turn were using him to exploit the people and to protect their own interests. Brecht's ideology motivated him to more intense anti-fascist activity throughout his exile than loyalty to Germany as a mythical or linguistic home ever did. Despite limited opportunities in the United States, he committed himself to a cause that had nothing to do with furthering his own name or with enriching him economically with the same tenacity and self-assurance he displayed in promoting his dramatic theories and writings. Brecht's anti-fascism represented what his Marxist ideology generally meant to him—a deep personal commitment to helping people by changing the world.

Early in December 1941, Brecht wrote Archibald MacLeish at the Library of Congress (someone had translated the letter into English for him) saying: "I'm burning to do my bit fighting the Nazis . . . I feel strongly that the psychological moment has come to broadcast from here right into Germany the truth which might easily act as an incentive to revolt . . . I would gladly participate in any such effort. I think you know that I could be helpful."[1] MacLeish never answered, and it was not until his first trip to New York City in the spring of 1943 that Brecht had an opportunity to enter the anti-fascist arena actively.

A number of Brecht's friends or acquaintances, including Berlau, worked for the Office of War Information in New York City. One of them, John Houseman, was head of the OWI's Radio Program Division of Overseas Broadcasting. During Brecht's visit, Houseman asked Brecht to liven up the pedestrian anti-fascist broadcasts being beamed into Germany by doing a program of his own works. Brecht agreed, and Houseman raised enough money to hire several instrumentalists to play and Lotte Lenya to sing. Houseman claims they recorded three or four programs.[2] Brecht's journal says only that "Lenya helps me with a recording of 'Song of a German Mother' for the Office of War

Information, composition by Dessau; the German desk sabotages it."[3]
In the early forties the OWI, often in conjunction with the BBC,
beamed dozens of foreign-language broadcasts each day to various
countries. Unbeknownst to Brecht, his own "Ballad of the German
Soldier's Bride" had already been transmitted to Germany by the BBC
in 1942.[4] Among material that survived this recording session are
three different discs of Lenya singing "Song of a German Mother" on
April 16, 1943.[5] Even with a free hand for the programs, Brecht felt
restricted—he wanted more instrumentalists and more time to experiment, neither of which was available. Houseman abandoned the project when the State Department's German desk and British Intelligence
objected that broadcasts by exiled Germans created hostility in their
German listeners, and the programs were never sent. Nor was burning
anti-fascism Brecht's sole motivation in preparing these programs. According to Houseman, Brecht briefly went on the U.S. government
payroll at Civil Service scale for daily work.

On April 3, 1943 Brecht attended a mammoth anti-war program
against Nazi Germany sponsored by German refugees, where his
works were among those read and sung. Under the slogan "We Fight
Back," Manfred George, editor of the German-language Jewish
weekly *Aufbau*, and Ernst Josef Aufricht arranged a four-hour-long
program of German and American anti-fascist music, poetry, drama,
speeches, slides, and a comedy act in the Hunter College auditorium.
Brecht's works stood out conspicuously on the program. Elisabeth
Bergner recited "The Children's Crusade 1939"; in a combination
slide-presentation and poetry reading, the exiled actor Herbert Berghof read Brecht's anti-war epigrams from his *Primer of War*, with slide
projections prepared by Piscator; and Lotte Lenya, accompanied by
Kurt Weill, sang three songs from *The Threepenny Opera* and *Happy
End*, as well as Weill's recent musical setting of Brecht's poem "And
What Did the Soldier's Wife Receive?"[6] Brecht's journal claims that
after the program Aufricht made and distributed records of Lenya's
singing these numbers, but she recalls nothing of it.

As part of the program the Kende Art Galleries in New York auc-
tioned off manuscripts, speeches, lithographs, and drawings by prominent refugees, with proceeds designated for the U.S. War Bond Drive.
The price that a Brecht poem fetched underscores his relatively
obscure status in America. A two-page radio address by Albert Einstein brought $2000; a two-page radio speech by Thomas Mann
$1500; and a poem by Franz Werfel $550. Brecht's manuscript of an
unidentified poem sold for $500.[7]

After returning to New York City in November 1943, Brecht increased his pace of activities. While staying at Berlau's apartment, he

received a telegram from Paul Robeson on December 11th, inviting him to participate in an anti-fascist rally on the tenth anniversary of the Reichstag Fire Trial. Robeson spoke as if he knew Brecht by reputation, if not personally: "Would be very happy if you can also participate as foremost representative [of] free German culture."[8] Brecht probably had not yet seen Robeson's performance of *Othello*, which he disliked so much, but he knew of him by reputation, and he liked recordings of his readings which Berlau had sent him the previous summer.[9] With evident enthusiasm he accepted. Within the previous two weeks Brecht had heard about Thomas Mann's lecture at Columbia University, had met Mann personally at Tillichs, and had written him a letter articulating his differences. Now he seized this invitation as an opportunity to continue the offensive against Mann's views.

When the program took place before three thousand people at Carnegie Hall on December 22nd, Brecht was the only German refugee to appear on it. Predictably he was out of step with the other participants. Speeches by Earl Browder, general secretary of the Communist Party, USA; Louis Adamic, an American leftist writer whom Brecht had read and admired years earlier;[10] Arthur Garfield Hays, an observer at the original Reichstag Fire Trial; and other prominent figures, turned into what *The New York Times* called "a series of eulogies of Mr. [Georgi] Dimitroff," an eminent witness in that trial.[11]

Brecht's statement, which had been formulated in German and polished into first-rate English by an unidentified friend, was read aloud in the company of messages from a group of unlikely bedfellows, among them President Fulgencio Batista of Cuba, the playwright Lillian Hellman, and Lord Marley. The statement glossed over Dimitroff in a single sentence and defended instead the issues Brecht had argued against Mann—that the Nazi regime and the German people were totally different; that resistance to Hitler had never ceased; and that this resistance tied down more than thirty divisions of elite SS troops on the home front (the English version says "a half million able-bodied men").[12] "Everyone who will can see that German enemies of Hitler, especially the German workers, are naturally aligned with the Allied peoples in the struggle against Hitler and his masters."[13] But Brecht's words went unreported in the press, and his efforts to refute the other foremost representative of German culture passed almost unnoticed.

Within a matter of days Brecht entered into further political activity with a body that came to be known as the Council for a Democratic Germany. As one of several groups that emerged after 1941, it functioned almost as if it were a German government-in-exile.[14] All these groups subscribed to a basic assumption shared by Brecht and

other German émigrés, but rejected by the U.S. State Department—
that German exiles were the only legitimate spokesmen for Germany.
Because the Council for a Democratic Germany included representatives of all the former workers' parties in the Weimar Republic, as well
as the Catholic Center Party, not to mention several "religious
socialists," i.e., theologians and pastors, it became the best known
(and most controversial) group within the limited and illusory power
structure of exile politics.

In the spring of 1943, Brecht met the exiled writer Hans Sahl. In late
November or early December 1943, and at Brecht's request, Sahl introduced him to Tillich, a former professor at the University of
Frankfurt who was now teaching at the Union Theological Seminary
in New York. According to Sahl, Brecht, who knew of Tillich's reputation and his willingness to promote a Free Germany-type committee in
America, was so eager to meet the theologian that he put on his best
flannel jacket and finest behavior. "He's very important to us," Brecht
reportedly said. At their meeting in Tillich's home, Brecht took pains
to be respectful and conciliatory, and Tillich welcomed him as a co-
worker to a group that was slowly coalescing.

Brecht was one of six present in Tillich's home early in January
1944 at the first recorded meeting of a group that announced itself
later that year as "The Council for a Democratic Germany." In the
nine weeks between January 11 and March 11, 1944, Brecht took part
in at least seven recorded conferences of the Council or one of its sub-
committees.[15] His was a dominant voice in forming the Council. According to Sahl, he argued that old differences needed to be put aside
and that representatives of the workers' parties in the Weimar Republic must form a coalition with their former enemies, the bourgeois parties. When it came to including Communists, Brecht stated "it's de-
meaning that no Communists have been invited." At his insistence,
two known Communists were asked to join. Others of whom Tillich
was unaware also joined, but he could report to someone, who reported it to the FBI, that "we have two and one-half Communist representatives on the Council. The half is Bert Brecht."

In attempting to speak for all German exiles in the western hemi-
sphere, the Council hoped to influence United States policy on rebuild-
ing Germany. It was "against the orientation of a democratic Germany toward East or West; against division, de-industrialization (a
reference to Henry Morgenthau's proposal to de-industrialize Germany, which Brecht and other refugees rejected); against [Allied] in-
tervention in the event Germany attempts a rebellion against Hitler
and the classes behind him; against Pan-Germanism." Strongly anti-
fascist, the Council wanted to counter misconceptions in the USA by

publicizing the underground movement in Germany, and to assist in the re-education of German prisoners-of-war interned in America.

Minutes of the Study Committee and of the Welfare Committee on which Brecht sat reflect his strong views on Germany as well as his pedagogical instincts. Amidst plans to document a democratic opposition to Hitler, to establish an Information Library, and to gather historical evidence refuting the Vansittart theory, Brecht was assigned to make suggestions for special radio broadcasts to be beamed into Germany at the time of the invasion.[16]

Another issue came up for repeated discussion—the protection of anti-Nazis in German POW camps in the United States. Brecht's journal expresses indignation that German officers responsible for discipline in these camps kept their men enthralled in Nazism.[17] Reports of homicides or suicides in the camps generated proposals to deal with this by segregation, by visits from refugees, and by determining what kind of reading material was available to prisoners. Finally, it was decided to have the clergymen in the Council contact United States Government officials about proposals for re-education of postwar Germany by Germans (they opposed American re-education of Germany).

According to an FBI informant, "Brecht had definite instructions from the Council to enlist as many famous writers as possible on the West Coast after he returned to Los Angeles." This may have been true, for Brecht wrote Heinrich Mann[18] inviting him to join the steering committee of an organization which his brother Thomas had refused to support (though Thomas Mann also refused to repudiate the Council when Clifton Fadiman challenged him to do so).[19] "In my opinion, this is an earnest attempt," writes Brecht, "to unify the German democratic forces in exile. The attitude of the State Department, initially rather cool, as Mr. Thomas Mann no doubt reported, is now very friendly."[20] Brecht's information came from a questionable source, for State Department skepticism eventually blocked the Council's activities. Heinrich Mann accepted Brecht's invitation, and his name appears along with Lion Feuchtwanger, Oskar Homolka, Peter Lorre, and Elisabeth Bergner, all of whom Brecht had persuaded to sign, in a public declaration of the Council reported in *The New York Times* on May 3, 1944.

Brecht relished working on the Council, and its members listened to him. Jacob Walcher, one of the Communist members who had been included at Brecht's insistence, urged him to consider settling permanently in New York, for, he wrote, "In our Council I miss your calm and well-considered argumentation very much. There have been several situations where your presence would have greatly served the common cause."[21]

Debates and discussions motivated Brecht to produce two political tracts during this New York visit. The one, "Report on the Position of Germans in Exile" (*GW* xx, 282-83), recapitulates his arguments against the Vansittart theory by claiming that, because the Germans were the first people Hitler conquered, Hitler and Germany could scarcely be equated. Brecht probably wrote the second essay as an outgrowth of his meeting with Tillich. He sent it to Bentley sometime in the spring of 1944, with a request to translate it and to submit it to a magazine like the *Saturday Evening Post*.[22] Bentley found no publisher, and today only his English rendering exists.

Brecht's title, "The Other Germany," refers to the Germany that most Americans failed to see. He claimed that 99 percent of Germany belonged to this "other Germany" which tolerated Hitler's war because it had tolerated a system that demanded war. To complain of this, he said, was to complain that the people had not brought about a social revolution. But "history shows that peoples do not lightly undertake radical changes in the economic system. They hate and fear the disorder which accompanies social change. . . . A world which expects the German people to revolt and turn itself into a peaceful nation is expecting much" (*GW* xx, 288-89).

By the time the Council for a Democratic Germany made its public debut on May 3, 1944, it was already under heavy attack. In *The New York Herald Tribune* William L. Shirer noted that it had not spoken a word of regret about the crimes committed by Germany against other countries, or about reparations for them.[23] Brecht and other Council members were not about to apologize for crimes that Hitler had also committed against the German people. The Jewish newspapers *Jewish Daily, Forward* and *Aufbau* attacked the Council for promoting its viewpoint so aggressively while remaining silent about Hitler's atrocities against the Jews.[24] Significantly, the large number of Jews on the Council shared Brecht's outlook on this point. They had suffered Nazi persecutions for political reasons before persecutions for racial reasons began, and they felt no personal guilt for Nazi anti-Semitism, nor any motivation to be philo-Semites. Eduard Heimann, one of Tillich's émigré friends, objected that "it never occurred to you that a just peace for Germany might be unfavorable."[25] Brecht refused to entertain such a notion, for he felt the Germany he was speaking for had already suffered enough. Rex Stout, the American murder-mystery writer, roundly declared that all signers of the Council's declaration ought to be shot.[26]

The Council might have resisted this type of criticism, and it might have survived weaknesses in its internal structure. But it could not have outlived the events of history or the opposition of the United

States State Department, which took a jaundiced view of a group they labeled "premature anti-fascists." To the State Department, the Council's radical anti-fascism had clear Marxist overtones. Consequently the Department blocked efforts by Council representatives to enter POW camps or to influence political events in Germany after its surrender.[27] FBI reports on Brecht's Council activities voiced a similar sentiment—that the Council was a Communist front, and that Tillich and others were being manipulated.

Tillich began to waver in January 1945 when emerging details of German atrocities caused him to doubt that he, in good conscience, could separate the German people from the Nazis.[28] Brecht, however, had neither abandoned his views nor lost his zeal. In August 1945 he wrote encouraging Tillich not to let the recent Potsdam conference create a crisis and urging the Council to continue. Although the Council by now was only an historical footnote, Brecht kept on trying to influence the shape of postwar Germany until the day he left for Europe.

Hidden in the shadows of this overt anti-fascist activity in New York was considerable behind-the-scenes involvement with Communist friends who counseled Brecht on various ramifications of his work for the Council. Hans Sahl claims Brecht met at this time with Dietrich Hildebrand, a professor at Fordham University, for regular discussion evenings on Marxist ideology, and Hermann Budzislawski remembers his own eagerness to hear about world affairs, i.e., European matters, from Brecht. There were also many discussions with Albert Norden and Jakob Walcher.

All this amounted to little more than an exile's personal politics of hope. Somewhat riskier was Brecht's contact with Gerhart Eisler, the brother of Hanns Eisler. Gerhart Eisler was accepted by German Communists in America as their political commissar. His direct contact with Russia made him the voice for the latest official views, and Brecht and others accepted him in this capacity. The FBI saw him in a more serious role—that of an agent for the Russian GPU engaged in Soviet espionage in America. Those of Brecht's FBI files released to date record one meeting with Gerhart Eisler on January 17, 1944, while Brecht was in New York, but there were others (Elisabeth Freundlich recalls being present at one in 1946). The playwright freely admitted playing chess and discussing the German Communist movement with Eisler, who, he stated, was a specialist in German politics. In a statement made before The House Un-American Activities Committee in 1947, Brecht admitted that he willingly submitted to Eisler's views on political matters. In reply to the House investigator's question whether Eisler was in fact a politician, as he had stated, Brecht replied: "Yes, he, of course, knew very much more than I knew about the situation in Germany."[29] This contact with Gerhart Eisler reveals that in American exile Brecht was neither as cautious nor as politically dormant as has been supposed.

Discussions in New York with Wieland Herzfelde and F. C. Weiskopf, two émigrés whom he knew as loyal to Stalin, not only centered on the prospects of a postwar Communist Germany; they resulted in the publication of anti-fascist literature directly tied to Brecht's work for the Council. Writing to Brecht, Herzfelde, who had begun to publish an edition of Brecht's works in Europe before fleeing the Nazis and coming to New York in 1939, announced plans to start a German language publishing house in America.[30] Brecht replied from Santa Monica with a suggestion about changing the proposed name to "Aurora"—he pointed out that too many institutions in America used "Tribune" in their name.[31] To emphasize his point, he wrote a poem called "Aurora" (*GW* x, 859) and sent it to Herzfelde.

During early 1944, Brecht, Herzfelde, Weiskopf, and several other leftist and Communist writers met in New York and agreed to organize what became the most widely known German émigré press in the United States, *Aurora Verlag*.[32] Those present welcomed Brecht's suggestion of the name "Aurora," for they sensed the implication of a word whose German equivalent, *Morgenröte*, meant "red sky at dawn." With some private backing, the journal was established as the joint property of its eleven founders. All profits were earmarked for expanded production, lower book prices, and more substantial author's royalties, which were paid after the sale of the first thousand books. Herzfelde became provisional managing director, and a committee of three was to select manuscripts for publication.

Herzfelde recalls Brecht's dominant role in determining the concept of what kind of works to publish. The dramatist demolished a proposal to commission and publish a history of *German Literature in Exile* by his observation that if space were allotted according to quantity written, Thomas Mann would have to receive the most attention.[33] Most of those present hoped to exert an influence in postwar Germany by marketing their works in the literary vacuum they expected would develop there. For this reason, Brecht insisted on "progressive" literature that would help to develop the proper political consciousness among German prisoners of war in the United States and among their countrymen at home. As the only founding editor who also belonged to the Council for a Democratic Germany, Brecht assured colleagues that an excellent market for their books existed in German POW camps in America, where they would serve as part of the Council-directed re-education program.

Brecht's colleagues accepted his suggestion, and their decision to publish German-language books in larger editions than market conditions warranted grew from this consideration.[34] But they made the mistake of announcing it publicly. Brecht's FBI files gleaned a notice from an issue of *New Masses* on the publication of an anthology by Aurora Verlag which, the FBI ominously notes, is intended for "German war prisoners."[35] American officials refused to cooperate, no books were allowed to be sold to POWs, and this miscalculation cost the publishing house dearly.

It managed nevertheless, between 1945 and 1947, to publish twelve separate titles by émigré writers in editions ranging in number from sixteen hundred to four thousand. A German version in three thousand copies of Brecht's play *Private Life of the Master Race* was the first volume it issued. But, like the work of the Council in particular and of exile politics in general, Aurora Press exerted virtually no influence on political or cultural events in postwar Germany. It remained one of the bright but ineffectual hopes that inspired leftist refugees as they looked toward a new Germany.

In a poem written in Danish exile that refers to Hitler as a house-painter, Brecht speaks of a tension in his works:

> In my songs, a rhyme
> Would almost seem presumptuous to me.
> Within me struggle
> Enthusiasm over the blossoming apple tree
> And horror over the house-painter's speeches.
> But only the second
> Drives me to the desk.
> (*GW* ix, 744)

In a sense this poem might be considered un-Brechtian, for it suggests an artificial dichotomy between his anti-fascist writings and his less engaged works. Yet he himself did not subscribe to this view. Since all his writings arose from the same ideological well-springs, he considered all of them in some degree anti-fascist. The "photograms" from his *Primer of War* published in the *Austro-American Tribune*, for example, are as artistically interesting as they are politically engaged. Nevertheless, some of the works Brecht wrote during his American exile were done with a more avowedly anti-fascist purpose than others. These were specifically intended to assist in the "denazification" of his countrymen which the Council for a Democratic Germany had envisaged.

Several such pieces arose in collaboration with Paul Dessau, the composer he met in New York during the spring of 1943. At Brecht's urging, Dessau came to Southern California the same year. For the next four years they worked together intermittently on plans for operas and musical settings of poems and plays. Virtually all these were intended as "political reorientation" literature for Germany.

In the midst of writing *Chalk Circle* in mid-1944, Brecht gave Dessau a number of epigrammatic quatrains from his *Primer of War* to set to music. Out of thirteen epigrams Dessau composed grew a full-scale oratorio called "Deutsches Miserere" which he worked on during the years 1944-1947. As with all his work, Brecht told Dessau precisely what he wanted. A journal note in mid-1944 says that "Dessau is making good progress with the 'Deutsches Miserere.' " For the instrumentation I suggested to him that he should eliminate the 'unified sound' and form separate instrumental groups for the individual pieces, and also individualize the choruses. . . ."[1] Even in areas where he could not match the technical competence of his collaborators, Brecht insisted they experiment until they achieved the effect he wanted.

Brecht's journal records another conversation with Dessau on plans for an opera based on his poem "The Jew-Whore Marie Sanders,"[2] which he had written in 1936 in reaction to the Nüremberg racial laws outlawing sexual relations between Aryans and Jews. Nothing came of this project, though Brecht noted in detail his specific ideas for a musical performance. But the motivation was identical—this self-appointed *Praeceptor Germaniae* did not want the German people to remain ignorant of the causes that had brought about Hitler and Nazi Germany.

In 1941 Brecht wrote a four-line epigram for Fritz Lang about the "God of Happiness" (*GW* x, 894), inspired by a Buddha-like wooden figure with arms stretched overhead and stomach protruding in sensuous enjoyment. Brecht had purchased the tiny figure for forty cents in Los Angeles's Chinatown.[3] At that time he also conceived of an opera entitled "The Journeys of the God of Happiness." Dessau joined him on it in 1943 and began to compose songs to individual poems as they were delivered to him. Brecht started writing the book for the opera in January 1945, and Dessau recalls receiving the epilogue and first scene, which he set to music.[4] The plan was complete, but the work remained a fragment of poems, sketches, and a few scenes. Despite its seemingly apolitical celebration of pleasure, Brecht was propagandizing. The text deals with an indestructible god of happiness who, despite poisoning and execution, cannot be killed. Brecht interpreted it to Dessau as a representation of the impossibility of killing people's desire for happiness, which, he told him, was Communism.[5] Brecht intended to see that the German people after the war were properly instructed in that ideology.

Dessau experienced Brecht's skill in trying to exploit rivalry between real or would-be collaborators. He relates how the dramatist assigned him to get in touch with Igor Stravinsky, who was living in Los Angeles, and to ask if he would compose music for his anti-war piece *The Trial of Lucullus* as an opera. Dessau did, but Stravinsky declined because of his work on *The Rake's Progress*.[6] Brecht, however, had planted a seed, and in 1949 Dessau himself composed the music for it. In 1944 Eisler agreed to write some music for the songs in *Chalk Circle*. He began work and had completed what he called "a few sketches"[7] when Brecht also gave Dessau the same assignment. After Dessau learned that Eisler had been asked, he withdrew.[8] Eisler did not finish his compositions, and it would be another decade before Dessau agreed to write the music.

A certain amount of Brecht's film-writing was done with an eye toward re-educating his countrymen. While writing the screenplay for *Hangmen Also Die* he devised scenes that he hoped to extract from the film and use for instructional purposes in post-Hitler Germany. Like

Lenin, Brecht viewed film as a means to mold ideological thinking in the masses. Early in 1945 he saw an opportunity to enlist film in the denazification process. Knowing that Allied authorities would control the postwar German film industry, he tried to use all the influence he could exercise in America.

An FBI report dated June 30, 1945, describes how Brecht tried to reach Billy Wilder, the Hollywood director recently selected to supervise postwar film production in the American-occupied sections of Germany: "On March 24, 1945, according to [informant] CNDI LA 2718, Bert Brecht attended a farewell gathering given for Billy Wilder of Hollywood, California, who had been selected by O.W.I. to handle American motion pictures in Germany after the war. Informant advised that in fact this gathering had been arranged principally so that Brecht might talk to Wilder, Brecht having previously expressed a desire to do so." Thirty years later, Wilder recalled only faintly meeting Brecht at this party, and, even if he had a chance to express them, Brecht's plans were ignored. But he did not abandon them.

Knowing of the many Nazis among German prisoners-of-war interned in the United States, Brecht planned to write films to be used in their re-education. His journal mentions a discussion of the topic with Dieterle in the spring of 1945.[9] Of two titles they planned—"Dr. Ley" and "The Two Sons"—only the second materialized into a film story.

One ambitious project Brecht undertook early in 1945 counts among his anti-fascist writings, since he intended it for use in re-educating German workers after Hitler's fall. His attempt to versify *The Communist Manifesto* counts as one of the most unusual activities of his American exile, if not of his life.

In 1939 Brecht conceived the idea of writing a counter-epic to Lucretius's *De Rerum Natura*, to prove that existing social orders were not necessarily the natural order of things.[10] This was clearly in mind when he set about to versify the *Manifesto*, using a meter every German schoolboy associated with the *Iliad* and *Odyssey*—dactylic hexameter. Throughout his prose and verse, Brecht referred to Marx, Engels, and Lenin as "classic writers." Now he hoped to "preserve in amber" what he considered to be a "classic" in world literature and, at the same time, to make it more accessible to German workers. He acknowledged that "even as a pamphlet the *Manifesto* is a work of art. Today, however, one hundred years later, it seems possible to me that its political impact, armed with new authority, can be rejuvenated by dispensing with its character as a pamphlet."[11]

While working with Laughton on *Galileo* in late December 1944 or in early January 1945, Brecht began this project. By January 25th he had completed fifty pages.[12] During the remainder of 1945 he produced four separate versions totaling over one thousand verses.[13] Perhaps at the outset, but more probably in the course of writing, the project expanded into a full-blown epic to be entitled *On the Unnatural Order of Bourgeois Society*[14] or *Didactic Poem on the Nature of Man*.[15] The second canto, the only one Brecht finished, contains a rather accurate rendition of the first section of the *Manifesto*, while the first and third cantos, which were to subsume the rest of its contents, remain fragments.

From the outset Brecht met two unaccustomed obstacles—strong opposition from his collaborators, and his own inability to handle classical hexameter. Eisler polemicized against this attempt to "poeticize" something that he felt the German workers after the war would scarcely understand in prose.[16] Brecht, he protested, was complicating Marx and assuming an unrealistically high niveau on the part of his readers. Most of all, Eisler objected to his use of this verse form. As a Marxist, he distrusted the form and formalism inherent in it; as a student of Greek (Brecht knew none), he found Brecht's "jazzed up hexameters"[17] to be faulty, or in many cases not hexameters at all. Consequently he and Feuchtwanger tried in vain to teach one of the most gifted twentieth-century German language poets the fundamentals of Greek verse by reading Greek poetry aloud to him.

Brecht held the theory that good poetry lent itself to oral transmission. Knowing that people remembered verse better than prose passages, he tried to make his own verse singable or recitable, and hence memorable. Wherever he could find an audience, he now read this poem aloud. Weigel, Kortner, Eisler, Feuchtwanger, and others listened to it. Egon Breiner, who was present with Eisler and Hans Reichenbach for one reading, remembers Brecht's asking for a response. Breiner answered, "You can't improve Marx." Stefan Brecht's sharp and detailed criticism also battered Brecht's confidence. But the judgments of Feuchtwanger did the most to undermine his efforts.

Among other things, Feuchtwanger stressed the futility of forcing words like "bourgeoisie" and "proletariat" into classical verse forms that resisted them, as dactylic hexameters clearly did. He proved to Brecht that, of two or three hundred hexameters he had written, perhaps two or three were correct. Brecht accepted this criticism of his hexameters and admitted in his journal that "in fact I really do not know enough about them."[18] Later he confessed in an interview that Feuchtwanger's objections created in him such an inferiority complex that it was difficult for him to continue.[19]

Brecht responded to each barrage of criticism with new revisions. Now he asked Breiner for suggestions. This literate worker went through the text with him, whereupon Brecht revised it again. Soon after he sent a copy of the second revised version to Karl Korsch, asking for constructive criticism of aesthetic or political weaknesses in the text. Korsch's enthusiastic response (he called it a "masterpiece")[20] contrasted so sharply with comments of other friends that Brecht welcomed every suggestion and exchanged several letters in the following weeks. Korsch promptly sent corrections and recommendations, which Brecht incorporated into the text.

Brecht labored over the poem until mid-May 1945. Summarizing a visit to New York in June 1945, his journal notes that he "read the didactic poem to Schreiner, Walcher, Duncker. Impression surprising." He was delighted by the enthusiastic reaction from two of these three Marxist comrades. Hermann Duncker considered it powerful; he stated that, in his view, the *Manifesto* needed to be read aloud to transmit the impact of the language, and that Brecht had not only done that; he had surpassed Marx in the process. Duncker even encouraged Brecht to poeticize and incorporate other writings by Marx into it.[21] Jacob Walcher concurred and, like Duncker, urged Brecht to publish it.[22] Only Albert Schreiner objected. He believed that Marx and Engels had mastered the form necessary to popularize their ideas, and that a new form would destroy the content.[23]

Ultimately the opposition Brecht met discouraged him enough to drop the project. In 1947 Korsch urged him to complete the fragmentary poem for the centennial celebration of the appearance of the *Manifesto*. By that time, however, Brecht was preparing to return to Europe. In 1950 and 1954 he briefly reworked earlier versions, but he did not finish it. Because *The Communist Manifesto* defied the attempts of the most gifted Marxist poet writing in its original language to preserve it in the amber of classic hexameters, it never reached the German workers whom it was to re-educate.

Though Brecht completed relatively few political poems in America, a notable exception was "The Anachronistic Procession" (*GW* x, 943), which he intended to use in instructing German readers on the dangers of the political institutions and modes of thought that had led to fascism. In 1938 Brecht already knew and had translated a number of stanzas from Shelley's "The Masque of Anarchy," which later served as his model, and included them in the essay on the "Breadth and Diversity of Realistic Writing Style." According to a journal notation in March 1947, he now completed his own poem, which he calls a "paraphrase of Shelley."[24] This bitter ballad describes a procession wending its way through ruined postwar Germany. Its two worn signs, inscribed with the words "freedom" and "democracy," attract all the reactionary and violent forces that ruled Germany during the Hitler era.

In 1932 Brecht had published a long political poem entitled "The Soldiers Three," which George Grosz had illustrated with biting caricatures. Presumably he had something similar in mind with "The Anachronistic Procession," for early in 1947 he sent part or all of it to Grosz with an invitation to supply illustrations. He hoped, Brecht said in a letter written early in 1947, to have it published as a booklet in America that could be sent "as a greeting to Germany." Grosz declined in a humorous letter which speaks of his efforts to invent a dictograph machine that would produce automatic caricatures from the printed word for you "political poets" in order to save himself the effort. Each time he tried, Grosz explained, his hands shook too much because of the nature of the material. Parenthetically, he mentioned that he was tired of working without pay, and that this machine would spare him the effort of friends wanting him to work gratis. For obvious reasons, Grosz provided no illustrations.

Concealed or overt anti-fascist messages occur in many of Brecht's poems and in most of the plays written in this period. Yet, like his work for the Council for a Democratic Germany, they had virtually no immediate impact on a German-language audience. Where they did circulate, it was usually in English, and without Brecht's knowledge or approval. Translations of several poems appeared in anti-fascist anthologies during the war.[25] One of them, "The Ballad of the German Soldier's Bride," was beamed into Germany by the BBC in a version sung to the music of Mischa Spoliansky. *Time* magazine published a shortened English version of that text in its February 1, 1943, edition, with a note reporting that it was being sung on BBC. But, generally, Brecht's anti-fascist writings remained unknown until after he returned to Germany.

When Brecht testified before the U.S. House of Representatives Committee on Un-American Activities in October 1947, he appeared in the company of eighteen Hollywood leftists and liberals, many of whom he had never met. This association raises the matter of his relationship to the American left during his exile years. Almost from the beginning, it had been an uneasy one, though it was not Brecht's fault alone. Mutual antagonisms arose from a variety of reasons, including widely differing understandings of Marxism; false preconceptions on the part of American Marxists about their European comrades, and vice versa; national and cultural differences; and artistic jealousy. Joseph R. Starobin, an active member of the American Communist Party at the time, recalls an experience that captures the atmosphere that often prevailed. In the company of other Communists, he met Brecht and Gerhart Eisler at a soiree in New York City in 1943 or 1944. It was, Starobin says, "a painful evening, with Brecht lying astride a bed, contemptuous of everybody." The exile, he claims, shared the "general European self-centeredness and arrogance" that American Communists sensed in their European counterparts. German Communists, states Starobin, were especially contemptuous and mordant to almost everyone else, and in this regard, he recalls, Brecht was "typically German."[1]

This perception of Brecht existed almost from the moment he first reached America. In part it arose from the native oppositional attitude which had brought him to Marxism in the first place. His disagreement or criticism on ideological or artistic issues was construed as lack of solidarity. Furthermore, he was considered to be ideologically devious, since the dramatic ideas and writings that he promoted struck American comrades as alien to accepted Marxist artistic theory and practice. But the uncompromising self-certitude with which Brecht represented his ideological views, his theatrical ideas, and his person probably alienated them more than all ideological differences combined. In a word, because American Marxists disliked Brecht as a person, they had no use for his ideological or artistic views. Almost involuntarily, he was forced into the role of an outsider.

The Theatre Union debacle in 1935 introduced American comrades to someone they perceived to be a tantrum-throwing, uncooperative European comrade who, in the words of George Sklar, considered himself a "superior Marxist" and who referred to them collectively as a *Misthaufen* (dung heap).[2] What they saw as arrogance and bad behavior in the name of Marxism made Brecht's name relatively unpopular among those leftists who knew him by reputation. John Howard

Lawson, an influential literary figure of the American left at the time, had never met Brecht, but he had read some of his pieces in translation and had heard of his abrasiveness from friends in the Theatre Union. Consequently he sided with them against him.[3] Lawson's aversion manifested itself in an attack on Brecht's theories of epic theater, allegedly based on ideological grounds. In the third issue of *Theatre Workshop* (April-July 1937), Gorelik had published an annotated version of some of *The Threepenny Opera Notes* that constituted one of the first statements of Brecht's ideas to appear in an American theater journal. The following issue carried a letter from Lawson polemicizing against Brecht's new ideas with the most damning label of all—"discredited and thoroughly un-Marxist theories." After attacking Gorelik's presentation for superficiality, he stated that "the 'new' ideas of Brecht are the old stand-bys of idealist philosophy, fully exploded by Marx and Engels in the middle of the last century."

Edmund Fuller's article "Epic Realism: An Analysis of Bert Brecht" in the April 1938 issue of *One Act Play Magazine*, though professing to be an ideological attack (from the left) on Brecht's theories, reveals that the dramatist's personality is behind at least part of the polemic. Responding to an outline of Brecht's distinctions between Aristotelian and epic theater published in the Moscow-based journal *International Literature* (no. 5, 1937) Fuller points out that, in his theatrical methods, Brecht is both an extreme collectivist *and* an extreme individualist. The first practice can lead only to "artistic anarchy," while the second makes Brechtian theater "essentially the theater of the director." Reflecting a knowledge of Brecht's working habits on the *Mother* production, Fuller agrees that "in such cases of group collaboration as typified by Brecht's style of work there is no true collectivism. There is always the influence of one dominant personality which stamps with its likeness the thoughts and responses of the others. When as forceful a personality as Brecht (an intense individualist in a collectivist's clothing) is present, something concrete will emerge."

These feelings of dislike were mutual. Shortly before coming to the USA, Brecht records in his journal an attack by John Howard Lawson in *The New Masses* on Gorelik's book *New Theatres for Old*.[4] The entry gives no clue to his own views and repeats only the substance of Lawson's critique, directed at Gorelik's account of epic theater. But Brecht in fact resented Lawson's ideology and aesthetics, and his real opinion became clear two years later when he met that writer personally. A journal entry treating their encounter reveals at least passing familiarity with Lawson's book *The Theory and Technique of Playwrighting* (1936). Brecht's notation begins "At Feuchtwangers [I] meet

Lawson, who has written about dramaturgy (reactionary stuff, 'back to Gustav Freytag') and represents the New Masses point of view."[5] The account which follows, dealing with Lawson's opinions on American labor figures and postwar political alignments, is formulated with the same hostility they expressed toward him. Viewed as an aesthetic reactionary and a retarded ideologue, Lawson did not measure up to Brecht's standards.

Even those American comrades whom Brecht treated warmly in public did not seem to merit his private respect. V. J. Jerome, who effectively functioned as the cultural commissar of the American Communist Party, befriended Brecht and became one of his strong supporters during the winter of 1935-1936. Before his departure, Brecht reciprocated by asking Jerome to take charge of American translations and performances of certain of his works. To judge by letters they exchanged over the next three years, they enjoyed a cordial relationship. But it must have been simulated cordiality, at least by Brecht. Sidney Hook, a disaffected Marxist philosopher living in New York, remembers two visits in 1935-1936 when Brecht (whom he knew from Berlin in 1929) launched into tirades against Jerome's stupidity, political crudity, and cultural pretensions.[6] This "idiot of the theater" was an "owl without wisdom," he remembers Brecht saying. Gorelik, too, recalls how he deprecated Jerome. This may explain why Brecht's journal fails to mention Jerome once, and why no contact between the two can be documented for the entire period of Brecht's exile.

The dramatist reserved his bitterest indignation for those who he felt had qualified or abandoned their commitment to Marxism. If accounts of his relationship to the dramatist Clifford Odets are accurate, Brecht considered him beneath contempt. No doubt Odets's success as a dramatist and screenwriter had created jealousy and resentment. More important, Brecht considered him to be an ideological traitor. After seeing a performance of his *Paradise Lost* in New York during the winter of 1935-1936, he declared Odets guilty of treason. Two plays by Odets—*Waiting for Lefty* and *Paradise Lost*—had appeared in 1935. When Brecht saw several scenes from *Waiting for Lefty* performed in Madison Square Garden late that year, he responded enthusiastically, perhaps because Odets's anti-illusory techniques approximated his own practice of involving spectators as participants (the play purports to be a strike meeting in a union hall, with the audience as the union membership). A member of the Communist Party at the time, Odets appealed to Brecht because he combined innovative dramatic ideas with a sound ideological perspective. But *Paradise Lost*, which Brecht saw a few weeks later, was another matter, for it portrayed with unusual compassion a middle-class American family which loses everything it possesses. This convinced Brecht that Odets had abandoned his Marxist tenets (Odets in fact left the Communist Party in late 1936). Writing to V. J. Jerome after his return to Denmark, he exclaims: "What a traitorous step from *Waiting for Lefty* (which I value highly) to *Paradise Lost*."[8]

When Eisler brought them together again in Hollywood in 1942, Odets was not only beyond redemption as a political person; Brecht felt convinced that as a successful screenwriter he had sold out to the American commercial establishment. His journal entry reflecting their first meeting sarcastically refers to him as "The White Hope of American Theater," a designation taken from the title of an article on Odets in *Time* magazine that Brecht probably knew.[9]

To judge from his account of that meeting, Brecht enjoyed their discussion on Hollywood, on American theater, and on Odets's own writings. After Odets held forth vividly on American vaudeville, Brecht mentioned his enthusiasm for the scenes from *Waiting for Lefty* played in Madison Square Garden during 1935, and surprised his guest by drawing a complimentary parallel between that play and vaudeville. But a gentle tone of mockery pervades his description of Odets's monologue on the decline and fall of American theater, character, morality, and personality. Taking his cue from that writer's lament at the downward leveling of writers, Brecht comments that Odets has not observed how differences between himself and second-rate film writers have begun to disappear. When Odets justified his type of psychological drama by saying, "I can't write if I don't know what I'm writing for," Brecht replied: "Write for Broadway . . . but remember that it will soon be in the center of the world. For the first time, America will have a role in world politics." He was challenging Odets to make his plays more political and to get away from portrayals of psychological problems among the middle class.[10]

Six days later Brecht met with Odets, Eisler, and Lang to discuss *Master Race* as a possible film story. His sardonic comment on Odets's attitude toward his anti-fascist play was: "Odets is looking for something uplifting."[11] Brecht's unvarnished opinion came out on another occasion when he found himself defending the esthete (and fascist) d'Annunzio against the smugness of Hollywood film-writers who belittled the Italian writer: "It's impossible for me to hear them speak contemptuously of him in company with [Franz] Werfel, [Ben] Hecht, and Odets."[12]

During the party at the Russian consulate at Los Angeles where Brecht clashed with Harold Clurman, he also found himself disagreeing with Odets. Brecht had praised Spencer Tracy's performance in *The Seventh Cross*; but, as he writes, "Odets did not see any such thing and was irritated by my advice to see the film again. He kept seizing his breast and swearing that he had felt nothing. For him a movie theater is a kind of electric machine, and he registers the shocks. Impossible to explain that one can go to a movie theater and curiously observe if any reflections of reality appear on the screen, hidden beyond childish plots, concealed in stock characters."[13]

Brecht's behavior toward Odets ranged from admiration to scorn to missionary zeal in trying to win back this political apostate. But they were too far apart. On May 14, 1944, Odets had written something in the *Los Angeles Times* that revealed the aeons separating him from Brecht: "I read in a book the other day that the Germans are intellectually complex, emotionally simple. We are just the opposite. Our future will have to come out of our emotional complexities." In part Brecht's refusal to accept emotional complexities as theatrical matter lay behind his condemnation of the playwright who made this assertion and of the majority of American dramas that confirmed it. Primarily, however, it was an ideological gap that could no longer be bridged.

The American labor movement appealed to Brecht as a source of potential dramatic material. He had learned about Eva Pastor, Emma Goldman, Molly McGuire, the "Wobblies," and other groups and personalities, and Reyher's information on Joe Hill supplied material that he later planned to use in a play about that figure.[14] He also knew of and might have met Ella Bloor ("Mother Bloor") during his 1935-1936 visit, for among his posthumous papers is a list in German and English arranged like a poem with the heading "Mother Bloor," showing gifts that labor unions and workers gave her in 1936.[15]

These heroes of the American workers' movement enjoyed the remoteness of time that allowed Brecht to admire them as semi-historic personalities suitable for literary treatment. This distance was lacking in his only recorded encounter with a living American labor leader. On January 19, 1945, his journal speaks of a meeting at Dieterle's with Sidney Hillman of the CIO, who by that time had succeeded John L. Lewis as the most powerful figure in American labor.[16] Brecht obviously respected Hillman, whom he describes as "a fox that bore the scars of having extricated itself from many traps." But as soon as the conversation turned to Nazi Germany, their views diverged. When Hillman stated that the Allies would prevent Germany from starting another war, Brecht replied that they first needed to abolish the capitalist system that caused war. Hillman then remarked that he had not heard of a German resistance movement. Brecht countered: "I have not heard that a German resistance movement has been liquidated." Obviously, Brecht believed this, in spite of repeated arguments with other Americans in which he insisted that the inconceivable degree of terror in Nazi Germany made resistance impossible. But Hillman had touched a sensitive nerve, and it provoked Brecht to an assessment that characterized his relationship to the American left generally: "It continues to be impossible to make clear the conditions in Germany to people who have not heard at least two tenets of dialectics—the tenet of opposites working to produce a unity, and the tenet of the leap from quantity into quality."

Brecht's critique of Hillman applied to most American leftists. He considered them to be retarded in the most fundamental aspect of Marxist thinking—dialectics. Brecht understood "dialectics" in Lenin's sense as the contradictions between conflicting forces and ideas that, taken together in their "synthesis," comprehend the essence of what is true. The importance of dialectics was its focus on paradoxes. For a man who thought like an acrobat, "dialectics" was made to order. One-sided, systematic logic demanded rigorous and narrow thinking. "Dialectics," which demanded and dealt with complexities found in opposing forces and seeming as well as real contradictions, allowed Brecht the luxury of contradicting himself and everyone else within a consistent framework. One friend claims that the contradictory mode which made this way of viewing the world so compatible to Brecht arose as much out of distrust of himself as of others.[17] Whatever the source, it was basic to his thinking, and it almost always cast him in an oppositional role.

Documented instances of Brecht's being in agreement on ideological and political matters with European or American leftists between 1941-1947 are rare. A harmony of views probably existed only with a handful of persons, such as the Eisler brothers and Hauptmann. But accounts of his disagreements are legion. Sometimes, if Brecht respected others, he was the model of Confucian courtesy. Breiner recalls a discussion with Helene Bauer which is also noted in Brecht's journal.[18] A well-known economist and revolutionary herself and the widow of Otto Bauer, an Austrian socialist, she patiently listened to his discourse on Marxist economics and politely dissented at the end with a remark that normally would have enraged him: "You, comrade Brecht, are of course a great poet." Brecht accepted it without a rejoinder. His correspondence in American with Karl Korsch, a renegade Communist living in Boston with whom he had once studied in Germany, was also conducted with unusual cordiality and courtesy. But these were exceptions. Brecht's normal behavior over ideological and political issues involved heated arguments and strong expressions of opinion.

Hans Viertel, whose Trotskyist position provoked repeated disagreement with the exile, once asked what would happen to those who refused to accept his views. Brecht's answer was simple: "They have to be shot." Viertel, Breiner, Gorelik, and Fritz Sternberg, another of Brecht's former teachers who had become a heretical Marxist and now was residing in New York City, all remember shouting matches when they disagreed with him. This is not to say that Brecht could brook no disagreement. It means only that when he believed he was right, Brecht did not normally try to be conciliatory for the sake of getting along.

One incident, however, in which Brecht did attempt to overlook differences for the sake of ideological unity occurred during his visit to New York in the winter of 1943-1944. Aufricht says he arranged for Brecht to invite Ruth Eisler Fischer, sister of Hanns and Gerhart Eisler, to dinner at Berlau's apartment. Brecht, who had never met her, was aware that she had been in Moscow and had known Stalin personally; he was probably unaware that, while still an ideological Marxist, she had become violently anti-Stalinist, and that she had written a vitriolic article against him entitled "Bert Brecht, Minstrel of the GPU." After reading a draft of the article, Aufricht tried to persuade Fischer to change her mind about publishing it by introducing her to her victim. Following a pleasant meal, Fischer turned on Brecht by saying that by the time he, with his schoolboy's brain, had begun to get interested in the Communist Party, Stalin had already subverted it. "In normal circumstances," continues Aufricht, "Brecht would have attempted to shout her down or throw her out." But for a time he continued to address her politely as "comrade" and tried to resolve their differences. It was no use. They quarreled bitterly, and at 3 a.m. they were still shouting at each other. When the article appeared in the April 1944 issue of *Politics*,[19] Brecht's solution for dealing with Fischer was simple: "The swine has to be shot." His reason: "One does not parade ideological differences between comrades in front of the police."[20]

Brecht knew of the heterogeneous makeup of the American left, and it bothered him. Members of the Communist Party USA were by no means the only ones who subscribed to the ideas of Marx. Anti-Stalinist Trotskyists; Socialists; apostate Communists without any party affiliation; fellow-traveling progessives of many persuasions; and some independent liberals shared a common ideological base in the teachings of Marx and were usually considered "Marxists." But their factionalism, and the broad spectrum of variations on a basic set of ideological beliefs, irritated Brecht. He believed that there was a right and a wrong kind of Marxism, and that he was in possession of the correct understanding. Hence he never ceased to correct or to attempt to convert improperly instructed American friends.

The non-party alignment of so many American leftists disturbed

Brecht for another reason. He held that external criticism of Stalin and the Communist Party was subjective. In his view, objective criticism was possible only from a firm position within the Communist Party, and criticism of Stalin and Communism by leftist friends who violated this code struck him as betrayal of a movement in which he deeply believed. Conservatives made it easy for him. He refused to tolerate their criticism and often stopped seeing them. Hans Sahl remembers a conversation with Brecht in Berlau's apartment in New York where, in a discussion of *The Good Woman of Setzuan*, he told Brecht that the methods of Stalin and Hitler were identical. Brecht asked him to get out, and that ended their relationship. But the dramatist was obliged to deal with criticism by Viertel, Breiner, Sternberg, Fischer, and others associated with the left. Their relative positions in respect to him are useful in defining Brecht's political orientation at the time.

Viertel, who had been active in the American section of the Fourth International, and Fischer were identified on the left as Trotskyists, which meant they were anti-Stalinists. In Brecht's view, Sternberg and Korsch, who were Marxist heretics, and the members of the Frankfurt Institute, who espoused an intellectual brand of Marxism that had nothing to do with a party or movement, were all salon Marxists. Breiner had been active in the Socialist party of Austria and continued to adhere to a Marxist brand of Socialism independent of the Communist Party. In contrast to these friends, Brecht was deeply committed to the teachings of Lenin, the practices and policies of Stalin, and the model of Soviet Russia, where, he felt, Marxist principles had been realized in their most perfect form. Lenin was one of his few heroes, and throughout American exile he continued to read and write about him. One journal entry reflects on eyewitness accounts of Lenin's inconspicuous but commanding behavior and expresses admiration for everything he had heard about him. It concludes: "he was authoritative; he had the authority of usefulness. He was primarily a functionary and proved it by functioning."[21] Another entry records the pleasure Brecht experienced in reading Trotsky's 1924 book about Lenin.[22] This entry, and Eisler's recollections,[23] confirm how much he admired Lenin's dedication to his principles and his cunning in dealing with enemies.

After losing many Russian and German exile friends to the purges that Stalin conducted between 1935 and 1938, Brecht's relationship to the Soviet leader had become ambivalent. Initially he had shared the shock and dismay of friends at the purge trials. In spite of his public efforts to justify them, Brecht expressed anti-Stalinist views in private conversations, in prose, in verse, and in his journal.[24] By the time he reached America, however, he had developed a battery of sophisti-

cated arguments to show that these trials were necessary, and they
made him sound like an apologist for Stalinist terror. Viertel and
Breiner, both of whom criticized the purges, recall that their most violent disagreements with him centered on this topic. Viertel remembers
Brecht's statement that Stalin had no way to make ninety million illit-
erate muzhiks understand why Bukharin and others were ideologically
wrong; he had to treat these men as criminals to make his point clear.
Whatever reservations Brecht may have had about Stalin during his
American exile, he seems to have repressed them, or at least not discussed them.

Journal entries of this period testify to Brecht's interest in and loyalty to the Soviet leader. A news clipping he included in his journal
without comment on December 2, 1941 dealt with the visit of an
American admiral to Moscow who described Stalin as being "sleepy
like a fox," which, translated, means "intelligently alert to what was
going on." Brecht clearly enjoyed this portrayal of a virtue he admired
in almost anyone—cunning.

In 1943 his journal records reading Boris Souvarine's biography
entitled *Stalin. A Critical Survey of Bolshevism*, which he found "depressing." According to him, it showed the "transformation of a
professional revolutionary into a bureaucrat" and of "an entire revolutionary party into a bureaucratic body."[25] This was not the first negative portrayal of Stalin that Brecht had heard or read, but it disturbed
him, nonetheless. Having committed himself to support the Soviet
Union as the center of International Communism, he seemed determined to be loyal to its leader, especially during the war years, when
Brecht considered Stalin to be the world leader in the fight against fascism.

Brecht possessed an ability to turn dross into gold, and he did just
that with Souvarine's unsympathetic Stalin biography. In addition to
drawing on it for places names and lore about the Caucasus for his
Caucasian Chalk Circle, Brecht transformed a bit of information from
it into a camouflaged paean to Stalin in the play. The first chapter of
the biography dealing with Stalin's boyhood was entitled "Sosso,"
after the Georgian diminutive for "Joseph," a name Stalin carried
throughout childhood and while doing illegal party work in Georgia.
As act three of the play opens, Grusha sings a song to buoy her courage. It recounts how four generals conducted unsuccessful campaigns
against Iran. But, it continues, when "Sosso Robakidze" came, he
fought a fierce war, won a quick victory, and inspired his soldiers.
Hence, it concludes, "Sosso Robakidze/ Is our man." When Brecht
showed this song to Hans Viertel immediately after writing it, the
young Viertel, who knew the background of "Sosso" and who recog-

nized the concealed praise of Stalin, confronted him. But Brecht refused to discuss it. "It's staying in," he said, and the matter ended
there.[26] Stalin's decisiveness and success as a leader where others had
failed were not open to question.[27]

In the eyes of most European and American leftists who knew him
in the forties, Brecht was a Stalinist. Viertel remembers challenging his
unequivocal support of the war effort, which from a Trotskyist position was an imperialist war. Brecht saw it as an anti-fascist conflict
conducted primarily by Stalin and the Soviet Union, and he discounted
its imperialist nature. Viertel also recalls Brecht's justification of the
Stalin-Hitler pact which had disillusioned so many American leftists.
Breiner, too, saw him as a hard-line Stalinist. Based on frequent contact and political discussions, he still holds the impression that the
Brecht he knew in America "suspended his critical faculties when con-
fronting the apparatus of the C. P." and displayed "a childish dependence on Russian Communism's ever changing policies."[28] When Albert Maltz met and dealt with Brecht again in 1947 as a fellow witness
before the House Un-American Activities Committee, he recognized in
Brecht a true-red Stalinist.[29] The matter, however, was not nearly that
simple, as later evidence will show.

Brecht's orientation toward the Soviet Union contributed to this
impression. On repeated occasions, his letters and journal borrow
Lenin's phrase in referring to the "grand disorder" of capitalist
America, as opposed to the "grand order" of the Socialist Soviet
Union, which he clearly preferred. Next to Germany, Russia was now
the center of Brecht's universe. This was reflected in other ways
throughout his journal. In it he pasted a number of newspaper and
magazine illustrations which serve to supplement articles he included
about fighting on the Russian front. Photos of the Soviet people and of
the Red Army give the impression that the fight against fascism is centered in that country, and that America and the other allies are ad-
juncts to the Russian war effort. In 1942, Brecht notes in his journal
how news that Radio Moscow might be able to use material prompts
him to write a poem for the Russian war effort entitled "To the
Hitler-Soldiers in Russia."[30] Obviously he hoped to have it broadcast.
A few months later he reflects in his journal that "the battle of
Smolensk is a battle for lyric poetry."[31] In his eyes, Russia was fighting
to make the world free for, among other things, poetry.

Throughout his American exile, Brecht maintained frequent contact
with Soviet consular and embassy officials in the United States. Friends
and acquaintances recall going with him to cocktail parties and to re-
ceptions given by the Soviet consulate in Los Angeles or seeing him
there, and his journal mentions several functions he attended there. In

testimony before the House Committee on Un-American Activities in 1947, Brecht spoke of going to parties at the Soviet consulate in Los Angeles "three or four times with, of course, many other writers."

His most sinister connection with a Russian was with Gregory Kheifetz, a Soviet vice-consul in San Francisco whom the FBI suspected of being an NKVD agent. According to its files, the FBI conducted surveillance of their meetings five different times between April 1943 and January 1944. In 1947 this known association with Kheifetz weighed heavily in Brecht's being summoned to appear before the House Un-American Activities Committee.

Brecht looked to the Soviet Union at this time as the model for society and the center of the world revolutionary workers' movement. From Breiner, Viertel, and others, he heard how politically backward American workers were.[32] In spite of a large number of wildcat strikes that took place throughout World War II and a bloody history of strikes and labor violence in America before that time, Brecht concluded that workers in the USA had no interest in staging a revolution. Like nearly all his opinions, this one he tempered dialectically with the view that, in spite of the lack of a true revolutionary party, the American bourgeoisie would not remain in power indefinitely.[33] But he dismissed relatively well-paid American workers, whose behavior looked suspiciously capitalistic, as reactionaries, though he probably had less direct contact with workers in America than in any place in his life.

An important consideration that put Brecht at odds with American leftists was his self-appointed role as a defender of Marxist ideological purity. His belief that he knew and understood the doctrines emanating from Moscow better than they made him react in one instance like a Jesuit encountering a heresy. Normally Brecht neglected his journal during trips to New York City and summarized the highlights in a single entry after he returned. But his reaction to what he thought was a major deviation from international Communism moved him to make a separate entry for a specific event on one trip. Incorrectly dated January 7, 1944 (he could not have known about it until two or three days later), it states: "The American Communist Party pays the heroic Red Army a little compliment by committing hari-kari."

Between January 7-9, 1944, the Communist Party of the USA held a meeting of its National Committee in New York while Brecht was there. He learned the results of its closed sessions either from a radio broadcast by William Z. Foster of the party secretariat on the evening of January 9th, or from *The New York Times*, which he read regularly. On the morning of January 10th it carried an article on page one with the headlines: "Reds Quit Politics as a Party in U.S. Accept Traditional Two-Party System, But Will Carry On 'Political Education'

Work." The article explains that Earl Browder, General Secretary of the Party, has announced that the Communist Party will "go out of business as a political party" and allow the country's political issues to be decided "within the form of the two-party system traditional to our country." It continues that Browder, who is scheduled to explain reasons for the decision that evening at a mass meeting in Madison Square Garden, had recommended that American Communists continue their existence with the name "American Communist Political Association."

Brecht was incensed. While Russian troops were suffering great losses, American Communists had the cowardice to surrender their role as the only revolutionary party in that country. This was tantamount to betrayal of the working classes. Moreover, Brecht took it to be a rebellion against Moscow's preeminence in party matters by politically immature, nationalistic Communists who were striking out on their own and subverting the international movement. Brecht did not know the background of this decision, but it would not have changed his views.

For several years the Communist International (the CI or "Comintern"), the general staff of world revolution in Moscow that cleared policies and directed the activities of the Communist Party in the United States, had tried to wean the CPUSA from its excessive dependence on foreign-language federations and models. Gradually the party had become more "American." When the Comintern was dissolved in May 1943, it was a signal to American Communists that their ties to Moscow could be loosened further. Earl Browder kept in touch with Georgi Dimitroff, former Comintern General Secretary, for approval of major decisions, but a feeling arose in the Party that, as Joseph Starobin describes it, "Their own creative thinking was being validated in Moscow," and that "their relative success entitled them to do some pioneering along the Marxist frontiers."[34] This, coupled with the meeting of Churchill, Roosevelt, and Stalin at Teheran in December 1943, led Browder to formulate a new program that constituted the sole item on the agenda at the January meeting of the Party's National Committee. His ideas, published the same month in a booklet entitled *Teheran and America. Perspectives and Tasks*, charted a course of polycentricism or "national Communism."[35]

Exuding optimism at the unprecedented cooperation of the three leaders, Browder announced that "Capitalism and Socialism have begun to find the way to peaceful coexistence and collaboration in the same world." Looking for the same "broad, democratic world-wide front" in the post-war world that had emerged from the Big Three's actions and communique at Teheran, he proclaimed that, guided by the theoretical heritage of Marxism, the "Teheran Declaration which was signed by Churchill, Roosevelt and the great Marxist Stalin represents the only program in the interest of the toiling masses of the whole world in the next period. . . . We could not unconditionally throw our forces into this new period while it was merely a possibility, but now that this possibility has been confirmed by the agreement of Teheran, we know we can feel absolutely certain that we have crossed the border-line from the past and have definitely entered the present" (pp. 45-46). Socialism, he declared, was not bent on world conquest, and free enterprise would continue in the United States. The Teheran agreement "preserves to each nation the ultimate right to determine for itself . . . the form of government and social organization it desires, without any outside pressure" (p. 14).

This did not mean dissolution of a Communist organization as such, but only of the party structure with separate candidates in elections. Recognizing that the two dominant parties were "coalitions of many groups which in most countries would be separate parties" (p. 40), and that the existence of a separate party was an obstruction to cooperation with other democratic groups, Browder called for a reconstitution of Communists. With the formation of an "American Communist Political Association," it would be easier for the Communist Party "to explain our true relationship with all other democratic and progressive groupings" operating within the two-party system, and its name would correspond "more exactly to the American political tradition and its own practical political role" (p. 41).

Brecht must have read *Teheran and America* shortly after it appeared. Hans Viertel remembers being present at a party in his home in 1944 when the playwright submitted Browder's booklet to an invective that embarrassed even his friend Eisler. Browder had declared invalid a cherished tenet of Marxism—that of world revolution. Another of Browder's heresies was to equate democracy in capitalist countries with real democracy, which meant rule by the working classes. In Brecht's view, American "democracy" was only a name for a capitalist political system, and it would never change until capitalism had been abolished.

Brecht considered Browder's deviant Marxism to be an example of what happened when politically backward American Communists were left on their own. He did not know that Browder believed that he had Moscow's sanction for his new course,[36] which he received after differences arose over this issue with William Z. Foster. After sending a transcript of the discussions to Georgi Dimitroff, Browder received instructions that Foster was not to press his arguments. Brecht knew none of this, nor would it have mattered; he knew only that the

American Communist Party had violated several unassailable dogmas, among them the hegemony of Moscow and the necessity for world-wide proletarian revolution. Brecht was vindicated the following year when the Communist Party USA was officially resurrected with its traditional goals intact. Wurtele later heard him cite a passage from an American leftist writer as further evidence that American Communism was rooted in its own peculiar form of nationalism. As Marshall Tito's expulsion from the Communist movement in 1948 for a similar heresy of "national Communism" proved, the exile understood Moscow's thinking at the time better than his American comrades did.

This distrust of American Communists was not without irony. Wurtele and Riker both claim they had experiences confirming that in the eyes of members of the CPUSA, Brecht himself had become suspect, allegedly for his association with Trotskyists and other non-Communist leftists. Through most of his life the political animal named Bertolt Brecht had strong resemblance to a maverick, and party members were not the only ones to recognize it. Those who knew him best detected something that made his hard-line Stalinism seem unconvincing.

Hanns Eisler, who was probably as close to Brecht politically as anyone in America, responded in detail to an interviewer's questions in the sixties as to whether Brecht was a Marxist and whether that categorization did him justice. After labeling it a "scholastic question," Eisler painstakingly attempted to explain how Brecht was and was not a Marxist: "In his use of language he was a Marxist, although I would rather say a Leninist. . . . Brecht learned the method of dialectical materialism from Marx and Lenin and used it in his own way in his poems, his dramas, and his prose . . . he always felt himself to be a Communist, to be, as they say in the Soviet Union, a 'Bolshevik without a party book.' "[37] This answer was more than an exercise in equivocation. Eisler was genuinely struggling to define a man who ultimately defied categorization. Brecht, as Eisler stated, clearly "felt himself" to be a Communist, but his sovereignty in thought and writing seemed to have made him much more, and surely not a conventional one.

Some non-leftists in America who knew Brecht's political persuasion agreed with the suspicions of American Communists. Laughton observed that "Brecht can't possibly be a Communist. He questions too much."[38] The apolitical actor's statement might have been an attempt to justify his association with a man of Brecht's known political views, but Florence Homolka had virtually the same impression: "I could never believe in Brecht's conversion to Communism . . . he did not seem submissive enough to fit into a hierarchy or conventional enough to be labeled."[39] Laughton and Homolka were seeing a character trait relating to Brecht's respect for authority on which the dramatist himself comments in a journal entry written in 1952: "By nature I am a difficult person to control. Authority that does not command my respect I reject out of hand, and I can view laws only as provisional suggestions for regulating community living that are constantly in need of change."[40] Roland Barthes has pointed out that in his works, "Brecht's greatness, and his solitude, is that he keeps inventing Marxism."[41] It was this almost total independence in his works and his thought that Hans Viertel captured in an apt description which comes as close as any to portraying the complexities of his enigmatic position: "Bertolt Brecht was a one-man political party in close coalition with the Communists."

American Communists probably knew that, for all his apparent Marxist orthodoxy, Brecht had never officially joined the Communist Party, notwithstanding Ruth Fisher's accusations to the contrary.[42] This kind of ambivalence irritated lesser spirits, and it was not the last time Brecht's behavior would raise suspicions about his ideological commitment. After returning to East Germany in 1949, he did not become a citizen of that country, but instead took out Austrian citizenship. When he won the Stalin Peace Prize in 1955 while living in East Berlin, he apparently deposited the money in a Swiss Bank. This was more than a "gambler hedging his bets," as W. H. Auden cynically put it;[43] it was Brecht's brand of "dialectical thinking" translated into behavior. Even the pieces he wrote in East Berlin criticizing or condemning Stalin,[44] some of which repose in the Brecht Archives and probably will never be published, should not be taken as a repudiation of his earlier views. He was merely subjecting his basic position to ongoing dialectical examination. In America the special conditions of exile, his attitude on the backwardness of American leftists, and a war he viewed as a struggle against fascism led by Russia, Stalin, and world Communism made Brecht appear to some more doctrinaire and less dialectical than he would ever seem again. But these considerations failed to obscure his own sovereign brand of Marxism. Brecht was and remained a "one-man political party," who, at least during his exile, was unable to form a coalition with American Communists. If he had, there is reason to think that better relations with leftist writers in Hollywood might have given him a chance for more screenwriting work and might have altered the conditions of his entire exile.

Brecht's highly personalized Marxist thought tended to be expressed in extreme formulations that made it difficult for listeners to distinguish between conviction and rhetoric. Sidney Hook describes a visit Brecht made in the winter of 1935-1936 to his Barrow Street apartment in New York. When Hook protested the travesty of justice in the events that had already signaled the beginning of Stalin's trials of innocent victims, Brecht allegedly replied that "the more innocent they are, the more they deserve to die."[45] Some have questioned whether Brecht ever said this,[46] but it seems ideologically and personally in character for him, especially if Hook's attack on Stalin had annoyed him. He had an impish mind, and he generally counterattacked with provocative statements geared to antagonize an opponent and to end further discussion. One critic has pointed out that Brecht's remark displays a deep insight into the nature and meaning of totalitarianism,[47] though Brecht obviously did not care to elaborate on it at the time.

Ideologically dictated claims and statements by Brecht ranged from wrong-headed and ridiculous to provocative and revealing. But they were never banal. Breiner recalls arguing with him early in the war about the fate of wealthy Jewish bankers in Nazi Germany. Brecht maintained that, according to the law of class struggle, Hitler must have struck an alliance with them and would leave them unmolested.[48] In later years, Breiner did not raise the subject again. Brecht's outlook on the fate of postwar Germany was dictated by the belief that a revolutionary uprising of workers would create a new German government for the entire country. He was an equally unreliable prophet on the future of America. In 1947 he strongly espoused the cause of Henry A. Wallace, who was emerging as a third party candidate for president. Bentley recalls hearing Brecht say that, if Wallace were not elected, the alternative for America would be World War III. There was no middle ground. And when the House Un-American Activities Committee launched its investigation of Hollywood in 1947, Brecht announced to friends the imminent destruction of America.[49]

An incident in Brecht's personal life demonstrates how his Marxist ideology informed his thinking on the most mundane matters. After complaining of depression, listlessness, and mental sluggishness in the early months of exile, he discovered vitamin pills, took them for five days, and felt rejuvenated. Even vitamin pills, he realized, had ideological implications for the Marxist theory of class struggle. A journal entry of December 2, 1942, written after he began taking vitamins, concludes with the observation that this was "striking proof of the social origins of the proletariat's 'inadequacy in thinking,' " a view doctors and sociologists have since confirmed.[50]

Another kind of material Brecht pasted in his journal not related to any aspect of the war or to the Soviet Union sounds a distinct ideological leitmotif—social protest by the common people, especially the working classes, in the United States. Photos of striking workers at

Bethlehem Steel; of pickets in front of a defense plant; of protest measures throughout the country when Congress voted to give its members a pension; and of the first "strike-to-work" in US history at Brewster Aeronautical's Long Island factory—all seem to reflect Brecht's optimism about the common sense of the common people to resist oppressive systems.

Brecht's lifelong sympathy with the underdog, as well as his own maverick nature, attracted him to one American labor leader who appeared to be an unlikely bed-fellow—John L. Lewis, head of the United Mine Workers, who had been associated with the isolationist "America First Committee." Four months after arriving in the USA, Brecht pasted a picture of the labor leader and his daughter Kathryn in his journal on a page symbolically opposite a photo of three steel magnates. In June 1943 he again inserted pictures of Lewis and his striking coal miners in his journal. One lengthy journal entry of May 31, 1942, testifies how this "great sinister figure" had become interesting for him as a dramatist. Brecht admitted that he found Lewis fascinating on a number of counts: his ability to organize barbers' apprentices, dirt farmers, and lumberjacks in his miner's union; his inscrutable ways (he had not yet taken a stand on the war); his naked ambition ("many call him a gangster, many a fascist"); and his singular devotion to his miners, whose interests he defended so vigorously. After remarking that the American working class was still too primitive to conduct dialectical politics and consequently had to choose leaders like this who represented "naked extremes," he concluded that if the "fifth act of the New Deal's gigantic drama were to end tragically or soberly, Lewis would be its Fortinbras."

Since before the war began, Lewis had carried on a private feud with Roosevelt, whose labor policies he generally opposed. In contrast to most of American labor, which supported the war effort, he had not hesitated to have his United Mine Workers strike the coal fields at the most critical moments. Brecht knew this from newspapers, and he admired Lewis's non-conformity and the strength that he displayed in his titanic clashes with FDR. He had dramatic interest in and personal regard for a strong man who in many ways was ideologically incompatible, but who reflected his own maverick spirit in watching out for the interests of the oppressed and the working classes.

A discussion with an unidentified leftist writer prompted Brecht to make a journal notation on April 3, 1947, that typifies his attitude toward writers of the American left generally—a degree of respect, but a stronger degree of critical disagreement. His refusal to surrender the right to instruct them by criticizing their ideological deficiencies never allowed him to become close to any Marxist writers, much less to other American men of letters.

As a youth, Brecht had read a good deal of American literature. In exile there, however, he displayed little interest in becoming acquainted with recent developments and writers. There is no evidence that he read anything by Dreiser, Farrell, Fitzgerald, or Faulkner, and little or nothing by Dos Passos or Steinbeck. Bentley's attempts to interest him in the writings of Robert Penn Warren were as futile as Reyher's invitations to read Sinclair Lewis. Reyher spoke frequently of *Moby Dick* as one of the great classics of all time, but there is no indication that Brecht took the bait.

The strongest reason behind this seeming disinterest was not the feeling of cultural superiority exhibited by many émigrés, but ideology. By the time he reached American soil, Brecht was so committed to Marxism that he sought out material which he thought or was told would interest him politically, or at least be compatible with his ideological views. Living near Hollywood as he did, he personally knew a number of American writers who were leftists, and much of his reading was devoted to their relatively undistinguished works, or to works they recommended. In addition to the plays by Stewart and Gorelik, Brecht had read Wexley's drama *They Shall Not Die* while they were working together on *Hangmen*.[51] This is not to say that he accepted this type of American literature uncritically. The opposite seems to have been the case, and Losey remembers Brecht's unflattering private opinions of the works by John Howard Lawson and by Albert Maltz. But it means that Brecht devoted much of his time to reading writers of the left, to the exclusion of many others, and that this was the only contemporary or recent American literature that he knew well. Ideology had not blinded him, but it had narrowed his field of vision when it came to a large segment of American letters.

The ideology of Brecht's informant was decisive. He was suspicious of critical opinions by friends like Bentley, who were not committed to Marxism. On the other hand, an apodictic judgment in one journal entry that Hemingway had no brain probably derived from fellow leftists who detested Hemingway, and not from first-hand reading.[52] Brecht's judgments of some writers whom he knew personally and liked seemed equally hasty. His view of Replansky as one of the three great American women poets was based in part on personal regard, but in larger measure on ignorance of American poetry. And to argue as he did with Bentley that the writings of John Howard Lawson were equal in quality to Hemingway's probably says less about Brecht's critical faculties than about his ideological convictions. Because

Bentley was not a Marxist, Brecht found it necessary to defend Lawson to him. Similarly, Paul Green, whom Brecht met through Gorelik, ranked in his eyes as a great American writer, while Tennessee Williams, whose *Glass Menagerie* he saw in a New York theater, did not. His calling Williams's play "an idiotic piece" had as much to do with ideology as it did with dramatic concepts. Brecht possessed a sure sense for a writer's political convictions, and he was quick to exclude from consideration those who failed to measure up.

In a sense turnabout was fair play. American writers and intellectuals, who traditionally have been unencumbered by any significant exposure to German literature, ignored or were ignorant of Brecht at the time. What Brecht learned of American literature likewise affected him so minimally that it was almost as though he had not been exposed. Ironically, those writers whom he did read, the well-known American leftists of the forties whose reputations surpassed his at the time, have been largely forgotten today, while the name of a maverick Marxist who lived in their midst has gradually achieved international prominence for its quality and for its exposition of Marxist thought.

IX. THE LAST ACT IN AMERICA

Almost from the day he landed, it was no secret that Brecht did not intend to stay in America. In contrast to Thomas Mann and to others who either took out American citizenship or declared their intent to remain in the country, Brecht continued to style himself an "exile." The FBI knew and understood this. Amid rumors circulating in the German exile colony in 1943, Brecht, according to an FBI informant, learned "that refugees now in the United States had already been listed by the government for purposes of custodial detention after the war. . . . Brecht is alleged to have stated that in view of this, he would escape from the United States with a Czechoslovakian passport which he could secure through Benes." On June 6th, 1944, Brecht and Hanns Eisler met with Benes, the Czech consul in San Francisco, and inquired about obtaining passports. The FBI notes: "They apparently believed that possession of Czech passports will facilitate their travel, particularly their departure from this country." A subsequent paragraph reads: "Brecht and Eisler, in response to a suggestion that possibly they would have to get exit visas from the United States government, indicated astonishment at this and then remarked, 'Well, the border is close by.' "

Sometime in the spring of 1945, as the war in Europe approached its end, an FBI informant reported "that Brecht continues to express himself as desiring to return to Germany with some sort of theatrical group. He makes reference to this matter in such a way, however, as to indicate that he does not contemplate the possibility of an early return. He further seems to indicate that whether or not he will be able to return depends upon who will be in authority in postwar Germany." Brecht was definitely playing a waiting game. He feared a resurgence of Naziism in postwar Germany or, worse still, what his friend Karl Korsch called a "reactionary Utopia" under the economic aegis of the Americans,[1] and he wanted to see how the situation would develop.

In contrast to many refugees who gradually became assimilated and who did not return to Europe, or who returned much later and often without enthusiasm, Brecht believed that his destiny lay in his homeland, and that he must not become too comfortable in America. Though he applied for his so-called "first papers" less than six months after arriving, he did not pursue the matter of acquiring citizenship after that. When Weigel wrote their mutual friend, the Finnish writer Hella Wuolijoki, in January 1946 that "we are waiting for the opportunity to return to Europe" and that "Thomas Mann's attitude is totally out of the question for us,"[2] she was alluding to Mann's decision to make America his home. Brecht had never entertained the idea.

Sternberg recalls hearing him say after the war that he was not writing for later generations, but for German-speaking stages and audiences of his time, and that, to see his own plays produced, he needed to be in Germany.[3]

In the postwar cultural vacuum, European theater directors looking for suitable plays remembered or discovered Brecht and rushed to produce him. Their requests to perform his plays after 1945 must have intensified his desire to return. Though eager to shape the cultural and dramatic institutions in postwar Germany, he felt he could not do it unless physically present. The consequence was his refusal to allow his works to be performed until he could be there to supervise each production.

Without Brecht's knowledge, his most popular work, *The Threepenny Opera*, had opened in July 1945 in the Hebbel Theater in Berlin. Its success reinforced his decision to block other productions. Hungry Berliners subsisting on a food ration of one loaf of bread and a quarter of a pound of butter per month and a quarter-pound of meat per week (cheese, milk, sugar, salt, and coffee were virtually unobtainable) found in it a welcome form of protest against the occupying powers who wanted to de-Nazify them without feeding them properly. Robert Joseph, a United States Army film officer in Berlin working with the four-power Kommandantura, describes the postwar premiere of Brecht's play in a letter written soon after the opening and printed in *The Los Angeles Daily News*:

"The people loved the show, and the house was packed . . . and when Mackie sings the song 'Zuerst Fressen, danach Moral' ('let us eat, and morality thereafter'), they applauded madly. Of course, this was meant for the Americans. The chorus for that song stood at the back of the house and sang the song, too, and this was a dramatic trick to make it seem as if this song was being sung by the people in the house itself. Naturally, this is a somewhat touchy subject. . . . I, and about five other American officers, were the only officers there in addition to two Russians. Naturally we were stared at, and everyone looked at us to see our reaction, first to that song, and second to the performance. I applauded the song like mad and probably shocked all of Berlin. . . . The Russians have decided, as of last evening, that they don't like the show. They think that song is inciting, and I think they'll insist on closing it. Well, that is the kind of problem we must solve at these subsection Kommandantura meetings."[4]

Brecht's journal notes that he agrees with the Russians: "We hear that *The Threepenny Opera* was performed to full houses in Berlin and then, at the insistence of the Russians, was closed. As ground for protest, the BBC (London) mentioned the ballad 'Food comes first,

morals follows on.' I myself never would have permitted a performance. In the absence of a revolutionary movement, the 'message' is
pure anarchy."[5] Writing soon afterward to Berlau, Brecht states that
"if there is *one* situation for which this is not appropriate, it's the
present one. *Galileo* is scheduled for performance by the Deutsches
Theater [in Berlin]. I'll also try to prevent that until I'm there myself."[6]

To stop the *Threepenny Opera* performances, this dramatist who
would not answer publishers, translators, or friends who wanted to
promote his works wrote two letters on October 14th. One he sent to
American authorities in Berlin; the second went to the director of the
performance, Karl-Heinz Martin. Brecht's objections touched on the
same matters that concerned him in any production of his work—the
quality of the cast and performance, and his own lack of control. In a
reply, Edward Hogan, an American occupation officer in the ISCS
Headquarters, Berlin, told him that his *Threepenny Opera* had not
caused any controversy. Hogan added that it was interestingly staged
and reasonably well cast, though Mackie Messer was perhaps not the
best. But, continued Hogan in response to Brecht's efforts to name his
own cast and production terms, "casting is always a problem, for the
actor you want is either in exile, dead, or unemployable under (N.S.)
rules against people tainted with Nazism. Martin's theater is the
cleanest in Berlin in this respect." In answer to Brecht's inquiry about
royalty payments, he urged him to let his works be performed through
arrangements with the stage publisher Felix Bloch Erben rather than in
pirated versions or not at all. "You may not realize it," he concluded
"but you are a very popular poet in Germany."[7]

After inferring correctly from Hogan's letter that his *Threepenny
Opera* had not been closed, Brecht wrote again in November or December 1945, asking how he could prevent *Galileo* from opening.
Hogan replied, stating that the *Threepenny Opera* "is still running, is
doing well, and will stay in the repertory of Martin for perhaps
another month." He had heard an announcement about a performance of *Galileo*, "but it is not in our sector, and I don't know the arrangements."[8] Apparently Brecht was not content with Hogan's responses, for he wrote to John Bitter, the civilian chief of the Theater
and Music Section of the Military Government, Berlin, about coming
there to supervise these performances. Bitter acknowledged that he
had received a note from Brecht and had passed it on to the director of
the *Threepenny Opera* as instructed. He urged the exile to inquire
with the State Department about travel; at the moment, the only reason for visiting Berlin was to conduct official business with the military government.[9]

From late 1945 until 1947 American occupational officials and theater directors in Germany and Austria eager to stage Brecht's plays wrote him requesting permission to perform them. Without exception he refused them on the grounds that he must be there personally to supervise productions.

Letters from the last half of 1946 reflect Brecht's uncertainty over where to settle. He looked to Germany as his ultimate destination, but he had no immediate plans to live there. Before 1933 he owned a house on Lake Ammer in the upper Bavarian township of Utting. In the spring of 1946 he informed his boyhood friend George Pfanzelt that, if the house still belonged to him, Pfanzelt would be welcome to move in. With characteristic generosity Brecht also invited Caspar Neher in November of that year to occupy it if he wished. His own property in Germany did not interest him, and his awareness of the devastation there, coupled with his fear of resurgent Naziism, increased an instinctive wariness that made him look for a base of operations outside Germany before venturing back.

After learning that pre-war royalties from performances of his *Threepenny Opera* had accumulated in Denmark, Brecht inquired in October if he could get the money out. When he learned it was blocked,[10] he apparently considered Denmark as a destination because of the available funds. An undated letter to Neher during the same period states that he was thinking of northern Italy, where he would work for several years and put together productions for Germany, while a letter to Reyher in early April 1947 mentions northern Italy as a place to work on films before returning to Germany. In early December 1946 Brecht wrote Neher, saying he hoped to be in Switzerland the following June and stating that "I would need certain actors from here and from Switzerland, etc. I also hope that by then, i.e., by the next theater season, guest productions by a traveling troupe will be possible in all of Germany."

In August 1946 Heinrich Mann wrote Alfred Kantorowicz, stating that he had received letters inviting him to return to the Russian occupation zone of Germany, and that the Soviet consul general from New York had invited Brecht and Feuchtwanger to settle there.[11] Either the Soviet consul general or someone else in the Russian occupation zone of Berlin communicated directly with Brecht during these months about using a Berlin theater, since Brecht mentions the offer to the stage designer Caspar Neher in a letter written in December 1946. Speaking of his hopes to be in Switzerland the following June, he adds that: "I also have offers from Berlin to use the Schiffbauerdamm theater [site of his 1928 triumph with *The Threepenny Opera*] for certain things."

Neutral Switzerland interested Brecht as a temporary stopping place, and he made inquiries in New York in the fall of 1946. In anticipation of a more temperate European climate, he complains in an undated letter to his wife in October or November that year of the unpleasant weather in New York, while instructing her on what to do: "In regard to Switzerland, we must go to the consulate in Los Angeles, but I believe that we also have to apply for American citizenship." He later discovered that American citizenship was unnecessary, but he learned that his own lack of national citizenship, coupled with restrictions imposed by European countries on displaced or stateless persons wanting to relocate, would require considerable paper work and a long waiting period for himself, his wife, and his daughter Barbara (their son Stefan, who had become an American citizen in December 1946, would not be accompanying them).

Brecht began submitting the necessary papers in December 1946. A letter to Reyher written during the first half of March 1947 transmitted good news: "We have applied for exit and re-entry visas (for Switzerland). Helli and Barbara have already received positive word; the photos on my application were not large enough. I hope that's all." Two weeks later his journal contains a one-sentence entry: "Received exit and re-entry permit for Switzerland."[12] Now Brecht needed only transit visas to allow his family to cross France, and he would be ready to depart. But six more months would elapse before he received them, a period marked by two significant dramatic performances. One of them, *Galileo*, was staged under his supervision. In the other, a hearing by the House Un-American Activities Committee, he himself was one of the principal actors.

When Egon Breiner first met Brecht in a Vladivostok bookstore before they sailed for America in June 1941, the dramatist was buying German editions of Lenin's writings. As they arrived at San Pedro, California, Breiner reports, Brecht threw these works into the harbor with the explanation: "I don't want any trouble with the U.S. authorities."

This anecdote contains an element of poetic truth regarding one aspect of Brecht's life in exile. In most respects, the revolutionary dramatist behaved like a law-abiding German burgher. He observed the curfew for enemy aliens while it was in force; he registered annually with the Immigration and Naturalization Service and he always notified them of his current address; he requested and received permission to travel from the local US District Attorney's office each time he went to New York; he registered for the draft; he took out a California driver's license; and, so far as is known, he paid income taxes. Brecht clearly had no desire to call himself to the attention of the authorities.

American authorities, however, had been aware of him almost since he landed. Documents released from his FBI dossiers reveal an interest in his political views and activities that persisted throughout his exile. Almost from the outset, the FBI viewed Brecht as a dangerous revolutionary. One report of March 6, 1943, states that "subject's writings . . . advocate overthrow of Capitalism, establishment of Communist State and use of sabotage by labor to attain its ends." Translations of part or all of several poems were included in this report to show the revolutionary nature of his writings. Another report of March 30, 1943, contains a plot summary of *The Measures Taken*, a play which, according to the FBI, "advocates Communist world revolution by violent means." And statements in Brecht's file gleaned from friends, enemies, and acquaintances whom FBI agents had interviewed, not to mention material from paid informants, transmit a clear picture of Brecht as a crypto-revolutionary. By 1944, reports on him no longer fall under the classification "alien control," but rather "internal security."

No later than 1946 the Brechts were aware of FBI surveillance of their home and of possible wire-tapping of their telephone. Helene Weigel seems to have taken it with equanimity, even humor. One chilly day, according to Rhoda Riker, she went to a car parked on their street where an FBI agent was watching their home. "You poor man," she said inviting him in, "you could watch us much better from inside the house." Riker remembers how Weigel read recipes from a Polish cookbook over the telephone to confuse those listening in.

Absorbed as he was with the *Galileo* production from mid-April through mid-August 1947, Brecht was nevertheless aware that in May of that year the House Committee on Un-American Activities had held special closed hearings in Los Angeles to investigate alleged Communist infiltration of the motion-picture industry. Among those called to testify was Hanns Eisler, whom the Committee suspected of being as dangerous as his brother Gerhart. The composer consciously avoided mentioning Brecht's name,[1] but the dramatist's close association with him was already known to investigators from FBI files. By the end of Eisler's testimony, the Committee apparently was considering a summons for Brecht. In light of this, Joseph Losey's declaration years later that Laughton denounced Brecht to the Committee seems unfounded.[2] Since they were deeply involved in rehearsals for the *Galileo* premiere, it is difficult to imagine that the normally timorous Laughton would have done something to jeopardize a production when bad publicity for him or for Brecht would have doomed the play. Eisler certainly told Brecht about his hearing, since he, too, was working on the *Galileo* production as the composer of the incidental music. But, like many others in Hollywood that summer, including some who later were summoned to testify before the Committee in Washington, Brecht paid little attention to what seemed like a minor threat that would pass quickly.[3]

After *Galileo* closed on August 17th, Brecht and his family were engrossed in preparations for their departure to Europe. In an undated letter of early September he wrote Reyher saying that "we wanted to sail in mid-September, but we did not get the French transit visas and could not sell the house. The house is now sold, and we want to leave for good from New York in mid-October, destination Zurich or Basel." *Galileo*, he added, had a good chance to make Broadway, but he would not wait. If, however, it reached Broadway, or if he sold film rights to it, "I'll bring along a car. Could you find out the best kind for me? It must not use too much gas. I hear that a Nash is difficult to repair. Is that right? How about a Chevrolet?"

Brecht's mind was on similar matters relating to his departure when a US marshal appeared at his home on September 19, 1947, and served him with a subpoena to appear before the House Un-American Activities Committee in late October. Brecht's daughter maintains that the marshal was not completely sober, and both she and Wurtele confirm that Weigel invited him in to drink coffee while Brecht listened to the man's complaints about a job that resulted in sore feet, ingratitude, and people who moved to avoid him. Barbara Brecht also relates that, while informing her father how the government paid round-trip expenses and per diem, he advised that by travelling on a train and by claiming reimbursement for auto mileage, he could collect more. Convinced as he was of the mild corruptibility of all humanity, Brecht was delighted with this representative of the US government who was helping him to take advantage of his employer. Nor did the subpoena seem to have disturbed him. Gorelik, who received a phone call from Brecht the same day, and Breiner, who visited him the next day, both remember that he expressed no fear. Brecht later asked Gorelik what the summons meant. When his friend inquired if he had done anything un-American, Brecht countered with "No, I'm not an American. If they had accused me of doing nothing for Communism, they would have been correct."

Brecht had been caught in the net of America's most notorious Congressional investigating committee. Soon after "HUAC" (its official name was the House Committee on Un-American Activities) was formed in 1938, it acquired the reputation of a witch-hunting body targeted against the American left. Originally known as the Dies Committee after its first chairman, Martin Dies, by its investigations it had caused the termination of the Federal Theater Project in 1939. In subsequent years the Committee's questionable tactics, which involved guilt by association and smear, brought it considerable notoriety. Soon after the beginning of the Cold War in 1946, it had begun to investigate charges that Communists had infiltrated Hollywood, and that the motion-picture industry had put subversive doctrine on the screen. Closed hearings held in Los Angeles in the spring of 1947 sent a few ripples through the film community, but, when public hearings in Washington were announced in September 1947, major shock waves were generated in Hollywood. Denials of subversive messages in films and a request for the Committee to name films in which they occurred met with silence. The Committee promised, however, to tell all in the hearings. With perfect hindsight, some Hollywood personalities who fell victim to this "red scare" began to detect evidence of anti-Americanism in films such as *Mission to Moscow* made during World War II when Russia was America's ally. Others saw the hearings as a ploy by members of the Committee to grab political headlines. There was widespread fear by liberals and conservatives alike that the government's inordinate interest in the content of films was the first step toward control of the industry, and that a witch-hunt was about to begin. In general, Hollywood became extremely nervous as it learned in the latter part of September the names of those who had been summoned to testify at hearings scheduled to open in Washington on October 20th.

Brecht's decision to accept the summons and to go to Washington was apparently easy, and certainly consistent with his previous behavior as a law-abiding revolutionary in exile. To travel to Washington meant only a slight detour in his return-trip to Europe, with the added incentive that the government would pay his round-trip fare and expenses. Apparently he never considered leaving the country without appearing.

Brecht soon learned that he would be in good company. On September 22nd the West Coast edition of *Variety* and of *The Hollywood Reporter* carried lists of more than forty persons who were being summoned to appear with him. Among those on the original lists he knew personally (not all those summoned would appear) were Charlie Chaplin, Clifford Odets, and Donald Ogden Stewart. For the first time, Brecht was part of a cause that involved some of the American left, and he seems to have welcomed being identified with their cause. Two days later, however, he began to realize that the Committee might threaten his planned return to Europe. On September 24th Hanns Eisler, who was already under suspicion of being a Communist, appeared again before the Committee in a postlude to the hearing of his brother Gerhart and heard the chief investigator, Robert E. Stripling, call him the "Karl Marx of Communism in the musical field." Eisler, who again scrupulously avoided using Brecht's name, dodged and double-talked. The answer Eisler gave when asked if he had appeared at US Communist Party headquarters with his brother Gerhart in 1935 was typical of his other replies: "My best recollection is I do not remember."[4]

It was clear from the questions put to Eisler that the Committee already knew of Brecht. In fact, some of the identical questions would recur in his hearing the next month. Eisler's refractory behavior prompted J. Parnell Thomas, chairman of the Committee, to instruct him not to leave the United States. Though the purpose was to initiate formal deportation proceedings against him, the order must have alarmed Brecht, who was eager to return to Europe and wished to avoid any delay. His subpoena, which had ordered him to appear in Washington on October 23rd, stated that he was "not to depart [Washington] without leave of said Committee." This fear of possible delay dominated Brecht's thinking and dictated his strategy and tactics during subsequent weeks.

Those summoned to appear in Washington included prominent Hollywood names that covered a spectrum from staunch conservatives like Walt Disney, Ronald Reagan, and Gary Cooper, to known leftists like John Howard Lawson and Albert Maltz. Out of this group emerged nineteen men determined to oppose HUAC's inquisitional methods. From the beginning, Brecht's name appeared in articles and on petitions as one of these "Hollywood nineteen," as they came to be known. Except for him, all were reasonably well-known members of the film community. Screen writers in the group included Alvah Bessie, Lester Cole, Richard Collins, Gordon Kahn, Howard Koch, Ring Lardner, Jr., John Howard Lawson, Albert Maltz, Samuel Ornitz, Waldo Salt, and Dalton Trumbo. Some of them, notably Lawson, Trumbo, and Lardner, were among the highest paid writers in Hollywood, with many successful screenplays to their credit. Two others, Herbert Biberman and Adrian Scott, were producers. Directors included Edward Dmytryk, Lewis Milestone, Irving Pichel, and Robert Rossen. The lone actor among the nineteen was Larry Parks. Because they were unfriendly to the committee's purposes, the group chose for itself the designation "the unfriendly nineteen," an unfortunate choice as it later turned out. Though Brecht knew only Cole, Lawson, Maltz, and Milestone personally, he found himself a full-fledged member of a loose coalition of American leftists and liberals. Nevertheless, he chose to remain something of an outsider even in this cause.

Before the hearings, individual members of the nineteen consulted with six different attorneys of their own choosing. They were Bartley Crum, Charles J. Katz, Robert W. Kenny, Ben Margolis, Martin Popper, and Samuel Rosenheim. Brecht had gone to Margolis, an attorney with a strong background in civil liberties and labor cases known for defending leftists and leftist causes (*The Hollywood Reporter* of October 27, 1947 calls him a "party-liner"). Before leaving for the East Coast, the attorneys and their clients held several strategy sessions at the homes of members of the nineteen. Brecht attended none of these, and Lawson, Maltz, and Trumbo all recall seeing him for the first time in Washington. Margolis, however, informed Brecht of the plan the other eighteen had worked out, and he was familiar with it when he joined the group in Washington several weeks later. But he felt the group's strategy was wrong, and he did not accept it.

The eighteen considered the House Un-American Activities Committee itself an un-American institution whose inquisitional methods violated constitutional rights to freedom of belief and expression. They decided to oppose it in the most effective way they knew—by making a case they could take to the courts. Realizing that J. Parnell Thomas, the chairman of the Committee, had a short temper, they knew that a refusal to answer the inevitable question about past or present membership in the Communist Party would probably draw a quick citation for contempt of Congress. But their attorneys informed them that an outright refusal to answer that question would, at least on the Supreme Court level, probably disqualify their appeal on purely technical grounds. Therefore they had to devise a way to avoid answering the question without appearing to refuse to answer. This could and did take various forms, such as the reading of a prepared statement in answer to the question, or the assertion that the witness was answering it in his own way. Had they all agreed to give the same answer, they would have violated existing conspiracy laws. Therefore each was left to answer as best he could without answering the question outright.

Kenny remembers that he and the other attorneys advised their clients not to invoke the Fifth Amendment to the Constitution, a practice that would not become common until the McCarthy era a few years later. Originally that amen•dment was conceived to protect a person from being forced to make self-incriminating statements under torture or duress. It had the serious drawback that, in the public mind in 1947, it vaguely implied that a serious crime had been committed. To avoid that implication, the group decided to invoke the First Amendment guaranteeing freedom of speech and belief as a right that was being violated by a group inquiring into political beliefs and affiliations arising from those beliefs. By challenging the Committee's right to ask such questions, they expected to draw contempt citations, but they planned to fight them in the courts as a constitutional issue.

Attorneys for the nineteen anticipated that they would lose their case in the local Washington, D.C., courts because juries consisted largely of government workers or those sympathetic to the government. They also expected to lose in the appellate court because of its make-up at the time. But they felt they could prevail at the Supreme Court level. Knowing they could count on the votes of Justices Hugo Black, William O. Douglas, Frank Murphy, and Wiley B. Rutledge, they anticipated that these four would swing Felix Frankfurter, and possibly one more Justice, in their favor. Thus they felt confident of a 5-4 or even a 6-3 vote in their favor.

Initially Brecht disagreed with this plan. He argued with Margolis that the others should state the truth about their party affiliation. Losey, too, remembers hearing him say that their tactics were wrong. Certainly Brecht recognized the Committee as a threat to individual freedom. He himself planned to oppose it through an outward show of cooperation that was really a brand of cunning. Outsmarting a powerful enemy was to him a valid form of opposition. He considered martyrdom to be folly in any political struggle, and the eighteen had adopted a course that smacked to him of precisely that. No matter that

Brecht had wanted to condemn Galileo's refusal to become a martyr for the truth in his play of that name; in *Schweyk* he had done the opposite by applauding an unheroic brand of behavior designed to do nothing more than save one's own skin.

Another consideration separated Brecht from the eighteen. They viewed themselves as loyal Americans who had a stake in their country and who wanted to fight for a principle. He was a European with no such commitment to the United States. He did not disagree with resistance, but rather with their form of resistance. He failed, however, to appreciate or to accept one serious ramification of their answering truthfully. Most of them were or had in fact been members of the Communist Party. Had they admitted this, the immediate consequence would have been a legal obligation to answer further questions by the Committee about others who were Communists. This left them with the choice of becoming informers or drawing a contempt citation and a jail sentence on that count.

As Brecht prepared his own defense with Margolis, the primary consideration in his plan was his desire to leave for Europe immediately after the hearings. As the only alien in the group, he felt he had a reason for marching out of step. Margolis in Los Angeles and Kenny again in Washington informed him that, in spite of being an alien, he enjoyed the same protection and rights under American law that citizens did. Out of skepticism or cunning, Brecht chose to act as though he did not, and he steadfastly insisted, both in his testimony and in later accounts, that he was a "guest" in the country who did not enjoy the same legal rights as citizens; consequently, he insisted, he was obliged to answer the Committee's questions. He could afford this luxury—he in fact had never been a member of the Communist Party and would have had no trouble replying in the negative. His general position was described to the other eighteen, who, according to Kenny and Margolis, agreed that Brecht should be free to answer as he wished, even if he broke ranks with them.

About the time Brecht received the subpoena in September 1947, Reynal and Hitchcock in New York brought out his first volume of poetry in the English translation of H. R. Hays. With his name again before the public, Brecht appears to have become unusually circumspect. Bentley was preparing an English translation of *Chalk Circle* for publication with the University of Minnesota Press at this time. In light of the new circumstances, Brecht instructed him to omit the prologue portraying a dispute in Russia between two collective farms.[5] It would not be restored in a later edition until long after his departure.

In addition to packing, arranging his literary affairs, and consulting with his attorney, Brecht took time to join with seventeen of the other unfriendly witnesses at a rally that Joseph Losey staged in the Los Angeles Shrine Auditorium on October 15th to raise money for their defense. Gene Kelly acted as master of ceremonies for this program on the eve of their departure, and Hollywood turned out *en masse*. Leaflets advertising the evening sponsored by the "Progressive Citizens of America" listed eighteen of the nineteen unfriendly witnesses who would "appear in person," among them "Berthold [sic] Brecht." But even in a matter as simple as terminology, he was out of step. Bessie, Cole, Kahn, Koch, Lardner, Lawson, Maltz, Ornitz, and Salt were identified on the leaflet as "writers." Characteristically Brecht chose another designation for himself—"author." Apparently he was inconspicuous at this rally attended by more than 5000 persons, since the other witnesses do not recall meeting him there, but a letter to Joseph Losey written the same day and signed by seventeen of the "unfriendly nineteen" that night includes his signature.

On October 16th Brecht left Santa Monica aboard the Los Angeles Limited, bound for New York City. Only he and two others of the nineteen went by train. His daughter claims that she and her mother stayed behind to close the house and to settle affairs, but a letter written from the train to the William Dieterles, who had given them a lunch to take, stated that "It's the second day, and we are still eating your meat, sugar, cake, homemade black bread and the butter from your cows." It was signed "the Brechts." Apparently at least some of Brecht's family accompanied him. He arrived in New York on October 20th, the day HUAC began its hearings. If his wife was not already with him, she joined him shortly, for his journal mentioned that Weigel was there on the 30th.

Brecht spent six days in New York before going to Washington. It is not known with whom he stayed, since Berlau was no longer living there, though the following week at his hearing he gave his current address as 34 West 73rd Street in New York. During this time he was settling literary affairs and preparing for his hearing. On October 22nd before a New York notary he signed a power-of-attorney authorizing Berlau to represent his literary interests in the Scandinavian countries.[6] He also spoke with Audrey Wood about handling his literary works in America. She remembers that Brecht instructed her orally before his departure that her agency was to represent him, but that Reyher was to have final say over any arrangements she made for productions of his plays. He later sent each of them documents outlining Reyher's role as his attorney-in-fact.[7]

Elisabeth Freundlich recalls an informal gathering during this week at which Brecht met with Hanns and Gerhart Eisler. Suddenly

Dear Joe Losey:

    We cannot leave our home town without expressing to
you our gratefulness for the unselfish and effective work
you have contributed to the common defense of our Constitution and our industry.

    You have launched a counterattack from which our
whole people will profit.

    This is small thanks, but you don't need any anyway.

Letter written by 17 of the "Hollywood 19," thanking Joseph Losey for sponsoring fund-raising rally at Los Angeles Shrine Auditorium on October 15, 1947, prior to their departure for HUAC hearings in Washington. Brecht's signature appears at bottom right.

Laughton, who was in New York to begin rehearsals for the *Galileo* production slated to open on December 7th, dropped in unannounced. Laughton did not know Gerhart Eisler, but undoubtedly he knew the name, for in recent weeks Eisler had received extraordinary publicity in the American press as a leading Communist agent. Brecht carefully avoided making an audible introduction. Since Laughton was beginning to fear that his association with Brecht might taint his reputation and produce bad publicity for *Galileo*, Brecht and the Eislers, who knew of his trepidation, carried on a conversation that Freundlich described as "dancing on eggs."[8] Politics were carefully avoided. Brecht had been meeting with the Eislers to discuss, among other things, tactics for his own appearance before HUAC the following week. Both had appeared before the Committee several times, and Hanns, who had testified the previous month, rendered special help with his description of questions about Brecht's works that the Committee had asked him.

A visit to Hermann Budzislawski during this stay in New York also proved to be useful in Brecht's preparation for HUAC. After seeing Brecht's subpoena and noticing that the dramatist did not seem frightened, Budzislawski asked: "What will you do?" "We'll rehearse," Brecht answered. "I'll give you copies of my works, and you question me about them." Brecht's theatrical imagination was again affecting his behavior—he could not visualize something without having it acted out. Shortly before coming to America he had noted that "the reason I really write down scenes that occur between people is because otherwise I have trouble visualizing them."[9] As a result the two men rehearsed for what might happen at the hearing as though they were preparing for a play. Budzislawski remembers asking in their rehearsal if he were a member of the Communist Party. Brecht promptly denied it. When he advised Brecht that any questions about how he voted in the Weimar Republic were protected by the right of secret ballot, Brecht replied that he had never voted anyway because he considered elections a swindle.

While rehearsing, they devised an answer to whether Brecht had written a given poem. He would reply that he had not written this poem, among other reasons because it was in English and was quite different from the German poem on which it was based. He not only used this ploy effectively before the Committee; he followed Budzislawski's advice on taking advantage of an interpreter during his testimony. Initially he did not want to, claiming his English was adequate. When Budzislawski commented that using an interpreter would give him time to think, he replied: "You're right. My English isn't very good. I do need an interpreter." Budzislawski reports that Brecht was determined not to lie; he stated that he had no desire to become a martyr and intended to answer the questions put to him. He was aware that defiance of the Committee might delay his departure, and he specifically inquired of Budzislawski how long it took before one's travel papers could be withdrawn by government officials. But his briefing by Eisler regarding questions that the Committee might put to him and his rehearsals with Budzislawski seem to have given him ample confidence. When Brecht arrived in Washington, he was the best rehearsed of the "unfriendly" witnesses who would testify.

After the hearings began on October 20th, Brecht followed them by radio and in the *New York Times*, one of many newspapers in the country that began to editorialize against what looked increasingly like a witch-hunt. Held in the caucus room of the Old House Office Building, which seated approximately 400 people, the hearings took on the air of a celebrity spectacle, with news coverage to match. *Variety* reported on October 20th that "nothing like it has ever been pulled before in a congressional committee investigation" and itemized the media representatives present on the first day: 90 reporters; five different newsreel companies, with cameras facing the witnesses; all the radio networks preparing live or delayed broadcasts, with microphones before witnesses and the Committee; news photographers operating at will throughout the hearing room; and television coverage to New York, Philadelphia, and Washington. Prophetically, *Variety* also noted that, if things went poorly, this degree of exposure could make the Committee a laughing stock.

Headed by J. Parnell Thomas (R., N.J.), the Committee was comprised of Representatives Herbert C. Bonner (D., N.C.); John McDowell (R., Pa.); Karl E. Mundt (R., S.D.): Richard M. Nixon (R., Ca.); J. Hardin Peterson (D., Fl.); John E. Rankin (D., Miss.); Richard B. Vail (R., Ill.); and John S. Wood (D., Ga.). At no time were all present, and in some hearings no more than two members were there in addition to Thomas and his chief investigator, Robert E. Stripling. Rankin, for example, was campaigning for re-election in Mississippi. Nixon's questioning of cooperative witnesses in the first week was restrained and almost shy and, when the "unfriendly nineteen" appeared during the week of October 27-30th, he disappeared altogether. Kenny and attorneys for the nineteen attributed it to the controversial nature of the hearings, which had already triggered a wave of protests throughout the country. For a first-term congressman from California, the home of the movie industry, too much opposition to Hollywood could be politically damaging, and they felt Nixon sensed this.

Since it had been announced publicly that the "unfriendly nineteen" intended to oppose the Committee, J. Parnell Thomas scheduled them for the second week (October 27-31st) and opened the first week of hearings (October 20-24th) with witnesses who were considered friendly. The "Barnum show" (as *Variety* called it) began with a parade of celebrities that played to packed houses. Witnesses such as actors Adolphe Menjou, George Murphy, Robert Taylor, Ronald Reagan, Robert Montgomery, and Gary Cooper; studio heads Walt Disney, Jack Warner of Warner Brothers, and Louis B. Mayer of MGM; Samuel (Sam) Grosvenor Wood, past president of the Motion Picture Alliance for the Preservation of American Ideals; and the screenwriter Ayn Rand—all testified during the first week that they thought Communists were in fact infiltrating Hollywood.

Sam Wood answered a question the first day that clearly identified the enemy. When asked what group in Hollywood must be watched more than the rest, he replied: "Writers. I know there are Communist writers in Hollywood." In the course of that week, the names of Lawson, Maltz, Trumbo, Lardner, and others of the "unfriendly nineteen" scheduled to appear the following week were named repeatedly by witnesses. Brecht's name never came up in one of the hearings, and the Hollywood movie publications (*Variety, The Hollywood Reporter*) which did mention it did not know what to say about him. From the outset he did not seem to fit.

The hearings of the first week were not without humor, but it was involuntary humor that bordered on lunacy. Several witnesses identified an MGM film made during the war called *Song of Russia* as a pro-Russian film. Ayn Rand found it blatantly propagandistic because it showed Russians smiling, and it did not show food lines in the streets of Moscow. Robert Taylor, who had starred in the same film, drew loud applause when he urged that all Communists "be sent back to Russia or some other unpleasant place." At one point he stated: "I have never worked with anyone knowingly who is a Communist. Moreover, I shall never work with anyone who is a Communist." In response Kenny passed a note to reporters in the room stating that the screen writer for Taylor's latest film, *The High Wall*, was Lester Cole, one of the nineteen.[10]

Before the hearings began, Hollywood had launched a counter-attack. After the subpoenas were delivered, directors John Huston and William Wyler had founded a "Committee for the First Amendment" and recruited some of the top names in Hollywood for a trek to Washington to protest the hearings. Humphrey Bogart and Lauren Bacall, Danny Kaye, Frederic March, Lucille Ball, Gene Kelly, Keenan Wynn, Henry Morgan, and other actors and actresses who, for the most part, counted as politically neutral, were in the nation's capital for the opening of the hearings to lend celebrity status to the opposition against the Committee. Careful to distinguish themselves from the "unfriendly nineteen," they nevertheless used some of the same arguments about the infringement of constitutional rights that motivated Brecht's fellow witnesses. On October 28th, this group left Washington for a barnstorming tour of several cities to help to stimulate the already audible public outcry against HUAC. As Brecht prepared to go to Washington during the second week of hearings, he, too, knew of this opposition and the swell of popular resentment running against the Committee.

On October 26th Brecht took a train from New York to Washington with Losey and Hambleton, who were in New York preparing the forthcoming *Galileo* production. Before leaving New York, Hambleton had booked a trans-Atlantic flight in his own name on Air France for the following Friday, October 31st. The ticket was intended for Brecht, who planned to leave as soon as his hearing ended. Losey meanwhile had advised Brecht to smoke a cigar during the hearings. J. Parnell Thomas was an avid cigar smoker, and Losey felt that Brecht might be treated more sympathetically by a fellow cigar smoker. The dramatist added this to a routine he was still rehearsing.

In Washington, Brecht went to the Shoreham Hotel, where the eighteen were staying and met individually with the two chief counsels, Robert W. Kenny and Bartley Crum, who were now acting as spokesmen for the other four attorneys and the nineteen unfriendly witnesses. Kenny was a former attorney general in California and the 1946 Democratic candidate for governor opposing Earl Warren. Crum, a practicing Catholic (something Brecht later emphasized to friends), had been a member of the American delegation to the United Nations in San Francisco in 1945 and belonged to the 1946 Anglo-American Committee of Inquiry on Palestine. He had written a book on his experiences with that committee, *Behind the Silken Curtain*, which received wide attention in 1947.

Out of fear that their hotel rooms might be "bugged," Brecht and the two attorneys conversed in the hotel's rose garden. Kenny remembers hearing him say how he had been forced to flee Germany, Denmark, Sweden, and Finland by an "Un-German Activities Committee," and that history was repeating itself in America. Neither of these attorneys knew of Brecht's strategy, and both were surprised to learn that he intended to answer the Committee's questions about party affiliation. According to Bentley, Brecht later claimed that Crum had counseled him to say that he was a member of the Communist Party. Crum argued that nothing could happen to him, since he was not a citizen, and it was the Communist Party in Germany to which he had belonged. When Brecht protested that he had not been a member in Germany, Crum said he should answer in the affirmative anyway, since the Committee doubtless would display a forged party membership card for him.[11] But Brecht resisted. He rehearsed parts of his testimony with Kenny, who advised him of his rights. Kenny claims, however, that, when Brecht testified, he and Crum had no sure idea what he would say except that he intended to answer the question about his party affiliation.

J. Parnell Thomas had announced that after hearing from Eric Johnston, head of the Motion Picture Alliance as the lead-off witness on Monday, October 27th, he would begin with the "unfriendly nineteen." Instead of calling Johnston, he reversed the order and began with John Howard Lawson, whose name had been mentioned most frequently the previous week as the leading Communist writer in Hollywood. After rejecting motions by Kenny and Crum to quash the subpoenas of Lawson and seventeen of the others and to cross-examine witnesses who had testified the previous week, Thomas engaged Lawson in a verbal brawl. Lawson asked to read a prepared statement. Thomas refused permission, and soon he and Lawson were shouting at each other. When Thomas admonished the writer not to disrupt the hearings, Lawson told him that "this Committee is on trial here before the American people. Let us get that straight." After several more angry exchanges, Thomas asked whether Lawson was or had been a member of the Communist Party. Lawson replied "It is unfortunate and tragic that I have to teach this Committee the basic principles of American—" but was interrupted mid-sentence by the Chairman, who had him removed from the room and later cited him for contempt of Congress. If convicted, Lawson faced a fine of $1,000 or a jail sentence of one year, or both.

Brecht had not been present at this turbulent hearing. Earlier he told Margolis that he preferred to listen to the hearings on the radio in his hotel room, where he could follow them free from distractions. When the other unfriendly witnesses returned to the Shoreham Hotel, he was there to meet them, some for the first time. As a result of Lawson's hearing, a mood of depression prevailed among the eighteen. Brecht, however, seemed elated. Margolis recalls that, when they asked him why, he congratulated them on their militant opposition. "Nothing like this ever happened in Germany," he claimed. "If it had, fascism never would have happened." He told them he was not only impressed with their stand; he was taken with the way liberals and conservatives across the country were rallying against the Committee's assault on the freedom of speech and political belief. With a sense of exhilaration that came from belonging to a significant cause, Brecht buoyed them up with his optimistic prediction that, under these circumstances, there would never be fascism in America.[12]

Brecht apparently did not attend any hearings before his own appearance on Thursday, October 30th. Losey claims that during this time he and Brecht tried to engage Archibald MacLeish to interpret for the playwright, but MacLeish denies he was ever approached.[13] Brecht followed in the newspapers and listened on the radio to what *Variety* had recently called the "Commie Carnival" going on before HUAC. Nine more of the unfriendly witnesses appeared before the Committee on October 28th and 29th and, according to plan, tried to avoid answering the question about their political affiliation without refusing to answer. Likewise according to plan, each was cited for contempt of Congress. With behavior that provoked Thomas' wrath, Dalton

Trumbo, Albert Maltz, Alvah Bessie, Samuel Ornitz, Herbert Biberman, Edward Dmytryk, Adrian Scott, Ring Lardner, Jr., and Lester
Cole appeared in hearings that ranged from heated to explosive.

Like Lawson, Trumbo had asked to read a statement. When denied
that privilege, he demanded to know what in the statement was not
pertinent and reminded the Committee that it had once allowed the
notorious right-winger, Gerald L. K. Smith, to read one. Exchanges
grew more heated as he refused to answer questions to the Committee's satisfaction. After being ordered from the witness stand, Trumbo
shouted: "This is the beginning of an American concentration camp."
Unexpectedly, Albert Maltz and Alvah Bessie, who followed him on
the afternoon of October 28th, were allowed to read prepared statements. But this did little to change the atmosphere of confrontation.
Maltz delivered an especially vitriolic polemic against the Committee,
which he accused of being anti-Semitic and Nazi, and its chief investigator Stripling, whom, toward the end of the hearing, he addressed
as "Mr. Quisling" after the Norwegian collaborator who betrayed his
country to the Nazis.

By now the Committee was under increasing fire from the press and
from the public at large. Clearly on the defensive, Thomas used the
hearing on October 29th to reiterate the Committee's authority to
conduct the investigation and to assert that no citizen's rights were
being violated. Interspersed with similar tactical skirmishes and the
testimony of Emmet Lavery and Dore Shary, who were cooperative in
answering but who clearly opposed the Committee's purpose, Samuel
Ornitz, Herbert Biberman, Edward Dmytryk, and Adrian Scott appeared on October 29th and were cited for contempt. In contrast to
the first four unfriendly witnesses, each of these four testified only a
matter of minutes before being cut off by Thomas. If this accelerated
pace and uncooperative behavior continued, the rest of the unfriendly
witnesses could be heard within two or three days.

After Lawson, Trumbo, Maltz, and Bessie had testified, *Variety*
(October 29th) had flippantly given the score of contempt citations to
that point as: "four down, fifteen to go." To buttress their case, investigators had produced Communist Party membership cards for each of
these unfriendly witnesses. Clearly the Committee, as well as Hollywood, expected the remaining unfriendly witnesses to be equally
hostile and to draw contempt citations, which the next four also did.
Ring Lardner, Jr. and Lester Cole, the first two witnesses to appear on
the morning of October 30th (Brecht was present, since he expected to
be called that day) did not disappoint them. Lardner interjected one of
the few notes of humor in the otherwise grim proceedings when the
sergeant-at-arms escorted him from the witness chair after Thomas

had ordered him to leave. He commented wryly: "I think I am leaving by force." Cole, too, who had ridden with Brecht in a taxi from the Shoreham Hotel that morning, was quickly cited for contempt and ordered to step down by a chairman who stated that he wanted to speed up the tempo. The hearing that morning had begun at 10:30 a.m., and there was a good chance several more witnesses could be heard before noon if each one followed suit. But neither the audience nor the Committee had reckoned with the next witness, Bertolt Brecht.

Because his reputation was almost a total mystery to the Committee and to spectators, and because he was the only foreigner among the nineteen, Brecht added what Kenny called a "flavor of international conspiracy" to the hearings. Neatly dressed in the suit Sam Bernstein had sent him five years earlier, he hardly seemed like a Communist agent from abroad. In a preliminary statement to establish Brecht's credentials, Kenny told the Committee that he had come to America as an immigrant in 1941; that he had taken out his first citizenship papers on December 8th of that year; and that he had had a son in the US Army during the war.[14] After being sworn in, Brecht found himself seated across from a committee comprised only of Chairman J. Parnell Thomas and Representatives McDowell and Vail. Contrary to a later erroneous report, Karl E. Mundt did not act as chairman and was not present at all that day.[15] Chief investigator Robert E. Stripling, who asked most of the questions, investigators Louis J. Russell and Robert Gaston, and Benjamin Mandel, director of research for the Committee, were seated in support of the Committee.

Brecht's testimony, which has been compared to a zoologist's being cross-examined by apes,[16] was a polite exercise in cunning and duplicity that lasted a full hour. From the moment he took an oath in the name of a God in whom he did not believe, he followed his carefully planned scenario, which included smoking cigars throughout. Stripling and Thomas offered the services of an interpreter, and Brecht accepted. The interpreter, David Baumgardt of the Library of Congress, appeared to have had less command of English than Brecht did. At one point he confused the Committee so badly with his own thick accent that Thomas complained: "I cannot understand the interpreter any more than I can the witness."

Before the preliminaries of identification were ended, Brecht had established the pattern he would follow—to give the appearance of answering the questions fully by addressing himself to them directly. The content of his answers was another matter, and he intended to control that content. Unexpectedly Stripling made a factual error at the outset which gave Brecht the advantage of being able to say that the Committee's information was inaccurate. As part of the identification process,

Stripling asked if Brecht had been born on February 10, 1888. Brecht's year of birth was 1898, and he politely told Stripling the accurate date. Four more times in the next hour Brecht corrected statements by the Committee in a courteous manner which seemed to reflect his eagerness to help it to obtain accurate information.

Asked next if he had ever been employed in the motion picture industry, Brecht replied: "Yes; I—yes. I sold a story to a Hollywood firm, *Hangmen Also Die*, but I did not write the screenplay myself." Technically he was correct, since he did not receive credit for the screenplay. But he had in fact worked on the screenplay, and four and one-half years earlier he felt strongly enough about his contribution to demand an arbitration hearing in order to receive credit. This would be typical of many responses.

Brecht answered the next two questions unequivocally. First he admitted that he had known Hanns Eisler for approximately twenty years. When asked if he was or ever had been a member of the Communist Party, Brecht replied that he would answer the question, but he asked if he might first read a prepared statement. Chairman Thomas perused it and declined on the grounds that it was not relevant to the hearing. Expecting a repeat of performances by previous witnesses, Stripling then asked the question again. To the apparent surprise of the Committee, Brecht replied: "Mr. Chairman, I have heard my colleagues when they considered this question not as proper, but I am a guest in this country and do not want to enter into any legal arguments, so I will answer your question fully as well as I can. I was not a member or am not a member of any Communist Party." It was almost the last question he would answer fully, but it won the day for him early in his hearing. Brecht had emphasized his status as a guest in America to underscore that he intended to cooperate with the Committee. His attitude contrasted so dramatically with the responses of earlier witnesses that it caught the Committee off balance. To be sure they understood what they had heard, Chairman Thomas and Stripling each repeated the question. Two more times Brecht replied that he had never been a member of the Communist Party.

The next bit of dialogue was one of many in which a man who has been called a "Marxist Till Eulenspiegel"[17] led his interrogators a merry dance:

> *Stripling*: "Mr. Brecht, is it true that you have written a number of very revolutionary poems, plays, and other writings?
>
> *Brecht*: "I have written a number of poems and songs and plays in the fight against Hitler and, of course, they can be

considered, therefore, as revolutionary because I, of course, was for the overthrow of that government."

At this point Chairman Thomas interrupted his chief investigator to say: "Mr. Stripling, we are not interested in any works that he might have written advocating the overthrow of Germany or of the government there." Brecht had successfully deflected the thrust of the question. Under instructions from the Chairman, Stripling changed his line and asked if he knew Alfred Kantorowicz, who had just published a scene from *Master Race* in an East Berlin magazine. Brecht acknowledged having known him in Berlin and again in New York, but, when asked if Kantorowicz were a Communist, he replied: "I do not know exactly whether he was a member of the Communist Party of Germany." Brecht knew very well that he was.

Stripling also asked him about meeting Sergei Tretyakov in Moscow and cited Tretyakov's interview with Brecht which portrayed him as an admirer of the ideas of Marx and Lenin. When asked if he remembered that interview, Brecht evoked laughter with his answer that "it must have been written 20 years ago or so." It was in fact written in 1934 and published in 1937. Stripling then asked: "Have many of your writings been based upon the philosophy of Lenin and Marx?" Brecht's response was: "No; I don't think that is quite correct but, of course, I studied, had to study as a playwright who wrote historical plays. I, of course, had to study Marx's ideas about history. I do not think intelligent plays today can be written without such study. Also, history now, written now, is vitally influenced by studies of Marx and history." In fact Brecht's writings since 1930 were undeniably based on Marxist-Leninist philosophy, and in any other context he would have insisted on it.

When Stripling inquired if he knew Gregory Kheifetz and gave a date when Kheifetz visited him, Brecht replied: "I don't remember that name, but I might know him." After Stripling mentioned two more dates when the FBI had observed their meetings, Brecht acknowledged that it was possible that someone with that name might have visited him along with others from the Russian consulate, but he simply could not recall their names. This again seems highly questionable. According to FBI records, Kheifetz had told various persons that Brecht was his "good friend." It seems improbable that Brecht met with him as often as he did without at least knowing his name.

Stripling then asked: "Are you familiar with the magazine *New Masses*?" Brecht: "No." Stripling: "You never heard of it?" Brecht: "Yes, of course." Stripling: "Did you ever contribute anything to it?" Brecht: "No." While the last answer may have been correct, Brecht was very familiar with *The New Masses*. In late 1935 he had assisted Eva Goldbeck in writing an article for *The New Masses* about his theater ideas. It appeared in the December 31, 1935 issue. After the Theater Union's disaster with his play *Mother*, he is said to have written *The New Masses* a letter protesting that production (it was never published).[18] His journal of April 16, 1941 describes reading Lawson's critique of Gorelik's *New Theatres for Old* in *The New Masses*; another entry on July 17, 1943, that identifies Lawson as a representative "of the New Masses viewpoint" suggests that Brecht was well-acquainted with the content of that journal.

Translations of Brecht's works provided a natural source of equivocation, and, unwittingly or otherwise, his interpreter supported him in this exercise. Citing the song "In Praise of Learning" from *Mother*, Stripling asked about a line that in German read: "Du musst die Führung übernehmen." Stripling read a translation that said: "You must be ready to take over." Literally it should have been rendered: "You must take over the leadership" or "assume control." But Brecht evoked laughter when he said, "No, excuse me, that is a wrong translation. That is not right." After brief consultation with Baumgardt, the interpreter announced that the correct translation should be: "You must take the lead," a rendering that vitiated the song's revolutionary message. The Committee accepted this harmless translation and went on to ask about the poem "Forward, We've Not Forgotten," which Stripling read aloud in an English version. When he asked: "Did you write that, Mr. Brecht?" the playwright repeated the answer he had rehearsed in New York: "No. I wrote a German poem, but that is very different from this." Amid laughter from the spectators, Stripling let the matter drop.

The heart of Stripling's inquiry centered on Brecht's collaboration with Eisler on *The Measures Taken*. A number of the questions on that work were identical to those asked Eisler. Had the Committee's memory been better, or had it done its homework, several of Brecht's answers about that play might have entrapped him. But the Committee let them go unchallenged. Stripling asked if the German title, *Die Massnahme*, could mean "disciplinary measures to be taken." To gain time, Brecht consulted with Baumgardt, who finally answered that it could not. Yet in his sworn testimony the previous month, Eisler had stated that it meant precisely that. Stripling then requested that he describe the substance of the play. Brecht claimed it was "the adaptation of an old religious Japanese play and is called Nōh Play, and follows quite closely this old story which shows the devotion for an ideal until death." The ending had in fact been based loosely on that idea from the Nōh play *Taniko*, which Brecht had read in Arthur Waley's translation some years before and had used as the basis for his learning plays *The Yea-Sayer* and *The Nay-Sayer*. But by no stretch of the imagination does *The Measures Taken* "follow quite closely" the old Japanese story. It deals instead with four Communist agitators sent to foment rebellion in a province of China. In the end the mission fails when, out of personal compassion with the poor, one of the four violates the orders of his comrades. To rectify his error, he voluntarily accepts the ultimate disciplinary measure taken against him in the name of the revolutionary cause—his own death.[19]

During Eisler's hearings in September, Stripling had inquired about this ending: "And three of the Communists murdered the fourth one because they felt he would be a menace to the cause; is that correct?" Eisler: "Yes." Stripling: "That is the theme of it?" Eisler: "Yes." When Stripling put the same question to Brecht, the answer came out totally different. Stripling: "Will you tell the Committee whether or not one of the characters in this play was murdered by his comrade because it was in the best interest of the Communist Party? Is that true?" Brecht: "No, it is not quite according to the story." He continued that the young man realized he had done damage to their mission and agreed to die. "So he asks his comrades to help him, and all of them together help him to die. He jumps into an abyss, and they lead him tenderly to that abyss." When Thomas interjected the question "so they kill him?" Brecht replied: "No; they did not kill him—not in this story. He killed himself."

The play Brecht described to the Committee here was unmistakably *The Yea-Sayer* and not *The Measures Taken*. A common denominator did link them—in the ending of each, a young man agrees he must die for the good of the mission being carried out. But in *The Yea-Sayer* he dies in the manner Brecht outlined to the Committee, whereas in *The Measures Taken* he is shot by his comrades and thrown into a lime pit. Had Stripling confronted him with the glaring discrepancy between his testimony and Eisler's, Brecht might have claimed that he confused the two plays. But the witness's earlier willingness to answer the question about his political affiliation and his cooperative, detailed answers contrasted so strongly with the belligerent testimony of the others that they must have dulled Stripling's critical faculties. He moved on to another area, and Brecht was safe again.

Toward the end of the hearing, and almost as an afterthought, Stripling asked a question that had caused Eisler considerable difficulty. He asked: "Have you ever made application to join the Communist Party?" Eisler, of course, had. Brecht replied emphatically: "No, no, no, no, never." Satisfied that this was a different breed of political animal from Eisler, the Committee asked only a few more questions before excusing him. Its treatment of him led *The New York Times* on October 31st to conclude: "Mr. Brecht apparently satisfied the Committee that his links with known Communists were principally on an artistic level." Chairman Thomas finally said: "Thank you very much, Mr. Brecht. You are a good example to the witnesses of Mr. Kenny and Mr. Crum," and recessed the hearing. Kenny claims that as it ended at 12:15 p.m., Representative John McDowell came to him and said: "If your client has any trouble with the immigration officials, let me know." But Brecht had no use for the offer. That afternoon he was already on a train to New York with Losey and Hambleton, and the following day he would be on a flight back to Europe.

A journal entry dated October 30, 1947 describes how Brecht listened to part of his hearing on the radio that evening in New York with his wife and Budzislawski. It notes that eighty reporters, a number of photographers and newsreel cameras, two radio stations, and theater people from Broadway had been present, the latter as "friendly observers." After commenting that the hearing was conducted with unusual courtesy and ended without a contempt citation, Brecht correctly analyzes the main reason why he had escaped without more difficulty: "It was in my favor that I had had almost nothing to do with Hollywood, had not been involved in American politics, and that those who preceded me on the witness stand had refused to answer the Congressmen."

Brecht also benefitted from Thomas's impatience. At one point in his hearing the Committee chairman had interrupted Stripling's questioning with "Mr. Stripling, can we hurry this along? We have a very heavy schedule this afternoon." Pressure to discontinue the hearings had been mounting. A recently completed Gallup poll showed that almost as many Americans opposed the hearings as favored them (37 percent for, 36 percent against),[20] and probably half the nation's press had come out against the Committee. Thomas intended to call as many of the nineteen as he could before he was forced to terminate the hearings, and he was in a hurry. Otherwise he might have allowed Stripling to probe more deeply. Without knowing it at the time, Brecht, number eleven of the Hollywood nineteen, rang down the curtain on HUAC's investigation of Communist subversion in Hollywood. After testimony by Louis J. Russell in the afternoon that had nothing to do with Hollywood directly, J. Parnell Thomas unexpectedly adjourned the investigation of the movie industry indefinitely. Though his statement emphasized that he had not called it off entirely and that he planned to hear at least sixty-eight more who had extensive records of Communist affiliation, Thomas never convened the hearings again.

Brecht's journal entry of October 30th contains one sentence about something very important to him. It reads: "The eighteen are very satisfied with my testimony." Brecht seems to have wanted their approval for the course he took. Lester Cole claims, that while riding back to the Shoreham Hotel in the same taxi, Brecht became emotional and asked Cole to try to understand why he had broken ranks with the eighteen. "I'm not a citizen," Cole recalls his saying. "They can hold me here for months before deporting me." Dalton Trumbo is reported to have said that, when Brecht reached their hotel, he apologized to others of the eighteen for the position he had taken.[21]

To some extent, Brecht's life seemed to be imitating his own art. By ironic coincidence, the play *The Measures Taken*, the central target of Stripling's questions to him that morning, focused on the problem he had just confronted—discipline and solidarity among leftists engaged in a common cause. In his play Brecht had settled the question of a young revolutionary who for personal reasons had broken ranks with his three comrades, by having him accept voluntarily the death sentence imposed by his comrades. In his present circumstances he expected no such drastic measure, but, to judge by his behavior, he did feel a degree of guilt for failing to maintain solidarity with a group of leftists whose devotion to a cause he admired. Now Brecht wanted their reassurance that his lack of solidarity was not construed as betrayal. Apparently he received it. Dalton Trumbo is reported to have felt that, in contrast to the others, Brecht in his hearing struck the right balance between belligerence and passivity,[22] while John Howard Lawson, who had not been present at the hearing, remembers how impressed he was when he heard the testimony. Brecht, he felt, was a born dialectician who had the makings of a great legal mind by the way he led the investigators in circles. Whether by dialectics or deceit, his outsmarting of the Committee made this group of men aware of what an unusual individual had been among them.

In the following months Brecht stylized his version of the hearing and of the events surrounding it. Soon after arriving in France, he met Don Ogden Stewart and his wife Ella Winter in Paris. They acted surprised to see him in Europe, to which Brecht replied: "When they accused me of wanting to steal the Empire State Building, I thought it was high time to leave."[23] Repeatedly he insisted that he was obliged to answer the Committee's questions because he did not enjoy the rights of an American citizen.[24] According to one anecdote, he boasted that even the great German exile writer Heinrich Heine did not have sufficient stature to merit having his works translated by the French police, as the FBI had done with him.[25] And in an unusually positive vein Brecht gave Thomas and his Committee credit for being reasonably courteous. "They weren't as bad as the Nazis," he said, "the Nazis would never have let me smoke."[26]

After the termination of the hearings, Brecht's name continued to be associated with the "unfriendly witnesses." A manifesto written in Washington and signed "the unfriendly nineteen" appeared in *The Hollywood Reporter* and in *Variety* the day after the hearings were adjourned. It declared their intention to continue to fight the Committee and it urged Hollywood not to create blacklists. Brecht's name also appeared in advertisements for a "Stop Operation Witch-Hunt" rally held at the Los Angeles Shrine auditorium on November 9, 1947. And from Europe Brecht followed the confirmation of the contempt citations against the ten by Congress and their legal battle as it made its way to the Supreme Court.

Brecht was perhaps unaware of a change in the Supreme Court in the summer of 1950 that derailed the plan worked out by the eighteen. Justices Murphy and Rutledge both died suddenly that summer, and their replacements could not be counted on to decide as they might have done. Albert Maltz remembers that, on hearing the news, he told his wife that he would be going to jail. The newly constituted Supreme Court did in fact deny their request to review the constitutional issues in the case, and the so-called "Hollywood Ten," the ten unfriendly witnesses who had preceded Brecht, were ordered to begin serving one-year prison terms.

When Brecht learned that the Ten were going to jail, he wrote a statement of solidarity entitled "We Nineteen."[27] Calling it "incredible" that this could happen, Brecht speaks of the blacklists that were already in effect, which meant that "the delinquent is not deprived of life, only of the means to life. He does not appear in the obituary lists, only on the blacklists." He continues that "The Constitution of the United States of America was written at a time when the goddess of liberty had oil in her lamp and not in her face. . . . My American colleagues were protected by the Constitution; it was the Constitution that was not protected." In a salute to their courage, Brecht says he is gratified to learn "that there are people ready to sacrifice themselves so that their countrymen as well as the rest of the people of the world may learn the truth."

In a bitter footnote to history, Ring Lardner, Jr. describes how, while serving his prison sentence in 1950, he met another inmate in the Danbury federal penitentiary who had been present at the 1947 hearings—J. Parnell Thomas, chairman of HUAC. Thomas had since been tried, convicted, and sentenced to eighteen months in prison for putting non-workers on the government payroll and for appropriating their salaries for himself. As a dramatist Brecht would have enjoyed this irony, and he would have had great sympathy for Lardner's description of his blacklisting as a "decree of exile."[28] The same events that ended more than six years of American exile for Brecht signaled the beginning of professional exile for some of Hollywood's most noted writers.

Through Reyher's daughter Faith, Brecht arranged for his wife and daughter to stay in New York for a few days until they could join him in Switzerland. Even on October 31, 1947, his last day in America, Brecht was still concerned with the theater. His journal records meeting Laughton that morning, who was in New York for the forthcoming *Galileo* production and who was already wearing a beard for it. The actor, Brecht noted, seemed overjoyed "that it will not require special courage to play Galileo." Fearing adverse publicity for the play, Laughton was relieved that Brecht's appearance before HUAC had not made the headlines in New York papers. Oskar Homolka also claims that Brecht phoned him that day and invited him to come to Europe to play the role of Galileo there. In addition, Brecht was bargaining until the last minute with Hambleton, who wanted a one-year option on performing *The Caucasian Chalk Circle*. One week after Brecht left, Hambleton contacted Weigel and paid her $500 for those rights.[29] In one form or another, it was theater until the very end. Unwittingly, Congressional investigators had given Brecht considerable assistance with the last act of his theater in exile. His departure, planned long in advance, now assumed the form of a dramatic escape from an American witch-hunt. One of the greatest dramatists of the century did not miss the cue.

X. EPILOGUE

In a letter written to George Pfanzelt in the spring of 1946 summarizing five years of American exile, Brecht remarks: "I have gone on writing plays . . . but of course not about America, which is not badly described in my earlier ones." As surprising as this seems in light of the mythical America portrayed in his earlier plays, Brecht's statement is not intended literally. It refers to the specific political/poetic idea called "America" that he had carried in his head since the early thirties. An outgrowth of his Marxist ideology and of his poetic imagination, that idea had been developed and had become firmly fixed before he ever came to America; it was reinforced and somewhat expanded during his exile; and it persisted until the end of his life.

Much like a social scientist, Brecht tended to see the world in terms of "models"—in this case models constructed out of Marxist ideological views and out of his poetic imagination. His sociological model for America when he arrived was based on the assumption that it represented the most advanced form of capitalism and consequently the most uncivilized, inhumane form of human existence. Knowing that class differences in America were less clearly defined than in Europe or in classical Marxist theory, Brecht seemed to have had only two groups in his American model—the moneyed ruling class, which included millionaires and politicians; and the "common people," whom the first group manipulated and controlled. Though neither group was precisely defined, power figures in capitalist society played the role of demons, and the common people were their victims. Predictably, Brecht sided with the "common people" in what he regarded as an ongoing struggle against their enemies.

One of Brecht's *Refugee Dialogues* written in 1940 or 1941 describes his pre-exile model of the American people by comparing their life to survival in the Wild West: "Take the American people, a great people. First they had to protect themselves from Indian attacks, and now they have millionaires on their necks. They are constantly attacked by the grocery kings, surrounded by the oil trusts, and burned down by the railroad magnates. The enemy is cunning and brutal and carries off women and children into the depths of the coal mines or keeps them prisoner in automobile factories. The newspapers lure them into ambushes, and the banks lay in wait during broad daylight. They can be fired at any moment, and when they are fired, they fight like savages for their freedom so that everyone can do what he wants, which the millionaires welcome" (*GW* xiv, 1447).

Brecht's autobiographical "Letter to an Adult American" (*GW* xx, 293-302), written five years after arriving in America, adds specific details but does not alter this basic model. "We live in an undignified city," he writes, attributing what he sees as a lack of basic human dignity among American adults to a capitalistic system that perverts social intercourse and corrupts its victims. Children, he states, are taught in school to adjust to society, but the society in question is riddled with violent conflict. In the lower classes "men shoot their inconstant wives, teenagers axe their fathers who beat their mothers, etc." In better circles, Brecht adds, similar conflicts are carried out as financial battles over alimony. He observes that the opinions of "the rulers," i.e., of "a few millionaires" who control the newspapers and radios, dominate national thinking so completely that a dissenter is considered maladjusted.

Beneath the easygoing optimism that is the social norm, Brecht writes, the threat of unavoidable financial crises keeps people in constant fear of losing their homes and savings. The sickness of a single person, for example, can destroy a family financially. The common people, he continues, are generally poorly informed, and their influence on the country is minimal. Political machines, controlled by "vested interests," determine the elections, and there are intimations that the president has been "made" by a group of gangsters: "Many have the feeling that democracy is of such a nature that it could disappear from one hour to the next." This is a direct result of the brutality that the capitalist struggle for survival breeds in its people. The wealthy control everything from universities (including private ones) to hospitals, and civil servants are merely the servants of political machines. "No wonder," Brecht concludes, "that something ignoble, loathsome, undignified attends all associations between people and has been transferred to all objects, dwellings, tools, even the landscape itself."

Brecht's basic perception of a conflict between an oppressed people and the wealthy few who controlled every aspect of life expanded as he experienced America directly. On April 8, 1942, his journal records a discussion with Dieterle about a film story that treated the final days of Julius Caesar. Dieterle wanted to use it, but he was sure that the studios had no interest in making "costume films" at the time. Brecht acknowledged his faith in the common people to accept such a film and directed his wrath at the capitalists who stood between the public and the artist: "Audiences surely would see something like this because their sense of history and grand politics has been awakened. But their owners, the film distributors and the cinema owners, who 'know' audiences, prevent it . . . it is a good example of democracy in appearance only." Repeatedly Brecht's journal and letters sound the leitmotif of film production controlled by the few (usually bankers and film ex-

ecutives) who stand between the artist and the public and who with-
hold what the people have enough common sense to appreciate.

In politics, too, Brecht admired the sound judgment of the little
man. In February 1942 the US Senate and House of Representatives
voted to put themselves on the Civil Service pension list. Brecht's journal documents the public outrage that this action triggered and the
subsequent nation-wide "bundles-for-Congress" drive that sent
thousands of packages of old clothes, artificial limbs, false teeth, rot-
ten vegetables, and table leftovers to "impoverished" Congressmen.
Using *Life* magazine photos with a brief commentary, Brecht lauded
an aroused people who succeeded in slapping down their elected officials. Congress, it should be noted, quickly abandoned the scheme.

When the US Government decided early in 1942 to intern all
Japanese-Americans on the West Coast, Brecht did not protest with
the vehemence one might expect. Instead, his journal on February 26,
1942, gives an underlying social reason for their actions (in addition to
the fear of their disloyalty)—the unpopularity of Japanese farmers
with American produce farmers. For him, protest became secondary
to his praise of the solidarity expressed by many "little people" in their
opposition to this obvious injustice. A journal entry of March 25,
1942 describes a surprising incident while Brecht was registering as an
enemy alien—the kindness and courtesy with which government officials and everyone present treated an old, half-blind Japanese woman,
now an official enemy, when she took too long filling out forms.
"Wonderful," Brecht added, "how humanity prevails against all
psychoses and agitation directed at the Japanese." He also spoke of
the solidarity of the "little people," many of whom had begun to buy
their vegetables from the Nisei. And a poem Brecht wrote at that time
mirrors the spontaneous sympathy that many people in Los Angeles
demonstrated for these victims of war hysteria. In listing various signs
of human kindness in dark times, it speaks of a cry from a crowd of
bystanders. To Japanese being evacuated from their homes, someone
calls out: "Chin up! It won't last forever!" (*GW* x, 859.)

Another entry on April 3, 1942 describes a discussion in which
Brecht and a friend think that the true spirit of democracy is present in
this opposition to the government's internment policy. He observes
that the common people, whose solidarity with the Japanese represents a challenge to their own political system, generally resent gov-
ernmental red tape and resist the government's call for "iron discipline" in such cases. The people, he believes, sense intuitively what
real "democracy" is.

Hans Viertel remembers an incident that he related to Brecht and
that appealed to him for a similar reason. While working in an

Alameda shipyard in 1941, Viertel had a shop steward who was a grizzled "Jimmy Cagney" sort of Irishman. On the day after Pearl Harbor, several workers were discussing the possible effects of the war. When someone speculated that President Roosevelt might freeze wages for the duration, the shop steward replied: "In that case the president and I are going to have a serious disagreement." This delighted Brecht, for it substantiated his belief in the willingness of the "little man" to oppose his leaders. Since he himself had no extensive contact with workers or with other representatives of the "common people," Brecht relied on the reports of friends like Viertel and Breiner, or on newspaper and magazine accounts, for information on daily life in his host country. Some friends felt that Brecht's preconceived American model restricted his ability to grasp the complexities of America's pluralistic society. Reyher especially labored to make him see things through American eyes. But Brecht resisted any extensive modification of his notions. He was not examining life in capitalist America in order to adjust his model of it, but to confirm it.

Dialectician that he was, however, Brecht felt compelled to criticize the faults of the common people. Usually they were character or social traits that did not fit his model. Gorelik reports that Brecht abhorred the back-slapping, hail-fellow-well-met attitude of many Americans, and, though essentially an optimist himself, that he disliked the shallow optimism of a people who, to his thinking, had little cause for hope. In one of the *Refugee Dialogues* (GW XIV, 1448) written before he came to America, Brecht has a character describe an earlier visit to Germany by an American uncle "who was optimistic all day long, the poor fellow, his face was fixed in a confident smile." After the uncle had praised the new car that he had brought to Germany with him, it broke down. The uncle optimistically noted that cars would continue to improve. Brecht also criticizes the mobility of American workers. In his view, a man who might be a taxi driver one day, a fry cook the next, and a construction worker the day after, would have difficulty developing a sense of class identity, as Marx described it. Brecht likewise censures the bourgeois aspirations and the reactionary political views of many American workers and trade unions whose highest goals seem to be middle-class affluence. To him, their disavowal of Marxist revolutionary sentiments is incomprehensible.

In spite of these and other reservations, Brecht showed a fundamental sympathy toward the "common people" of his model. Almost without exception, he ascribed their faults to the insidious influence of capitalistic society. This was the context of his observation to Gorelik that American children are the most beautiful on earth, but American adults the most damnable. The same motif of people as the products and innocent victims of a cruel society recurs in his "Letter to an Adult American" (GW xx, 300). There he speaks of the country's "national ideal, the grand planlessness which is created by the varied and intense plans of many individuals who are in the dark about each other's plans." This situation, Brecht maintains, casts Americans into a constant state of fear and neurosis. Many, he says, escape their anxieties through the help of psychiatry. The poor have an exceptional number of neuroses, but he has heard that they disappear when the poor find employment: "When the patient finds work, the psychiatrist is thrown out of work." This is a classic Marxist answer to the cause of psychic disturbances in the lower classes. While traveling cross-country in October 1947 on the way to Europe via Washington, Brecht made an observation that again underscores his compassion for the little man. He wrote Dieterle that, in contrast to his trips during the war, "the trains are empty, the big boom is past. The shops in the stations reflect the inflation. The people lose *every* war." War-generated inflation, in his view, was inflicting further suffering on those least able to deal with it.

This same sympathy for the "people" of America followed Brecht back to Europe and colored much of what he said in his last years about that country. Increasingly he ignored the realities of American life and stylized the oppositional role of the people to their government and social system to fit his model. Bentley recalls that, when Communist friends damned America in his presence, Brecht contradicted them, explaining that one has to distinguish between the people of the country and the system and its leaders. And, in 1950, after learning that the Hollywood Ten had lost their appeals and were going to jail, Brecht wrote the essay "We Nineteen," which transformed what had been real public opposition against HUAC into an imaginary solidarity of the American people with the Russians. Reconstructing the circumstances that led to their subpoenas in 1947, he recalls that Hollywood had been put under pressure to write anti-Communist films, but that its good writers would not do so, and its bad writers could not. Brecht states that the same defiant attitude extends to the entire population and claims: "The American people were not ready to allow the heroes of Stalingrad, who had spared America so many sacrifices, to be maligned" by this action (GW xix, 491). In reality, most Americans hardly knew or scarcely cared about the "heroes of Stalingrad" who were supposed to have spared them so much, since the Cold War was underway by 1947. Most Americans by this time viewed the Soviet Union with distrust.

In 1953, when news reached Brecht of the execution of Ethel and Julius Rosenberg, who had been convicted of passing atomic secrets to the Russians, Brecht declared them innocent and used their case to reiterate his view of an American people at odds with a repressive group of rulers: "One hundred and fifty million intelligent, attentive people trained in many trades and occupations find themselves under a regime that scorns their intelligence and scoffs at their love of justice. They know nothing of the glaring injustice. All the large newspapers of the country, the radio networks, movies, and television take part in the conspiracy. Thus the hundred and fifty million hardly know what happens to one of their number. Even if they found out, they could do little" (*GW* xx, 338). By this time in Brecht's life, the "people" had come to include one hundred and fifty million Americans, or the entire population. Whatever positive appreciation he had developed for America as the country of the "common man" had again begun to assume the mythical dimensions it had possessed in his early dramas.

During his final years, Brecht remembered an America that sprang primarily from his political-poetic imagination. America, on the other hand, seems to have remembered Brecht scarcely at all. Yet an interesting footnote to Brecht's exile proves that there was at least one exception. Shortly before he returned to Europe, his name had entered the consciousness of a few influential Americans.

Before Brecht's departure in 1947, someone had nominated him for an award by the prestigious American Academy of Arts and Letters and the National Institute of Arts and Letters. On March 19, 1948, he, along with Dudley Fitts, Harry Levin, James F. Powers, Genevieve Taggard, and Allen Tate, was named as one of the recipients of a $1,000 grant. A letter to him of that date sent in care of his publishers states that it was awarded "in recognition of your creative work in literature." Brecht responded with a letter on April 15, 1948, thanking them for the honor and saying, in his own English: "In a time like this, such an award is especially encouraging. Unfortunately, I will be unable to attend the annual ceremony as I am at present living in Switzerland. I am, however, enclosing the material which your assistant wished." He included an abbreviated version of the same biographical statement that he had prepared to be read before HUAC, but without some of its political statements. The citation Van Wyck Brooks read at a ceremony held on May 21, 1948, states that the American Academy of Arts and Letters awarded this grant "to Bertolt Brecht, now living in California, preeminent from his early youth in both the dramatic and lyric poetry of his native Germany, in recognition of the international value and the import of his work. In his name we also thank other European authors who have come here as exiles and remained to contribute to our culture."

Brecht, of course, was no longer living in California, nor had he contributed to contemporary American culture. But from a historical perspective it was symbolically correct that this award followed his departure. Distance, to be sure, lends enchantment, but it is a maxim of his own epic theater that it also lends perspective. Brecht was probably too far ahead of his time and too uncompromising in promoting his kind of theater in his own way to have succeeded in an alien environment like America. Only after leaving did his influence begin to make itself felt. And only in his absence did American theater gain perspective on the genius of this writer whom it harbored during a productive and bitter "exile in paradise."

A WORD ON SOURCES

The sources cited in the following footnotes do not represent all those consulted for this work. Wherever possible, I have attempted to state my sources in the text itself. This is the case, for example, with many citations from Brecht's own writings which are identified in parentheses following a cited passage. They bear the letters *GW* for *Gesammelte Werke* [Collected Works] followed by volume and page number. This principle also applies to material obtained from interviews. If information attributed to a clearly identifiable person is not footnoted, it derived from an interview on the following list. With letters written by Brecht himself, the matter is somewhat more complicated, since he was notoriously careless in dating letters. Sometimes he excluded the date altogether; at other times he gave only a partial date. The fullest possible identification has always been made, either in the text itself or in a footnote.

In most cases I have not attempted to identify the location of unpublished Brecht documents cited here. Because of their wide dispersion at this time, it would be cumbersome, not to say inaccurate, since many are in the process of changing hands. Gradually, most of them are finding their way to the Bertolt Brecht Archives in East Berlin, where, ideally, copies of everything Brecht wrote ultimately will be kept. The majority of letters by Brecht cited here were examined there. Other materials were viewed at Harvard University's Houghton Library; Yale University's Beinecke Library; the Morris Library of the University of Southern Illinois, Carbondale; the University of Wisconsin Library; the Wisconsin State Historical Society; and the UCLA Library. Unpublished or obscure documents by and pertaining to Brecht were made available to me by the following persons: Eric Bentley, Elisabeth Bergner, Samuel Bernstein, Egon Breiner, Joseph Breitenbach, Brainerd Duffield, Leo Fiedler, Gerda Goedhart, Mordecai Gorelik, Lotte Goslar, Ernst Halberstadt, H. R. Hays, Faith Reyher Jackson, Elsa Lanchester, Fritz Lang, James Laughlin, Kate Drain Lawson, Albert Maltz, Henry Marx, Dorothy Norman, Walter Nubel, Gwen Pascal, Frederick Z. Reitler, Naomi Replansky and Hans Sahl.

A number of citations in the text derive from Brecht's FBI files. In a letter of December 11, 1973, Clarence M. Kelley, Director of the FBI, informed me that "our files concerning Bertolt Brecht consist of approximately 1,000 pages." At the time this manuscript was completed, I had in my possession 427 pages from that file released under the Freedom of Information Act. Though the file makes interesting reading, and though it corroborates much that I had already discovered, it is not an especially reliable source of biographical information. Factual material is intermingled with hearsay, while masses of uncorroborated data based on rumor and, in many cases, error are indiscriminately interwoven into allegedly objective reports. Information from telephone wire taps, copies of letters written by Brecht and Berlau, newspaper and magazine clippings, and records from the Immigration and Naturalization Service were useful, but often the value of these documents as curiosities outweighs their usefulness as solid biographical evidence. Hence I have used them cautiously and sparingly.

INTERVIEWS CONDUCTED BY JAMES K. LYON

Anders, Günther 6-30-73;
  7-1-73
*Auden, W. H. 3-15; 12-9-71
Bentley, Eric 6-14, 12-8-71;
  10-22-74
Bergner, Elisabeth 6-15-73
Berlau, Ruth 10-23, 24-70,
  9-12-72
Bernstein, Sam 5-17-74
Brecht, Barbara 10-29-70;
  9-19-72; 10-15-74
Brecht, Stefan 12-28-70
Breiner, Egon and Leopoldine
  6-28, 29-72; 11-13-74
Breitenbach, Joseph 10-23-74
Budzislawski, Erna 6-28,
  30-72
Budzislawski, Hermann
  6-25-73
Burrows, Abe 12-29-72
Clurman, Harold 12-10-71
Cole, Lester 10-14-77
Dessau, Paul 6-28-73
Dieterle, William 9-21-72
Drews, David 6-14-73
Duffield, Brainerd 6-21, 22-72
Feuchtwanger, Marta 5-26-71
Freundlich, Elisabeth 7-3-73
Froeschel, George 8-6-73
Goedhart, Gerda 10-20-74
Gorelik, Mordecai 4-30-74

Guggenheim, Felix 8-6-73
Hagen, Anna Harrington
  6-15-16-73
Halberstadt, Ernst 3-15, 19-71
Hambleton, T. Edward
  12-9-71
Hauptmann, Elisabeth 10-26,
  29-70; 9-19-72
Hays, H. R. 12-11-71
Henreid, Paul 8-10-73
Herzfelde, Wieland 6-22-73
Homolka, Oskar 6-16-73
*Houseman, John 12-28-72
Hubley, John 12-29-72
*Isherwood, Christopher 6-25,
  26-72
Jackson, Faith 10-10-70;
  1-29-71, 4-4, 5, 6-71;
  8-29-71
Kaus, Gina 6-23-72
Kenny, Robert 8-8-73
*Lahn, Ilse 6-20-72
Lanchester, Elsa 6-19, 20-72
Lang, Fritz 8-8-73
Lang, Olga 12-28-72
Laughlin, James 11-14-74
Lawson, John Howard
  5-30-74
Lawson, Kate Drain 8-10-73
Lenya-Weill, Lotte 4-25-73
Ley-Piscator, Marie 12-10-71

Losey, Joseph 9-12-72
MacDonald, Dwight 3-14-77
Maltz, Albert 8-5, 6, 8-73
Margolis, Ben 5-17-74
*Melnitz, William 12-20-74
Mierendorff, Marta 6-21-72
*Mostel, Zero 10-23-74
Neumann-Viertel, Elisabeth
  6-30-73
Norman, Dorothy 12-10-71
Nubel, Walter 12-29-70;
  1-25; 12-10-71
Pecker, Rhoda Riker 6-19,
  27, 29-72
Pozner, Vladimir 9-28-72
Rainer, Luise 9-11-72
Reichenbach, Marie 6-22-72
Reitler, Frederick Z. 8-8-73
Renoir, Jean 6-22-72
Replansky, Naomi 12-9-71;
  12-27-72

Rosenberg, Meta 6-27-72
Roth, Wolfgang 10-23-74
Sahl, Hans 12-12-71
Sklar, George 8-7-73
Slochower, Harry 10-22-74
Starck, Taylor 2-17-71
Stewart, Don Ogden 9-11-72
Tabori, George 8-7-73
Viertel, Hans 7-22, 30;
  8-11-71; 4-28-73
Viertel, Salka 9-22, 23-72
Weigel, Helene 10-27, 28-70
*Wilder, Billy 1-20-75
Wilson, Richard 6-22-72
Winter, Ella 9-11-72
Wood, Audrey 12-10-71
Wurtele, Morton and Zivia
  6-26, 27-72
Youngkin, Douglas 8-12-75

In addition to the interviews conducted by the author, information was also drawn from notes based on:

1. Interviews carried out by Elsa Lanchester and Ned Hoopes with:

Anderson, Herbert 7-9-68
Brocco, Peter 7-3-68
Brown, Stephen 8-27-68
Feuchtwanger, Marta 6-26-68
Hambleton, T. Edward 1-4-68
Goslar, Lotte 12-15-67

Heflin, Frances 7-8-68
Houseman, John 1-7-68
Lloyd, Norman 1-18-68
Merin, Eda Reiss 2-15-68
Winters, Shelley 12-27-67
Wood, Audrey 12-19-67

2. Interview by Wolfgang Gersch with John Wexley, 5-8-65

* = Telephone interview.

NOTES

PART I. CHAPTER 1

1. Harold Clurman, *Lies Like Truth. Theatre Reviews and Essays* (New York: MacMillan, 1958), p. 228.
2. Bruce Cook, "Brecht was no Box-Office Hit, but His Influence Lingers On," *The National Observer* (Sept. 6, 1971), 18.
3. Bertolt Brecht, *Gesammelte Werke* (Frankfurt/Main: Suhrkamp, 1967), VIII, 69. Unless otherwise noted, citations from Brecht's published works come from this twenty-volume German edition, the most complete to date. Future references to it will appear in parentheses, using the abbreviation *GW*, followed by the volume number in Roman numerals and the page number in Arabic numerals. Unless another source is given, all English translations are my own.
4. See Martin Esslin, *Brecht. The Man and His Work* (New York: Norton, 1974), pp. 251-269.
5. Patty Lee Parmalee, *Brecht's America* (Columbus, Ohio: Ohio State University Press, 1980). See also Helfried Seliger, *Das Amerikabild Bertolt Brechts* (Bonn: Bouvier Verlag Herbert Grundmann, 1974).

PART I. CHAPTER 2

1. Reported for the first time in *Twentieth Century Authors*, eds. Stanley J. Kunitz and Howard Haycraft (New York: H. W. Wilson, 1942), p. 186.
2. John Willett, *The Theatre of Bertolt Brecht. A Study From Eight Aspects* (third revised edition, New York: New Directions, 1968), p. 34.
3. Hella Brock, *Musiktheater der Schule* (Leipzig: Breitkopf und Härtel, 1958), p. 66.
4. James K. Lyon, "Der Briefwechsel zwischen Bertolt Brecht und der New Yorker Theatre Union von 1935," *Brecht-Jahrbuch 1975* (Frankfurt/Main: Suhrkamp, 1975), 136-155.
5. Mordecai Gorelik, "Brecht," *Theatre Arts* (Mar., 1957), 72, and "On Brechtian Acting," *The Quarterly Journal of Speech* (Oct., 1974), 266.
6. Lee Baxandall, "Brecht in America, 1935," *The Drama Review* (Fall, 1967), 69-87.
7. *Ibid.*, p. 74.
8. Hans Bunge, *Fragen Sie mehr über Brecht. Hanns Eisler im Gespräch* (Munich: Rogner & Bernhard, 1970), p. 233.
9. Written contract dated Oct. 22, 1935 between Brecht, Eisler, and Paul Peters of the Theatre Union. Located in files of the Dramatists Guild of America.

10. Cited in *Materialien zu Bertolt Brechts 'Die Mutter,'* ed. Werner Hecht (Frankfurt/Main: Suhrkamp, 1969), p. 99.

11. Interview, Albert Maltz.

12. Baxandall, p. 85.

13. Interview, Mordecai Gorelik.

14. Stage name of Mrs. Elisha Cook. In a letter of Nov. 9, 1936, Brecht speaks of her "great talent."

15. In his *Arbeitsjournal 1938-1955* (Frankfurt/Main: Suhrkamp, 1973) under the date of May 30, 1942, Brecht speaks approvingly of vaudeville as the "only [theatrical] form which has any tradition here." Future references to this journal will use the abbreviation *AJ*.

16. *Ibid*.

17. A translation is published in *Progressive Labor* (Dec., 1965), 74.

18. Interview, George Sklar.

19. Baxandall, p. 81.

20. *Ibid*., p. 74.

21. *Ibid*., p. 75.

22. Klaus Völker, *Bertolt Brecht. Eine Biographie* (Munich: Hanser, 1976), p. 241.

23. Cf. Diderot's *Paradox sur le comédien*. See also Mordecai Gorelik, "Bertolt Brecht's 'Prospectus of the Diderot Society,' " *Quarterly Journal of Speech* (April, 1961), 113-117.

24. Letter dated "beginning of March, 1937."

25. Well-acquainted with Loyola's *Spiritual Exercises*, which his 1927 volume of poems entitled *Bertolt Brechts Hauspostille* had parodied (Engl. *Manual of Piety*), Brecht owned a copy of Loyola's work during the final years of his life in East Berlin.

26. John Fuegi, *The Essential Brecht* (Los Angeles: Hennessy & Ingalls, 1972); and Reinhold Grimm, *Bertolt Brecht. Die Struktur seines Werkes* (Nuremberg: Hans Carl, 6th ed., 1972).

27. "Epic Realism: An Analysis of Bert Brecht," *One Act Play Magazine* (April, 1938), 1124-1130.

28. Unpublished letters of Jan. 20 and 21, 1936, Eva Goldbeck to V. J. Jerome, and unpublished letter of Jan. 21, 1936, V. J. Jerome to Eva Goldbeck, found in Marc Blitzstein's posthumous papers, Wisconsin State Historical Society, Madison, Wisconsin.

29. Unpublished letter of Feb. 13, 1936, Eva Goldbeck to V. J. Jerome, *ibid*.

30. Unpublished letter of Feb. 15, 1936, V. J. Jerome to Eva Goldbeck, *ibid*.

31. A translation of Brecht's letter to Jerome is found in *Progressive Labor* (Dec., 1965), 74.

32. *Ibid*. In addition to an English version of the poem which appears in German in *GW* IX, 684, Jerome publishes here another letter from Brecht dated June 3, 1939.

33. An unpublished transcription is found in the Bertolt Brecht Archives under the number 341/46-51. References to materials in the Brecht Archives will be abbreviated BBA, followed by the relevant number.

34. Among Brecht's posthumous papers (BBA 403/08) is a copy he retained

of MacLeish's talk that evening entitled "The Hope·for Poetry in the Future," which was published in *New Theatre and Film* (Nov.-Dec., 1935), 9.

35. Foreword to Marc Blitzstein's *The Cradle Will Rock* (New York: Random House, 1938), p. 7.

36. John Gassner, "Mother," *New Theatre and Film* (Nov.-Dec., 1935), 13.

37. Minna Lederman, "Memories of Marc Blitzstein, Music's Angry Young Man," *Show Magazine* (June, 1964), 21.

38. His fragmentary novel is known as the *Tui-Roman*. It was written for the most part in America. The play is *Turandot, or the Congress of the Whitewashers* (1955).

39. Minna Lederman, "Some American Composers," *Vogue* (Feb. 1, 1947), 232.

40. John Houseman, "Brecht in Hollywood," interviews with Houseman, Elsa Lanchester, Marta Feuchtwanger, and William Melnitz published in *Annual Annual* (Berkeley: Pacifica Foundation, 1965), p. 6. Hereafter references to these interviews will identify the person by name and by the title "Brecht in Hollywood."

41. "The Individual Eye," *Encore* (Mar., 1961), 11.

42. *The New Theatre Handbook and Digest of Plays*, ed. Bernard Sobel (New York: Crown, 1959), p. 429, claims that "elements of the Living Newspaper technique were used by Brecht in the development of his 'epic theatre.' "

43. "The Individual Eye," 12.

44. Unpublished letters dated Feb. 13 and Mar. 12, 1936, Eva Goldbeck to V. J. Jerome; unpublished letter to Minna Lederman dated Jan. 11, 1936; undated note M. J. Olgin. All material found in Marc Blitzstein's posthumous papers, Wisconsin State Historical Society.

45. Located in BBA 341/75.

46. Harold Clurman, *All People Are Famous* (New York: Harcourt, Brace, Jovanovich, 1974), pp. 134-135.

47. *The Daily Worker* (Oct. 31, 1935), 5.

48. The most widely circulated was probably *Songs of the People* (New York: Workers Library Publisher, 1937). In addition to Brecht texts for "In Praise of Learning" (p. 24) and "United Front Song" (p. 55), a third by him, "Forward, We're Not Forgotten" (p. 16), erroneously bears the name "Erich Weinert" as the author of the original German text.

49. Bunge, p. 234.

50. Unpublished, undated note, Martha Dreiblatt to Wilella Waldorf found in Marc Blitzstein's posthumous papers, Wisconsin State Historical Society.

51. Eisler, reported by Bunge, p. 233; Sklar, reported by Baxandall, p. 81; Mordecai Gorelik, conversation of April 23, 1977, also recalls watching a number of gangster movies with him.

52. Located in BBA, folders no. 469 and 470.

53. Undated FBI documents.

54. Undated FBI documents quoting from Brecht's immigration records.

55. Published in the *Deutscher Reichs- und Preussischer Staatsanzeiger*, no. 133 (June 11, 1935), 2.

56. Letter written sometime in July, 1936, Brecht to Piscator.

PART I.   CHAPTER 3

1. Robert Conquest, *The Great Terror. Stalin's Purge of the Thirties* (New York: MacMillan, 1968) gives a comprehensive picture of these years.

2. Quoted by Walter Benjamin, *Versuche über Brecht* (Frankfurt/Main: Suhrkamp, 1966), p. 133.

3. James K. Lyon, *Bertolt Brecht's American Cicerone* (Bonn: Bouvier Verlag Herbert Grundmann, 1978), pp. 4-7.

4. Letter dated May 17, 1940, Brecht to Piscator.

5. Geoffrey Perrett, *Days of Sadness, Years of Triumph. The American People 1939-1945* (New York: Coward, McCann & Geoghegan, 1973), pp. 96-97, reports that sometimes refugees were forced to return to Nazi Germany because U.S. officials refused to admit them.

6. According to a letter dated Mar. 16, 1939 from Ferdinand Reyher (who was corresponding with Brecht) to George Seldes.

7. *Ibid*.

8. Letter dated June 13, 1939, from Margarete Steffin (who was quoting Brecht) to Reyher.

9. Letters dated July 24, 1939 from Reyher to Lang, and Oct. 4 and Dec. 4, 1939, from Lang to Reyher.

10. Fritz Kortner, *Aller Tage Abend* (Munich: Deutscher Taschenbuch Verlag, 1969), pp. 318-319; interview, Marta Feuchtwanger; Baxandall, footnote, p. 85.

11. Letter of June 15, 1939, Piscator to Brecht.

12. Interview, H. R. Hays. Letter dated February, 1941, Hays to Brecht.

13. Letter dated May 2, 1940, Johnson to Brecht, reporting on the telegram and confirming the offer.

14. Laura Fermi, *Illustrious Immigrants. The Intellectual Migration from Europe, 1930-1941*, revised second edition (Chicago: U. of Chicago Press, 1971), pp. 74-76.

15. Brecht, *AJ*, p. 285.

16. Letter dated June 12, 1940, Brecht to Johnson.

17. Letter dated Dec. 6, 1940, Johnson to Brecht.

18. *GW* XIV, 1448-1449.

19. Letter dated Mar. 3, 1941, Brecht to Hays.

20. Salka Viertel, interview of Sept. 22, 1972, claims Henry Manckiewicz signed affidavits of support for fifteen people at one time whom she helped bring to the United States.

21. Interview, William Dieterle.

22. Interview, Marta Feuchtwanger.

23. Interview, Marta Mierendorff.

24. Brecht's *AJ*, in an entry of July 13, 1941 recording the events of the past two months, erroneously gives the date as May 2nd.

25. *AJ*, April 25, 1941.

26. Undated letter written from Helsinki in April or May, 1941, Brecht to Gorelik.

27. *AJ*, July 13, 1941.

28. *GW* x, 830-831.

29. Perrett, p. 97.

30. Reinhold Grimm, *Brecht und Nietzsche oder Geständnisse eines Dichters: Fünf Essays und ein Bruchstück* (Frankfurt/Main: Suhrkamp, 1979), 11-54 interprets this and related poems. See especially pp. 26-27.

PART I. CHAPTER 4

1. Contrary to the account in Brecht's *AJ*, Dieterle had sent his secretary, Erna Budzislawski, to locate and rent the apartment. Interview, Erna Budzislawski.

2. *AJ*, Aug. 9, 1941.

3. *AJ*, Sept. 20, 1942.

4. *AJ*, Oct. 4, 1941.

5. Ernst Bloch, "Disrupted Language, Disrupted Culture," *Direction*, Special issue on "Exiled German Writers. Art, Fiction, Documentary Material" (Dec., 1939), 17.

6. *GW* xx, 298-299.

7. Esslin, p. 22.

8. "Brecht in Hollywood," p. 11.

9. According to John Willett, *Brecht on Theatre. The Development of an Aesthetic* (New York: Hill and Wang, 1964), p. 170, "the cryptic title derives from the analogy with a man who buys a brass instrument for the metal it is made of rather than for the music it makes. The theatre, in other words, is being cross-examined about its content, from a hard-headed, practical point of view."

10. "Der Zweifler" in *GW* ix, 587.

11. "Besuch bei den verbannten Dichtern," *GW* ix, 495, and "Die Auswanderung der Dichter," *GW* ix, 663.

12. *AJ*, Aug. 1. 1941.

13. *AJ*, Aug. 9, 1941.

14. Undated letter written in late August, 1941, Brecht to Hays.

15. *AJ*, Mar. 23, 1942.

16. *AJ*, Jan. 21, 1942.

17. *AJ*, Mar. 23, 1942.

18. Interview, Morton Wurtele.

19. Undated letter of May, 1940, Brecht to Tombrock.

20. Undated letter of late May, 1940, Brecht to Tombrock.

21. Undated letter of June, 1940, Brecht to Tombrock.

22. *GW* xii, 499.

23. *GW* xii, 491.

24. Bunge, p. 195.

25. *Ibid*.

26. According to Hans Viertel, interview.

27. *AJ*, Dec. 19 and 20, 1941.
28. According to FBI files.
29. Interview, unidentified neighbors, June 22, 1973.
30. According to an undated FBI report drawn from files of the Immigration and Naturalization Service, Brecht registered on Feb. 2, 1942.
31. Brecht, *Tagebücher 1920-22. Autobiographische Aufzeichnungen 1920-1954* (Frankfurt/Main: Suhrkamp, 1975), p. 232.
32. Salka Viertel, *The Kindness of Strangers* (New York: Holt, Rinehart and Winston, 1969), p. 240. For a poem Brecht wrote to accompany a photo of this event which he saw in an unidentified American newsmagazine, see his *Kriegsfibel* (Berlin: Eulenspiegel Verlag, 1967), pp. 59-60.
33. *AJ*, Aug. 9, 1941.
34. Quoted from a letter by Karl Korsch to Brecht in Wolfdietrich Rasch, "Bertolt Brechts marxistischer Lehrer," *Merkur* (Oct., 1963), 992.
35. *AJ*, undated entry of Aug., 1941, p. 295.
36. Brecht registered on Feb. 16, 1942 with Local Draft Board no. 243.
37. Letter dated August, 1941, Brecht to Hays.
38. *AJ*, Feb. 13, 1942.

PART II. CHAPTER 5

1. *GW* xx, 299.
2. *AJ*, Jan. 21, 1942.
3. Peter Bauland, *The Hooded Eagle. Modern German Drama on the New York Stage* (Syracuse, N.Y.: Syracuse University Press, 1968).
4. On February 3, 1939 the San Francisco Theatre Union produced *Señora Carrar's Rifles* and the scene "The Informer" from *Private Life of the Master Race*. That scene, and one entitled "Yes, I'm Going Away" ("The Jewish Wife") from *Master Race* appeared in *The Living Age* magazine (1938-39). *Theatre Workshop* published a translation of *Señora Carrar's Rifles* in 1938. "The Informer" appeared in the anthology *Six Anti-Nazi One-Act Plays* (1939), ed. Stephen Moore. The Desmond Vesey/Christopher Isherwood rendering of his *Threepenny Novel* was published in England and the USA (1939) as *A Penny for the Poor*. Translations of Brecht's poems appeared in *The Christian Century* (1937), *Diogenes* (1940), *The New Republic* (1940), and *Decision* (1941). Essays on his writings appeared in *Theatre Arts* (1937), the *Kenyon Review* (1940) and the *Partisan Review* (1941). H. R. Hays's English translation of *Mother Courage* appeared in *New Directions in Prose and Poetry* (1941).
5. Letter dated Mar. 4, 1941, Hays to James Laughlin.
6. Perrett, p. 133, 176.
7. Alfred Döblin, *Briefe*, eds. Walter Mersche and Heinz Graber (Olten and Freiburg im Breisgau: Walter, 1970), p. 242.
8. *AJ*, July 22, 1941.
9. Letter dated Sept. 14, 1941, Brecht to Piscator.
10. Hans Kafka, "What Our Imagination Did for Hollywood—and Vice Versa," *Aufbau* (Dec. 22, 1944), 40. See also "Berlin und Wien am Broadway," *Aufbau* (Dec. 22, 1944), 55.

11. Interview, George Froeschel.
12. Interview, Elsa Lanchester.
13. *GW* x, 848.

PART II.   CHAPTER 6

1. Bertolt Brecht, *Galileo*, transl. Charles Laughton (New York: Grove Press, 1966), p. 122.
2. *Life* (Sept. 15, 1941), 42.
3. Unpublished notes and outline in BBA 158/65 and 286/59.
4. *AJ*, Jan. 16, 1942.
5. *AJ*, Oct. 4, 1941.
6. Gottfried Reinhardt, *Der Liebhaber. Erinnerungen seines Sohnes Gottfried Reinhardt an Max Reinhardt* (Munich: Droemer-Knaur, 1973), p. 268.
7. Interview, Erna Budzislawski; confirmed by Dieterle in an interview.
8. *AJ*, Dec. 17, 1941.
9. *Bertolt-Brecht-Archiv. Bestandsverzeichnis des literarischen Nachlasses*, ed. Herta Ramthun (Berlin: Aufbau, 1972), III, 216-226, lists unpublished notes for all extant film materials written by Brecht in America. Thirteen published film stories or outlines written in America are found in Bertolt Brecht, *Texte für Filme*, eds. Wolfgang Gersch and Werner Hecht (Frankfurt/Main: Suhrkamp, 1969), II, 401-631.
10. *AJ*, Nov. 18, 1941.
11. *AJ*, Dec. 2, 1941.
12. John Houseman, "Brecht in Hollywood," p. 9.
13. *AJ*, Mar. 24, 1942; BBA 158/10.
14. *AJ*, Apr. 8, 1942.
15. *GW* XII, 674.
16. Interview, William Dieterle.
17. *GW* IX, 549.
18. *AJ*, Jan. 16, 1942.
19. The complete text is published in *Texte für Filme* II, 401-405. Douglas Youngkin, Lorre's biographer, thinks this story was written in 1946-47. Textual evidence suggests the earlier date.
20. *AJ*, Apr. 23, 1942 and Apr. 27, 1942.
21. *Texte für Filme* II, 406-413.
22. *AJ*, May 30, 1942.
23. *AJ*, Jun. 5., 1942.
24. Bunge, p. 235.
25. *AJ*, June 5, 1942.
26. *Texte für Filme* II, 413-429, publishes the text of "Die Fliege."
27. Letter to Walter Benjamin, cited by Walter Oehme, "Brecht in der Emigration," *Neue deutsche Literatur* 11 (1963), 182.
28. Perrett, p. 245.
29. *AJ*, Jul. 27, 1942.
30. Letter dated Aug. 31, 1943, Brecht to Berlau.

31. Werner Hecht, in a panel discussion devoted to "Brecht und der Film," *Brecht 73. Brecht-Woche der DDR. Dokumentation*, ed. Werner Hecht (Berlin: Henschel, 1973), p. 262.

32. *GW* ii, 651.

PART II.   CHAPTER 7

1. Peter Bogdanovich, *Fritz Lang in America* (London: Movie Magazine Limited, 1967), p. 38.

2. *AJ*, June 27, 1942.

3. Unless otherwise noted, information from Lang is contained in a letter dated Aug. 23, 1971 he wrote to this author. See also Wolfgang Gersch, *Film bei Brecht* (Berlin: Henschel, 1975), pp. 200-217.

4. Bogdanovich, p. 60.

5. John Wexley, interview with Wolfgang Gersch. Also letter dated June 17, 1972 from Wexley to this author.

6. *AJ*, June 29, 1942.

7. Undated letter of late June or early July, 1942, Brecht to Berlau.

8. Letter dated Dec. 5, 1971, Lang to this author.

9. Interview with Wolfgang Gersch; letter to Hans Teuchert, Dec. 30, 1974.

10. *AJ*, Oct. 22, 1942.

11. Joseph Losey, "L'Œil du Maître," *Cahiers du Cinema* (Dec., 1960), 30.

12. *AJ*, Oct. 19, 1942.

13. *AJ*, Sept. 14, 1942.

14. *AJ*, Oct. 18, 1942.

15. Letter dated "October, 1942," Brecht to Korsch.

16. *AJ*, July 20, 1942.

17. *AJ*, Aug. 18 and Oct. 5, 1942.

18. *AJ*, Nov. 2, 1942.

19. *AJ*, Nov. 4, 15, 24, 1943.

20. *AJ*, Nov. 4, 1942.

21. *AJ*, Nov. 15, 1942.

22. Henry Marx, "Eine Unterredung mit Bert Brecht," *New Yorker Staats-Zeitung und Herold* (Mar. 7, 1943).

23. *AJ*, Jan. 20, 1943.

24. *Ibid.*

25. Bogdanovich, p. 60.

26. *AJ*, Jan. 20, 1943.

27. They did not include it in *Texte für Filme*.

28. *AJ*, Oct. 18, 1942.

29. Bogdanovich, p. 62.

29a. Hans Teuchert, "Bertolt Brecht's Contributions to the Screenplay of 'Hangmen Also Die,' " unpublished Ph.D. dissertation, University of California, San Diego, 1980.

30. Interview, William Dieterle.

31. Interview, Morton Wurtele.

32. According to undated FBI reports summarizing Brecht's activities in the USA during 1942 (reported by unidentified informants).

33. Interview, Salka Viertel.

34. *AJ*, Oct. 25, 1942.

35. *AJ*, Jan. 20, 1943.

36. Interview, Oskar Homolka.

37. Bogdanovich, p. 62. Also reported in a letter dated June 17, 1972 from Lang to this author.

38. *GW* xx, 305.

PART II.   CHAPTER 8

1. *AJ*, Oct. 22, 1941.

2. *AJ*, July 7, 1943.

3. *Texte für Filme* ii, 430-432.

4. Letter dated June 5, 1943, Brecht to Berlau.

5. Letter dated June 28, 1943, Brecht to Berlau.

6. Undated letter written from Lake Arrowhead, Brecht to Berlau. See also *AJ*, July 3-6, 1943.

7. The plot was reconstructed by Hans Viertel in an interview.

8. Interview, Ilse Lahn.

9. James K. Lyon, "Kinderkreuzzug 1939. Zu einem unbekannten Filmexposé von Bert Brecht," *Film und Fernsehen* 6 (1978), 25-29.

10. *AJ*, Dec. 12, 1941. See also Benjamin Britten's score of "Children's Crusade" (New York: Schirmer, 1970).

11. Letter dated July 19, 1943, Brecht to Berlau.

12. According to Goldschmidt's widow, Vera Caspary Goldschmidt, letter dated Nov. 15, 1973 to this author.

13. Salka Viertel, *The Kindness of Strangers*, pp. 194-308.

14. *Ibid.*, p. 283. See also Vladimir Pozner, "bb," *Erinnerungen an Brecht*, ed. Hubert Witt (Leipzig: Philipp Reclam, Jr., 1964), pp. 271-283.

15. Salka Viertel, p. 284.

16. For the complete English text, see *Texte für Filme* ii, 538-597.

17. Salka Viertel, p. 284.

18. *AJ*, May 12, 1945.

19. Interview, Marta Feuchtwanger.

20. Letter dated Mar. 27, 1943, Feuchtwanger to Brecht.

21. Telegrams dated Feb. 19 and 24, 1944, Feuchtwanger to Brecht.

22. Letter dated June 25, 1971, Marta Feuchtwanger to this author.

23. According to contract dated Mar. 27, 1944.

PART II.   CHAPTER 9

1. *AJ*, Sept. 20, 1945.

2. *Texte für Filme* ii, 438-475.

3. Letter dated Mar. 23, 1947, Reyher to Brecht. Probably Lorre or one of his associates rejected the offer, since Lorre had no agent at the time.

4. Reported by Brecht's friend John Hans Winge, "Brecht and the Cinema," *Sight and Sound* (Winter, 1947), 146.

5. Norman Lloyd, interview by Elsa Lanchester and Ned Hoopes.

6. Reported by the editors of *Texte für Filme* in an annotation found in II, 666. This is not a journal entry.

7. Interview, Anna Harrington Hagen.

8. *Losey on Losey*, ed. Tom Milne (Garden City, New York: Doubleday, 1968), p. 169.

9. Interview, George Tabori.

10. *AJ*, Oct. 12, 1943.

11. Interview, Naomi Replansky.

12. Völker, *Bertolt Brecht*, p. 326.

13. Esslin, p. 80.

14. Bunge, p. 59.

15. Charles Chaplin, *My Autobiography* (New York: Simon & Schuster, 1964), p. 434.

16. Unpublished manuscript by Berlau entitled "Wie ich Barfrau in New York wurde."

17. *AJ*, Nov. 7, 1944.

18. *AJ*, Mar. 4, 1945.

19. Bunge, p. 58.

20. Bunge, pp. 58-59.

21. *AJ*, Mar. 24, 1947.

22. Undated letter of late March or early April, 1947, Brecht to Reyher. See also *AJ*, Mar. 24, 1947.

23. Leslie Halliwell, *The Filmgoer's Companion. Revised and Expanded Edition* (New York: Hill & Wang, 1967), p. 104.

24. Erwin Leiser, "Bert Brecht und der Film," *Neue Züricher Zeitung* (Aug. 22, 1970); and Klaus Völker, "Nur die Unterlegenen liebte er. Bertolt Brecht und der Film," *Frankfurter Allgemeine Zeitung* (Sept. 18, 1976).

PART III.   CHAPTER 10

1. "Brecht in Hollywood," p. 10.

2. *Ibid*.

3. BBA 720/79.

4. *AJ*, May 28, 1944.

5. *AJ*, June 12, 1944.

6. *AJ*, July 30, 1944.

7. Clurman, *The Fervent Years* (New York: Alfred Knopf, 1945), pp. 137-140; 160.

8. *AJ*, Oct., 1944.

9. *All People Are Famous*, p. 137.

10. Letter dated July 24, 1946, Reyher to Brecht.

11. Undated letter of late July, 1946, Brecht to Reyher.

12. According to letter dated Aug. 15, 1946, Reyher to Brecht.

13. *All People Are Famous*, pp. 140-141.

14. According to information from Günter Glaeser, archivist at the Bertolt Brecht Archives.

15. *All People Are Famous*, pp. 140-141.

16. "Bertolt Brecht and His Work," afterword to *The Private Life of the Master Race*, pp. 119, 121.

PART IV. CHAPTER 11

1. Henry Marx, "Eine Unterredung mit Bert Brecht."

2. Lyon, *Bertolt Brecht's American Cicerone*, pp. 61-64.

3. Letter dated Apr. 11, 1939, Piscator to Brecht.

4. According to letter dated Mar. 4, 1941, Hays to James Laughlin.

5. Undated letter written in Aug., 1941, Brecht to Piscator.

6. Undated letter written in Oct., 1941, Piscator to Brecht.

7. Letters dated Sept. 23, 1941, Jan. 21, and Dec. 1, 1942, Piscator to Brecht.

8. Undated letter, H. R. Hays to Brecht.

9. Letter dated April 11, 1939, Piscator to Brecht.

10. See Hans Christof Wächter, *Theater im Exil. Sozialgeschichte des deutschen Exiltheaters* (Munich: Hanser, 1973), pp. 136-137.

11. Erwin Piscator, "Amerikanisches Theater," *Die andere Zeitung* (Hamburg, June 13, 1957), p. 11.

12. Letter dated Sept. 23, 1941, Piscator to Brecht.

13. *AJ*, Nov. 22, 1941.

14. Letter dated Nov. 20, 1972, Muse to this author.

15. Letter dated Mar. 3, 1942, Weill to Brecht.

16. *AJ*, Apr. 15, 1942.

17. Performed at the "Fraternal Clubhouse," 110 West 48th Street.

18. Brecht's letter of early June, 1942, has been published in *Nachrichten aus dem Kösel-Verlag. Berthold Viertel. Eine Dokumentation*, ed. Friedrich Pfäfflin (Munich, 1959), pp. 41-42.

19. Interview, Elisabeth Neumann-Viertel.

20. *AJ*, Aug. 17, 1942.

21. *AJ*, Aug. 12, 1942.

22. Interview, Barbara Brecht.

23. *AJ*, Nov. 19, 1942.

24. *AJ*, Oct. 30, 1942.

25. *AJ*, July 7, 1940.

26. *AJ*, Jan. 3, 1943.

27. *AJ*, Nov. 11, 1942.

28. Bunge, p. 184.

29. Lion Feuchtwanger, "Zur Entstehungsgeschichte des Stückes Simone,"

Neue deutsche Literatur (June, 1957), 57. See also *AJ*, Oct. 30, 1942, and Nov. 15, 1942.

30. Bunge, p. 182.

31. Feuchtwanger, p. 57.

32. *AJ*, Nov. 25, 1942.

33. *AJ*, Dec. 2., 1942.

34. *AJ*, Dec. 8, 1942.

35. Feuchtwanger, p. 57.

36. *AJ*, Dec. 2, 1942.

37. Feuchtwanger, p. 58.

38. Letter dated Dec. 1, 1942, Piscator to Brecht.

39. Undated letter written near the end of October or beginning of November, 1946, Brecht to Caspar Neher.

PART IV. CHAPTER 12

1. Interview, Olga Lang; Völker, p. 332.

2. Reported by Henry Marx, "Bert Brecht Abend der Tribüne im Studio Theater," *New Yorker Staats-Zeitung und Herold* (Mar. 8, 1943).

3. Interview, Paul Dessau, in *Brecht-Dessau. Lieder und Gesänge* (Berlin: Henschel, 1963), p. 5; and Fritz Henneberg, *Dessau-Brecht. Musikalische Arbeiten* (Berlin: Henschel, 1963), p. 541.

4. Interview, Eric Bentley.

5. Letter dated Mar. 3, 1941, Brecht to Hays.

6. Letter dated January, 1942, Brecht to Hays.

7. Interview, H. R. Hays.

8. Letter dated June, 1943, Brecht to Hays.

9. According to Hays's written account of Oct. 18, 1971; confirmed by Brecht's *AJ*, July 21, 1943.

10. Arthur Braunmuller, "Introductory Note" to *The Duchess of Malfi* in *Bertolt Brecht. Collected Plays*, eds. Ralph Manheim and John Willett (New York: Random House, 1975), VII, 331.

11. Letter dated June, 1943, Brecht to Hays.

12. Undated letter written in early December, 1943, Brecht to Auden.

13. *Ibid*.

14. Interview, H. R. Hays.

15. Joseph Losey, "Speak, Think, Stand Up, *Film Culture* (Winter-Spring, 1970), 57.

16. Found in BBA 1945/1-2; 7.

17. For more on Brecht's relationship to Piscator, see Herbert Knust, "Brecht and Piscator: Affinity and Alienation," *Essays on Brecht. Theater and Politics*, eds. Siegfried Mews and Herbert Knust (Chapel Hill: University of North Carolina Press, 1974), pp. 44-68, and C. D. Innes, *Erwin Piscator's Political Theatre. The Development of Modern German Drama* (Cambridge, England: Cambridge University Press, 1972).

18. "We Fight Back," *Aufbau* (April 9, 1943), 14.

19. *AJ*, entry dated "March, April, May, 1943."

20. Ernst Josef Aufricht, *Erzähle, damit du dein Recht erweist* (Berlin: Propyläen, 1966), p. 256.

21. *Materialien zu Bertolt Brechts "Schweyk im zweiten Weltkrieg,"* ed. Herbert Knust (Frankfurt/Main: Suhrkamp, 1974), p. 153.

22. Interview, Wolfgang Roth, who claimed he heard it from Brecht.

23. John Willett, "Piscator and Brecht. Closeness Through Distance," *ICarbS* (Spring-Summer, 1974), 88-90.

24. Letter dated June 30, 1943, Brecht to Berlau.

25. Interview, Zero Mostel.

26. Letter dated June 30, 1943, Brecht to Berlau.

27. Undated letter, Brecht to Berlau, quoted by Knust, p. 154.

28. *AJ*, May 29, 1943.

29. *AJ*, June 24, 1943; letters dated June 25 and 28, 1943, Brecht to Berlau.

30. *AJ*, June 28, 1943.

31. Letter dated June 23, 1943, Brecht to Berlau.

32. Letter dated July 2, 1943, Brecht to Berlau.

33. Aufricht, p. 256.

34. Letter dated Sept. 14, 1943, Brecht to Berlau.

35. Letter dated Sept., 1943, Brecht to Berlau.

36. Douglas Youngkin, interview of Aug. 12, 1975. Youngkin has written a biography of Lorre.

37. A letter dated Nov. 8, 1943, Brecht to Berlau, states that Gorelik translated one entire scene. Gorelik, in a letter to this author dated Jan. 8, 1977, claims he translated only two pages.

38. Knust, p. 295.

39. Willett, p. 89.

40. Letter dated Sept. 23, 1943, Piscator to Brecht, cited in Knust, pp. 296-297.

41. Letter dated Sept. 18, 1943, Brecht to Berlau.

42. Letter dated Jan. 30, 1944, Weill to Brecht.

43. Undated letter to Reyher received on Feb. 8, 1944.

44. Letter dated Apr. 2, 1944, Brecht to Berlau, cited by Knust, p. 297.

45. The reading took place on Apr. 17, 1944. Reported in letter dated Apr. 18, 1944, Brecht to Berlau, cited by Knust, p. 297.

46. According to Martin Magner, its director, the first professional production of *Schweyk* in the United States took place in the Studio Theater, Hoover High, Glendale, California, on Sept. 15, 1977. See "Schweik: A Military Anti-hero," *Los Angeles Times* (Sept. 8, 1977), IV, 12.

47. Frederic Ewen, *Bertolt Brecht. His Life, His Art, and His Times* (New York: Citadel Press, 1967), p. 406.

48. *AJ*, May 27, 1943.

49. Letter dated July, 1943, Brecht to Berlau; letter dated July, 1943, Brecht to Weill.

50. Letter dated July, 1943, Brecht to Weill; cited by Knust, p. 292.

51. According to letter dated June 23, 1943, Brecht to Berlau.

52. Knust reproduces the cartoon cover, p. 263.

53. *AJ*, June 24, 1943.
54. Fuegi, p. 100; Esslin, p. 47.

PART IV. CHAPTER 13

1. BBA 1155/15-20. The contract is dated "January, 1944."
2. Letter dated Jan. 30, 1944, Weill to Brecht.
3. Letter dated Apr. 20, 1944, Brecht to Berlau.
4. Undated letter written in early July, 1944, Brecht to Berlau.
5. Letter dated Dec. 29, 1943, Hays to Laughlin.
6. *AJ*, Apr. 6, 1944.
7. Letter dated Apr. 20, 1944, Brecht to Berlau.
8. Perrett, p. 321.
9. *AJ*, entry dated mid-November, 1943 to mid-March, 1944.
10. *Ibid.*, p. 386.
11. *Materialien zu Brechts "Der kaukasische Kreidekreis,"* ed. Werner Hecht (Frankfurt/Main: Suhrkamp, 1966), p. 17.
12. Bertolt Brecht, *Schriften zum Theater* (Frankfurt/Main: Suhrkamp, 1964), VII, 196. This section is not included in Brecht's *GW*.
13. Homolka, p. 111.
14. Interview, Elsa Lanchester.
15. Interview, Luise Rainer.
16. Letter dated Jan. 24, 1944, Rainer to Brecht.
17. According to supplement to Dramatists Guild Contract dated Dec. 7, 1944. A letter of Feb. 28, 1944, from the Samuel French agency which represented Brecht, to Frank J. Sheil states that Leventhal has already paid $200 on the contract. A letter from Samuel French to Brecht dated Mar. 6, 1944 informs him that another $50 payment has been deposited to his credit with the Dramatists Guild.
18. Interview, Rainer. See also Leonard Lyons, "The Lyons Den," *New York Post* (Sept. 16, 1962), magazine section, p. 7, who reports on an interview with her.
19. Letter dated June 7, 1944, Brecht to Berlau.
20. Letter dated Apr. 2, 1944, Brecht to Berlau.
21. *AJ*, Apr. 10, 1944.
22. *AJ*, May 8, 1944.
23. Interview, Luise Rainer.
24. Interview, Christopher Isherwood.
25. *AJ*, May 17, 1944.
26. *AJ*, June 15, 1944.
27. *AJ*, Aug. 8, 1944.
28. *AJ*, June 15, 1944.
29. *GW* XVII, 1206. For additional information on Brecht's reworking of the play, see Betty Nance Weber, *Brechts 'Kreidekreis', ein Revolutionsstück: Eine Interpretation* (Frankfurt/Main: Suhrkamp, 1978).

30. Letter dated June 7, 1944, Brecht to Berlau.

31. According to a supplement to the Dramatic Production Contract held by the Dramatists Guild, dated Dec. 7, 1944.

32. Letter dated "Jan., 1945," Brecht to Auden.

33. Undated letter of late Mar. or early Apr., 1945, Brecht to Berlau.

34. *Ibid*.

35. Letter dated Aug., 1946, Brecht to Berlau.

36. Letter dated May 6, 1974, Gorelik to this author.

37. *GW* xv, 470.

38. Henry Glade, "Brecht and the Soviet Theater: A 1971 Overview," *Brecht heute/Brecht today. Jahrbuch der internationalen Brecht-Gesellschaft* II (Frankfurt/Main: Athenäum, 1972), 171-172.

PART IV.   CHAPTER 14

1. Letter dated Jan. 15, 1944, Bentley to Laughlin.

2. BBA 1762/1-2. Contract is dated May 25, 1944.

3. "Introducing Bertolt Brecht," *The Saturday Review of Literature* (Jan. 27, 1945), 12.

4. Letter dated Apr. 2, 1945, Bentley to Laughlin.

5. Letter dated Apr. 30, 1945, Bentley to Laughlin.

6. Wilella Waldorf, "Two on the Aisle," *The New York Post* (June 6, 1945).

7. Interview, Eric Bentley.

8. *Ibid*.

9. Willett, "Piscator and Brecht," 90.

10. Cited by Willett, *ibid.*, 90-91.

11. Interview, Naomi Replansky.

12. Interview, James Laughlin.

13. Kappo Phelan, "The Private Life of the Master Race," *The Commonweal* (June 29, 1945), 262-263.

14. Interview, Elisabeth Neumann-Viertel.

15. *Ibid*.

16. Interview, Brainerd Duffield.

17. *New York Women's Wear Daily* (June 13, 1945).

18. Burton Rascoe, *New York World Telegram* (June 13, 1945).

19. "The Private Life of the Master Race," *Variety* (June 20, 1945).

20. Otis L. Guernsey, Jr., "Bertolt Brecht's Play 'The Private Life of the Master Race' at Pauline Edwards," *New York Herald Tribune* (June 13, 1945).

21. Wilella Waldorf, "Bertolt Brecht's 'Private Life of the Master Race' is Staged," *New York Post* (June 13, 1945).

22. George Freedly, "Produce Incredibly Dull Version of Bertolt Brecht's 'Master Race,'" *New York Morning Telegraph* (June 14, 1945).

23. Robert Coleman, "'Master Race' Lags in Stage Derby," *New York Daily Mirror* (June 13, 1945).

24. Burton Rascoe, *New York World Telegram* (June 13, 1945).

25. Wilella Waldorf, *New York Post* (June 13, 1945).

26. Lewis Nichols, *New York Times* (June 13, 1945).

27. Robert Garland, *New York Journal American* (June 13, 1945).

28. Letter dated Feb. 13, 1939, Reyher to Brecht.

29. Robert Garland, *New York Journal American* (June 13, 1945).

30. Burton Rascoe, *New York World Telegram* (June 13, 1945).

31. See also Garland, *New York Journal American*.

32. Kappo Phelan, *The Commonweal*, 263.

33. Bentley, p. 132.

34. Letter dated Feb. 14, 1945, Flanagan to Laughlin.

35. *AJ*, "June through mid July, 1945."

36. Telegram dated June 8, 1945, Schnitzler to Brecht, BBA 1185/48.

37. Ed Smith, "Opening Night of 'Master Race' Pronounced Definite Success," *The Daily Californian* (June 8, 1945).

38. *AJ*, entry dated June to mid-July, 1945.

39. Letter dated June 15, 1945, Piscator to Brecht, quoted in Willett, "Brecht and Piscator," 91.

40. Letter dated Feb. 5, 1949, Brecht to Reyher.

41. *AJ*, entry dated June to mid-July, 1945.

42. Interview, Wolfgang Roth.

43. Interview, Elisabeth Neumann-Viertel; *Nachrichten aus dem Kösel Verlag. Berthold Viertel*, p. 50.

44. Carl Zuckmayer, *Als wär's ein Stück von mir. Horen der Freundschaft* (Frankfurt/Main: S. Fischer, 1966), p. 537.

45. Interview, Hermann Budzislawski.

46. Undated letter from "Rosalie" to Brecht, BBA 1188/72-75.

PART IV.   CHAPTER 15

1. Letter dated Feb. 16, 1946, Brecht to Bergner.

2. Braunmuller, "Introductory Note" to *The Duchess of Malfi*, pp. 331-334.

3. Letter dated Oct. 22, 1946, Ann Elmo to Richard Rodgers, stating that the contract was signed on Sept. 19, 1946.

4. Braunmuller, p. 331-332.

5. *Ibid.*, p. 449.

6. Letter dated July 15, 1945, Brecht to Berlau.

7. Letter dated Feb. 16, 1946, Brecht to Bergner.

8. Interview, Ruth Berlau.

9. Interview, Elisabeth Bergner.

10. *The Duchess of Malfi*, pp. 403-414.

11. Cited by Braunmuller, p. 424.

12. Letter dated Feb. 16, 1946, Brecht to Bergner.

13. *Ibid.*

14. For examples, see Braunmuller's discussion in "Notes and Variants," pp. 421-450.

15. Braunmuller, p. 434.

16. Interview, Elisabeth Bergner.

17. Braunmuller, p. 424, citing a passage taken from Brecht's *Schriften zum Theater* IV, 194.

18. Letter dated Jan. 21, 1974, Rylands to this author.

19. Interview, Elisabeth Bergner.

20. Braunmuller, Text for *The Duchess of Malfi*, p. 400.

21. Letter dated Jan. 21, 1974, Rylands to this author.

22. *Variety* (Sept. 25, 1946).

23. According to entry in Ferdinand Reyher's unpublished diary.

24. *Boston Post* (Sept. 22, 1946).

25. Braunmuller publishes an English translation of this complete letter, pp. 423-424.

26. Letter dated Oct. 22, 1946, Ann Elmo to Richard Rodgers.

27. Letter dated Sept. 26, 1946, Brecht to Czinner.

28. Interview, Elisabeth Bergner.

29. Braunmuller, p. 331.

30. Letter dated Jan. 21, 1974, Rylands to this author.

31. *Theatre World (Season 1946-47)*, ed. Daniel Blum (New York: Stuyvesant Press Corp., 1947), p. 27.

32. Letter dated Nov. 15, 1946, Speiser to Brecht.

33. Letter dated July 17, 1947, Stabile to Brecht.

34. Letter dated Dec. 9, 1946, Speiser to Brecht.

35. Letter dated Feb. 11, 1975, from Richard O. Fowkes of the Dramatists Guild, Inc. to this author.

36. Braunmuller, pp. 422-423, who translates from Brecht's *Schriften zum Theater* IV, 196.

37. Reyher, diary entry of Sept. 30, 1946.

38. Interview, Wolfgang Roth.

39. Letter dated May 28, 1949, Reyher to Brecht.

PART IV.   CHAPTER 16

---

1. Interview, Taylor Starck. Brecht's letter to Starck cannot be located.

2. Eric Bentley, "Introduction," *Parables for the Theatre. Two Plays by Bertolt Brecht. The Good Woman of Setzuan and The Caucasian Chalk Circle* (Minneapolis: University of Minnesota Press, 1965), pp. 4-5.

3. Letter dated June 19, 1945, Bentley to Laughlin.

4. Letter dated July 5, 1945, Bentley to Laughlin.

5. Letter dated July 7, 1945, Bentley to Laughlin.

6. BBA 1762/56 gives the date as Mar. 26, 1946.

7. Letter dated Feb. 27, 1946, Brecht to Bentley.

8. Letter dated Feb. 28, 1946, Bentley to Laughlin.

9. BBA 1762/45.

10. Letter dated June 12, 1946, Hauptmann to Brecht.

11. Letter dated Dec. 29, 1943, Hays to Laughlin.

12. Undated letter written in Jan. or Feb., 1945, Hays to Eisler.

13. BBA 1762/39-42.

14. Letter dated May 28, 1946, Brecht to Hauptmann.

15. Interview, H. R. Hays.

16. Letter of June 29, 1945, Hartmann to Brecht, BBA 1185/24.

17. Letter dated Jan. 31, 1972, Dorothy Norman to this author.

18. Interview, Dorothy Norman.

19. Letter dated June 2, 1946, Winston to Norman.

20. Letter dated June 24, 1946, Winston to Norman.

21. Letter dated July, 1946, Berlau to Norman.

22. Letter dated Sept. 12, 1947, Norman to Brecht.

23. Elisabeth Freundlich, "Der sonderbare Nachruhm Bertolt Brechts," *Spectrum. Wochenendbeilage der Wiener Presse* (No. 10-11, 1973), I.

24. *AJ*, June 20, 1944.

25. Reinhold Grimm, "Marxistische Emblematik. Zu Bertolt Brechts 'Kriegsfibel,' " *Wissenschaft als Dialog. Studien zur Literatur und Kunst seit der Jahrhundertwende*, ed. Renate von Heydebrand and Klaus Günther Just (Stuttgart: J. B. Metzler, 1969), pp. 351-379.

26. Freundlich, "Der sonderbare Nachruhm Bertolt Brechts."

27. Letter dated August, 1946, Brecht to Bentley.

28. Undated letter written in Aug. or Sept., 1946, Bentley to Brecht.

29. *AJ*, Apr. 2, 1945.

30. Gorelik, "On Brechtian Acting," *The Quarterly Journal of Speech* (Oct. 1974), 271.

31. Interview, Mordecai Gorelik.

32. Letter dated Sept. 3, 1946, Schnitzler to Brecht.

33. See *The New York Times* (May 2, 1947) for a discussion of its premiere at Princeton one week later.

34. Letter dated June 19, 1947, Gassner to Bentley.

PART IV. CHAPTER 17

1. Bruce Cook, *The National Observer* (Sept. 6, 1971), 18.

2. According to an undated flyer by Pelican Productions announcing the forthcoming premiere of *Galileo*.

3. *GW* xvii, 1119.

4. Interview, Elsa Lanchester.

5. *AJ*, Sept. 4, 1943.

6. Interview, Donald Hall. Hall was doing research for a biography of Laughton at the time of the interview.

7. *AJ*, Oct. 17, 1942.

8. Elsa Lanchester, unpublished, undated manuscript, "The Sound of Words vs. The Meaning of Words."

9. Letter dated Nov. 17, 1958, Brainerd Duffield to Eric Bentley.

10. Interviews, Brainerd Duffield and Elsa Lanchester.

11. See Brecht's essay on their collaboration, "Aufbau einer Rolle," *GW* xvii, 1118.

12. *AJ*, Apr. 29, 1944.

13. *AJ*, July 30, 1944.

14. Hans Viertel, unpublished manuscript, "The Brecht of Nigel Dennis: Review of a Review."

15. *AJ*, May 3, 1945.

16. Interview, Elsa Lanchester.

17. *AJ*, Aug. 28, 1944.

18. *AJ*, Apr. 29, 1944.

19. Brecht, *Tagebücher. 1920-1922. Autobiographische Aufzeichnungen*, 1920-1954, p. 214.

20. Brecht, *Galileo*, transl. Charles Laughton, p. 109.

21. Letter dated Nov. 17, 1958, Brainerd Duffield to Eric Bentley.

22. An unpublished copy of this "secretary's version" is found among Ferdinand Reyher's papers owned by Mrs. Melvin Jackson, Washington, D.C.

23. Three undated letters written in the fall of 1944 from Duffield to Charles Laughton and owned by Elsa Lanchester report on their work and its completion.

24. Letter dated Aug. 27, 1966, Duffield to Bentley.

25. Telegram dated Nov. 25, 1944, Laughton to Duffield.

26. A copy of the Duffield-Crocker translation is found among Laughton's papers deposited in the UCLA Special Collections library.

27. *AJ*, Dec. 10, 1944.

28. *AJ*, December, 1944.

29. *GW* xvii, 1120.

30. *GW* xvii, 1119-1120; x, 938.

31. *GW* xvii, 1120-21.

32. *GW* xvii, 1119.

33. Interview, Oskar Homolka.

34. *AJ*, Feb. 11, 1945.

PART IV.   CHAPTER 18

1. *AJ*, May 14, 1945.

2. Undated letter of late July, 1945; letter dated Oct. 10, 1945, Brecht to Berlau.

3. Undated letter written in late Sept. or early Oct., 1945, Brecht to Berlau.

4. *The Autobiography of Science*, eds. Forest Ray Moulton and Justus J. Schiffer (New York: Doubleday, Doran, 1945).

5. *AJ*, Sept. 10, 1945.

6. *GW*, xvii, 1106.

7. Eric Bentley, "The Science Fiction of Bertolt Brecht," introduction to Charles Laughton translation of *Galileo*, p. 14.

8. Cited from Duffield-Crocker translation of fall, 1944.
9. Brainerd Duffield, interview by Elsa Lanchester and Ned Hoopes.
10. Interview, Elsa Lanchester.
11. *AJ*, Oct. 10, 1945.
12. *GW* xvii, 1120.
13. Guy Stern, "The Plight of the Exile: A Hidden Theme in Brecht's 'Galileo Galilei,' " *Brecht heutelBrecht today. Jahrbuch der internationalen Brecht-Gesellschaft* i, 110-116.
14. *AJ*, Dec. 10, 1945.
15. Interview, Morton Wurtele.
16. A slip pasted in the rear of the UCLA library copy showing "date due" as Dec. 31, 1945 indicates this book was checked out at the time to Morton Wurtele.
17. Interview, Morton Wurtele.
18. *AJ*, Dec. 10, 1945.
19. BBA 582/13-15.
20. BBA 582/16-19.
21. *AJ*, Dec. 17, 1945.
22. Lewis B. Funke, "News and Gossip of the Rialto," *New York Times* (Feb. 10, 1946).
23. Audrey Wood, interview by Elsa Lanchester and Ned Hoopes.
24. Letter dated Feb. 23, 1946, Welles to Brecht.
25. Letter dated Apr. 16, 1946, Berg to Brecht.
26. Undated letter written in late April or early May, 1946, Welles to Laughton.
27. Reyher, diary entry dated May 4, 1946.
28. *Ibid.*, May 7, 1946.
29. Letter dated June 25, 1946, Wilson to Laughton.
30. Interview, Meta Reis Rosenberg.
31. Letter dated June 25, 1946, Wilson to Laughton. See also announcement in *Variety* (July 3, 1945), 45.
32. Letter dated Aug. 15, 1946, Reyher to Brecht.
33. Undated letter written in late Aug., 1946, Brecht to Reyher.
34. Losey, "The Individual Eye," 10.
35. Interviews with Nahum Tschabasov and Ernst Halberstadt.
36. *Losey on Losey*, p. 170.
37. Eda Reiss Merin, interview by Elsa Lanchester and Ned Hoopes.
38. Letter dated Oct. 16, 1946, Berg to Brecht.

PART IV.   CHAPTER 19

1. Interview, T. Edward Hambleton.
2. Contract signed on May 12, 1947.
3. Memo appended to Laughton's Actors Equity contract for *Galileo*.
4. Norman Lloyd, interview by Elsa Lanchester and Ned Hoopes.

5. Houseman, "Brecht in Hollywood," p. 10.

6. According to interview with Lotte Goslar.

7. Guy Flatley, "Remembrances of Joseph Losey's Past," *Los Angeles Times* (Mar. 9, 1975). Also interview, Joseph Losey.

8. Houseman, "Brecht in Hollywood," p. 10.

9. Frances Heflin, interview by Elsa Lanchester and Ned Hoopes. Eda Reiss Merin, interview by Lanchester and Hoopes.

10. Houseman, interview by Lanchester and Hoopes.

11. Interview, John Hubley.

12. *GW* xvii, 1122.

13. Interview, Abe Burrows. Dialogue reconstructed in a letter dated Feb. 9, 1972 from Burrows to T. Edward Hambleton.

14. *Materialien zu Brechts "Leben des Galilei,"* ed. Werner Hecht (Frankfurt/Main: 1963), p. 66.

15. "'L.A. Premiere for 'Galileo' Set," *Los Angeles Times* (July 20, 1947).

16. Stephen Brown, interview by Elsa Lanchester and Ned Hoopes.

17. *Materialien zu Brechts "Leben des Galilei,"* p. 76.

18. *Ibid.*, p. 69.

19. *Ibid.*, p. 76.

20. Fuegi, *The Essential Brecht*, pp. 171-173.

21. Cited by Fuegi, *Ibid.*, p. 175.

22. *Los Angeles Herald Express* (July 31, 1947).

23. *The Hollywood Reporter* (Aug. 1, 1947).

24. *Citizens News* (July 30, 1947).

25. Shelley Winters, interview by Elsa Lanchester and Ned Hoopes.

26. Interview, John Viertel.

27. Houseman, "Brecht in Hollywood," p. 10.

28. *Materialien zu Brechts "Leben des Galilei,"* p. 79.

29. Letter dated Aug. 21, 1947, Wead to Reyher.

30. *Losey on Losey*, p. 168.

31. Stephen Brown, interview by Elsa Lanchester and Ned Hoopes.

32. Letter dated Sept. 15, 1947, Brecht to Reyher.

33. *Galileo*, transl. Charles Laughton, p. 22.

34. *Materialien zu Brechts "Leben des Galilei,"* p. 53.

35. Lloyd, interview by Elsa Lanchester and Ned Hoopes.

36. *Vogue* (Sept. 1, 1947), 181.

PART V.   CHAPTER 20

1. *Boswell's Life of Johnson* ed. Robert Hunting (New York: Bantam Books, 1969), p. 321.

2. See *Erinnerungen an Brecht*, ed. Hubert Witt, as an example.

3. Nigel Dennis, "Alienating Brecht," *The New York Review of Books* (June 3, 1971), 17.

4. "Introduction," *Parables for the Theatre*, p. 5.

5. Letter dated January, 1946, Brecht to Reyher.

6. A possible source for this dialogue across a mountain stream occurs in Act II of Ibsen's *When We Dead Awaken*.

7. *AJ*, Nov. 16, 1941.

8. Interview, Mordecai Gorelik.

9. Interview, Samuel Bernstein.

10. Letter dated Mar. 11, 1942, Brecht to Bernstein.

11. *AJ*, Oct. 20, 1942.

12. See Grimm, "Brecht und Nietzsche," *Brecht und Nietzsche oder Geständnisse eines Dichters*, pp. 146-245.

13. Döblin, *Briefe*, p. 284.

14. Freundlich, "Der sonderbare Nachruhm Bertolt Brechts."

15. Florence Homolka, *Focus on Art. Photographs by Florence Homolka* (New York: Ivan Obolensky, 1962), p. 111.

PART V.   CHAPTER 21

1. Letter dated Feb. 9, 1972, Burrows to this author.

2. Doug Youngkin, unpublished manuscript on Lorre's life.

3. *Texte für Filme* ii, 401-405.

4. Interview, Oskar Homolka.

5. *AJ*, July 11, 1943.

6. Letter dated May 18, 1948, Losey to Brecht.

7. *GW* x, p. 20 of *Anmerkungen*. Replansky's translation has also been published in Hanns Eisler, *Lieder und Kantaten* ii (Leipzig: Breitkopf und Härtel, 1957), pp. 145-147, to Eisler's musical setting.

PART V.   CHAPTER 22

1. Lyon, *Bertolt Brecht's American Cicerone*. See especially their published correspondence, pp. 160-218.

2. Interview, Helene Weigel.

3. *AJ*, Feb. 13, 1942.

4. Letter dated Aug. 15, 1946, Reyher to Brecht.

5. Undated letter, Brecht to Reyher, received on Feb. 8, 1944.

6. Undated letter of mid-April, 1947, Brecht to Reyher.

7. Unpublished diary owned by Mrs. Melvin Jackson.

8. *Ibid.*, Jan. 17, 1951.

9. Interview, Dale Van Every.

10. Letter dated July, 1946, Brecht to Reyher.

11. BBA 286/58.

12. Letter dated May 14, 1972, Mrs. Edgar Lee Masters to this author.

13. Reported in interviews with Helene Weigel and Rhoda Riker Pecker.

14. Letter dated May 21, 1949, Brecht to Reyher.

15. At this writing, Brecht's notes on *Tin* still have not been published.
16. Undated letter written in Oct. or Nov., 1950, Brecht to Reyher.

PART V. CHAPTER 23

1. Interview, Salka Viertel. Viertel declined to identify the actress.
2. Guy Flatley, "Remembrances of Joseph Losey's Past."
3. *AJ*, Dec. 2, 1945.
4. Letter dated Jan. 11, 1946, Ida Bachmann to Brecht.
5. Fritz Sternberg, *Der Dichter und die Ratio. Erinnerungen an Bertolt Brecht* (Göttingen: Sachse & Pohl, 1963), pp. 53-54.
6. Letter dated January, 1946, Brecht to Reyher.
7. Interview, Ruth Berlau.
8. Gisela Bahr, unpublished paper, "Brecht's Fellow Exile in America: Ruth Berlau," p. 3, delivered at the International Brecht Symposium, College Park, Maryland, March 29, 1979. Bahr is citing a statement by Brecht from an unpublished biography of Ruth Berlau written by Hans Bunge.
9. According to Bahr, *ibid.*, p. 1, Berlau by her own count donated to the East German Academy of Arts a total of 1007 letters which Brecht wrote to her.
10. Letter dated June 23, 1943, Brecht to Berlau.
11. Letter dated May 2, 1943, Brecht to Berlau.
12. BBA 1185/35.
13. Quoted from an unpublished agent's report in Brecht's FBI files.
14. Interview, Joseph Breitenbach.
15. Interview, Rhoda Riker Pecker.
16. Interviews with Rhoda Riker Pecker; Anna Hagen Harrington; and Salka Viertel.
17. Interview, Anna Hagen Harrington.
18. Letter dated Jan. 11, 1946, Ida Bachmann to Brecht.
19. Interview, Rhoda Riker Pecker.
20. Lanchester, "Brecht in Hollywood," p. 7.
21. Interview, Salka Viertel.
22. Interview, Rhoda Riker Pecker.
23. *The Kindness of Strangers*, p. 285.
24. "Brecht in Hollywood," p. 7.
25. Unpublished screenplay of "Hangmen also Die," University of Wisconsin Library.
26. *AJ*, Nov. 24, 1942.
27. Letter dated Aug. 23, 1971, Lang to this author.
28. Interview, Morton Wurtele.
29. See her "biography" in *Helene Weigel zu Ehren*, eds. Werner Hecht and Siegfried Unseld (Frankfurt/Main: Suhrkamp, 1970), p. 132.
30. Interviews, Barbara Brecht and Günther Anders.
31. Interview, Morton Wurtele.
32. According to interview with Barbara Brecht, who accompanied her mother.

PART VI.   CHAPTER 24

1. "Bertolt Brecht (1898-1956)," *The New Republic* (Aug. 27, 1956), 19.

2. Günther Anders, *Bert Brecht. Gespräche und Erinnerungen* (Zürich: Verlag die Arche, 1962), p. 38.

3. Kortner, p. 319.

4. Alfred Kantorowicz, *Deutsches Tagebuch I* (Munich: Kindler, 1959), p. 559.

5. Florence Homolka, p. 111.

6. Bunge, p. 173.

7. Interview, Herbert Marcuse.

8. Elsa Lanchester, "Brecht in Hollywood," p. 8.

9. Clurman, *All People Are Famous*, pp. 136.

10. "Bertolt Brecht (1898-1956)," *The New Republic*.

11. Postcard dated Feb. 10, 1948, Bentley to Reyher.

12. "Bertolt Brecht (1898-1956)," *The New Republic*, 19.

13. Letter dated Mar. 4, 1941, Hays to Laughlin.

14. *AJ*, June 12, 1942.

15. *AJ*, Sept. 20, 1943.

16. Interview, Ruth Berlau; interviews, Mrs. Melvin Jackson, who heard it from her father, Ferdinand Reyher.

17. Stated in interview with M. S. Handler, *New York Times* (Nov. 2, 1958), 133.

18. Robert Craft, *Stravinsky. Chronicle of a Friendship 1948-1971* (New York: Alfred Knopf, 1972), p. 287.

19. Letter dated Mar. 11, 1971, Auden to this author.

20. Letter dated Nov. 2, 1971, Auden to this author.

21. Interview, W. H. Auden.

22. Breon Mitchell, "W. H. Auden and Christopher Isherwood: The 'German Influence,' " *Oxford German Studies* (1966), 163-171.

23. Aug. 19, 1943. Interview, Christopher Isherwood.

PART VI   CHAPTER 25

1. Material in this chapter is based on interviews with Anna Hagen Harrington, Rhoda Riker Pecker, Naomi Replansky, Hans Viertel, and Morton and Zivia Wurtele.

2. Interview, Hermann Budzislawski.

PART VII.   CHAPTER 26

1. "Disrupted Language, Disrupted Culture," p. 17.

2. Undated letter written in the fall of 1941, Brecht to Viertel.

3. Interview, Naomi Replansky.

4. Henry Pachter, "On Being an Exile. An Old-Timer's Personal and Political Memoir," *Salamagundi* (Fall, 1969 - Winter, 1970), 46.

5. Unpublished diary entry made by Mann sometime in 1938. Cited by Nigel Hamilton, *The Brothers Mann. The Lives of Heinrich Mann 1871-1950 and Thomas Mann 1875-1955* (New Haven: Yale University Press, 1979), p. 305, 353.

6. Fritz Sternberg, p. 55.

7. Interview, Egon Breiner.

8. Kortner, p. 304.

9. See Joachim Radkau, *Die deutsche Emigration in den USA. Ihr Einfluss auf die amerikanische Europapolitik 1933-1945* (Düsseldorf: Bertelsmann Universitätsverlag, 1971), pp. 73-79.

10. *AJ*, Apr. 12, 1945.

11. *AJ*, Nov. 14, 1941.

12. *AJ*, Apr. 27, 1942.

13. Golo Mann, "Die Brüder Mann und Bertolt Brecht. Einige Klarstellungen zu den eben veröffentlichten 'Arbeitsjournalen,' " *Die Zeit* (Mar. 2, 1973), 9.

14. In a letter to Brecht dated June 13, 1945, Charlotte Dieterle reports that Döblin is receiving $150 a month from the European Film Fund. BBA 1185/77.

15. Interview, Barbara Brecht.

16. *AJ*, Dec. 31, 1941.

17. *AJ*, June 25, 1944.

18. Interview, Fritz Lang.

19. *AJ*, Sept. 30, 1943.

20. Interview, Hans Sahl.

21. Interview, Egon Breiner.

22. Hanns Eisler, "Bertolt Brecht und die Musik," *Sinn und Form, 2. Sonderheft Bertolt Brecht* (1957), 440.

23. Bunge, p. 172.

24. *AJ*, Apr. 27, 1942.

25. Letter dated Aug. 12, 1943, Brecht to Berlau. See also Hans Hess, *George Grosz* (New York: Macmillan, 1974), p. 222.

26. Döblin, *Briefe*, p. 292.

27. *AJ*, Aug. 14, 1943.

28. Martin Jay, *The Dialectical Imagination. A History of the Frankfurt School and the Institute for Social Research 1923-1950* (Boston: Little, Brown, 1973), pp. 201-202.

29. H. Stuart Hughes, *The Sea Change. The Migration of Social Thought 1930-1965* (New York: Harper & Row, 1975), p. 143.

30. Interview, Herbert Marcuse.

31. Jay, p. 202.

32. Interview, Hans Viertel.

33. *AJ*, June 16, 1942.

34. *AJ*, Jan. 18, 1942.

35. *AJ*, Mar. 27, 1942.
36. *AJ*, Apr. 24, 1942.
37. *AJ*, Dec. 18, 1944.
38. *AJ*, Oct. 10, 1943.
39. *AJ*, Aug. 2, 1943.

PART VI.   CHAPTER 27

1. Reprinted in Barbara Glauert, review of Helfried W. Seliger, *Das Amerikabild Bertolt Brechts* in *Brecht-Jahrbuch 1976* (Frankfurt/Main: Suhrkamp, 1976), p. 211.
2. Hamilton, *The Brothers Mann*, p. 218.
3. *Ibid.*, p. 315.
4. Günter Hartung, "Bertolt Brecht und Thomas Mann," *Weimarer Beiträge* (1966), 407-435.
5. *GW* XVIII, 49.
6. *Ibid.*
7. *GW* XVIII, 23-24.
8. Rasch, p. 992.
9. *AJ*, Dec. 3, 1941.
10. *AJ*, Nov. 11, 1943.
11. Golo Mann, "Die Brüder Mann und Bertolt Brecht."
12. Letter dated June 13, 1945, Charlotte Dieterle to Brecht.
13. Golo Mann, "Die Brüder Mann und Bertolt Brecht."
14. *AJ*, Sept. 30, 1943.
15. Bunge, p. 61.
16. *AJ*, Oct. 19, 1944.
17. Golo Mann, "Die Brüder Mann und Bertolt Brecht."
18. Cited that year by Eric Bentley in "Bertolt Brecht and His Work," an afterword to *The Private Life of the Master Race*, p. 129. Bentley heard it from Brecht or other refugees.
19. Bunge, p. 62.
20. Unpublished letter by Thomas Mann to Agnes Meyer dated Dec. 5, 1943. This and subsequent citations from unpublished Mann letters taken from Herbert Lehnert, "Bert Brecht und Thomas Mann im Streit über Deutschland," *Deutsche Exilliteratur seit 1933. Kalifornien*, ed. John M. Spalek and Joseph Strelka (Bern: Francke, 1976). The present citation is found on p. 79.
21. *AJ*, July, 1938.
22. *AJ*, Sept. 9, 1943.
23. *AJ*, Sept 30, 1943.
24. Bunge, p. 62. See also André Müller and Gerd Semmer, *Geschichten vom Herrn B.* (Frankfurt/Main: Insel, 1967), p. 33.
25. *Ibid.*
26. Ludwig Marcuse, *Mein 20. Jahrhundert. Auf dem Weg zu einer Autobiographie* (Munich: List, 1960), p. 241.

27. Sternberg, p. 52.

28. UPI wire service story reported in the *St. Petersburg Times* (Jan. 21, 1972), 3-A, under the heading "FDR Eyed a Mann for Germany."

29. Letter of July 8, 1943, Mann to Agnes Meyer, cited by Lehnert, p. 64.

30. Reported later in *AJ*, Aug. 1, 1943.

31. Thomas Mann, *Gesammelte Werke* (Frankfurt/Main: S. Fischer, 1960), XI, 1076. Translation is mine.

32. Mann's statement, dated July 26, 1943, was published in the Mexico City German exile newspaper *Freies Deutschland* (Aug. 6, 1943), 3.

33. Mann, *Gesammelte Werke* XI, 1077-79. The speech was delivered on July 27, 1943.

34. Unpublished letter dated Aug. 9, 1943. Cited by Lehnert, p. 71.

35. *AJ*, Aug. 9, 1943.

36. *AJ*, Sept. 9, 1943.

37. *The Atlantic Monthly* 5 (1944), 78-85. The German title was "Schicksal und Aufgabe."

38. See his essay "Betrachtungen eines Unpolitischen" ["Reflections of a Non-Political Person"] published in 1918. To date it has not been translated into English.

39. Lehnert, p. 78, quotes a memo by Adolf Berle reporting on his conversation with Mann.

40. Thomas Mann, *Briefe 1937-1947*, ed. Erika Mann (Frankfurt/Main: S. Fischer, 1963), p. 341.

41. Nov. 16, 1943.

42. Unpublished letter of Dec. 5, 1943, cited by Lehnert, p. 79.

43. Mann, *Gesammelte Werke* XII, 934.

44. Unpublished letter of Dec. 5, 1943, cited by Lehnert, p. 79.

45. Brecht, *GW* XIX, 478-480. The letter, dated Dec. 1, 1943, was written in New York City.

46. Mann, *Gesammelte Werke* XI, 188.

47. Mann, *Briefe 1937-47*, p. 341. Mann's letter is dated Dec. 10, 1943.

48. Mann, *Gesammelte Werke* XI, 188.

PART VIII.   CHAPTER 28

1. Letter dated Dec. 8, 1941, Brecht to MacLeish.

2. Houseman, "Brecht in Hollywood," p. 6.

3. *AJ*, single entry covering March, April, May, 1943.

4. *Germany: A Self-Portrait*, ed. Harlan B. Crippen (London: Oxford University Press, 1944), p. 431.

5. According to James R. Smart, reference librarian, Recorded Sound Division, Library of Congress, letter dated Sept. 20, 1974 to this author.

6. Advertisements for the program "We Fight Back," *Aufbau* (Mar. 19, 26, Apr. 2, 1943); and unsigned article "We Fight Back," *Aufbau* (April 9, 1943), 14.

7. "Autoren-Manuskripte bringen $8,900." *Aufbau* (Apr. 9, 1943), 13.

8. BBA 1185/76.

9. Letter dated middle of July, 1943, Brecht to Berlau.

10. Brecht had read a translation of Adamic's book *Dynamite* some time before 1935. See Michael Morley, "The Source of Brecht's 'Abbau des Schiffes Oskawa durch die Mannschaft,' " *Oxford German Studies* 2 (1967), 149-162.

11. *New York Times*, Dec. 23, 1943.

12. The English version exists in BBA 116/43.

13. Translated from the German version in *GW* xx, 292-293. The editors fail to identify this as the text Brecht wrote in response to Robeson's invitation to participate in the Carnegie Hall rally on the tenth anniversary of the Reichstag fire trial.

14. Radkau, pp. 193-195, describes the activities of the Council and several other groups with similar purposes.

15. Minutes of the meetings kept by Dr. Felix Boenheim are found in BBA 2061/61-98. Other minutes of a single meeting are listed under BBA 1959/32.

16. BBA 1158/615, meeting of Feb. 21, 1944.

17. *AJ*, July 18, 1943.

18. Letter dated Mar. 13, 1944, Brecht to Heinrich Mann.

19. Mann, *Briefe 1937-1947*, p. 366.

20. Letter dated Mar. 13, 1944, Brecht to Heinrich Mann.

21. BBA 1329/27.

22. According to Bentley's introduction to the essay, which he published in *Progressive Labor* (Mar.-Apr., 1966), 46-49. Confirmed in an interview with Bentley.

23. July 7, 1944.

24. Radkau, p. 200.

25. *Ibid.*

26. *Ibid.*

27. Interview, Hermann Budzislawski.

28. Minutes of Council meeting, Jan. 6, 1945, BBA 2061/61-98.

29. United States Congress Committee on Un-American Activities, *Hearings Regarding the Communist Infiltration of the Motion Picture Industry, Devoted to the Hearings of October 20, 21, 22, 23, 24, 27, 28, 29 and 30, 1947* (Washington: U.S. Government Printing Office, 1947), p. 500. Reprinted in Eric Bentley, *Thirty Years of Treason. Excerpts from Hearings Before the House Committee on Un-American Activities 1938-1968* (New York: Viking Press, 1971), p. 216.

30. Letter dated Sept. 17, 1942, Herzfelde to Brecht.

31. Interview, Wieland Herzfelde. Brecht's letter, which has been lost, was written sometime in 1943.

32. Robert E. Cazden, "The Free German and Free Austrian Press and Book-trade in the United States 1933-1950 in the Context of German-American History" (unpublished doctoral dissertation, University of Chicago, 1965), p. 169.

33. Interview, Elisabeth Freundlich. Also reported by Freundlich in "Der sonderbare Nachruhm Bertolt Brechts."

34. According to Oskar Maria Graf, "Kleine Indiskretion in Bezug auf die 'Morgenröte,' " *Austro-American Tribune* vi, no. 5 (Dec., 1947), 3.

35. FBI report dated April 27, 1945.

PART VIII.   CHAPTER 29

1. *AJ*, July 30, 1944.

2. *AJ*, Oct. 5, 1944.

3. *AJ*, Nov. 16, 1941.

4. *Brecht-Dessau. Lieder und Gesänge*, p. 20.

5. *Ibid.*

6. Interview, Paul Dessau.

7. Bunge, p. 240.

8. Interview, Paul Dessau.

9. *AJ*, Apr. 3, 1945.

10. Hans Bunge, "Das Manifest von Bertolt Brecht," *Sinn und Form* 15 (1963), 187.

11. *AJ*, Feb. 11, 1945.

12. Bunge, "Das Manifest," p. 199.

13. *Ibid.*, p. 185.

14. *Ibid.*, p. 186.

15. *GW* x, 895.

16. Bunge, pp. 81-94.

17. Bunge, p. 87.

18. *AJ*, Mar. 3, 1945.

19. Letter, Feuchtwanger to Bunge, cited in "Das Manifest von Bertolt Brecht," p. 198.

20. Bunge, "Das Manifest," p. 195.

21. Interview with Duncker, cited by Bunge, *ibid.*, p. 193. See also BBA 1185/48.

22. Interview with Walcher, cited by Bunge, *ibid.*, p. 193.

23. Interview with Schreiner, cited by Bunge, *ibid.*, p. 193.

24. *AJ*, Mar. 20, 1947.

25. "The Ballad of the German Soldier's Bride" in *Germany. A Self-Portrait*, ed. Harlan R. Crippen (London: Oxford University Press, 1944), p. 432; "Yes, I Live in a Dark Age," *Heart of Europe. An Anthology of Creative Writing in Europe, 1920-1940*, eds. Klaus Mann and Hermann Kesten (New York: L. B. Fischer, 1943), pp. 719-720; "Yes, I Live in a Dark Age," *Decision* (Oct., 1941), 74-75; "To Those Born After," *War Poems of the United Nations*, ed. Joy Davidman (New York: Dial Press, 1943), pp. 112-118.

PART VIII.   CHAPTER 30

1. Letter dated Dec. 12, 1974, Starobin to this author.

2. Interview, George Sklar.

3. Interview, John Howard Lawson.

4. *AJ*, Apr. 16, 1941.

5. *AJ*, July 17, 1943.

6. Sidney Hook, "A Recollection of Berthold [sic] Brecht," *The New Leader* (Oct. 10, 1960), 22.

7. *AJ*, May 30, 1942.

8. Letter of Feb., 1936, published in *Progressive Labor* (Dec., 1965), 74.

9. "The White Hope," *Time* (Dec. 5, 1938), 44-47; *AJ*, May 30, 1942.

10. *AJ*, May 30, 1942.

11. *AJ*, June 5, 1942.

12. *AJ*, July 18, 1942.

13. *AJ*, Oct., 1944.

14. Interview, Helene Weigel. See also BBA 1080/26; 238/62.

15. BBA 400/70.

16. According to Perrett, p. 404.

17. Interview, Egon Breiner.

18. *AJ*, Apr. 16, 1942.

19. Ruth Fischer later expanded her essay and included it in her work *Stalin and German Communism. A Study in the Origins of the State Party* (Cambridge, Mass.: Harvard University Press, 1948), pp. 615-625.

20. Aufricht, pp. 258-260.

21. *AJ*, Jan. 25, 1942.

22. *AJ*, Dec. 10, 1942.

23. Bunge, *Fragen Sie mehr über Brecht*, p. 96.

24. *GW* IX, 741; *AJ*, entry dated "January, 1939"; Benjamin, *Versuche über Brecht*, pp. 117-135. See also Peter Bormans, "Brecht und der Stalinismus," *Brecht-Jahrbuch 1974* (Frankfurt/Main: Suhrkamp, 1975), 53-76.

25. *AJ*, July 19, 1943.

26. Interview, Hans Viertel.

27. See Betty Nance Weber, *Brechts Kreidekreis*, for an interpretation of Brecht's entire *Caucasian Chalk Circle* as a political statement relating largely to Stalin and the Soviet Union.

28. Letter dated July 30, 1972, Breiner to this author.

29. Interview, Albert Maltz.

30. *AJ*, Jan. 9, 1942.

31. *AJ*, Apr. 5, 1942.

32. *AJ*, Apr. 16, 1942.

33. *AJ*, July 25, 1945.

34. Joseph Starobin, *American Communism in Crisis, 1943-1957* (Cambridge, Mass.: Harvard University Press, 1972), p. 54, 64. See pp. 51-102 for a detailed account of these events.

35. *Teheran and America. Perspectives and Tasks* (New York: Workers Library Publisher, 1944), p. 13. All subsequent quotes are from this edition.

36. Starobin, pp. 75-76.

37. Bunge, *Fragen Sie mehr über Brecht*, p. 95, 98, 107.

38. Interview, Elsa Lanchester.

39. Florence Homolka, p. 111.

40. *Tagebücher 1920-1922. Autobiographische Aufzeichnungen 1920-1954*, p. 236.

41. Roland Barthes, "The Tasks of Brechtian Criticism," *Critical Essays*, trans. Richard Howard (Evanston, Ill.: Northwestern University Press, 1972), p. 74.

42. Fischer, *Stalin and German Communism*, p. 615.

43. Quoted by Robert Craft, *Stravinsky*, p. 287.

44. Andrzej, Wirth, "Brecht: Writer Between Ideology and Politics," *Essays on Brecht*, ed. Siegfried Mews and Herbert Knust, pp. 199-208. See also Bormans, pp. 53-76.

45. Hook, 22-23.

46. Eric Bentley, letter to *The New Leader* (Dec. 30, 1968 and Mar. 17, 1969).

47. Henry Pachter, letter to *The New Leader* (Apr. 28, 1969); See also Bormans, p. 61.

48. Letter dated July 6, 1972, Breiner to this author.

49. Florence Homolka, p. 111.

50. Alvin L. Schorr, *Poor Kids. A Report on Children in Poverty* (New York: Basic Books, 1966), p. 14.

51. Wexley, interview by Wolfgang Gersch.

52. *AJ*, July 25, 1945.

PART IX.   CHAPTER 31

1. Letter dated Apr. 18, 1947, Korsch to Brecht. Cited by Klaus Völker, *Brecht-Chronik. Daten zu Leben und Werk* (Munich: Hanser, 1971), pp. 115-116.

2. Letter dated Jan. 27, 1946, Weigel to Wuolijoki.

3. Sternberg, p. 55.

4. *Los Angeles Daily News*, Oct. 23, 1945.

5. *AJ*, Sept. 25, 1945.

6. Undated letter of late Sept. or early Oct., 1945, Brecht to Berlau.

7. Letter dated Nov. 1, 1945, Hogan to Brecht.

8. Letter dated Jan. 3, 1946, Hogan to Brecht.

9. Letter dated Jan. 17, 1946, Bitter to Brecht.

10. Letter dated Oct. 23, 1946, Brecht to Berlau.

11. Letter dated Aug. 22, 1946, Heinrich Mann to Kantorowicz. Cited by Kantorowicz, pp. 136-137.

12. *AJ*, Mar. 29, 1947.

PART IX.   CHAPTER 32

1. Bunge, *Fragen Sie mehr über Brecht*, pp. 204-205.

2. Flatley, "Remembrances of Joseph Losey's Past."

3. Interview, Albert Maltz.

4. *Hearings Regarding Hanns Eisler Before the Committee on Un-American Activities* (Washington: U.S. Government Printing Office, 1947), p. 28. Reprinted in Bentley, *Thirty Years of Treason*, p. 88.

5. Bentley, "Introduction," *Parables for the Theatre*, p. 8.

6. BBA 1/042.

7. BBA 585/01.

8. Freundlich, "Der sonderbare Nachruhm Bertolt Brechts."

9. *Tagebücher 1920-1922. Autobiographische Aufzeichnungen 1920-1954*, p. 226.

10. Reported in *Variety* (Oct. 23, 1947). Confirmed by Robert W. Kenny, interview.

11. Eric Bentley, "Bertolt Brecht Before the Committee on Un-American Activities," Introduction and Commentary accompanying Folkways Record Album No. FD 5531 (1961), p. 10. Confirmed by Ben Margolis, interview.

12. Interview, Ben Margolis. Confirmed by Bruce Cook, interview of Nov. 19, 1976, who claims Dalton Trumbo told him the same story.

13. Letter dated Mar. 18, 1973, MacLeish to this author.

14. Reported in the *Los Angeles Daily News* (Oct. 30, 1947). These preliminaries were not included in the official transcript.

15. "The Hit Tune that Earns $$$ for the Reds," *Top Secret* (June, 1956), 50. Senator Mundt, in a letter of June 29, 1965, to Eric Bentley, confirms that the article is incorrect, and that he was absent on that day.

16. Esslin, p. 89.

17. Stefan Kanfer, *A Journal of the Plague Years* (New York: Athenaeum, 1973), p. 70.

18. Interview, Eric Bentley.

19. For an excellent discussion of this play, see Reinhold Grimm, "Ideologische Tragödie und Tragödie der Ideologie. Versuch über ein Lehrstück von Brecht," *Zeitschrift für deutsche Philologie* LXXVIII-IX (1959-60), 394-424.

20. Kanfer, p. 72.

21. According to R. G. Davis, interview of Nov. 17, 1976, who reports that he heard it from Trumbo.

22. According to Bruce Cook, interview of Nov. 19, 1976, who reports that he heard it from Trumbo.

23. Interview, Don Ogden Stewart and Ella Winter.

24. Interview, Robert Kenny. Also reported by Eric Bentley, *Getting Busted. Personal Experiences of Arrest, Trial, and Prison*, ed. Ross Firestone (New York: Douglas Book Corp., 1970), p. 124.

25. Müller and Semmer, *Geschichten vom Herrn B.*, p. 39.

26. Bentley in *Getting Busted*, p. 124.

27. *GW* xix, 490-492. English version by Bentley, *Thirty Years of Treason*, pp. 223-224.

28. Ring Lardner, Jr., "My Life on the Blacklist," *Saturday Evening Post* (Oct. 14, 1961). Reprinted by Bentley, *Thirty Years of Treason*, pp. 189-94.

29. Letter dated Nov. 6, 1947, Hambleton to Weigel.

PUBLISHED WORKS CONSULTED

I. Brecht Editions Cited

Brecht, Bertolt.
Arbeitsjournal 1938-1955. 2 vols. Frankfurt/Main: Suhrkamp 1973.
Galileo. Transl. Charles Laughton. New York: Grove Press, 1966.
Gesammelte Werke. 20 vols. Frankfurt/Main: Suhrkamp, 1967.
Schriften zum Theater. Vol. IV, Frankfurt/Main: Suhrkamp, 1963. Vol. VII, Frankfurt/Main: Suhrkamp, 1964.
Kriegsfibel. Berlin: Eulenspiegel, 1967.
Tagebücher 1920-22. Autobiographische Aufzeichnungen 1920-1954. Ed. Herta Ramthun. Frankfurt/Main: Suhrkamp, 1975.
Texte für Filme. 2 vols. Eds. Wolfgang Gersch and Werner Hecht. Frankfurt/Main: Suhrkamp, 1969.
"The Other Germany: 1943." Translation and introduction by Eric Bentley. *Progressive Labor*. Mar.-Apr. 1966, 46-49.
The Private Life of the Master Race. A Documentary Play. Transl. Eric Bentley. New York: New Directions, 1944.
The Good Woman of Setzuan and the Caucasian Chalk Circle. Parables For The Theatre. Two Plays By Bertolt Brecht. Transl. Eric Bentley. Minneapolis: University of Minnesota Press, 1965.

II. Secondary Works

Anders, Günter. *Bert Brecht. Gespräche und Erinnerungen*. Zurich: Verlag die Arche, 1962.
Aufricht, Ernst Josef. *Erzähle, damit du dein Recht erweist*. Berlin: Propyläen, 1966.
"Autoren-Manuskripte bringen $8,9000." *Aufbau*. Apr. 9, 1943, 13.
Barthes, Roland, "The Tasks of Brechtian Criticism." *Critical Essays*. Translation by Richard Howard. Evanston, Ill.: Northwestern University Press, 1972.
Bauland, Peter. *The Hooded Eagle. Modern German Drama on the New York Stage*. Syracuse, N.Y.: Syracuse University Press, 1968.
Baxandall, Lee. "Brecht in America, 1935." *The Drama Review*. Fall, 1967, 69-87.
Benjamin, Walter. *Versuche über Brecht*. Frankfurt/Main: Suhrkamp, 1966.
Bentley, Eric.
"The Science Fiction of Bertolt Brecht." Introduction to Brecht's *Galileo*. Transl. by Charles Laughton. New York: Grove Press, 1966.
"Bertolt Brecht and His Work." Afterword to *The Private Life of the Master Race. A Documentary Play*. New York: New Directions, 1944.
"Bertolt Brecht before the Committee on Un-American Activities. An Historic Encounter?" Ed. Eric Bentley. New York: Folkways Records, FD 5531.

"Bertolt Brecht 1898-1956." *The New Republic*, Aug. 27, 1956, 19.

"Introduction" to *The Good Woman of Setzuan and The Caucasian Chalk Circle. Parables For The Theatre. Two Plays by Bertolt Brecht*. Minneapolis: University of Minnesota Press, 1965.

Bertolt-Brecht-Archiv. Bestandsverzeichnis des literarischen Nachlasses. Ed. Herta Ramthun. Berlin: Aufbau, 1972. Vol. III.

Blitzstein, Marc. *The Cradle Will Rock*. New York: Random House, 1938.

Bloch, Ernst. "Disrupted Language, Disrupted Culture." *Direction*. Special Issue on "Exiled German Writers. Art, Fiction, Documentary Material." Dec., 1939, 16-19.

Bogdanovich, Peter. *Fritz Lang in America*. London: Movie Magazine Ltd., 1967.

Bormans, Peter. "Brecht und der Stalinismus." *Brecht-Jahrbuch, 1974*. Frankfurt/Main: Suhrkamp, 1974, 53-76.

Braunmuller, Arthur. "Introductory Note," *The Duchess of Malfi* in *Bertolt Brecht. Collected Plays*. Eds. Ralph Manheim and John Willett, New York: Random House, 1975, vii, 331-334.

"Brecht in Hollywood." *Annual Annual*. Berkeley: Pacifica Foundation, 1965, 6-19.

Brecht on Theatre. The Development of an Aesthetic. Ed. John Willett. New York: Hill and Wang, 1964.

"Brecht und der Film." *Brecht 73. Brecht-Woche der DDR, 9-15. Februar 1973. Dokumentation*. Ed. Werner Hecht. Berlin: Henschel, 1973, 255-267.

Brock, Hella. *Musiktheater der Schule*. Leipzig: Breitkopf und Härtel, 1958.

Browder, Earl. *Teheran and America. Perspectives and Tasks*. New York: Workers Library Publishers, 1944.

Bunge, Hans.
   Fragen Sie mehr über Brecht. Hanns Eisler in Gespräch. Munich: Rogner & Bernard, 1970.
   "Das Manifest von Bertolt Brecht." *Sinn und Form* 15, 1963, 184-203.

Burnshaw, Stanley. "The Theater Union Produces 'Mother.'" *New Masses*. Dec. 3, 1935, 27-28.

Carver, John Lewis. "The Hit Tune that Earns $$$ for the Reds." *Top Secret*. June, 1956, 25, 49-51.

Cazden, Robert E. "The Free German and Free Austrian Press and Booktrade in the United States 1933-1950 in the Context of German-American History." Unpublished doctoral dissertation, University of Chicago, 1965.

Chaplin, Charles. *My Autobiography*. New York: Simon & Schuster, 1964.

Clurman, Harold.
   Lies Like Truth. Theater Reviews and Essays. New York: MacMillan: 1958.
   The Fervent Years. New York: Alfred Knopf, 1945.
   All People are Famous. New York: Harcourt, Brace, Jovanovich, 1974.

Coleman, Robert. "'Master Race' Lags in Stage Derby." *New York Daily Mirror*. June 13, 1945.

Conquest, Robert. *The Great Terror. Stalin's Purge of the Thirties*. New York: MacMillan, 1968.

Cook, Bruce. "Brecht was no Box-Office Hit, but His Influence Lingers On." *The National Observer*. Sept. 6, 1971.

Coser, Lewis A., with the assistance of Julius Jacobsen. *The American Communist Party. A Critical History*, 1919-1957. Boston: Beacon Press, 1957.

Craft, Robert. *Stravinsky. Chronicle of a Friendship 1948-1971*. New York: Alfred Knopf, 1972.

Dennis, Nigel. "Alienating Brecht." *The New York Review of Books* XVI, 10, June 3, 1971, 17-20.

Dessau, Paul. *Brecht-Dessau. Lieder und Gesänge*. Berlin: Henschel, 1963.

Deutscher Reichs- und Preussischer Staatsanzeiger. No. 133. June 11, 1935.

Döblin, Alfred. *Briefe*. Eds. Walter Mersche and Heinz Graber. Olten and Freiburg im Breisgau: Walter, 1970.

Dreiblatt, Martha, "Interview with Bertolt Brecht," *The Daily Worker*, Oct. 31, 1935, 5.

Edel, Leon. *Literary Biography*. Bloomington, Ind.: Indiana University Press, 1973.

Eisler, Hanns.
"Bertolt Brecht und die Musik." *Sinn und Form. 2. Sonderheft Bertolt Brecht. 1957*, 439-441.
Lieder und Kantaten II. Leipzig: Breitkopf und Härtel, 1957.

Erinnerungen an Brecht. Ed. Herbert Witt, Leipzig: Philipp Reclam, Jr., 1964.

Essays on Brecht. Theater and Politics. Eds. Siegfried Mews and Herbert Knust. Chapel Hill: University of North Carolina Press, 1974.

Esslin, Martin. *Brecht: The Man and His Work*. New York: Norton, 1974.

Ewen, Frederic. *Bertolt Brecht, His Life, His Art and His Times*. New York: The Citadel Press, 1967.

Fassman, Kurt. *Brecht. Eine Bildbiographie*. Munich: Kindler, 1958.

"FDR Eyed a Mann for Germany." UPI wire service story. Jan. 21, 1972.

Fermi, Laura. *Illustrious Immigrants. The Intellectual Migration from Europe, 1930-1941*. Rev. 2nd ed. Chicago: University of Chicago Press, 1971.

Feuchtwanger, Lion. "Zur Entstehungsgeschichte des Stückes Simone." *Neue deutsche Literatur*. June, 1957, 56-58.

Fischer, Ruth.
Stalin and German Communism. A Study in the Origins of the State Party. Cambridge, Mass.: Harvard University Press, 1948.
"Bert Brecht, Minstrel of the GPU," *Politics*. April, 1944, 88-89.

Flatley, Guy. "Remembrances of Joseph Losey's Past." *Los Angeles Times*. March 9, 1975.

Freedley, George. "Produce Incredibly Dull Version of Bertolt Brecht's 'Master Race,' " *New York Morning Telegraph*. June 14, 1945.

Freundlich, Elizabeth. "Der sonderbare Nachruhm Bertolt Brechts." *Spectrum. Wochenendbeilage der Wiener Presse*. March 10-11, 1973.

Fuegi, John. *The Essential Brecht*. Los Angeles: Hennessy & Ingalls, 1972.
Fuller, Edmund. "Epic Realism: An Analysis of Bert Brecht." *One Act Play Magazine*. April 1938, 1124-1130.
Funke, Lewis B. "News and Gossip of the Rialto." *New York Times*, Feb. 10, 1946.
Garland, Robert. " 'Life of Master Race' Opens at City College." *New York Journal-American*, June 13, 1945.
Gassner, John. "Mother." *New Theatre and Film*. Nov.-Dec. 1935, 13.
Gersch, Wolfgang. *Film bei Brecht*. Berlin: Henschel, 1975.
Germany: A Self-Portrait. Ed. Harlan B. Crippen. London: Oxford University Press, 1944.
Gilliam, Dorothy Butler. *Paul Robeson. All-American*. Washington, D.C.: New Republic, 1976.
Getting Busted. Personal Experiences of Arrest, Trial, and Prison. Ed. Ross Firestone. New York: Douglas Book Corp., 1970.
Glade, Henry. "Brecht and the Soviet Theater: A 1975 Overview." *Brecht heute/Brecht today. Jahrbuch der internationalen Brecht-Gesellschaft II*. Frankfurt/Main: Athenäum, 1972, 164-173.
Glauert, Barbara. Rev. of *Das Amerikabild Bertolt Brechts* by Helfried W. Seliger. *Brecht-Jahrbuch 1976*. Frankfurt/Main: Suhrkamp, 1976, 205-211.
Gorelik, Mordecai.
    "Epic Realism: Brecht's Notes on the Three-Penny Opera," *Theatre Workshop*. April-July, 1937, 29-40.
    "Brecht: 'I Am the Einstein of the New Stage Form.' " *Theatre Arts* 41. March, 1957, 72-73, 86-87.
    "Bertolt Brecht's 'Prospectus of the Diderot Society.' " *The Quarterly Journal of Speech*. April, 1961, 113-117.
    "On Brechtian Acting." *The Quarterly Journal of Speech*. Oct., 1974, 265-278.
Graf, Oskar Maria. "Kleine Indiskretion im Bezug auf die 'Morgenröte.' " *Austro-American Tribune* VI, No. 5, Dec. 1947.
Grimm, Reinhold.
    "Bertolt Brecht." *Deutsche Dichter der Moderne. Ihr Leben und Werk*. Ed. Benno von Wiese. Berlin: Erich Schmidt, 1965, pp. 500-524.
    Bertolt Brecht. Die Struktur seines Werkes. Nuremberg: Hans Carl, 6th. ed., 1972.
    Brecht und Nietzsche oder Geständnisse eines Dichters. Fünf Essays und ein Bruchstück. Frankfurt/Main, Suhrkamp, 1979.
    "Ideologische Tragödie und Tragödie der Ideologie. Versuch über ein Lehrstück von Brecht," *Zeitschrift fur deutsche Philologie*. LXXVIII-IX, 1959-60, 394-424.
    "Marxistische Emblematik. Zu Bertolt Brechts 'Kriegsfibel.' " *Wissenschaft als Dialog. Studien zur Literatur und Kunst seit der Jahrhundertwende*. Ed. Renate von Heydebrand and Klaus Günter Just. Stuttgart: J. B. Metzler, 1969, pp. 351-379.

Grimm, Reinhold und Schmidt, Henry J. "Bertolt Brecht and 'Hangman also Die.'" *Monatshefte*. Fall, 1969, 232-240.

Guernsey, Otis, L. "Bertolt Brecht's Play 'The Private Life of the Master Race' at Pauline Edwards." *New York Herald Tribune*. June 13, 1945.

Halliwell, Leslie. *The Filmgoer's Companion. Revised and Expanded Edition.* New York: Hill and Wang, 1967.

Hamilton, Nigel. *The Brothers Mann. The Lives of Heinrich Mann 1871-1950 and Thomas Mann 1875-1955.* New Haven: Yale University Press, 1979.

Hartung, Günter. "Bertolt Brecht und Thomas Mann." *Weimarer Beiträge*, 1966, 407-435.

Hearings Regarding Hanns Eisler Before the Committee on Un-American Activities. Washington: U.S. Government Printing Office, 1947.

Heart of Europe. An Anthology of Creative Writing in Europe, 1920-1940. Eds. Klaus Mann and Hermann Kersten. New York: L. B. Fischer, 1943.

Helene Weigel zu Ehren. Eds. Werner Hecht and Siegfried Unseld. Frankfurt/Main: Suhrkamp, 1970.

Henneberg, Fritz. *Dessau-Brecht. Musikalische Arbeiten.* Berlin: Henschel, 1963.

Higham, Charles. *Charles Laughton. An Intimate Biography.* Garden City, New York: Doubleday, 1976.

Himelstein, Morgan V. "The Pioneers of Bertolt Brecht in America." *Modern Drama*. Sept., 1966.

Homolka, Florence. *Focus on Art. Photography by Florence Homolka.* New York: Ivan Obolensky, 1962.

Hughes, Stuart H. *The Sea Change. The Migration of Social Thought 1930-1965.* New York: Harper & Row, 1975.

Hook, Sidney. "A Recollection of Bertold [sic] Brecht." *The New Leader.* 10 Oct., 1960, 22.

Innes, C. D. *Erwin Piscator's Political Theatre. The Development of Modern German Drama.* Cambridge, England: Cambridge University Press, 1972.

Jay, Martin. *The Dialectical Imagination. A History of the Frankfurt School and the Institute for Social Research 1923-1950.* Boston: Little, Brown, 1973.

Jerome, V. J. Letters to and from Brecht (in translation), *Progressive Labor.* Dec., 1965, 74.

Kafka, Hans. "Berlin und Wien am Broadway." *Aufbau.* Dec. 22, 1944, 55. "What Our Imagination did for Hollywood—and Vice Versa." *Aufbau.* Dec. 22, 1944, 40.

Kantorowicz, Alfred. *Deutsches Tagebuch I.* Munich: Kindler, 1959.

Kanfer, Stefan. *A Journal of the Plague Years.* New York: Athenaeum, 1973.

Kerz, Leo. "Brecht and Piscator." *Educational Theater Journal* 20, 1968, 363-369.

Klabund (Henschke, Alfred). "Wie der Kreidekreis entstand." *Blätter der Württembergischen Volksbühne* LX, no. 1 (no date), 7.

Kortner, Fritz. *Aller Tage Abend*. Munich: Deutscher Taschenbuch Verlag, 1969.

"L.A. Premiere for 'Galileo' Set." *Los Angeles Times*. July 20, 1947.

Lardner, Ring, Jr. "My Life on the Blacklist." *Saturday Evening Post*. Oct. 14, 1961, 38-44.

Ledermann, Minna.
"Memories of Marc Blitzstein, Music's Angry Young Man." *Show Magazine*. June, 1964, 18-24.
"Some American Composers." *Vogue*. February 1, 1947, 184-187, 231-234.

Lehnert, Herbert. "Brecht und Thomas Mann im Streit über Deutschland." *Deutsche Exilliteratur seit 1933. Kalifornien*. Eds. John M. Spalek and Joseph Strelka. Bern: Francke, 1976, pp. 62-88.

Leiser, Erwin. "Bert Brecht und der Film." *Neue Zürcher Zeitung*. Aug. 22, 1970.

Losey, Joseph.
"L'Œil du Maître." *Cahiers du Cinema*. Dec. 1960, 21-32.
Losey on Losey. Ed. Tom Milne. Garden City, New York: Doubleday, 1968.
"Speak, Think, Stand Up." *Film Culture 48-49*. Winter-Spring, 1970, 53-61.
"The Individual Eye." *Encore*. Mar.-Apr., 1961, 5-15.

Lyon, James K.
Bertolt Brecht's American Cicerone. With an Appendix Containing the Complete Correspondence Between Bertolt Brecht and Ferdinand Reyher. Bonn: Bouvier Verlag Herbert Grundmann, 1978.
"Der Briefwechsel zwischen Bertolt Brecht und der New Yorker Theatre Union von 1935." *Brecht-Jahrbuch 1975*. Frankfurt/Main: Suhrkamp, 1975, 136-155.
"Kinderkreuzzug 1939. Zu einem unbekannten Filmexposé von Bert Brecht." *Film und Fernsehen 6* 1978, 25-29.

MacLeish, Archibald. "The Hope for Poetry in the Future." *New Theatre and Film*. Nov.-Dec., 1935, 9.

Mandler, Jean Matter and George. "The Diaspora of Experimental Psychology: The Gestaltists and Others." *The Intellectual Migration. Europe and America, 1930-1960*. Eds. Donald Fleming and Bernard Bailyn. Cambridge, Mass.: Harvard University Press, 1969, pp. 371-419.

Mann, Golo. "Die Brüder Mann und Bertolt Brecht. Einige Klarstellungen zu den eben veröffentlichten 'Arbeitsjournalen.' " *Die Zeit*, Mar. 2, 1973, 9.

Mann, Klaus and Erika. *Escape to Life*. Boston: Houghton-Mifflin, 1939.

Mann, Thomas.
Briefe 1937-1947. Ed. Erika Mann. Frankfurt/Main: S. Fischer, 1963.
Gesammelte Werke. Frankfurt/Main: S. Fischer, 1960. Vol. xi.
"What is Germany," *The Atlantic Monthly 5*, 1944, 78-85.

Marcuse, Ludwig. *Mein 20. Jahrhundert. Auf dem Weg zu einer Autobiographie*. Munich: List, 1960.

Massing, Hede. *This Deception*. New York: Duell, Sloan and Pearce, 1951.

Materialien zu Brechts " 'Der Kaukasische Kreidekreis.' " Ed. Werner Hecht. Frankfurt/Main: Suhrkamp, 1966.

Materialien zu Bertolt Brechts 'Die Mutter.' Ed. Werner Hecht. Frankfurt/Main: Suhrkamp, 1969.

Materialien zu Bertolt Brechts 'Schweyk im zweiten Weltkrieg.' Ed. Herbert Knust. Frankfurt/Main: Suhrkamp, 1974.

Marx, Henry.
  "Bert Brecht Abend der Tribune im Studio Theater." *New Yorker Staats-Zeitung und Herold.* Mar. 8, 1943.

  "Eine Unterredung mit Bert Brecht." *New Yorker Staats-Zeitung und Herold.* Mar. 7, 1943.

  "Exiltheater in den USA 1933-1945," *Theater heute* xv, no. 2, February, 1974, 1-4.

Mayer, Hans. "Über Brechts Gedichte." *Études Germaniques* 20, 1965, 269-274.

Mitchell, Breon. "W. H. Auden and Christopher Isherwood: The 'German Influence.' " *Oxford German Studies*, 1966, 163-171.

Morley, Michael. "The Source of Brecht's 'Abbau des Schiffes Oskawa durch die Mannschaft.' " *Oxford German Studies* 2, 1967, 149-162.

Müller, André and Gerd Semmer. *Geschichten vom Herrn B.* Frankfurt/Main: Insel, 1967.

Nachrichten aus dem Kösel-Verlag. Berthold Viertel. Eine Dokumentation. Ed. Friedrich Pfäfflin, Munich, 1959.

Oehme, Walter. "Brecht in der Emigration." *Neue deutsche Literatur.* 11, 1963, 180-185.

Pachter, Henry. "On Being an Exile. An Old-Timer's Personal and Political Memoir." *Salamagundi*, Fall, 1969 - Winter, 1970, 12-51.

Parmalee, Patty Lee. *Brecht's America.* Columbus, Ohio: Ohio State University Press, 1980.

Perrett, Geoffrey. *Days of Sadness, Years of Triumph. The American People 1939-1945.* New York: Coward, McCann and Geoghegan, 1973.

Phelan, Kappo. "The Private Life of the Master Race." *The Commonweal*, June 29, 1945, 262-263.

Radkau, Joachim. *Die deutsche Emigration in den USA. Ihr Einfluss auf die amerikanische Europapolitik 1933-1945.* Düsseldorf: Bertelsmann Universitätsverlag, 1971.

Rasch, Wolfdietrich. "Bertolt Brechts marxistischer Lehrer." *Merkur.* Oct., 1963, 988-1003.

Rascoe, Burton. " 'Master Race' Due for Mighty Few Laps," *New York World-Telegram.* June 13, 1945.

Reinhardt, Gottfried. *Der Liebhaber. Erinnerungen seines Sohnes Gottfried Reinhardt an Max Reinhardt.* Munich: Droemer-Knaur, 1973.

Reinhardt-Thimig, Helene. *Wie Max Reinhardt wirklich lebte.* Percha am Starnberger See: R. S. Schulz, 1973.

Ronch, Isaac. A. "Bertolt Brecht's Years in California." *Morning Freiheit.* 8 Aug. 1971.

Roth, Wolfgang. "Working With Bertolt Brecht." *The University of Dayton*

Review, Fall, 1971. 45-48. Also published in *Brecht heute/Brecht today.*
Jahrbuch der internationalen Brecht-Gesellschaft. II. Frankfurt/Main:
Athenäum, 1972, 131-135.

Rühle, Günther. *Theater für die Republik. 1917-1933 im Spiegel der Kritik.*
Frankfurt/Main: S. Fischer, 1967.

Schnorr, Alvin L. *Poor Kids. A Report on Children in Poverty.* New York:
Basic Books, 1966.

Schürer, Ernst. "Revolution from the Right: Bertolt Brecht's American Gangster Play 'The Resistable Rise of Arturo Ui.' " *Perspectives in Contemporary Literature* II, 2, 1976, 24-46.

Seliger, Helfried. *Das Amerikabild Bertolt Brechts.* Bonn: Bouvier Verlag
Herbert Grundmann, 1974.

Singer, Kurt. *The Laughton Story. An Intimate Story of Charles Laughton.*
Philadelphia: John C. Winston, Co., 1954.

Smith, Ed. "Opening Night of 'Master Race' Pronounced Definite Success."
The Daily Californian. June 8, 1945.

Songs of the People. New York: Workers Library Publisher, 1937.

Starobin, Joseph. *American Communism in Crisis, 1943-1957.* Cambridge,
Mass.: Harvard University Press, 1972.

Stern, Guy. "The Plight of the Exile: A Hidden Theme in Brecht's Galileo
Galilei,' " *Brecht heute/Brecht today. Jahrbuch der internationalen
Brecht-Gesellschaft* I, Frankfurt/Main: Athenäum, 1971, 110-116.

Sternberg, Fritz. *Der Dichter und die Ratio. Erinnerungen an Bertolt Brecht.*
Göttingen: Sachse und Pöhl, 1963.

Tallmer, Jerry. "The Art of an Uncomfortable Man." *The Nation.* Sep. 17,
1960, 161.

Tar, Zoltan. *The Frankfurt School.* New York: Wiley, 1977.

Theatre World (Season 1946-47). Ed. Daniel Blum. New York: Stuyvesant
Press Corp., 1947.

The Autobiography of Science. Eds. Forest Ray Moulton and Justus J. Schiffer. New York. Doubleday, Doran, 1945.

The New Theatre Handbook and Digest of Plays. Ed. Bernard Sobel. New
York: Crown, 1959.

"The White Hope." *Time*, Dec. 5, 1938.

*Thirty Years of Treason. Excerpts from Hearings Before the House Commit-
tee on Un-American Activities 1938-1968.* Ed. Eric Bentley. New York:
Viking Press, 1971.

Twentieth Century Authors. Eds. Stanley J. Kunitz and Howard Haycraft.
New York: H. W. Wilson, 1942.

United States Congress House on Un-American Activities Committee. *Hearings Regarding the Communist Infiltration of the Motion Picture Industry, Devoted to the Hearings of October 20, 21, 22, 23, 24, 27, 28, 29
and 30, 1947.* Washington: U.S. Government Printing Office, 1947.

Viertel, Salka. *The Kindness of Strangers.* New York: Holt, Rinehart and
Winston, 1969.

Völker, Klaus.
Bertolt Brecht. Eine Biographie. Munich: Hanser, 1976.

Brecht-Chronik. Daten zu Leben und Werk. Munich: Hanser, 1971.

"Nur die Unterlegenen liebte er. Bertolt Brecht und der Film." *Frankfurter Allgemeine Zeitung*. Sep. 18, 1976.

Wächter, Hans Christof. *Theater im Exil. Sozialgeschichte des deutschen Exiltheaters, 1933-1945*. Munich: Hanser, 1973.

Waldorf, Wilella.

"Two on the Aisle." *The New York Post*. June 6, 1945.

"Bertolt Brecht's 'Private Life of the Master Race' is Staged." *New York Post*. June 13, 1945.

War Poems of the United Nations. Ed. Joy Davidman. New York: Dial Press, 1943.

"We Fight Back," *Aufbau*. Apr. 9, 1943, 14.

Weber, Betty Nance. *Brechts 'Kreidekreis,' ein Revolutionsstück. Eine Interpretation von Betty Nance Weber. Mit Texten aus dem Nachlass*. Frankfurt/Main: Suhrkamp, 1978.

Weiskopf, F. C. "Introducing Bertolt Brecht." *The Saturday Review of Literature*. Jan. 27, 1945, 12.

Weisstein, Ulrich. "Brecht in America: A Preliminary Survey." *MLN* 78. Oct., 1963, 373-396.

Willett, John.

The Theatre of Bertolt Brecht. A Study from Eight Aspects. 3rd. rev. ed. New York: New Directions, 1968.

"Piscator and Brecht. Closeness Through Distance." *ICarbs*. Spring-Summer, 1974, 88-90.

Winge, John Hans.

"Brecht and the Cinema." *Sight and Sound*. Winter, 1957, 144-147.

"Der Dramatiker Bertolt Brecht im Exil," *Österreichisches Tagebuch* 14, July 6, 1946, 7-8.

Wirth, Andrzej. "Der Amerika-Gestus in Brechts *Arbeitsjournal*," *Die USA und Deutschland. Wechselseitige Spiegelungen in der Literatur der Gegenwart*. Ed. Wolfgang Paulsen. Francke: Bern and Munich, 1976.

Zuckmayer, Carl. *Als wär's ein Stück von mir. Horen der Freundschaft*. Frankfurt/Main: S. Fischer, 1966.

SELECTED BIBLIOGRAPHY
OF BRECHT'S WORKS IN ENGLISH

Brecht, Bertolt. *Brecht on Theatre*. Trans. John Willett. New York: Hill & Wang, 1964.

———. *Caucasian Chalk Circle*. Trans. Eric Bentley and Maja Apelman, New York: Grove Press, 1966.

———. *Collected Plays Vol. 1*. Eds. Ralph Manheim and John Willett. New York: Random House, 1971.

———. *Collected Plays Vol. 5*. Eds. Ralph Manheim and John Willett. New York: Random House, 1972.

———. *Collected Plays Vol. 6*. Eds. Ralph Manheim and John Willett. New York: Random House, 1976.

———. *Collected Plays Vol. 7*. Eds. Ralph Manheim and John Willett. New York: Random House, 1975.

———. *Diaries 1920-1922*. Trans. John Willett. Ed. Herta Ramthun. New York: St. Martin's Press, 1979.

———. *Galileo*. Trans. Charles Laughton. Ed. Eric Bentley. New York: Grove Press, 1966.

———. *Good Woman of Setzuan*. Trans. Eric Bentley. New York: Grove Press, 1966.

———. *Kriegsfibel*. New York: International Publishing Service, 1978.

———. *Manual of Piety*. *Die Hauspostille*. Trans. Eric Bentley. Ed. Hugo Schmidt. New York: Grove Press, 1966.

———. *Mother Courage and Her Children*. Trans. Eric Bentley. New York: Grove Press, 1963.

———. *Mr. Puntila and His Man Matti*. Trans. John Willett. London: Methuen, 1977.

———. *Parables for the Theatre: Two Plays by Bertolt Brecht*. Trans. Eric Bentley. Minnesota: University of Minnesota Press, 1965.

———. *Poems on the Theatre*. Trans. John Berger and Anna Bostock. Lowestoft, England: Scorpion Press, 1961.

———. *Selected Poems*. Trans. H. R. Hays. New York: Harcourt, Brace, Jovanovich, 1971.

———. *Selected Poems, Nineteen Thirteen to Nineteen Fifty-Six*. Trans. John Willett and Ralph Manheim. London: Methuen, 1979.

———. *The Measures Taken, and other Lehrstücke*. Trans. Carl L. Mueller et al. London: Methuen, 1977.

ENGLISH VERSIONS OF CITED SECONDARY WORKS

Benjamin, Walter. *Understanding Brecht*. Trans. Anna Bostock. London: NLB, 1973.

Mann, Thomas. *Letters of Thomas Mann 1889-1955*. Trans. Richard and Clara Winston. New York: Alfred Knopf, 1971.

Reinhardt, Gottfried. *The Genius: A Memoir of Max Reinhardt*. New York: Alfred Knopf, 1979.

Völker, Klaus. *Brecht, A Biography*. Trans. John Nowell. New York: Seabury Press, 1978.

———. *Brecht Chronicle*. Trans. Fred Wieck. New York: Seabury Press, 1975.

Zuckmayer, Carl. *A Part of Myself*. Trans. Richard and Clara Winston. New York: Harcourt, Brace, Jovanovich, 1970.

INDEX

Library of Congress Cataloging in Publication Data

Lyon, James K.
    Bertolt Brecht in America.

    Bibliography: p.
    Includes index.
    1.   Brecht, Bertolt, 1898-1956—Biography—Exile—
United States.   2.   Authors, German—20th century—
Biography.   3.   Brecht, Bertolt, 1898-1956—
Appreciation—United States.   I.   Title.
PT2603.R397Z74593   832'.912   [B]   80-7543
ISBN 0-691-06443-1